ISBN 978-1-330-19238-2
PIBN 10049087

1 MONTH OF
FREE
READING

at

www.ForgottenBooks.com

By purchasing this book you are
eligible for one month membership to
ForgottenBooks.com, giving you
unlimited access to our entire
collection of over 1,000,000 titles via
our web site and mobile apps.

To claim your free month visit:
www.forgottenbooks.com/free49087

English
Français
Deutsche
Italiano
Español
Português

www.forgottenbooks.com

Mythology Photography **Fiction**
Fishing Christianity **Art** Cooking
Essays Buddhism Freemasonry
Medicine **Biology** Music **Ancient
Egypt** Evolution Carpentry Physics
Dance Geology **Mathematics** Fitness
Shakespeare **Folklore** Yoga Marketing
Confidence Immortality Biographies
Poetry **Psychology** Witchcraft
Electronics Chemistry History **Law**
Accounting **Philosophy** Anthropology
Alchemy Drama Quantum Mechanics
Atheism Sexual Health **Ancient History**
Entrepreneurship Languages Sport
Paleontology Needlework Islam
Metaphysics Investment Archaeology
Parenting Statistics Criminology
Motivational

Autobiography

of

OLIVER OTIS HOWARD

MAJOR GENERAL UNITED STATES ARMY

VOLUME ONE

New York

THE BAKER & TAYLOR COMPANY

1907

THE TROW PRESS, NEW YORK

Dedicated

TO

MY WIFE

WHOSE ABIDING INFLUENCE FOR SIXTY YEARS
HAS SUPPORTED MY EFFORTS
TO UNDERTAKE AND ACCOMPLISH THE
WORK GIVEN ME TO DO.
CHILDREN AND GRANDCHILDREN HAVE ALREADY
RISEN UP TO CALL HER BLESSED;
AND HER HUSBAND HONORS HER AFFECTION
AND STRENGTH OF CHARACTER

TABLE OF CONTENTS

VOLUME ONE

PART I

PREPARATION FOR LIFE

PART II

THE CIVIL WAR

Lieutenant to Major General, and in Command of an Independent Army

Table of Contents

Table of Contents

LIST OF ILLUSTRATIONS

VOLUME ONE

PART I

PREPARATION FOR LIFE

AUTOBIOGRAPHY OF

OLIVER OTIS HOWARD

MAJOR GENERAL UNITED STATES ARMY

CHAPTER I

CHILDHOOD AND YOUTH

IT is difficult for the human mind to determine what is its earliest recollection. Connected with the place where I was born, the remembrance that is most distinct is of an occurrence which took place when I was three years old. There is a dreamy sensation connected with the preceding, and with much of that which was subsequent to this one event.

My parents lived in a large, plain, two-story frame house, facing toward a north and south road about a quarter of a mile westward from it. The front hall on the west side was remarkable for the broad frieze extending around it, on which was inscribed in plain letters, near the ceiling, the name of my grandfather, Seth Howard, repeated as often as necessary to the completion of the border. The kitchen part, the sheds, the corn building, and the barn began at the northeast corner of the house and extended in broken lines to the orchard. The main house had npon it a roof comparatively flat, with a small portion fenced in at the crest by a balustrade. The house was upon the

3

northern slope of " the great hill " of Leeds. With its tall chimneys, its balustrade, its white color, and green blinds, the structure was as noticeable as a lighthouse upon a promontory. It was seen and known for miles around as the residence of Captain Seth Howard.

At that time the family consisted of my father (Rowland Bailey Howard), my mother, and my grandfather, who was a little past seventy.

Occasionally a neighbor, assisting father in the work of the farm, sat at our table, but habitually we four made up the household.

During the winter, probably in February, 1834, just before night set in, I was looking out of the south window of mother's sitting room and saw something new and startling to me. It was a team of horses hauling a pung with high, brightly painted sides. Just above the pung body on a cross box were seated two men, warmly dressed, having on mufflers, fur caps, and mittens. One of them was driving the horses. Openmouthed sleigh bells were attached to the shafts. The team stopped near our side door, the driver gave his reins to the other man, and ran up to the house and knocked. My father went out to meet him, and after a little conversation the horses were taken from the pung, properly stabled, and the men came in and took supper with the family. I was permitted to sit up during that memorable evening, being too excited to think of sleep.

In the front hall my father's cornsheller was placed. Why it was put there that night I never could tell. There was a bin of unshelled corn in the northwest room where stood my mother's loom and all that belonged to it, not used in the winter. The corn on the cob was brought and put through the machine, one of the men turning the crank and the other feeding it in. I saw the cobs fly in one direction, the dust in another, and the shelled corn fall into its proper receptacle. It was put into bags and carried out every now and then by the men and emptied into the body of the pung. This went on till that singular sleigh was heavily loaded.

After this operation, so absorbing to a child, we all gathered in the sitting room, where a table was spread with refreshments. There was a cheerful fire in the old-fashioned fire-frame. As the party drew their chairs in social order so as to look at the fire, everything appeared unusually pleasant, and I am sure that my grandfather and one of the strangers had lighted their pipes. My father said, as his curious little boy was noticed: "Otis, you must speak your piece. Step up on the bench there beside the door."

I did so. My father then said: "Now, Otis, make your bow and go on."

I did the best I could and stammered through that wonderful speech which children learn without knowing for many years its meaning:

> You'd scarce expect one of my age
> To speak in public on the stage,
> And if I chance to fall below
> Demosthenes or Cicero,
> Don't view me with a critic's eye,
> But pass my imperfections by.

This was the event, and the whole sweet picture of it is still before me, more than seventy years after its occurrence.

Grandfather, with his thin, silvery hair and very genial face, was already infirm with age. He helped mother about the house more than he did father in the farm work, yet he did many chores in the woodhouse and in the garden and around the barn, which gave father hours of time. My father, a man about five feet eleven in height, with dark-brown hair and sandy whiskers, which he wore at the sides of his face, was not very strong and often tortured with rheumatic attacks, yet he resolutely did the farm work. To me now it is wonderful how much he accomplished in the course of a year, for the winter never set in till the cellar was well replenished with meat, vegetables, and fruit, ample for a comfortable living and sufficient for our wants.

Coming with his young wife to his father in Leeds, Me., some four years before, he had succeeded in freeing the farm from a heavy mortgage and in giving support to all his household.

That farm, nearly half of which was wood and pasture land, did not exceed eighty acres. We had several cows, a yoke of oxen, and between fifty and sixty sheep. We raised hens and turkeys in sufficient numbers for our home use, and had also a beautiful apple orchard, which never failed the family in its fruitfulness.

My father's fondness for horses helped increase his income. He would buy up six or eight, as many as his stables would hold, and train them carefully, feeding them well for a few months, then lead or drive them to the nearest market. He succeeded in this trading so well that he was able to clear the farm of its obligation sooner than he could have done by the ordinary profits from the crops.

I love to think of my father and to remember how fond he was of music and how sweetly he played of

an evening upon his flute, while my mother and sometimes others sang to this accompaniment. He was
fond of books, and poetry was his delight. To me he
seemed, as a rule, stern and unbending, but I am sure
from what many have told me that there was never
a man prouder of his children or more faithful to them
during his short life.

My grandfather, Captain Seth Howard, was, next
to my mother, my favorite companion. His usual
stories concerned the Revolutionary War, in which
he had served, during the last part, as a private.
Subsequently during Indian troubles he obtained the
rank of captain in the militia. He was born in Bridgewater, Mass., and was known as "Captain Seth
Howard" in Massachusetts, as in Maine after his
migration to that State, which was on his arrival but
a province, a part of Massachusetts. His father was
Jesse Howard, who at the breaking out of the Revolutionary struggle entered the service against the
British as a lieutenant in Captain Ames's company;
he was subsequently a captain himself, according to
the Bridgewater record.

Tracing the family back through three generations
beyond Jesse, we find John Howard, who was an aide
and helper to Miles Standish. This John Howard
came from England to America shortly after the
arrival of the *Mayflower*. If a Howard can trace his
relatives in the line of heredity to Bridgewater, he is
almost sure to belong to the very numerous family of
which John Howard was the progenitor. The English
connection is not so very clear and to me it does not
seem important. It is, however, a source of gratifica-
tion to a man to find his family tree representing men
exceptionally industrious and respectable.

A little later, during that same winter of the corn-shelling incident, another event impressed me. Early one day my mother dressed me and herself with warm wraps and we joined my father in his sleigh. The weather was exceedingly cold, so that to keep me from being nipped with the frost I was made to sit down on a little bench under the "buffalo." I am confident that there was a piece of oak wood there which had been previously heated before the fireplace. It kept my mother's feet warm and was a comfort to me, so that I soon fell asleep. When I wakened we had reached the lake, then called Wayne Pond, and were riding across it on the ice. The crushing of the snow, the sound of the bells, and the peculiar gliding motion of the sleigh have left their impression upon my memory.

Just at dark we stopped at a tavern in New Sharon. My mother and I entered the tavern through a dark entry. The office room was heated by an old-fashioned Franklin stove and we went to it to get warm, for in spite of all precautions we were chilled by the ride.

My mother not noticing me, I started back to join my father and opened the door, as I supposed, into the dark entry, but it proved to be the cellar way, equally dark. I rolled down the stairs from top to bottom, making my nose bleed and bruising my forehead, but without much other damage. A tall man came and picked up the little bundle of a boy and brought him to his mother. Just then my father came in, and I never quite forgave him for reproving my mother for not having taken better care of Otis. Indeed, Otis was wholly to blame.

The next day we proceeded to Bangor, Me. There

two things occurred which have become part of my life. One was the impression produced by Mrs. Richmond's large music box that she wound up several times for my benefit, and the other was a misfortune which I had while playing with a little girl about my age. I shut the door upon her fingers, without meaning to do so, nearly crushing them. A young man with a stiff leg, supporting himself on crutches, rushed upon me, seized me, gave me a shaking, and a good scolding. My heart was broken already when he came because of the afflicting accident. Imagine then my complete prostration and long sobbing after the chastisement. Surely I learned a wholesome life lesson from that occurrence.

In the summer of 1834, when I was four years of age, I began to go to the district school, nearly one mile south of our home. From that time I continued, summer and winter, to attend till my father's death, which occurred during the spring after I was nine years of age. This school-going was a marked period in my boyhood life. We had a change of teachers each summer and winter term, and I recall to-day the names and faces of those teachers.

When there were fifty or sixty scholars and the school was not graded, it was an exceedingly hard task which any teacher had to so arrange that every scholar should have an opportunity to receive his personal instruction in some branch of the curriculum. Reading, writing, and spelling were for all. Geography, arithmetic, and English grammar were for those who were advanced enough to be classified in these branches. I was fond of my teachers, and remember distinctly that I could be governed by kindness and by praise, interspersed with an occasional punishment.

9

One of my earliest instructors was Ben Murray. To keep me out of mischief he would take me and put me in his lap and let me play with his watch chain. A little later Elizabeth Moore would try to shame me by making me sit with the big girls. Hannah Knapp, on one occasion, kept me in at recess on a back seat. Here I shed some tears and meanwhile surreptitiously drew out the ginger cake from my dinner, which had been placed for safety on the little shelf below the desk. I had hard work to eat the dry cake for the crying and the scattering of the crumbs from my over-full cheeks.

Thomas Bridgham, one winter, was obliged to punish me with the ferule, giving several smart slaps upon the palm of the hand, because I went off with some other boys at recess to search for spruce gum and did not return in time.

Indeed, I had learned to read by my mother's care before the first school, and progress was always steady and rapid enough. As a lad I was not complained of for want of quickness or intelligence.

The larger schooling came from the outside, from the three-score of boys and girls with whom I associated. Scarcely one of them is alive to-day. There were among the boys those who had every characteristic of sturdy New England lads. As a rule, the roughest plays were our delight, and I had a very early ambition to be a leader. Rufus Knapp was at least sixteen when I was eight, jovial with the younger boys, but huge in size, strong and sinewy as an athlete. I used to combine my forces from the small boys and lead them to attack him simply with a view of throwing him to the ground. I would first dive for his legs, and no matter how much I was bruised I led those attacks with success. Rufus never was angry and laughed at the rest of us when we piled upon his prostrate form and held his arms and legs.

On one occasion something that has been a characteristic in later life showed itself. Several boys were on their way to school. There had been a freshet, and the deep ditches were full of water. At one place there was quite an excavation comparatively full. The surface in the early morning was skimmed over with thin ice. Henry Millet, one of the companions of about my age, called out and said: " Ote, you dasn't slide across that ditch!" As quick as thought I sprang forward and started to slide. When I reached the middle I went through to my neck in the cold water. Of course I sprang out as quickly as I went in, but I had to go on to school drenched to the skin. Indeed, all my life it has been hard for me to resist a challenge.

The year I began school my brother Rowland was born. Just after he was old enough to accompany me the fearful excitement attending the settlement of the northeast boundary came to a head. With other lads we ran from school to find the Leeds Company drilling with fifes and drums in Mr. Millet's large front yard. On arriving we were delighted with the beautiful uniforms and bright plumes of the company and excited as boys always are by the music. This was a new experience. Suddenly one of the boys told us that our father, Rowland B. Howard, had been drafted and would have to go to war. Little Rowland and I ran home sobbing and crying, not half understanding what the thing meant. Our mother soon explained that father accepted the draft, but on account of his rheumatism would send a substitute. He did so. The substitute's name was George Washington George. He was cross-eyed, but avoided the examining surgeon, declaring that he could shoot as well as anybody by closing one eye. George's full equipment in the old style, with the flint-lock musket and all that went with it, so much interested me that I have never forgotten any article of its make-up.

The so-called war was brief, for the controversy was settled by General Winfield Scott in 1838 before there was any actual exchange of shots. This was called the " Madawaska War."

Before I was six years old my father, having some business in the valley of the Hudson, made quite a long visit among his mother's relatives, living there. My grandmother's name was Desire Bailey, a sister of Dr. Rowland Bailey. On my father's return he passed through the city of Troy. For some benevolent reason he there befriended a little negro lad and brought him to our house in Leeds, Me. I remember well the night the boy first made his appearance in the household. His large eyes, white teeth, woolly head, and dark skin kept my eyes fixed upon him for some time, while my father was telling the story of his advent. This boy lived with us for four years. As he was vigorous and strong we had our plays together. The coasting, the skating, the ball playing, the games with marbles and with kites—all such things found us adepts. Also in work, such as comes to every New England farm lad, we toiled side by side, or at our respective stints in which we competed for success and finish. Edward Johnson, for that was his name, was always kind to me, and helpful. Indeed, I never remember quarreling with him, but he was never cringing or slavish. I have always believed it a providential circumstance that I had that early experience with a negro lad, for it relieved me from that feeling of prejudice which would have hindered me from doing the work for the freedmen which, years afterwards, was committed to my charge.

In the year 1838 my younger brother, Charles, was born.

In the early settlement of Leeds, before there were any school privileges, Mr. Francis, a young Englishman, came with a party of prospectors from England. They were entertained by my great-grandfather, Thomas Stanchfield. After leaving his home, situated then in a wilderness near the eastern border of Leeds, the party kept on westward. After a few days, Mr. Francis, much broken and bruised by the journey, returned alone and accepted the offer of Mr. Stanchfield to remain and teach the children of the scattered families in that section of Maine. At a later period, seeing the moral and religious condition of this frontier, he began to give religious instruction to the adults as well as to the children, and was soon after ordained as the first Baptist minister in that community. He was still preaching in the meetinghouse before mentioned when my father and mother were young people. Through his influence and that of other ministers who followed him, a thriving church resulted, and the community of Leeds, far and near, became remarkable in its attention to religious matters.

Into this atmosphere I was born. In a letter written by my mother, which lies before me, of date July 14, 1833, I find not only expressions of deep affection for her husband and her then only son, but utterances which indicate piety and a simple trust in God, and also express a proper ambition subdued by humility of heart. She wrote:

Autobiography of Gen. O. O. Howard

I think if we cannot fill so high a station in life as we could desire, we may possibly do as much good in some less exacting situation. Our children, though humbly educated, may fill important stations in life. Let us hope for the best and bear with patience whatever crosses our path in life.

At the church on Sunday there was preaching in the morning and in the afternoon. During the recess between the sermons the children were gathered into a Sunday school. Deacon Cobb had six or eight of us boys shut into one of those old-fashioned pews with back and front and door so high that we could not look out of the pew when on the floor. The usual routine was to recite verses previously learned at home. My parents must have been very faithful in having me prepare my lessons, for I committed to memory a great deal of Scripture about that time that has since been of great service to me. There was no sign of religiousness in my first home. We did not even have family prayer. Once during my father's illness I came from a prayer meeting at my uncle's house much impressed with a desire to be a Christian. My father, sitting in his high-backed chair, asked me about the meeting. After telling him, I said, " Father, do you ever pray? "

He was silent for a few moments and then said: " My son, would you like to have me pray? "

I said " yes " and we knelt together beside his chair and he repeated our Lord's Prayer. This was the only time that I heard my father thus offer a petition. My mother, however, had taught me the simple prayers of childhood and rendered me familiar with Bible stories too early in my life for distinct recollection.

One Sunday morning I was keeping the cattle out of the upper grain field. The wind was blowing hard

14

from the west. Just before church time my father called for me at the top of his voice, using all his strength to make me hear. At last I saw him and faintly heard his call and ran home at once. He told me to get ready for meeting. The meetinghouse was on the southern slope of the great hill, about two miles away. My father had been rebuilding the church edifice for the people and was much interested in it and in the meetings. I begged to be allowed to stay at home that day. My father, mother, and brother went and left me behind. Early in the afternoon they came back. Sitting in the church my father had been attacked with a sudden hemorrhage of the lungs, due undoubtedly to the strain of his morning call to me against the wind. He was never well again, and on April 30, 1840, he died. The scene at his death has . always appeared to me to be a tragic one—the hemorrhage, the cries of my mother, and the tearful friends gathered around his bed. It was indeed my first idea of a death scene.

The whole ceremony following was like that in a country place in New England where one is taken away who is much respected and beloved by his neighbors. Every office from the undertaker to the bearers and the burial party was filled by a kind friend and late associate. The pastor of the Baptist church read the hymns and made the prayer, and with trembling voices the choir, which had so often sung to his accompaniment with his flute in social entertainments, sang precious hymns.

The family followed the improvised bier which was carrying my father to the little graveyard situated on the east side of his uncle's farm, and the people in a long column of twos and threes followed on in silence and gathered around the grave, full of kindness and respectful bearing, while the last simple rites were there performed.

It was a sad house for my mother and the little boys after our return for many days, but my mother did not give way to grief so much as not to be able to perform the new tasks that devolved upon her, the care of the family, and the carrying on of the farm.

For the first year after father's death my mother employed a good strong Englishman to perform the farm labor and do anything necessary for our support under her supervision.

My grandfather did not remain with us long, but soon went to live with his eldest son, Stillman.

Two years after, my mother married a prosperous farmer, Colonel John Gilmore, living some six miles away in the southern part of Leeds. He was a widower and had a considerable family of his own. I was nearly eleven years of age when we moved to the new home. There were three boys. For all of us this marriage with the removal from the old place began a new era.

CHAPTER II

DURING the interval between father's death and
the marriage of my mother, I had been much
·leaned upon and trusted as the eldest. To harness and
control a horse attached to a carriage, or to drive one
or two yoke of oxen, were no uncommon tasks. Of
course, the praise for this precociousness set me up not
a little. The new home changed all this. My stepfather was very kind always and humored my whims;
but his youngest son, two years my senior, by his criticisms and odd speeches soon made me feel that I was
not yet a man. He evidently meant "to take the con-
ceit out of Otis." This discipline while I was learning
and participating in all the farm work, which a lad ten
years of age could do, was really needed and wholesome. But the new conditions and neighborhood associations made my watchful mother very anxious for a
change.

The first autumn before I was eleven in November,
she sent me away to a "high school" at Wayne Village. Improvement in all elementary instruction came
with these two months. I learned, too, how to live
away from home without too much homesickness.

Soon followed another advantage. My mother's
brother, Hon. John Otis, living in Hallowell, offered
me a place in his family, if I would do the chores for

17

my board. I was to take care of his horse and cow and perform such tasks as the situation might demand. The object was to give me the privilege of Mr. Burnham's High School. These privileges overshadowed everything and hindered criticism.

At Mr. Burnham's I joined a class of six lads of about my age. This class was just beginning Latin, but the class did not give itself exclusively to this study, keeping abreast of others in the books essential to a high school graduation. Before the close of the two years at Hallowell the teacher had added the elements of Greek. The class made considerable progress not only in the Latin but in the Greek grammar. It was my uncle's wish and my mother's delight that I should begin a preparation for college and we had Bowdoin College in view.

At thirteen my health was perfect and Mr. Burnham chose me with my ruddy cheeks to illustrate his talks, as a specimen of a healthful New England boy.

The home instruction under my Aunt Frances, usually given to her son William and daughter Maria and myself, embraced everything that was best. She read to us by the hour. She saw that we prepared our lessons for the Sabbath school at the Old South church, and she sympathized with us in our youthful troubles that often seemed so hard to bear. Surely I was treated by her and by my uncle as a son.

Again, as always, the outside schooling cannot be ignored. I met in the village, and, in fact, at the school, a conclave of boys who insisted that I had too much pride and it must be taken down. One would insist that I did not properly pronounce words which ended in *ow*, such as *now* and *cow*, and that I could not

18

properly pronounce such words as *round* and *found*. I declared that I did pronounce them properly, when a sharp contest would often ensue.

One day I was caught by the arms and legs and hurried forward to be bumped against a brick wall. I cleared myself and fought till one opponent had fallen and another been bruised, but one of my eyes was swollen and closed. In this plight my aunt was not very proud of me and discouraged my strong inclination to resist every intrusion. The youngsters, not being satisfied with their own efforts to humble me and bring me into a proper frame of mind, had a sudden accession to their company of a boy called Joe Marshall. He was fourteen or fifteen years old and had been to sea in some training ship long enough to teach him the skillful use of his arms and fists. On one Saturday afternoon as I was working in the garden a troop of boys came along the street with " Joe " at the head. A flat-topped stone wall separated me from them. Being near the wall myself I did not wait for an attack, but knocked off his cap. With fierce anger he sprang over the separating fence and began his assault upon me. Understanding the disadvantage of fencing with a trained lad, I sprang upon him, lifted him in my arms and put him down between a tree and the wall and believed that I had gained a victory, but Marshall so punched and pulled my nose that it bled profusely. As I disengaged myself from this brutal fight I set out for the house and saw my uncle and aunt on the porch looking at me, and I felt ashamed. Some of the boys called out, " Coward! " but I resisted every inclination to turn back to the fight and went to the house. My aunt gently chided me for my impulsiveness, but my good uncle said, " I glory in your spunk." After that all the boys were on my side and I was not further molested.

Who can say but that this training in a little community, which represents the great world, may not have been essential to the subsequent work which necessitated not only intellectual development but a hardy spirit.

My good mother, however, always leaned to the idea that kindness, shown even to enemies, would win in time. It may, if not misunderstood, but how often kindness is imputed to want of courage.

There was another proverb that affected me: "Be sure you are right and then go ahead."

While at Hallowell, first my beloved grandfather, Captain Seth Howard, passed away at the age of eighty-four; and a little later my grandfather, Oliver Otis, the noble man for whom I was named. A few days before his death I went in to see him. He was still able to be dressed and sit in his armchair. He called me to him and said, while my right hand rested in his, " Otis, always be kind to your employees." I did not know then precisely what he meant, because I hardly realized the possibility that Otis would ever have men under his charge and subject to his will, but the message he gave me then has been with me to influence my conduct toward the thousands whom I have been called upon to command. There has been with me a steady purpose to be kind to any and all of those who looked to me for direction.

My grandmother, Elizabeth Stanchfield Otis, was a very devout Christian and never neglected an opportunity to say something to me that she thought would help me to a right purpose in all my undertakings.

The spring and summer of 1844, when the political

excitement which preceded the Mexican War was upon us and so much interested my stepfather, Colonel Gilmore, that he would never miss reading his weekly journal, and, of course, needing some time for this, I was kept at home. After my return I soon found myself among the working "boys" on his farm. His three sons with myself, besides often hired men, were admirably led by Colonel Gilmore, who directed all from the seed sowing to the harvest. Here follows a suggestive schedule which long ago I made of things done:

"Spring plowing, harrowing, sowing, bushing, rolling—this for the grain fields. Dressing, furrowing, manuring in the hill, planting the corn and the potatoes. Stones are to be picked up and drawn off, year by year; fields are to be cleared, lowlands to be drained, fences to be made and kept in repair. There is a hoeing time when the farmer fights against weeds, thistles, and grasses; the haying time, mowing, spreading, raking, loading, stowing on the cart and in the barn. The harvest season closely follows with all its various labors. The sheep, the cattle, the pigs, and the fowls all demand constant care. The orchards and the garden cannot be neglected. From the March snows to the October frosts the New England farmers keep up their unceasing work with only Sundays and a few holidays to rest."

I fell into line and adjusted myself to all this till September 1st. It was during that summer when my strength for a time became overtasked and I felt jaded. The trouble was on account of a foolish ambition. In plowing I must hold the plow; in haying swing the scythe; and in loading pitch the hay. I wanted before being fully grown and properly developed in sinews

21

and muscles to do a grown man's part. After trials and some suffering the true lesson was learned, to try and do the boy's part well. It was better than to do the man's part poorly.

My good mother went with me to the vicinity of Monmouth Academy the day before the beginning of the term. My boarding place was already secured at the house of Captain Wilcox, a retired sea captain. My room was chosen, some pictures put on the wall and little changes made by my mother to make the chamber tidy and cheerful. My mother's injunction as she parted with me and set out for home was a message often repeated in her letters through all my school and college life, " Do the best you can, Otis, with your studies, and try hard to do right, ever seeking God's help." Surely with such a mother one ought not to go astray.

I pursued my preparation for college diligently. My Greek as I went on became more and more difficult to me; and the principal of the academy, Mr. True, began to doubt whether I would have the capacity to master the preparatory course in that study. A schoolmate older than I and of excellent ability and strong character, showed me why I was losing ground. It was because I sought too much help from translations and did not get a sufficient vocabulary in my mind, nor trust enough to my memory in the class room, but interlined my book so as to make a fair showing at the academy. On his advice I acted at once and so persevered that by the close of the term my Greek was abreast of my Latin, which had never been a hard subject to me.

Here I formed some associations which proved to be for life. I had the usual experiences of a very ardent nature with strong attachments and a few antipathies, and some quarrels not at all to my credit.

The Monmouth term, however, I can now see carried me along so that at its close I was far ahead of my Hallowell class.

The following winter there was an excellent teacher, Stephen H. Dean, at what we called the brick schoolhouse, two miles and a half from our home; so, with my mother's strong approval, I went there. During this season I boarded part of the time on the north road with a Mr. Henry Foster, always returning home for Saturday and Sunday.

It was at this school that I made a very fair review of all the studies, excepting the foreign languages, essential for a Bowdoin examination. Arithmetic and algebra were always easy of attainment and a pleasure, and I began to comprehend better and better all that pertained to English grammar.

We did not have the athletics of to-day, but the young men of that school, several older than myself, engaged in many a contest. Wrestling at arm's length and in close hug were favorite sports. Running, jumping, snowballing, and ball playing, as soon as practicable, added to the health and strength of our boys quite as much, I think, as the sports of to-day.

Warren Lothrop, who distinguished himself in Mexico and who became a colonel afterwards during the Civil War, was then a fellow student. He was about twenty years of age and of gigantic frame. Henry Mitchell was always his contestant in the sports. The latter was light of weight, slight of figure, and not so tall as Warren. In wrestling they would contend again and again for the mastery, but at last by his skill and quickness Henry would lay Warren prostrate at every contest. Then they would both laugh, Warren the loudest, though he was defeated.

In such sports I always bore my part and sometimes gained the victory. Henry could always throw me at arm's length, and on our long walks together from the Lothrop home through the storms and snows, Warren took a special delight in catching me in his strong arms and tossing me into a snow bank. I fought hard, and it was not easy for me to keep my temper under restraint in defeat. These stout and athletic companions, however, in spite of my resistance, often forced a wholesome lesson of patience and self-control upon me.

My stepfather had a large flock of sheep and there was plenty of wool, which in due time was taken to Wayne Mills to be worked up into handsome gray cloth. By the help of a good tailoress, who periodically spent several happy and busy days at our house, mother made up for me a suit of gray that fitted me well. I remember the trousers flaring a little at the bottom, the vest and the coat each having its proper braided trimmings. With warm underclothing, a pair of roomy boots and home-knitted socks, and with a bright comforter around my neck, I did not need an overcoat.

My stepfather took me, thus newly attired, in his pung from Leeds to North Yarmouth. He used the pung so as to transport my small trunk which contained books and other equipments, such as my mother had stowed in it for my use and comfort.

The long ride with Colonel Gilmore, my stepfather, early in March, 1845, was a pleasant and profitable journey. The weather was rather cold and blustering and the snow still of considerable depth. My stepfather was reminiscent and revealed to me much of his past experience in his early life in Massachusetts. He made me feel the force of a New England character, always upright, industrious, frugal, and usually successful in what he undertook. He was a partisan in politics, first a Whig and later a Republican, but always extremely patriotic and devoted to what he believed to be the best interests of his country. He strengthened me in my budding convictions of political duty, hardly yet blossoming out. I never questioned the rightness of the views which he so graphically revealed on that ride to a lad of fourteen.

On arriving at North Yarmouth he took me to the house of Allan H. Weld, the head of the Classical Department, who with marvelous brevity assigned me to a room in what was called the Commons Building. In that building were the classical students and the recitations for those who were taking the classical course, with a few other students who attended the English academy near by. The latter was under the supervision of Professor Woods, who a little later became the president of the Western University of Pennsylvania, located at Pittsburg and Allegheny. He developed that institution from small beginnings, attained a national reputation in educational circles and was, as long as he lived, my warm personal friend.

The next morning after my arrival I sat with a class of twelve bright-looking young men facing Mr. Weld in a room filled with writing desks. He had become famous for fitting boys for college. Only one of the class, John Bullfinch, of Kennebunk, was younger than myself.

Mr. Weld gave me a searching examination after the class had been dismissed, and told me that if I was diligent enough I might possibly enter college in 1846. His very manner aroused my ambition and made me determine to do everything in my power to accomplish that result.

I had for a roommate John Pettengill, whom I had known at the Leeds brick schoolhouse. He belonged to the English Department and had studies entirely different from mine. He was kind and companionable, always ready to perform his part in the care of the room. The room was small and the Commons a building poorly furnished from bottom to top. In the basement were the kitchen and the dining room. At the first meal I found myself at a long table, serving a "mess" of some fifteen to twenty young men. One was the president of the Commons. With a business-like manner he asked a blessing while the students were yet standing, then all sat down. Sitting on rough benches instead of chairs, we saw before us but little table furniture. There were on the board bottles of molasses, which was used every day, except Sunday, for butter. Loaves of bread were scattered at irregular intervals interspersed with some thin slices of cold meat. We had water for drink and no tea or coffee; these with meats were not allowed at every meal.

This was my first experience at such a table, and it was indeed the most economic of any that ever befell me. Soldiers would have complained if they had had such short rations; yet the young men were healthful and fairly well contented. It was their own choice to be thus frugal. Our mess bill never exceeded $1 per week, and sometimes was as low as eighty cents. We always had both meat and butter on Sundays.

My attention was very soon called to the most popular and the most singular of our young men. His

26

reputation as a student was such that I took an early fancy not only to know him, but to see how he made such rapid progress. He took very little exercise out of doors and that by rapid walking or running by himself. He had a standing desk where he stood when not in recitation or at his meals. He could so prolong his studies as to do with but five hours' sleep in the twenty-four.

As I was so anxious to keep up with the advanced class which I had entered, I imitated Spencer Wells for a part of the time. I took more exercise, but I kept myself many hours at the standing desk and I tried hard to shorten my sleep. At times I succeeded in getting along with only five or six hours by a rigid persistency, and it is a wonder that I did not impair my health.

Toward the latter part of the course the students of my class, with two or three exceptions, were inclined to dissipation. They had all their preparation quite complete and to them the review to put on the final touches was easy. To me much of it was in advance.

During the last term I roomed with Arthur Mc-Arthur. He was a splendid specimen of a youth, having a perfect physique, with mental talents above the ordinary, that is, in the outset, when I first knew him. Fearful headaches and depression followed his frequent indulgences, and I did my best to care for him. His example, with that of the more dissipated of the young men, was a constant warning to me and I think deterred me from giving way in those days to temptation.

The time finally came to take the preparatory examinations before entering college on September 1st. We had no railways then. There was a stage line, wearisome to boys, between Yarmouth and Brunswick. McArthur proposed to me to hire a chaise and take the ride comfortably, remain in Brunswick till after the examinations at Bowdoin, and then return to Yarmouth to take our final leave of that institution. There was a tavern at the halfway house, in front of which was a half hogshead, which was full and running over with fresh water. Arthur sprang out to let down the check rein that the horse might drink. He had been meditating upon getting a drink of whisky at this tavern and had reasoned with me about it. His reasons for urging me to join him were the common ones: "Howard, you are ambitious, you would like to make something of yourself in the future; you do not expect to do it without ever taking a glass of liquor, do you?" I answered that I did not see what the taking of a glass of liquor had to do with the subject. Then he gave me the names of several public men of distinction, both State and national; he said they all drank and in his judgment drink helped them to their greatness. I answered that I did not care to be great and that I was already on a pledge to my mother and would not drink. I recall this instance only to show how I felt with regard to strong drink at that period of my life.

Before we graduated from Bowdoin Arthur McArthur had so suffered from drink that he had hard work to secure his diploma. The eminence and worthiness of his father, who had graduated years before from Bowdoin, pleaded strongly for him.

The entrance examination was held in what was then the medical college building, where Professor Cleveland gave his lectures on chemistry, mineralogy, and astronomy.

Professor Boody, who taught composition and elocution and sometimes Latin in the college, met us young men at the hall door and took us into a grewsome sort of room where there were a few chairs and every sort of article from specimen boxes and chemical retorts to articulated skeletons. Here we were examined in everything required. I succeeded very well in my reading and translations and in my mathematics, but was conditioned upon scanning. That I had never studied, so I could not scan at all from Virgil or the Odyssey. I think, too, that I was a little weak in the line of Greek roots, still my heart was filled with intense satisfaction when I found that I was to enter with the class. I have passed through many ordeals since then, but I do not think that any of them impressed me more than that preliminary examination. I was fifteen years old at that time.

CHAPTER III

AFTER rising every day except Sundays for three weeks at four o'clock and continuing work until near midnight during the final preparation for college; and after the subsequent trying examinations early in September, one may imagine, weariness and apathy succeeded. I was glad enough to get home to my friends and have a short vacation. The good air, the good water, and the wholesome food at home soon restored me to my normal condition, and father took me to Bowdoin for the fall term, which at that time commenced during the last week in September.

Soon after reaching Bowdoin, before I was fairly settled in my college room in the south end of North Hall, I met a young man, Peleg Sprague Perley, who had belonged to the previous freshman class, but being kept away by illness so much of the year he had concluded to join the class to which I belonged. He was a year my senior in age, and his mother had been in early life my mother's neighbor and school friend, so we readily formed an acquaintance and agreed to room together. He was about my height, with a fair physique, but one hardly strong enough in our trying climate to give him the endurance which his mental capacity and his ambitions demanded. He had a large head and a very active brain. In the languages no

30

man could excel him, but in anything akin to mathematics he had a hard struggle. In these respects he was the reverse, or I might say the complement, of myself. To me mathematical studies were easy and a pleasure and the languages not so readily mastered. We two roomed together during our entire college course. We became fast friends and always exchanged confidences. During the first term at Bowdoin we were, I may say, "broken in" to systematic study. The daily routine embraced "Livy" under Professor Upham, a continuance of the "Odyssey" under Professor Packard, and algebra under Prof. William Smyth. At least once a week every member of our class was obliged to "declaim" before the class under the supervision of Professor Boody. He also caused every student to write *themes*, which must fill at least two pages of foolscap.

Professor Boody took great pains with our speaking, endeavoring to train us in the right way in all that pertained to elocution. He was equally careful in reviewing and correcting our compositions.

One of the professors was always present in the "Old Chapel" where all the students met at dawn for prayers, and President Leonard Woods presided at the evening chapel exercises; his singularly sonorous voice so impressed every student that he never forgot it nor the dignified lessons which came gently yet forcibly from his lips.

As I run over my college diary, and letters which I wrote to my mother and which she always preserved with care, prizing them far beyond their merits, I see the glaring faults of composition in, first, the gradual but slow emancipation from the stiffness of paragraphs, from the stilted manner of conducting a correspondence, and from the use of words that hardly conveyed the meaning intended, to a freer and easier style.

Herein I discover something of the great benefit to a young man taking a classical course simply in this line of review and examination. I realize now the fidelity of our professors, and rejoice in the unfailing personal supervision which they gave to the work of every student under their charge. Our studies went on to embrace the entire course of four years. No important department was neglected. We had not only the *dead* languages, but considerable instruction in French and German. Attention to chemistry, mineralogy, geology, and astronomy was abreast of that in any college. The harder studies which pertained to metaphysics, such as Butler's " Analogy," Paley's " Evidences," and Upham's " Moral Philosophy " were explained by the teachers and mastered by the students.

I feel that I was too young and had too poor a preparation to receive all the benefit that was needful, or the help and discipline which came to many of my classmates who were older and more mature before entering college, but, after all, this classical training was for me in every way a good foundation for my subsequent professional life and for the various requirements of what followed in my career. Indeed, I count the great gain of a college course to be the impression made upon the character of a young man, first, by the professors, and then by daily intercourse with the students.

President Leonard Woods, by his example, earnest, dignified, and sincere, always exacted a high standard of deportment. His corrections were given with such fidelity and kindness that a student was never discouraged, but rather stimulated by them to do better.

Prof. Thomas C. Upham, a tall man of sixty with head modestly drooping, sat at his desk and reasoned with any delinquent lad in such a fatherly way that even the boy's wrongdoing seemed to be a source of drawing him nearer to a fatherly heart; though the professor had, without any severity of manner or method, a way of getting from a youth anything he wanted to know. In spite of his modesty and retiring disposition, scarcely able to give an address on his feet, Professor Upham was a natural and polished diplomat.

Prof. A. S. Packard differed from the others. He had a fine figure, was very handsome, and wore a pair of gold spectacles; his hair and clothing were always in perfect condition. He was quick to see a student's fault and sometimes corrected it with severity, sometimes wittily, but he conveyed the impression of the highest order of gentility. He was, in fact, the student's beau ideal of a Christian gentleman.

When we came to modern languages we had Professor Goodwin, whose mind was replenished with knowledge and so clear cut in its action that every student felt at once his superiority. He was quick-tempered and at times irascible, and resented any attempted humor on the part of a pupil; but the lessons he gave were settled in his own mind, and the student could not well forget them. Besides his teaching the languages, he often gave us brief historical lectures of a high order.

Professor Smyth's unruly hair had already begun to whiten; he had good health, was interested in everything that concerned the college or the welfare of the village. He was rather above the medium height, had a fine head and face, models for an artist. His large gray eyes when not abstracted beamed with kindness; yet the students who disliked mathematics called him " Ferox," more from his earnest pursuit of a matter in hand, regardless of chalk and dust, than from any severity of look or act.

Prof. Parker Cleveland was the oldest teacher when I came. He had been for over forty years connected with Bowdoin. His forte was chemistry. His lectures to students, including the medical classes, were plain, clear, and beautiful, not at all behind the times. Chemistry, geology, mineralogy, and astronomy could not be pursued as now with the new splendid opportunities for individual experiments, but in these subjects the venerable professor made ours the equal of any existing college. The man himself was grand. His face was strong, like that of Bismarck. No student would willingly receive a reprimand from him. His looks with a few words were enough for a delinquent lad. Though he was a great scholar and indeed a manly man, yet he had, it was said, a peculiar weakness. He was nearly paralyzed with fear in a thunder storm and resorted to an insulated stool for safety; he would never step into a railway coach, but rode in his own chaise from Brunswick to Boston when duty called him to Massachusetts. In spite of his rough exterior he had a tender heart for young men and we all loved him.

During the freshman year a young man had all the old trials in the way of hazing; holdings-in at the chapel; football miscarriages; smokings-out; baths at the pump; casting the remains of nightly feasts into his room and such like performances, that some sophomores, aided by other fun-loving boys from the higher classes, could give him. When my roommate and I came to the sophomore year we determined to abstain from such practices. In fact, as he had belonged to the previous class he proved to be quite a mascot of prevention to his roommate during the first and second years.

As I think of my college course, and in fact of all my school life, I see that I had in mind very clearly defined one purpose, and that was to accomplish what I undertook in spite of the obstacles thrown in my way. The means of my family, so far as I was concerned, were very limited, and I desired greatly to teach a district school the first winter, but in spite of every effort which I made I could not at sixteen convince the school committees that I was old enough to undertake the teaching and government of forty or fifty scholars. Though fully grown, I had no beard, and my face was yet that of a youth emerging into manhood. " O Otis, you are too young altogether!" the Chairman of the Leeds Committee declared.

That winter vacation, however, was a very important one to me. It was a complete rest from study and very much enlivened by social intercourse with young people in Leeds and the neighboring towns. My roommate, Perley, lived with his parents, brothers, and sisters in Livermore, which was separated from Leeds by the Androscoggin River. He invited me to visit him. I did so for a few days. His mother gave him and me a pleasant evening party of young people from the neighborhood. Among the girls there came to the party a young lady visiting her relatives in the vicinity, who was a cousin of Perley. During the evening I made her acquaintance. She was about two years younger than I, but very mature for her age. As two or three of us were chatting together that evening, I related some of my mischievous performances, probably exaggerating them, when with her large, dark eyes she looked into mine and said, " Mr. Howard, do you think that was right? "

I may here say that this little *contretemps* eventuated in a lifelong relationship. The acquaintance ripened into a correspondence which absorbed my heart and much of my leisure during the college course. After this my purpose to do well, to accomplish what I undertook, and to make a success of life never faltered.

The next winter I was able to get a school in the district where I was born. Here I began to teach for $14 a month. The following winter I had a large district school in East Livermore and received for my hard work $18 per month, and part of the time I had the very pleasant experience of " boarding round." Of course, the master, during his week with a family, always had the very best. After a month, however, I was relieved from the wear and tear of it by an aged widow who found me so useful and companionable that she requested the privilege of boarding the master at her house.

In the fall of 1849 I stayed out of college and conducted a high school at Wayne Village; and the following winter was employed in our home district and enabled to board at home under my mother's care. This was the most difficult and trying of all my experiences in school-teaching, owing to the school being composed of boys and girls of all ages from five years to twenty-one and without any proper classification, and further, owing to the fact that I had previously been a scholar in the same school. I managed, however, to get through the winter without any serious difficulty. There were threatenings from some of the young men who felt sure that they could " put the master out " in a contest of strength, and there was at times a troublesome independence on the part of some of the larger girls who had known me as their companion in social life. To them I was hardly " master," but simply Otis Howard.

The help that came from my school wages and from my mother's economy and self-denial paid all the expenses at Bowdoin which, including my preparatory course, cost a sum in the neighborhood of $1,100. So small an expense seems to-day hardly possible, but at Brunswick I joined what was called a club where the students themselves, twelve or less, organized and chose a good purveyor from their own number to serve without pay. He employed a family which did the cooking and served the table. The table furniture descended from generation to generation, being added to, now and then, when there was a deficiency or a breakage. During my course I belonged to four different establishments of this kind. Habitually the cost to each of us in the club was $1 per week. Sometimes it slightly exceeded this amount. The highest that was paid at any club was $1.75 per week.

During my last year, with several classmates of special selection, I boarded at Mrs. Hall's, not far from the Tontine Hotel, for $1.50 per week.

This board did not include what was called the term bill, which, for room rent, tuition, and incidentals, was paid to the treasurer of the college.

In my class were thirty-six students. One only, Dr. Holmes, a surgeon in the army, died during the Civil

War. Another, William P. Frye, of just my age, truly a most distinguished citizen, is now a United States Senator and President *pro tem.* of the United States Senate. John S. Sewall, D.D., for a time in the United States Navy, has just retired with accumulated honor from the Presidency of the Bangor Theological Seminary. Carroll S. Everett was, long before his death, a professor in Harvard College and at the head of the Divinity School of that institution.

My classmates were scattered hither and thither over the country. Some were lawyers, some were physicians, and several were clergymen of different denominations. With scarcely an exception the record of each has been most worthy, and I am proud to-day of those living; they are still doing important work in the world.

The oldest, most dignified, and perhaps the hardest worker when in college was John N. Jewett. His parents had moved from Maine to Wisconsin and he came back from Madison to take the Bowdoin course. He was really, while a student, the head of the class. I remember to have tried my hand with him in mathematics, which study we completed at the end of the junior year. The test problem was to be solved by using the calculus. This was the problem as I remember it:

"Find the volume generated by revolving a circle about an axis exterior to it; given the radius of the circle and the distance of the axis from the center of the circle."

We both worked at it for some time. One morning I wakened quite early and went to my small blackboard and wrote out its solution. It seemed to have come to me in the night. I ran to Jewett's room. He had not yet obtained the answer; so that my class-mates gave me the credit of being the mathematician of the class, though Professor Smyth, with better discrimination, taking in the entire course, gave the palm to my friend Jewett. Jewett and Fuller were for years in the same firm in Chicago. "Mell Fuller," as we called him, was a college friend, though not a class-mate, of mine. He is now the Chief Justice of the United States.

As I have said, in the winter vacation of 1846 I met at her cousin's house one who was but a girl just budding into womanhood. She arrested my attention and impressed me more deeply than I then thought. Our acquaintance very soon after that winter ripened into something more than an ordinary friendship. I met her during her visits to Livermore in vacations and I had several times visited her father's house in Portland. I may say that with the approval of our parents we had come, before my graduation, to have a constant and intimate correspondence.

In the fall, while I was conducting a high school at Wayne Village, something happened that threw a heavy cloud of sorrow upon the household to which she belonged. Her father, Alexander Black Waite, super-intending a number of workmen engaged in calking one of his vessels, accidently fell through the hatchway to the deck below. This fall gave him such a terrific blow on the head that he never spoke again. He was carried unconscious to his house, where every remedy was applied, but to no purpose, and he very soon breathed his last.

His remains, accompanied by his wife and daughter, were brought to his father's house in Livermore and he was buried with proper ceremony in the cemetery in that vicinity. The news of this fearful calamity came to me with the suddenness of lightning from a clear sky. I went over and was present during those saddest of days.

Alexander B. Waite was still a young man when thus so tragically arrested in the midst of a most promising career. His wife was never quite herself again. The only child, Elizabeth, seemed at first completely overcome. She gave evidence of intensity of affection for her father and could not repress her grief. From that time it was understood by everybody connected with our two families that we young people were betrothed.

I left the stricken ones to return to my school and as soon as the term was completed went back to Bowdoin for a short time. Then, hard pressed as I was for means, I took my school in the winter.

During the hardest part of that winter, when the snow was deep and a storm raging, my mother on one occasion worked her way on foot from our home to the schoolhouse to bring me an important message. That trip of my good mother, so full of exposure and danger to herself, gave me the strongest impression that I ever had had of my mother's love.

During that year, while I was hard at work in the summer term, preparing for graduation, and while even to my sanguine mind the future was dark enough, I received a letter from my uncle, the Hon. John Otis, then at Washington:

WASHINGTON, June 20, 1850.

MY DEAR NEPHEW: From what William (William Otis, his son) writes me to-day, I am of opinion that he will not be accepted at West Point on account of the narrowness of his chest, and want of general physical strength. . . . What I wish to know is whether, in case he is not accepted, you would like to have me recommend you or Rowland Bailey (my brother). The advantages you would have are a good constitution and strength for endurance, and you have a good acquaintance with the languages and are fond of mathematics. . . . The applicant must be full sixteen years of age. Is that Rowland's age? He must not be over twenty-one. Please write me your own thoughts before you apply at home.

Yours sincerely,

[Signed]   JOHN OTIS.
Oliver Otis Howard.

This was a turning point in my career. What my uncle anticipated with reference to his son took place. He was rejected upon the physical examination. I did not accept the offer at once. It occasioned too radical a change in all my thoughts and plans. I had desired to do something to enable me to lay by money enough to commence and go through a professional course without interruption, and I wanted to be, like my uncle, a lawyer. It had never entered my mind before to be a soldier, and I knew scarcely anything with regard to the Military Academy; but the prospect of bettering my education and having a support while I did so and, if I graduated successfully, a career open which would relieve me from the anxiety of toiling too much for a support, soon determined the case in favor of acceptance. As we were so young, Miss Waite and her friends made no serious objection.

I went home to my mother and laid the whole case before her and think I should have been governed by her wisdom had she decided that I ought not to go into the army, but she looked into my face and said, " My son, you have already made up your mind." It was the nearest to an objection that she ever made. Her chief thought, often expressed, was that I must be upright in all my intercourse at the Military Academy and take a high stand.

By diligent study I was able to pass all my examinations at Bowdoin and secure my proper degree at graduation, though it was impossible for me to remain with my classmates for the final " commencement."

It has been my privilege to attend ceremonials at home and abroad of every description and to take in as well as I could notions of precedence, arrangement, and dignity, but I have never been so much impressed as I was with the seniors of Bowdoin College during the last term of our class. Their display at chapel exercises was particularly noticeable, especially at the time of evening prayers. As a rule they wore tall silk hats and a majority of them carried canes. They attached considerable importance to their long coats, their well-selected cravats and standing collars. They usually came with a quick step, to be observed by the other classes, the professors and President Woods, who, through his large spectacles, never let anything escape his attention. As soon as the seniors were seated President Woods arose and gave out a hymn, which was well sung by a choir of selected voices. Then he read a portion of Scripture. Always reverent and yet always cheerful, he offered a prayer, simple and direct, as a prayer should be. It covered the usual ground of confession and entreaty, but always wound up with asking a blessing upon the college, upon our rulers, State and national, and upon " all our fellow men, for the sake and in the name of our Blessed Lord." The seniors never waited for the last benediction, but as soon as they heard the words " all our fellow men " they rose *en masse* and marched out with their dignified tread and deportment, much impressing, as it should, the under classmen who were to follow them. The hats were resumed, and the canes, carried under the arm, were taken in hand at the door.

The present beautiful chapel is not the one I found at Bowdoin in 1846, but is a new one, handsomely constructed, which, for a time, answered the purpose of a chapel and a library. After half a century the library, having become altogether too small, has been, through the generosity of an alumnus, General Thomas H. Hubbard, of New York, replaced by a new structure four times as large and in every way conformable to the wonderful growth of the college itself.

Perhaps at no time in my life did I feel so much that I had attained substantial greatness as when, among the seniors with their hats and canes, I passed in and out of the college chapel for the last time.

CHAPTER IV

IT was after the middle of August, 1850, when I left my home for West Point. I had my trunk packed with those things that were required in the way of underclothing, but as the uniform, whatever that might mean, and everything pertaining to the furnishing of a cadet's room were to be had from the public store after my arrival, I did not overburden myself with articles which would be of no use to me if I succeeded in passing the entrance examinations. On the way from Boston to New York I was fortunate enough to meet on the train Lieutenant Alley, who had been my predecessor. A predecessor is the cadet from my same district whose graduation caused the vacancy which I filled. He gave me some very wholesome suggestions and I saw at once that it would not do to appear there with a silk hat or a cane. I found that they called a freshman a " plebe " and that I should not escape the hazing process whatever might be my character, my age, or previous experience.

New York City, now visited for the first time, was much enjoyed. I had relatives in Brooklyn and remained a few days with them. The old omnibuses were running on Broadway, and at times every day the street was blocked with them, so that nothing could pass one way or the other till a gradual clearing was

44

had under the direction of the police. The St. Nicholas Hotel, said to be much needed, was just open for guests. The Hudson River Railroad had its depot in Chambers Street and the cars were taken in and out of the city from that point by horses. There was substantially no city above Forty-second Street.

The first time I stayed overnight in New York proper, I had a room in the old Washington Hotel near Bowling Green. The Astor House was at that time in best repute as a family hotel.

On August 26th I took the Hudson River Railway and after a two hours' run was left at Cold Spring, a small New York village just above West Point. Here again I counted myself very fortunate in meeting an officer of the army, Captain E. Kirby Smith. He was dressed in citizen's clothes and was on his way to the Military Academy. Two flat-bottomed rowboats were found at the wharf just at the foot of the main street. Captain Smith being my guide, I got my trunk on board one of them. He and I seated ourselves in the stern and a single oarsman began to row us, a distance of a mile and a half, to the West Point landing.

The captain explained to me very kindly what I must do, and some things that I must not do, when I reached the post — the whole military station was called a post. He advised me not to report at once to the superintendent, but to go to Roe's Hotel and stay at least one night, visit the cadet encampment close by and take observations. The orders which I had in my pocket were for me to report to the adjutant of the academy on or before September 1, 1850.

Indeed, I think that Captain Smith's kind warnings saved me from a good deal of annoyance and from

45

some laughable mistakes that a candidate is almost sure to make unless he is thus befriended.

It was not long before I reported to Captain Seth Williams, then adjutant of the Military Academy. He, too, was very pleasant and thoughtful for me. He was always a genial gentleman and took pleasure in doing something for the comfort of anybody who came in contact with him.

The superintendent, Captain Brewerton, was a tall military man dressed in the uniform of the corps of engineers. Every officer at West Point was in uniform, and every cadet also. The cadet's dress consisted of the well-known gray coat, with the tail so short you might call it a coatee. . It was double-breasted, with three rows of bell buttons and a stiff collar. During the encampment, and for some time after, the trousers were of white duck. When off duty the cadet, outside of his quarters, wore a small cap of blue cloth, diminishing toward the top, which was flat and round, and having a chin strap with a brass button at each extremity. The cap was essentially like the ordinary undress cap of officers. When on duty, at that time, the cadet wore a singular stiff felt hat shaped like a section of stovepipe with a leather band around it at the bottom, and a band at the top. It was finished with a stiff visor, and pompon at the crest. Each hat was ornamented in front with a handsome bronze castle. The cadet officers, instead of a pompon, wore a plume of dark feathers which floated in the breeze and covered the top of the hat. The waist belt was of white canvas with a brass breastplate, and the shoulder belt, which sustained the cartridge box, was also of the same material.

As I looked upon the battalion for the first time

when in line of battle in two ranks, I thought I had never seen anything handsomer. There did not appear to be a motion throughout the line, and later, the movement in column presented an appearance even more beautiful. Every cadet held his musket in his left hand, and the drill in the manual of arms was nearly perfect. Though the motions were angular and stiff enough, the effect upon the beholder was that of a complete machine which could make no failure as long as it was in order.

When the cadets were at drill or on parade there was, not far off, a squad of young men dressed in old clothes of different descriptions. They all had caps, but caps differing from each other. This squad afforded interest and amusement to a number of visitors who clustered about the encampment to observe the drills and parades. I was very soon attached to that squad. At drill we were divided into two such squads and each was under the command of a cadet corporal of the class above us.

They called us "Septs" because we came in September. The officers said we were September cadets. The main portion of my class, 102 in number, had reported for duty before June 1st, and so had had the benefit of the summer encampment. It really meant a constant drill and discipline, covering the whole new life of a young man, every day and every hour, from which he was never for a moment relieved, even at night; because with only blankets and a single pillow he was obliged to lie upon the hard floor of his tent and be subject to annoyance, he knew not when—to be plagued by the other cadets—some of whom would pull him out of his bed or otherwise attempt to haze him. I escaped this severe trial because I slept in the encampment only four nights; then the battalion was sent to the barracks. Still our squad drill continued once a day while the uniforms of the September cadets were in making. The corporal of one of our squads was Cadet Boggs, of Georgia. He was a capital drill master, severe enough, but always dignified and respectful to the boys under his charge; but the other corporal, Cadet Walker, never let an opportunity slip for an irritating speech to the squad and to individuals in it.

It was hard enough for a young man to put himself into what was called the military attitude, the little fingers on the seams of the trousers, palms to the front, head drawn back, and shoulders squared. I held myself in this position of apparent awkwardness till it became natural to be thus set up. I think the most difficult thing for each of us was to so walk as to strike the ball of the foot first. To point the toe and do this were required, and it gave a cadet a peculiar gait.

As soon as I received my uniform, my coat neatly fitting and keeping me in shape, with a clean white linen collar turned over the stiff binding, and trousers like my comrades, it was easier than before to escape expressions of amusement, and when we were divided into sections and sent to the class rooms I became daily more and more reconciled to the new life. In the recitation room I was more ready to compete with my companions.

At first the young men of my class when getting acquainted with each other were reasonably harmonious in their social life, but I very soon found that unpleasant feuds existed in the corps of cadets, and, as a rule, the subject of slavery was at the bottom of the controversy. I would not have owned at that time that I was an abolitionist, but in sentiment I indorsed the speeches of William H. Seward, which were against slavery and demonstrated the desirability of its non-extension. However, I said but little about politics, yet once in a while in conversation with a companion I did let my sentiments be known.

When we first went into quarters the room to which I was assigned was in what was called the Old South Barracks, a very large room without alcoves. There were four separate iron bedsteads and four iron tables, with other meager furniture for four cadets. My mates were Thomas J. Treadwell, from New Hampshire, a student of Dartmouth; Levi R. Brown, from Maine, my own State; and Henry M. Lazell, of Massachusetts. No young men were ever more studious or more desirous to get a fair standing in the institution than we.

The only single room on the same floor had been at one time used as a " light prison," and this room was occupied by a cadet of the third class by the name of Elmer S. Otis. He had done some foolish thing while in the camp which the majority of his class condemned. There was no criminality in it, but his comrades declared that no gentleman would do such a thing. A few of them started the cry to ostracize him, or, as the cadets say, " cut him." The idea went from man to man till there was scarcely a cadet who would speak to him. I remember two of his classmates who were exceptions. One was McPherson, who was a man of independence and noble instincts, and another was William Sooy Smith, who was a professing Christian. They occasionally visited him. As he had my mother's maiden name, my attention was early called to him and his situation. Frequently I stepped in to see him, and sometimes during leisure hours played checkers with him to relieve his loneliness.

The next day after my arrival at the post I went to the engineer's barracks situated near the northwest corner of the reservation to look up Warren Lothrop from my home town. He was the first sergeant of the Engineer Company then called the " Sappers and Miners." This company had achieved success in the Mexican War and was considered the first of all the companies of enlisted men in the service. Warren himself had gained quite a distinction for his bravery and work during the campaign. He was now a magnificent-looking man, straight, tall, and of fine figure, and his officers were proud of him and trusted him fully in the management of the company. He was earnestly seeking a commission, and his friends thought he had a good prospect of receiving one. As he was a worthy man and the son of my guardian, and as our families at home were intimate, I felt it a duty and a privilege to visit him. For a time he came to see me during release from quarters, always making short calls. One Saturday afternoon, when the limits of cadets were extended to embrace the public lands generally, I went to the engineer barracks to make a call. Two army officers saw me and the next night my name was published before the battalion, " Cadet Howard off limits Saturday afternoon." The next Saturday I took to the acting commandant, Lieutenant John M. Jones, of Virginia, a written request to go and see that friend. In my presence, with a show of anger, Mr. Jones tore up my request and threw the fragments on the floor. Feeling outraged I wrote another and carried it to the superintendent, Captain Brewerton. This request was disapproved and I was reported for forwarding a permit to the superintendent over the head of the commandant. A day or two afterwards Captain B. R. Alden, the commandant, sent for me and gave me a lecture, a very kind and fatherly one, for which I was grateful. He had been temporarily absent. The purport of what he said was, " There has been nothing wrong in your conduct; on the contrary, it is to your credit to recognize your friend as you have done, but it is contrary to the regulations and spirit of this institution. The sergeant is an enlisted man and it will not do for you to recognize him in any social way."

Captain Seth Williams, the adjutant, also sent for me and advised me kindly in the matter: " You must remember that it will be for your own advantage to separate yourself from your friend while he is in the unfortunate position of an enlisted man." I wasn't yet wise enough to be silent on the subject of what I regarded as wrong.

About the year 1854 Lothrop became a second lieutenant and was assigned to the Fourth Artillery. He was promoted, step by step, till he became, during the Civil War, the colonel of a regiment, and he would probably have had higher promotion still had not typhoid fever seized him in camp and terminated his life. I have never regretted my show of friendship to him in our younger days and the incident always affected me, when considering the subject of discipline in the army, inclining me strongly against martinetism in whatever form it presented itself.

For a time I was very intimate with one of my classmates from the East, and finding him a man of high culture, I constantly sought his companionship, as he did mine. A few months had passed when I began to feel that there was something in the social atmosphere of my class unfavorable to me. I need not go into details, but simply state that a few individuals with a view to promoting the interest of a rival in academic standing, formed a cabal. They were all of them Southern men. It was the beginning of a feud such as I had observed in other classes. Against me certain things were alleged: First, that I was an abolitionist; second, that I associated with " cut men "; third, that I visited and made companions of enlisted men; and fourth, that I had joined the Bible class and curried favor with the professor of ethics. We were accustomed to salute each other as we passed, or give some sign of pleasant recognition. I now saw that individuals who belonged to the small conspiracy passed me without recognition or took some other method of showing that my society was not desirable. I became suspicious and turned a cold shoulder upon any classmate who might pass me by without notice, even when done by accident. My friend and associate, of whom I have spoken, changed his place in ranks to remove from me, and completely withdrew his fellowship. For this I called him to account with indignation. On the Sabbath the professor of ethics, who was also the chaplain, preached a sermon against slander and ostracism. The case fitted so well that my late friend asked of me an interview. We had a walk and talked over the whole matter, when he told me frankly that he wanted to stand high in the academy, not only in his studies but socially, and as he saw that I was becoming unpopular for the reasons I have alleged, he thought it would be better for him completely to forego my companionship. In a proud spirit I agreed to this. He said, however, something that comforted me a little, that he believed there was nothing against me as a gentleman. He and I from that time did not speak to each other for over three years.

This feud, for it became one, entered into the following summer encampment and for a time I confess that my life at West Point was wretched. Several of those who were opposed to me became cadet officers and they gave me reports with demerit on every possible occasion. Seeing how matters went, Captain Alden at last sent for me and said that he had noticed how I was being treated and how unjustly demerit was being given me and he said, "Now, Mr. Howard, I want to give you some advice. Mind you, I do not give you this advice as Commandant of Cadets, for I shall punish you for any infraction of regulations. Yes, sir, I shall punish you severely, but I give it to you as a father to his son. If I were in your place I would knock some man down."

I understood Captain Alden thoroughly, and from that time on my friends had nothing to complain of from my want of spirit. I had some conflicts, some wounds, and was reasonably punished for breaking the regulations, and my demerits increased.

My friends might be curious to know if I had any following in my own class. Indeed I did, and it wasn't long before I had nine-tenths of the class in sympathy with me and my defenders. I never can forget the manliness of J. E. B. Stuart, of Virginia, who became, in the Civil War, the leader of the Southern cavalry. He spoke to me, he visited me, and we became warm friends, often, on Saturday afternoons, visiting the young ladies of the post together. While I was made to feel keenly the hatred which accompanies ostracism, yet by a straightforward course I first robbed it of its sting; and finally the majority of those who opposed me were ashamed of the course they had pursued and before graduation there were few indeed with whom I was not on good terms. I did not go to the offenders and ask any favors, but one by one they came to me.

At one time during my first winter the horizontal bar turned with me and I fell in the gymnasium. The injury to my head was very severe and ended in a serious attack of erysipelas and for a time my life was despaired of. The gentle care and nursing of Dr. Cuyler, the surgeon, saved my life.

While I was in the hospital the superintendent, then Colonel Robert E. Lee, paid me a visit, sat down by my bedside and spoke to me very kindly. After I was restored to health, with Cadet Stuart I visited Colonel Lee's family and was well received by every member of it.

Notwithstanding this accident and my detention for some weeks from the recitation rooms, I kept up my studies and did not lose my standing. At the end of the first year I was at the head of my class, already reduced in numbers from resignations to sixty-three, and I had the privilege and honor of marching the class whenever it went *en masse* to any exercise.

The difficulties which had assailed me prevented me for a year from receiving military advancement, and in fact I entered my second class year without promotion. One day our new commandant, Captain Robert S. Garnet, who relieved Captain Alden, came into our recitation room and heard several cadets recite, myself among the number. He was a Southern man and a just and impartial commandant. He inquired why Cadet Howard was without chevrons. A few days after this inquiry I had the pleasure of hearing my name published as promoted to a sergeancy, and a little later, after some cadet officer was reduced for a military offense, I was made quartermaster sergeant of the cadet corps and held that office till the end of the year.

The last year at the Military Academy I was promoted to a cadet lieutenancy and a little later was made cadet quartermaster of the corps. In this I followed in the footsteps of Cadet J. B. McPherson, who had had the same office during his second and his first class years.

My unpopularity had, at the beginning of my last year, so far passed away that I was elected to the presidency of our only literary association, the Dialectic Society. In this also I followed McPherson.

It has often been said to me, " You had the advantage over your companions in a college training, did you not?" I did have the advantage of some of them, but it should be remembered that we had in our class fifteen young men who also had had a college education, and as many as twenty more who had received an equivalent training, many of them in those studies that had special reference to the West Point course. We were all on a par in tactical exercises, both in the theoretical and the practical. Much time was then given to right line and topographical drawings, and as much more to sketching and painting. In this branch I was without any experience whatever. At the end of the first year of drawing I was ranked thirty-seven, but by perseverance and great care I kept rising till I graduated ninth in that division of work.

The most difficult of our course was the second class year, and the most trying study of that year was Bartlett's " Mechanics," usually denominated " The application of Algebra to Geometry." Professor Bartlett was a man of great research and very able in the preparation of text-books, but he was of a nervous temperament and not a very successful instructor on that account. His digestion was so bad at one time that he ate scarcely any meat. It was said that they selected for him the tenderest birds in order to tempt his appetite and keep up his strength.

One day I remember that he had me at the blackboard and was very impatient and indignant that I did not follow him as he made his lightning demonstration. I remained after the class had gone so as to have a talk with him, and I said to him: " Professor Bartlett, I have a good mathematical mind, but I move slowly through a demonstration. If you hurry me or disconcert me I lose my chance. You are so familiar with this complicated work that it is very plain to your mind, but not to ours " (referring to myself and fellow cadets).

Professor Bartlett instantly changed. He was kindness itself, and said that I was right and that he would try to remember what I said in the interest of the class.

As a rule no professors conducted our recitations, but had their several instructors, who were detailed from the army, do this work under their supervision. During the recitations the professors would go from one section to another, sometimes taking part in the recitation and sometimes simply looking on and listening to the questions and answers. Professor Bartlett usually deviated from this custom.

I did not succeed so well in " English studies," as they were called, such as Blair's " Rhetoric," logic, and international law. Some of my mates would recite several pages word for word. How they could so memorize in the limited time given to preparation for the next day's recitation was a mystery to me. However, I could give the meaning in my own terms and obtained fairly good marks. I enjoyed the study of international law and never forgot the principles which were then learned. Even without books, when in the field, I could have decided most questions that arose involving our relations with other nations, as at Atlanta and Savannah; but I do not think that any of us could have equaled Sherman in his thorough mastery of that study. He never forgot what he once learned.

Those of our class who were able to systematize and seize upon the principles of any study were in the end able to retain the knowledge. The recitations at first of those who memorized were seemingly the best, but on the final examinations, after a month or more had elapsed, those who memorized were not so proficient. Many officers fail with large commands, and the reason is traceable to their encumbering their minds with the detail.

There were many things about my last year as a cadet which were very pleasant. Being the cadet quartermaster I was relieved from the irksome part of military duty and had more time for study during "call to quarters," and was more at leisure to extend my acquaintanceship to the families of the garrison. I think now that I had become quite a favorite in the social circle made up of the professors' and officers' families.

Henry W. Closson, a classmate from Vermont, who was retired as a colonel of artillery, became my favorite companion. He was a poet and very quick-witted. He and I exchanged confidences, read books together, and made visits in each other's company. Closson was small of stature, with light hair, of pale complexion, and had as finely formed a head as if it had been chiseled from marble by the best of sculptors. One lady with her two little children always took my friend's attention. She was beautiful and especially so in her little family, so that no visits were pleasanter than those that he and I made at her house. These and other visits gave us glimpses of home life that we very much needed while cadets.

I also became quite intimate with two of my classmates. One was Cadet Charles G. Sawtelle, the other his roommate, John T. Greble. Sawtelle was from Maine, and we were naturally thrown together, and through him I became associated with Greble. The latter belonged to a large Philadelphia family. Father, mother, and sisters often paid him visits. They invited me to see them at the hotel whenever they came, and I was treated by them with much attention and reciprocated the kindness as well as I could by attending them in their walks about the post and to the parades.

After graduation Mr. Edwin Greble always insisted that I make his house in Philadelphia my home whenever I came to that city.

CHAPTER V

GRADUATION FROM THE UNITED STATES MILITARY ACADEMY, 1854; BREVET SECOND LIEUTENANT IN ORDNANCE DEPARTMENT, 1855-56

AFTER a term of hard study away from home there is probably no more real enjoyment for a student than the vacation. Each vacation has its specialty. There are relaxations and rests which in themselves are refreshing. The constant call to duty, the constant pressure of mental work, and the exactions of instructors are by no means without their rewards, but such things always need the relief of a vacation. Then there is the comfort of meeting old friends; the bright welcome in the homes of old neighbors; the parties gotten up especially for you; and the increasing charm of the old homestead where are the father, the mother, the brothers, and the visiting friends, young men and young women. All these things had been mine and were delightfully reminiscent. What was called my cadet furlough at the close of the first two years of West Point life had been indeed the richest of all my vacations, so that when I returned to the severe discipline and confinement of the Military Academy I was for some time discontented and inclined to tender my resignation and return to my people, but no vacation was equal to that which came at the close of the West Point course.

The continued hardship of unremitting study; the freedom of action fettered; the orders and requirements which could never be evaded were now over forever. With the graduation a commission had followed the diploma, not a high one, but that of a brevet second lieutenant in the Army of the United States. It was something gained, something that looked larger to me then than any of the subsequent commissions which I received. On graduation in June, 1854, our class numbered forty-six members. As I graduated fourth in the class I had the right to choose any arm of the service from that of topographical engineer to the infantry arm inclusive. For several reasons I signified my choice to be that of the Ordnance Department.

Thus I went forth well equipped for enjoyment. The Ordnance Department had in charge all the United States arsenals and armories of the country with a few powder stations, and at every one of these there was a house ready for a married officer, so that as soon as I could get the assent of my *fiancée*, we could be married and have immediate provision for a home. The Ordnance Department had many other advantages over the line of the army, but this one of a house, which in the army we called quarters, was just then to me of special interest.

On the way to New York on board the old *Thomas Powell*, I met General Winfield Scott, accompanied by several of his staff and some young officers whom I knew. I had met him before and been presented, but this time his attention was called to me and he said some pleasant things welcoming me to the army. But when one of my classmates indicated that Howard would soon be married, the general shook his head and said, " No, no, don't do that; a lieutenant must never get married." I was glad enough to have the conversation turned to some other topic. I had no intention of

REVET SECOND LIEUTENANT HOWARD'S COMMISSION FROM PRESIDENT PIERCE
AND JEFFERSON DAVIS, SECRETARY OF WAR.

heeding Scott's advice on the subject of marriage, because I knew well enough the limitations of his authority, and the inalienable rights of even a brevet second lieutenant.

New York had never been so delightful, but there were stars in the East which drew me away from even the social life of New York. In Boston and Cambridge and Arlington welcome was extended to the young lieutenant with enough of cheer to turn his head, but the brighter visions were still farther on.

Portland, Me., was at that time the most beautiful of cities, and it had the center of all the attractions of that vacation. It will be impossible, of course, to interest others very much in the two succeeding months after my arrival in Maine; but as I look back and think of the rides into the country, the visit to my home and to friends in the towns round about, I say to myself that those days in the retrospect are genial and cloudless.

My mother had followed me with devoted affection, all the way from the day I left home at eleven years of age to begin my preparation for college at Hallowell, till then. No week had passed without a cheerful letter, and of course at no time did she ever go to rest without a prayer for her son; now imagine the welcome home when the first round of the ladder of his achievements had been reached. I think she had never been so happy as when she had her children together again around her table. I often hear the expression " American " or " That is an expression of our American life." It covers so much; energy in preparation; fearlessness in undertakings; bravery in action; endurance under every hardship. It involves a healthful and well-developed body; mental powers well in hand;

61

and an upright heart. Now who accomplishes this so much as an American mother, and who would deprive her of the joy of the home welcome which she gives to her sons as they come from or go to their world's work?

The vacation ended, I reported for duty to Major John Symington, commanding Watervliet Arsenal at West Troy, N. Y., in September, 1854.

Major Symington was a typical officer of the old school, already not far from the age of retirement. He was from Maryland and had married a sister of General Joseph E. Johnston. He was a tall man, very modest and retiring, but one who always stood up to his convictions of duty. After talking with me a few minutes in a kind and manly way he said that if I wished to go beyond the arsenal grounds all I would have to do was to put my name on a certain book, recording my departure and my return. Every day I was to have certain duties which would be easily performed, but twice a week I would be detailed as officer of the day. When officer of the day I would inspect the barracks, which then contained about forty enlisted men, and be responsible for the marching on of the guard and for the location of the sentinels, two being on duty at a time. I would further go through all the arsenal shops at least twice during my tour and note everything that was taking place.

So much freedom when on duty I had never had before since entering West Point, and never had afterwards till I came in command of a department.

I have already spoken of my strong leaning toward a paternal government as against that of a martinet. Here with Major Symington I realized the full blessing of the paternal; a man extraordinarily observant and conscientious, but always kind and considerate in his requirements.

Mrs. Symington was a strong character. She was of large size and rather stout, a woman of unusual accomplishments. The major's quarters were ample and commodious. He had a family consisting of his wife and five children, two daughters and three sons. The family was always hospitable. Nieces and nephews from Virginia and Maryland were generally part of the household. The large parlor gave a reception nearly every evening to the young officers, where there were music, innocent games, and delightful social converse. At that time there was but one other married officer, Major Laidley. He was a first lieutenant who had been in the Mexican War and was brevetted major for gallantry in action. He and his wife and child occupied a set of stone quarters. The other set under the same roof contained the unmarried officers' mess and rooms.

Ellen McCarty, who could do everything in the line of housework, was a treasure to them. Her husband worked in the shops and her children aided her when she needed any assistance. I think Ellen became well known throughout the entire Ordnance Department. Our quarters were always as neat as they could be made from garret to cellar, and everything was done by her for us young men to make the entire house as homelike as possible.

Lieutenant W. R. Boggs, of Georgia, who, it will be remembered, was at times my drill master when at West Point and who afterwards became a general in the Confederate service, was now my constant companion. Lieutenant F. J. Shunk, of Pennsylvania, whom I had known as a cadet captain, was a choice comrade to Boggs and myself. He was full of humor and oddities and entertained us often by his violin and by the anecdotes that he picked up from his abundant reading and daily observations. We three seldom were at table without a guest from outside, and in those days young gentlemen from Troy were frequent visitors.

One evening we were introduced at Mrs. Symington's reception to Miss Jennie Pickett. She was sister to Captain George E. Pickett of the Ninth Infantry, who became celebrated at Gettysburg. She was a beautiful girl, a niece of Mrs. Symington's, and soon captured all our hearts, especially by her exquisite singing. I never had heard before, and only once or twice since, such a voice. Every time she sang she thrilled and delighted all present.

Miss Carrie Symington, the major's niece from Baltimore, was with us in that garrison for at least two months. She was as remarkable for her personal beauty as Miss Jennie was for her music. Dignified in deportment, tall and commanding, she always had around her many admirers.

One can imagine, then, something of the manner in which we spent the fall and winter of 1854 at Watervliet. The outer high wall inclosed an immense space which included not only the buildings which I have named and also the warehouses of great length that contained gun carriages and every sort of artillery equipment, but small groves of trees, gardens always well kept, and roads and paths which were a delight. Our outdoor parties in pleasant weather are kaleidoscopic in my recollection.

The young officers did much reading at that time, each choosing books according to his taste. Major Symington, on one occasion, introduced to us a young

Frenchman, Eugene de Courcillon, who had met with some singular misfortune and was seeking employment. I was somewhat fascinated by him and hoped that my intercourse with him would improve my French, but he soon proposed to write a book revealing some of the customs of the part of France from which he came, interesting especially to Protestant minds. As he knew very little English I aided him in the translation of his book. This took all my leisure time for months. The book was published in New York. I aided him in its publication and was to receive a return for my advances whenever he disposed of his manuscript. Without my knowledge he managed to sell his work out and out and then disappeared without communicating with me, rewarding me only with this singular dedication:

"To Lieutenant Oliver O. Howard, my friend in adversity."

My comrades laughed and wondered at the double meaning of the dedication, that is, as to which was really in adversity, de Courcillon or myself.

In those days, in addition to the commissioned officers, we had an official called the military storekeeper. Accounts of the material in this arsenal of construction were carefully kept upon his books. He took care to receive everything coming in and to issue everything going out from the arsenal, making careful storage and record. An elderly man, Mr. Lansing, occupied that place. He and his wife, not much younger than himself, lived nearer to the arsenal entrance than any of us. For really charming hospitality Mr. and Mrs. Lansing excelled and very often entertained the young officers, among whom I was a welcome guest. Frequently Mr. Lansing, who was fond of fishing, would take me in his carriage and spend an entire day going to different fishing grounds. A favorite place was near Waterford in the upper waters of the Hudson. We caught there several varieties, but the favorite was the bass. Mr. Lansing declared that the bass was of better flesh and flavor than any other fish.

While these days were passing I kept up a constant correspondence with my friends, and the time for the long-anticipated wedding was at last fixed for February 14, 1855. It was necessary for me to have a leave of absence, so I applied to the head of our Ordnance Department at Washington, Colonel Craig, who very kindly gave me twenty days, and, of course, those twenty days embraced the principal event of that year.

Mrs. A. B. Waite had a comfortable home on Chatham Street in Portland, Me., where she and her daughter, Elizabeth, were then living. Every necessary arrangement was made for a private wedding, but as the relatives on both sides were numerous and intimate friends were not wanting, Mrs. Waite's apartments were soon filled by a happy company. All agreed then and thereafter that no more charming bride and none more appropriately dressed ever went to the altar. The only criticism came from the bride's mother, and that was with reference to the bridegroom — dressed in full uniform with sash and belt. She said "it seemed too much like war."

An event occurred the night of the wedding which, at least, was remarkable in the history and development of Portland. The large theater took fire and burned to the ground. It was difficult to keep down the fire and preserve the houses in the neighborhood. In those days the young men worked at the brakes of the engine, among whom the bridegroom very properly performed his part.

Before the expiration of the twenty days Lieutenant Howard and his bride appeared at Watervliet and began their social and domestic careers, which have now been continued beyond the golden wedding.

I remember that Mr. Hillhouse, who had been a graduate of West Point and resigned, lived not far from Watervliet Arsenal; he with his wife had been a constant visitor in the families of the officers. Hearing that I was to be married, Mrs. Hillhouse entreated me to give a description of the lady who was to be my wife. Out of mischief I gave her a description, naming every particular the exact opposite. For example, I said *tall*, with *reddish hair, bright blue eyes*, etc. Very soon after our arrival Mrs. Hillhouse came in her carriage to pay her respects to Mrs. Howard. As soon as she saw her she cried out with amazement, " Oh, Mr. Howard, how could you have sold me that way? " I know that she and the many others who promptly paid us visits were better satisfied with the actuality than with the imaginary figure which I had painted.

During the first few months after we had become settled in the north quarters we had a visit from Colonel Craig, the Chief of Ordnance, and I think we won his heart from the start. The result of it, however, seemed to be this: Captain Callender, in command of the Kennebec Arsenal at Augusta, Me., was to go to another post in the Far West, and there was no ranking ordnance officer available to fill his place; so I was selected and sent to Augusta to relieve him.

It was a favor for a second lieutenant to have an independent command, and it was indeed a promotion; but after you have furnished your quarters, planted your garden, provided yourself with a horse and buggy, and settled down to real life, it is not so easy to conform to a sudden change, and I would have been inclined to have said, " Let me remain here with my comforts for a while as a subordinate," but the army principle was: " Never decline promotion."

The Kennebec Arsenal was beautiful; large grounds; fine quarters, both for officers and men; a garden five times as large as the one we left; perfect roads, well shaded, and fruit trees in abundance. Only five or six enlisted men were allowed, but at the head of them was Sergeant McGregor, a Scotchman of great native talent, who not only knew how to put before you in perfect order all the papers that pertained to the commanding officer, the quartermaster, commissary, and the surgeon, but could refresh you at any time with the most apt quotations from Burns. McGregor had but one drawback. It may be stated in this way: That he was fond of preparing fireworks to properly celebrate the Fourth of July, and it was exceedingly difficult for him to use the alcohol essential to that operation without some of it getting into his mouth. The wounds without cause that afterwards marked his face and the humility that came into his heart were consequent. When I forgave him out and out, only subjecting him to a brief sermon, his gratitude reached the highest water mark. I did not stay at Augusta long enough for a second trial of Independence Day.

It was while on duty at this arsenal that I became acquainted with James G. Blaine, then editor of the *Kennebec Journal,* a Republican paper. The day I first saw him he had a controversy with the editor of the *Argus* of opposite politics. I had never before heard a man who had a better command of language than he; but his rejoinders to the other editor, a young man of about his age, were incisive and extremely forcible.

Blaine soon after that became a member of the Maine Legislature and later the Speaker of the House. While doing his part in this capacity I went to him with an important request to the effect that the children within the arsenal grounds should have the privileges of the common schools. He saw to it at once, and the proper bill was drafted and went through both Houses without opposition. From that time on we became very warm personal friends and remained such all his life.

On December 16, 1855, our first child was born. We named him Guy. The incidents of his career will appear here and there in connection with my own. His was an ideal life from his babyhood to his death in the service in the Philippines.

One of the most intimate friends that I had had when preparing for college was Charles H. Mulliken, of Augusta. He was now married and had a small family. He and I renewed our intimacy and our families enjoyed the social life of Augusta together. It was very much to me personally then and for many years afterwards to have such a friend. He was healthful, hearty, and always congenial.

The father and mother of Captain Seth Williams opened their hospitality to the commander of the arsenal and his wife, and various other members of the Williams family gave us their fellowship and the *entrée* into their homes. The Fullers, the Lamberts (Allen and Thomas), the Morrills, the Childs, the Tappans, the Manleys, Governor Coney, and many others afforded an entrance into society which has always been gratefully recalled by Mrs. Howard and myself.

Here we first became acquainted with the Rev. E. B. Webb, D.D., pastor of the Congregational church, who was perhaps Mr. Blaine's strongest friend, and, if I may say so, he and his were even more intimate with my family and always unselfishly devoted to my best interests.

We sometimes, while in Augusta, attended the Episcopal church. Rev. Mr. Armitage, then a young man, made a strong impression upon us. He was an able and efficient minister, who subsequently became the Bishop of Ohio.

It was while at Augusta that I spent much of my leisure in training horses. I had brought on with me from Watervliet a beautiful Arabian called Mallach, and it was a great pleasure, on his back, to gallop over the country. Pure white, with silver mane and tail, rather tall, with slender limbs and small feet, Mallach in his best days was ideal.

Two army officers during their first vacation from instructing cadets at West Point made a trip to Canada. One of them was Lieutenant A. J. Perry, who afterwards became a brigadier general and quartermaster of high order, and another was Lieutenant George B. Cosby, of Kentucky, who became a general in the Confederate Army. The third was Lieutenant William Silvey, then an assistant professor at the Military Academy. They had gone to Canada by rail and steamer, but concluded to purchase horses and ride across the country from Quebec to Augusta, Me. Mrs. Howard and myself entertained them at the arsenal, and Lieutenant Perry sold me his horse, which I called a " Canuck." He was jet black, fat and round, and very swift in his motions. Being taught entirely in the French language, it was for some time difficult for me to manage him. If I said *whoa*! and drew the reins taut, he would go fast, and if I drew them more or with a view to checking his speed, he would go faster.

Later I purchased an unbroken colt and trained him.

My brother, R. B. Howard, at the time a college student at Bowdoin, paid us a visit. He took as much interest in the horses as I did, and I remember giving him his first lessons in scientific riding. On one occasion, with some show of pride, he complained that I corrected him too severely in the presence of witnesses, men and women, who were looking on; but I think that the riding lessons did him much subsequent service.

The latter part of July, 1856, after one year's stay, I was relieved by Captain Gorgas, of Georgia, and received orders which sent me back to Watervliet. I left my family behind with my mother at Leeds. Mrs. Waite now formed part of it. They remained there till they could come on with my brother Rowland, who was to live with us at Watervliet and attend the Law School at Albany. I went ahead with our belongings to get everything in order for them.

Very few changes had taken place at Watervliet during my absence, but I saw very soon that the political struggles in the country were having a serious effect upon the relations of our families. The officers themselves were not yet particularly estranged from each other, but differences were becoming very sharp and sometimes chronic. Mrs. Symington was a great leader in all discussions. She could not bear to be beaten at euchre or whist, and she was very pro-

71

nounced in her expressions of dislike toward any who were inclined to favor the abolition of slavery. Lieutenant Boggs had married the eldest daughter, Miss Mary Symington. He and I had the north stone house, he occupying the south quarters. Boggs, though from Georgia, was always very mild in his statements. I remember that an escaped slave came to the arsenal for assistance. He needed food and money enough to get to Canada. Boggs laughed at him but told him he would give him food as he would anybody that was hungry. He then turned to me and said laughingly, "Howard, it is against my principles to help a slave escape from his master. You can do what you choose." That poor black man, at any rate, avoided the marshal and succeeded in reaching the Canada line.

I was not yet very pronounced in my sentiments, but my brother, already an ardent Republican, was educating me to a completer expression, especially against the extension of slavery into the new territories.

It was not long before my family came and we established the household anew, thinking that we would be at Watervliet for at least a year.

None of us in the family were at this time members of any church, but I had made up my mind to have family gathering in the morning just before or just after breakfast, at which time a chapter of the Scriptures should be read. My brother, who was then a little inclined to skepticism, said to me, "Otis, why do you do that?" I replied to him that I could not tell him why, but that I had made up my mind to do just that.

The Hon. Ira Harris, afterwards the United States Senator for New York, was the Dean of the Law

School at Albany. My brother entered there under
his supervision and went through a part of the course.
He had a comfortable room with us and immensely enjoyed our home life. He was particularly devoted to
our little boy, and as the latter grew they had lively
times together. Everything went on smoothly until
the latter part of December, 1856, when I was surprised, as I would have been by a clap of thunder from
a clear sky, by an order from Washington instructing
me to proceed at once to the Department of Florida
and report to General W. S. Harney, who was commanding that department—war existed and I was to
be " Chief of Ordnance " in the field. It was another
promotion, but it cost my family and myself a complete breaking up, for I could not take them with me.
It would not be safe for me to do so in any event. I
made no ado; did not ask for delay, but hastened
every preparation. After the storing of such things
as could be retained and the selling of much of our
goods at a loss and parting with the carriage and
horses, I was ready to obey the orders.

It was the coldest season that I had ever known on
the Hudson. I set out from Watervliet on December
23d. It showed how well I had studied up the route,
.for I wrote home from Brooklyn: " It is by steamer to
Savannah; thence by steamboat to Palatka on the St.
John's River; thence by stage to Tampa." Tampa was
then a small village near Fort Brooke, and Fort
Brooke was at the time the headquarters of the Department of Florida.

CHAPTER VI

AFTER the most fatiguing ride through the sand and over palmetto roots for three successive days and nights from Palatka to Tampa, I arrived at Fort Brooke and found several officers of General W. S. Harney's command out in the offing of Tampa Bay, and ready to start southward as soon as the tide would permit. Getting my supper and a change of clothing, I had myself rowed out to the long and queerly constructed steamer.[1] The surface of the water was smooth in the bright moonlight and the atmosphere as warm as that of a summer evening in the highlands of the Hudson.

General Harney, the department commander, was then at Fort Myers and wished me to report to him there. The steamer swayed back and forth, tugging at her anchor, and, weary as I was, I enjoyed the gentle breeze, just cool enough for comfort. It seemed to me, while walking the deck for a few minutes, that I had passed from winter to summer into a new and charming world.

Early the next morning I was again on deck watching the new scenes as we sped along southward. We never went out of sight of the pretty coast line. The

---

[1] This steamer, named *The Fashion,* had subsequent to this a most remarkable career, ending up as an ironclad in the Confederate Navy.

land presented a variety of colors bordered all along with the white streak of the sandy beach, and was quietly beautiful though without a single elevation in view. By one o'clock we were at Punta Rassa, a military post at the mouth of the Caloosahatchee River. Here was stationed one company of the Fifth Infantry, Captain N. B. Rossell in command. What I remember particularly about Punta Rassa is that the forests came down very near to the mouth of the river, and that the mosquitoes were more abundant and of a larger size than any I had ever seen before. They were so greedy that they attacked not only the soldiers but the animals; the dogs would run out into the water of the bay to escape from them.

We ascended the river in a small boat on which we could use a sail in case of a favorable breeze. The river was as charming as could be, a simple succession of green-bordered lakes. Of course, in military company our attention was called to the point where General Harney had been surprised by the Indians and obliged to escape in his night clothes. There he had had some forty men killed. We were shown where he ran down the river some seven or eight miles and was saved by being taken off in a skiff.

Against a head wind we made our way, and at last, between eight and nine o'clock at night, landed at Fort Myers. How kind the officers were in those days to one another! Lieutenant W. W. Burns, though he had never seen me before, extended to me his hospitality. From his quarters I promptly visited my commander, General Harney. Harney was very cordial and evidently glad to see me. He rose before me like a giant, six feet and a half, straight and well proportioned; said at one time to have been the handsomest man in the service. He was already gray, with just enough red in his whiskers to indicate what they had been in their best days. His characteristics were peculiar; always impatient when things went awry, his language was then rough in the extreme. I noticed, however, that occasionally a good-natured oath would escape him even when he was pleased. At this time of life Harney's memory was not very good. He did not appear to reason at all, but jumped to his conclusions. Notwithstanding this weakness, everybody said, " Harney has always been a good soldier."

Captain Pleasonton of the dragoons was in the same room with his general when I reported. Very young looking, pleasant in his speech, though always serious, Pleasonton, as Harney's adjutant general, usually managed to improve his administration of affairs, whether commanding an expedition or a department.

The next morning we left Fort Myers to return to Tampa. In the small boat were General Harney, Captain Pleasonton, Dr. McLaren, the surgeon, eight soldiers, and myself. We had hardly started out before our general was in a rage. First the mast was improperly set; then one of the men was behaving badly, interlocking his oar with the others at every stroke. When reproved, the man laughed in the general's face, sprang behind the mast and defied him. As Harney seized a boat hook to chastise him, Dr. McLaren interfered, saying that the man was unquestionably insane.[1] Then Harney instantly desisted, smiled, and said, " I suppose the fellow thought I would kill him."

By noon of January 9, 1857, we were on board *The*

[1] The doctor's opinion later proved to be true.

Fashion, which we found ready at the mouth of the river. Our return journey was very pleasant, and the next morning we anchored close to the city of Tampa, running in to shore with a small boat.

When we arrived, the steps which were usually let down to the boat were not in readiness, and the general was angry again. When at last the steps were properly planted he cried out, "Too late, too late!" for he had managed to spring ashore without them.

That afternoon I was assigned to ordnance duty at the Tampa depot. This depot consisted of two rough main buildings and a separate office far from the garrison of Fort Brooke, but on its grounds. One of the buildings was a small magazine where powder and fixed ammunition were stored, and the other held everything that belonged to the equipment of the troops.

The population of Tampa at that time did not exceed six hundred people, half of whom were negroes. The officers' quarters ran along the bay. A beautiful shell walk was on the city side with some shrubbery and flowers; the whole front was charming. There were very many large live oaks which, with their broad evergreen branches, rendered the reservation habitable even in the warmest season of the year.

There was in the town a small public house at which all the officers who were in Tampa without their families boarded. It was called "Duke's Hotel." At this place I took my meals in a dining room always filled with flies.

At first Major W. W. Morris, Fourth Artillery, who later became colonel and then general, was in command of the post. He was a good specimen of the severe

disciplinarian of the old school and known to all the
officers who had served in the Mexican War. His good
wife, Mrs. Morris, was very kind to me as a young officer, and rests in my mind as my beau ideal of what we
call an " army woman." She knew how to make the
commanding officer's quarters a place for constant and
pleasant reunions, and every young man was ready to
do anything he could to make her life pleasant, no matter how great were the privations of the frontier. Our
garrison was made up partly of the Fifth Infantry and
partly of the Fourth Artillery. Colonel John Munroe,
who was the lieutenant colonel of the Fourth Artillery, returned from a furlough and immediately assumed command. Munroe was a peculiar character,
inclined to conviviality, but always full of those resources which delighted young men around him. His
humor was constant and he had a fund of anecdote
which never failed him. He had a very black little
colored boy about twelve years old, who had a broad
mouth, white teeth, and large eyes that were constantly
blinking and rolling in a droll way. One day when I
was at the colonel's quarters he took pains to illustrate
his ideas of the discipline and government of such a
boy. He said, " William, come here! "

As he approached, the lad said, " What is it? " and
he began to back away when he saw that the colonel
had a couple of small withes in his hand.

" Oh," he said, " you come here! "

The little fellow would approach and work his
mouth and roll his eyes and pull back and say, " What
want, colonel? what want? "

" Oh," said Munroe, " I want to whip you."

" What for? hain't done nothing; what for? "

" Why, just to make you a good boy; whip you in

78

the morning before you have done anything, and then you will be a good boy all day."

The colonel undertook to switch him, though not very hard, but William danced about, laughed aloud, and kept crying, "Hain't done nothing; hain't done nothing; don't whip me, colonel."

On one occasion Munroe took me to task because I had concluded not to drink and declined a treat.

"What!" he said, "why so, why so?"

"Because," I said, "I have found that when I haven't much to do if I accept a treat in the morning the desire for the repetition keeps growing upon me."

"That's it, is it?" he said. "Do you know what I do when I feel that desire?"

"No," I said, "I can't conceive what you do."

"Ah," he said, "I always take a little more."

And I think that he often did. He was always serious and ready for business in the early morning, but got through with whatever he was obliged to do by twelve o'clock; after that he gave the rest of the day to his enjoyments. His adjutant, Lieutenant Geo. W. Hazzard, was a scholarly man of rather a skeptical turn of mind. During the summer his wife joined him at the garrison and I knew them both very well. During the war Hazzard became at first the colonel of an Indiana regiment, but the severity of his discipline seemed to displease the patrons of the regiment, and he was induced to resign, and went back to his place in the artillery.

I saw Hazzard in battle and I never knew an officer who could bring a battery into place and serve it with more rapidity. His great vigor kept all his command well in hand and made his battery of twice the value of any other that I ever saw.

79

Major McKinstry was our department quartermaster, a large, fine-appearing man of strong character. One day McKinstry, Kilburn, the able commissary, Lieutenant Oscar A. Mack, who was an assistant in the commissary, and I were talking together when the subject of dueling came up. It was already against the law for an officer to engage in a duel, but the practice was not yet fully over. I made a remark that I would not fight a duel. I remember that McKinstry took me to task for it and gave me several instances where he said it was imperative that an officer should accept a challenge. He made this assertion: " Suppose, Howard, you should be challenged to fight, and you declined, then you would be posted."

I hardly knew what that meant, but I declared that my contestant might " post " me if he chose.

" Why," he said, " you would be proclaimed as a coward."

" That would not make me one," I answered. " I am not a coward, and probably the time will come, if I live long enough, to show that I am not."

The conversation dropped at this point, but the recollection of it recalls the feeling that existed among my comrades that it would be difficult in the army to carry out the new law against dueling.

From the time I left home till June 1st my duties of receiving ordnance supplies and issuing them to the troops were constant, though not very onerous. At that time I was taking great interest in books, especially in religious reading.

I cannot tell for what reason, but after considerable activity in operations in every direction from Tampa as a center, Harney asked to be relieved, and Colonel L. L. Loomis, of the Fifth Infantry, became the commander of the department. This was a very helpful change to me. Colonel Loomis, a member of the Presbyterian Church, soon showed great interest in whatever concerned me. As often as he could he would converse with me and give me books, booklets, and tracts, for he said, "Howard, you have an inquiring mind." I absorbed all these books with great avidity. About this time my brother Rowland became a pronounced Christian, gave up his law studies and went into the ministry. He naturally wrote me accounts of his Christian experiences and sent me well-selected books. Among them was the life of Captain Hedley Vicars of the British Army.

I had a small office building near those of the arsenal, which I fitted up for use and made my sleeping room. In that little office, with my Bible and Vicars's Life in my hands, I found my way into a very vivid awakening and change, which were so remarkable that I have always set down this period as that of my conversion. It was the night of the last day of May, 1857, when I had the feeling of sudden relief from the depression that had been long upon me. The joy of that night was so great that it would be difficult to attempt in any way to describe it. The next morning everything appeared to me to be changed—the sky was brighter, the trees more beautiful, and the songs of the birds were never before so sweet to my ears.

Captain Vicars, who had been a good man and a Christian in the Crimea, and a consistent member of the Church of England, afterwards, under the influence of a single verse of the First Epistle of John, "The blood of Christ cleanseth us from all sin," had experienced a wonderful change, so that his influence over his comrades in arms was more marked and his Chris-

tian work in the hospitals among the sick and wounded
so increased and so enthusiastic as to leave a striking
record. My own mind took a turn like that on reading
the account of it: What was it that made him such a
different man from what he had ever been before?
Later, the influence of the same Scripture produced
that strong effect upon me and caused me ever after
to be a different man, with different hopes and different purposes in life.

There are always epochs in the lives of young people, and surely this was an epoch in my own career.
There was only one church of any activity in Tampa—
the Methodist. The clergyman, Mr. Lynde, had been
at one time a Catholic priest, and was a very earnest
preacher. He showed me so much kindness that I have
always remembered him as just the kind of a friend
that I needed at that time. One night I was sitting in
the back of his church when, after the Methodist fashion, amid continuous singing, he called people to come
forward to the altar. Quite a number arose and
worked their way down to the front; among them was
a poor hunchback woman whose gait in walking was
very peculiar. I noticed some young men on the other
side of the church, that I knew, laughing at her gro-
tesque appearance. I asked myself, "Which would you
rather be, on the side of those who were trying to do
God's will, or on the side of the scoffers?" I instantly
rose and went to the front and knelt at the altar. Mr.
Lynde, in tears, put his hands upon my head and
prayed for me. I was not conscious of any particular
change in myself, but I had taken the public stand,
which caused quite a sensation in our garrison. Some
of the officers said that I had disgraced the uniform;
others that I was half crazy; but a few sympathized

with me and were my friends then, and, in fact, ever after.

Great sickness came upon the garrison during that summer and fall, and several officers were helpful in the care of the poor fellows who were prostrated with malarial fever. Many died and were buried in the little cemetery close at hand. Tampa was a field for self-denial and Christian work.

Hazzard at one time took me to task in a jocose manner and pointed out to me in his scholarly way certain discrepancies in the Bible and asked me how I accounted for them. I answered him that I could not then tell, but perhaps I might be able to explain them at some future time.

At Yorktown, during our Civil War, Hazzard and I were walking together back of McClellan's works when a single round shot came rolling along the road and I thought I could strike it with my foot, but Hazzard cried out, " It is going too fast! " and pulled me back. At that time even he was asking me to explain to him how to become a Christian and get such peace as he thought that I had obtained. Of course I explained the matter to him as well as I could. It was not very long after that before one of those same round shot struck him in the thigh and gave him a mortal wound. His friends have told me that he became a very decided Christian before his life ebbed away in the hospital to which they carried him.

Our new department commander in Florida was very active in his operations with a view to close out the war with the Seminoles, but there was no great battle. The regulars had little faith in the war itself. It was a frequent remark by our regular officers: " We haven't lost any Indians." Of course, however, they did their duty, but without much ardor or enthusiasm. It was not the case, however, with the volunteers. They usually had well-selected officers, but the majority of the companies were made up of the roughest element. Very often they would involve in their attacks Indian men, women, and children and take very few prisoners. As far as the Indians were concerned, they behaved very much like the Bashi-bazouks of Turkey. Our department commander did not like the reports that came from this rough campaigning and he made up his mind to try hard to secure some sort of peace with the few remaining Indians in Florida.

One day in June Colonel Loomis sent for me and told me that he wanted me to go as a peace commissioner to the Indians in the Everglades, and explain to them how easy and advantageous it would be for them to submit to the Government and end the war. If possible I was to find Chief Billy-Bowlegs and use all the influence I could with him to get him to take his tribe and join the remainder of his people in the Far West.

I undertook the mission, first going to Fort Myers and getting the interpreter, Natto Joe, and an Indian woman with her child, who was still detained at that post. This I did as quickly as possible. The woman in her miserable condition, poorly clad, wrapped in an army blanket, looked as if she were beyond middle age, but her child, who was perhaps five years old, with a comfortable gown and two or three necklaces of blue beads, had a healthy look and was really pretty. She would, however, shake her hair over her face and act as shy as a young broncho. When white men were about she generally clung to her mother's skirt, endeavoring to hide herself in its folds.

With some difficulty Natto and I took these people

with us to Fort Deynaud. There we found Captain Brown with two companies of the Second Artillery. A classmate, Lieutenant S. D. Lee, was in command of one of the companies.

Captain Brown, leaving but a small guard behind, took with him the two companies, his and Lee's, and wagons with supplies for ten days, and escorted me and my charge into the interior. We went toward Lake Okeechobee. Lee and I were close friends and we had a happy expedition. The forests through which we made our way, the sweet open glades within which we encamped for the night, and the easy marches of every day, I have never forgotten. All this experience was new and fresh to me and everything in nature filled me with an enthusiasm which much amused my companion. While *en route* I found a short sleep of twenty or thirty minutes better than any other refreshment, and here began my habit of taking short sleeps at the halts in the midst of active campaigning. Lee said, " Howard thinks a nap better than a toddy "; and so indeed in time it proved to be.

On arriving at Lake Okeechobee a wonderful transformation took place in our Seminole woman. She bathed her face again and again; she managed to repair her clothing; she beat the tangles out of her matted hair. Taking some roots, powdered and soaked in water, and thus producing a soapy substance, she washed her hair till it was smooth and glossy. She also found ways of beautifying her child. From a haggard old squaw she was transformed into a good-looking young woman. She promised us so faithfully that she would bring us into communication with her people that with some reluctance I gave her instructions and let her go.

Natto was afraid to accompany her. He had been too long and too evidently a friend of the white man to risk the journey. I hoped almost against hope that Mattie, as we called the Indian woman, would prove true and bring about a meeting with her tribe, but I was to be disappointed. I could not, after many trials, get an interview with any chief. My mission was, to all appearances, a failure. Still, it is probable that the news the woman carried helped to bring about the peace which was secured by Colonel Loomis soon after I had left his department—a peace which has lasted without interruption from that time till to-day.

On our return, not far from Lake Okeechobee, while we were crossing a long strip of meadow land which the daily showers had refreshed and brightened, I witnessed for the first time a wonderful mirage. Lee and I were riding some distance from the command. Suddenly we saw what appeared to be the whole command, soldiers, ambulances, and army wagons, lifted high in air and moving along with regularity amid the clouds in the sky. Such a mirage was familiar to officers and soldiers who had served on the plains, but to my vision it was a startling sight. It was a complete illusion. My companion and I rode on toward the point where we supposed Captain Brown and his men were marching and had come, as we supposed, quite near them before the vision disappeared.

After my peace expedition into the interior I hastened back as quickly as possible to Tampa and found on my office desk a bundle of letters which greatly delighted me. The first one I opened was from my mother, giving me the news of the birth of our second child, whom we subsequently named *Grace Ellen*. She was born on June 22d in our home at Leeds, Me.; I myself was that day at Fort Deynaud, Fla.

One evening, July 15th, found me at the Methodist prayer meeting. Our department commander, Colonel Loomis, with his white hair and beard, was leading the meeting when I entered. He was reading a portion of Scripture, after which he spoke in his quiet, confident style, making remarks very edifying to the people, and then, standing erect and looking up, he led in a simple prayer. It was a great comfort to me at that time to find a commanding officer so fearless and exemplary and so sympathetic with every Christian effort.

About this time the sickness among the volunteers, some of it extending to the regulars, increased, and there were many deaths. I remember one poor fellow who had become almost a skeleton. He was very anxious to be baptized as a Baptist and he was not satisfied that Mr. Lynde, the Methodist clergyman, should perform the ceremony. He was too weak to go where there was sufficient water. Before long we found in the neighborhood a farmer (Mr. Branch) who had at one time been ordained as a Baptist minister. As soon as he heard of the earnest entreaty of the sick man he came, and I aided him to fill a large bathing tub with water, and with the doctor's assent and coöperation we let the invalid gently down into the water while Mr. Branch baptized him with the usual formula of his Church. The result of the baptism revived the man and for some days he was much better, but the fever had reduced him too much for a complete recovery. Before I left Tampa he died and received a soldier's burial.

Tampa was the center to which all the officers of

that station in Florida came. The garrison was usually changeable, but there were many companies of volunteers and several of the regulars, particularly of the Fourth Artillery, who served for some time at Fort Brooke, so that I came in contact with a great many officers of the regular army and of the volunteers and made their acquaintance. Recently I have thought of the names of nearly all who remained for any length of time at Tampa Bay. Of these, all except one or two became pronounced Christian men and united with the Church, though many of them not till years after our Florida experiences.

That remarkable summer when there was so much sickness and death and such faithful preaching, with our commander sympathizing with every Christian effort, influenced most of the officers and many of the men to change the character of their lives. Our experience there constituted an epoch in the religious history of Tampa to which evangelists in writing and speaking have since often referred.

On August 17, 1857, my friend Captain Kilburn, the chief commissary of the department, told me that he had been informed that I was to go to West Point as an instructor. I made this note concerning the news: "I hope it is a mistake, for it seems that I could not, for any reason, now desire to go there." This remark indicates to me that I did not in any way seek the detail.

Captain Kilburn was right. The orders soon came for me to proceed from the Department of Florida and report to the superintendent of the Military Academy. I left Tampa August 20th, going north by the ordinary stage route, reaching Palatka the 23d. At Palatka, to my delight, I found a new steamer called the

Everglade, instead of the old *General Clinch,* which had taken several days to bring me from Savannah to Palatka. The *Everglade* had modern conveniences, so that the numerous passengers, many of them army officers changing station or going on leave, had a short and delightful passage down the St. John's River and up the coast to Savannah. By Friday, the 28th, I was in Washington and visited the office of our Chief of Ordnance. By September 9th I was speeding away from the capital northward. Some accident to a train ahead of me hindered our baggage so that I could not get my trunk Saturday night or Sunday morning, and had to borrow clothing of Cousin Frank Sargent to attend church. This was at Brooklyn, but I managed to go on to Boston Monday night, an aunt and cousin with me, having taken the steamer by the Stonington route, so that not till Tuesday afternoon did I meet my family at Lewiston, Me.

Guy was then a little lad of a year and eight months, and Grace a babe in the cradle. A home-coming after that first separation at Watervliet and long absence was delightful, indeed. It was not necessary for me to be at West Point this year till the latter part of September, so that I had quite a vacation and very delightful visits with my family and friends before I reported, in accordance with instructions, to the superintendent of the Military Academy.

CHAPTER VII

AT WEST POINT AS INSTRUCTOR, 1857-61; THE OUTBREAK
OF THE CIVIL WAR

WITH my little family I left New York for West
Point, September 23, 1857. We ascended the
Hudson on the steamer *Thomas Powell,* and immediately after landing went to Roe's Hotel, the only public house upon the military reservation. Here we took a suite of rooms and were rather crowded for about a month. At first, there being no quarters vacant, I could get none assigned to me on account of my low rank.

According to the orders from Washington I joined the corps of instructors; and Lieutenant J. B. Fry, of the First Artillery, the adjutant, issued the following necessary orders: " First Lieutenant Oliver O. Howard, Ordnance Corps, having reported to the superintendent . . . is assigned to duty in the Department of Mathematics and will report to Professor Church for instructions."

Immediately I entered upon my duties, and for a time had under my charge the first and second sections of the fourth class. At first I was very careful to prepare myself daily by reviewing the studies in mathematics, with which, however, I was already familiar; later less study was required.

The fourth class was composed of new cadets, and, before many days, had been so sifted that the best prepared students were in the two sections, called first and second, committed to my charge. Beginning at eight in the morning my recitations were an hour and a half for each section. I think I never in my life had a pleasanter duty than this school work.

The professor in a West Point department of instruction habitually visited the rooms of his teachers from day to day. Professor Church was very attentive to this inspection and remained with me, from time to time, till I was thoroughly conversant with his methods of teaching and recording the daily progress of the cadets. If I had occasion to be absent any day for a good reason, the professor would hear my section for me.

On October 22d my family moved into the smallest officer's house at West Point. It was a little cottage just beyond the north gate and near the house and studio of Prof. Robert Weir. Our dwelling was called "The Elm Cottage." It was a story and a half house with tiny rooms, in which we made ourselves very comfortable, having escaped from the closer confinement of the hotel. The front hall of this cottage was just one yard square.

At the time I came to West Point I was exceedingly desirous to help the chaplain, Professor French, in any way I could, and to open up more general religious privileges to the cadets, to the soldiers, and to the families in the neighborhood. I had it in mind then that I should soon leave the army and enter the Christian ministry. This caused me to use all my leisure time in systematic study of a religious nature, in fact, my reading took that direction.

Very early, with the permission of the commandant and the chaplain, I opened with a few cadets a social meeting for prayer and conference. The first meeting was in a room in what was called the " Angle " of the new barracks. Lieutenant Henry M. Robert of the Engineers and myself carried in a table, two or three chairs, and some benches. Only five cadets came to the first meeting, though the invitation had been quite extensively circulated. All the meetings were held during recreation hours, just after the cadets' supper.

The attendance kept increasing, while the meetings were held at first twice a week, till our room was filled. Many of the young men who attended this gained later a national distinction. Among them was Cadet Emory Upton, who, after he had attained the rank of brigadier general, was for a few years the superintendent. He then made a change, allowing the young men to have their meetings on Sunday evenings in the dialectic hall of the academy. Instead of being confined to a half-hour's service, they were permitted to remain together until tattoo. This was a great privilege. Later the Young Men's Christian Association was formed and took charge of the meetings. Nearly the whole corps of cadets are now members of this association, and the meetings have been continued without interruption for fifty years.

Our commandant in 1857, Lieutenant Colonel William J. Hardee, had a family of two daughters and one son. One day Colonel Hardee and myself had a long walk together beyond the limits of our reservation. He had previously expressed a desire that I should teach his children and allow him to compensate me privately for it. At that time the officers had no private school for their families. I consented to do this, and so began an intimacy with the family that was only interrupted by Hardee's relief from duty before the end of my term. He declared that he was fond of the Union, but he had made up his mind that there would be two governments, and as he was from the extreme South, he told me that he could not bear the thought of belonging to a Northern confederacy.

I took up the Hebrew language and recited with some regularity to an Episcopal clergyman near Highland Falls. He was a scholarly man and interested himself greatly in my progress. Lectures, in connection with Bible study, I delivered habitually once a week in what we called "the little church under the hill." This church where the soldiers' families attended was so arranged that a partition separated the altar and all that belonged to it from the main room. This enabled the Catholics to have their services in the morning, when the partition doors were opened, and the other people in the afternoon and evening, when the doors were closed. Here we had, every Sabbath for nearly four years, a thriving Sunday school, of which I was the superintendent. In this active Christian work, cadets, the chaplain's daughters, and other ladies of the post assisted regularly with the music and as teachers. Usually in the evening we had a Methodist clergyman to preach and conduct the services. Sometimes our chaplain, who was an Episcopalian, would give an address, and sometimes the clergy of other denominations.

I always endeavored to do something in addition to what my military duties proper and the preparation for them required. It may be said that this was not a fair preparation for what might be required of me sooner or later in the army proper; but I do not think so. This training to which I subjected myself enlarged my sympathies and acquaintanceship and was, indeed, a stepping-stone to all that followed.

One thing that troubled me was a class distinction, which seemed too intense for our republican ideas, and, indeed, made the army itself disliked by the people at large. I gave much reflection to the subject of discipline and came to fully believe that it was possible to have a higher grade for our enlisted men and a better system of government by officers, especially by those of high rank. While considering this subject in 1858 I wrote an article entitled " Discipline in the Army." There I advocated with as much force as I could a paternal system over against the martinet system in vogue. I endeavored to show that the general who cared for his men as a father cares for his children, providing for all their wants and doing everything he could for their comfort consistent with their strict performance of duty, would be the most successful; that his men would love him; would follow him readily and be willing even to sacrifice their lives while enabling him to accomplish a great patriotic purpose.

Indeed, I am now glad that my mind took that turn, for I never met a soldier who served with me in the great war who does not now come to me with an expression of appreciation and fellowship. Others, doubtless, have had similar experiences, but I know that during the Civil War the general who loved and cared for his men and diligently showed this disposition to all under his command, won good will and affection above all other commanders.

My article, published in a New York monthly, caused quite a commotion at West Point, at the time, among the thirty or forty officers stationed there. Even the superintendent was annoyed because he thought that I reflected upon his management of affairs. Some agreed with my sentiments, but the majority said that they were contrary to a proper military spirit.

In March, 1858, the War Department sent our Sapper and Miner Company, about one hundred strong, to Utah Territory, where some difficulty between the Mormons, the Indians, and the emigrants had already begun. Lieutenant E. P. Alexander was at that time in command of that company. He became an officer in the Confederate Army and was Chief of Artillery under Longstreet, planting his numerous batteries along our front at Gettysburg. One day at West Point he overtook me on the sidewalk and we conversed together for some time, continuing our discussion till after we reached my home. He gave me two books of a religious character and $5 to be expended in Christian work. One remark that he made I well remember. " I wish to be thought by my men to be a Christian and have their sympathy and interest during the expedition to Utah."

I have met Alexander since the Civil War and found him the same kind-hearted, good man that he was when on duty at West Point.

Two days after that conversation with Alexander I addressed the Sapper and Miner Company. The little soldiers' church was filled, and the men, some of whom had families to leave, appeared deeply interested in my lecture. I presented to them the idea that a Christian soldier was the highest type. In him the sense of duty and contentment were combined.

On April 21st an incident occurred in our family that made quite a sensation. Mrs. Howard and I had taken a walk toward the mountain Crow-Nest. We had been away about half an hour when the nurse, completely out of breath from running, overtook us and said that the baby (Grace) was sick, very sick. We were near the cadets' garden. Mrs. Howard and I ran as fast as possible; I reached the house first, and found Mrs. Robert Weir holding the child; she stretched her hands toward me, holding the baby, and said, "Your dear little lamb!" Grace was as white as a sheet, with a little blood around her mouth. I instantly caught the child and turned her head downward, put my finger into her mouth and removed from her throat one of Guy's marbles that had remained there choking her for more than half an hour. The nurse had first run in the other direction to the cadets' hospital for the doctor, whom she did not find, before going for us.·

On December 20th a court of inquiry brought together Colonel Robert E. Lee, Major Robert Anderson, Captain R. B. Marcy (McClellan's father-in-law), and Captain Samuel Jones. Colonel Lee had been very kind to me when a cadet.

I had known Major Anderson before — noticing then how tenderly he was caring for his invalid wife. Captain Samuel Jones had been my instructor when a cadet, and Captain Marcy and myself were on duty at the same posts in Florida. To pay my respects to them at the hotel was a real pleasure.

A little later came the funeral of Colonel John Lind Smith of the Engineers. The whole corps of cadets acted as an escort. Lieutenant Fitz John Porter commanded the corps during the exercises, and I was exceedingly pleased with his military bearing that day.

During the summer vacation of 1859, extending from the middle of June to August 28th, I made quite a tour northward for recreation. First, with my family, I visited my friend, Lieutenant C. C. Lee, at Watervliet Arsenal, and there I met the venerable Major Alfred Mordecai and his family. Mordecai loved the Union, but, being from North Carolina, he concluded that he would not fight in a civil war, and so early in 1861 tendered his resignation. His son Alfred is now a brigadier general on the retired list. He has had an honorable and useful life in the army, always on active duty in the Ordnance Department, and very successful in his profession.

From Watervliet we passed on to Niagara Falls. On this journey I was attacked with rheumatism, which bowed me down, gave much pain, and made all who saw me think I was hopelessly disabled, yet for the sake of those with me I would not interrupt the journey.

We went forward by way of Lake Ontario and down the St. Lawrence, stopping at Montreal to take in that beautiful city and its surroundings. We had a few days at Quebec, a city which impressed me more than any other in Canada, reviving the old accounts of the Revolutionary struggle and all that preceded it.

We passed on to the Glen House in New Hampshire near Mount Washington, ascended that mountain and enjoyed the magnificent scenery.

At last we reached my mother's home in Leeds about June 30th. Before this, though my suffering diminished the pleasure of my trip, I recovered from my rheumatism. The remainder of the vacation we passed in visiting friends.

It was during this vacation that I began to be invited to give addresses and lectures in Maine: one at Farmington on July 4th; one at the city schoolhouse in Leeds; another at North Leeds on a Sabbath, and at a church in Auburn the following Sunday, July 24th. A little later I undertook to give an extempore lecture, the first time I had tried one of any length, at an old schoolhouse in Livermore. My classmate in college, P. S. Perley, was present; which caused me some embarrassment. He, however, encouraged me to keep on trying.

After the outing we returned slowly by the way of Boston and New York to the Military Academy. The work of the ensuing years, 1859 and 1860, was much like that of the preceding.

It was after we had returned from another vacation, in 1860, that Prince Edward of England with his suite visited the Military Academy. It was quite an event to us and absorbed the attention of both officers and cadets. The prince came up October 15th, arriving at 2 P.M. on the steamer *Harriet Lane*. His suite consisted of eight or ten gentlemen. There rushed in from far and near a large crowd of people, but they were very orderly except a few overcurious mortals who crowded into places where they were not invited.

The prince was a good-looking young man of nineteen, rather small of stature, modest and gentle in his bearing. He took much interest in everything he saw at West Point. He visited our buildings and received military honors extended to him by the corps of cadets on the plain. He partook of a collation at Colonel Delafield's quarters, in which a few invited guests, ladies and gentlemen, participated. He then went to Fort Putnam on horseback, having a small escort with him, and passed down to Cozzen's Hotel, where he spent the night. The next morning he returned and visited the section-rooms. He stayed in mine long enough to hear one recitation from Cadet A. H. Burnham, of Vermont. He was pleased with this. His suite of gentlemen continued with him as he went from room to room.

This was the Prince of Wales as I saw him at West Point, kind, courteous, genial, without any attempt whatever at display, and showing no egotism. I do not wonder that he proves to be a good sovereign.

During my fourth year of teaching I had been promoted to " assistant professor," which was equivalent to being a captain in the army.

Here at our national school there was naturally a commingling of the divers elements which then constituted the personnel of our nation, and the lines of attempted separation near the outbreak of 1861, running as they did between comrade and comrade, neighbor and neighbor, and even through the heart of families and households, were as a rule less marked here than elsewhere.

Probably no other place existed where men grappled more quickly, more sensitively, and yet more philosophically with the troublesome problems of secession. Prior to any overt act, however, a few members of our community were much disturbed, and by almost morbid anticipations experienced all the fever of the subsequent conflict.

All the preceding winter, for example, our worthy professor of ethics, J. W. French, D.D., who had been a lifelong friend of Jefferson Davis, worked day and night in anxious thought and correspondence with him with ever-decreasing hope that he might somehow stay the hands which threatened a fratricidal strife. This excellent professor seemed to be beside himself in his conjectures and in the extreme fears which he manifested. But his soul was truly prophetic and thus early did he feel the blasts of a terrible war which even the radical men of the country as yet deemed improbable.

A Southern man, a true patriot, Dr. French, when the storm broke, offered all the money he had to strengthen the government exchequer. There were cooler minds who believed that these first symptoms of rebellion were merely dark days of passion—the sheer embodiments of windy fury which time under the sun rays of good sense would dissipate.

My immediate official chief was Prof. A. E. Church. From the first his heart and speech were bubbling over with patriotic fervor. Our superintendent, ex-officio commander of the post, was Colonel Richard Delafield. Twice had he served at West Point, twelve years in all, so that more than a thousand graduates felt the direct influence of his inflexible example and the impress of his rugged nature.

Delafield was the embodiment of able administration; very exacting in his requirements, and, like the just judge, precise and severe in his awards of punishment—so much so that he appeared to us subordinates at times to have eliminated all feeling from his action; but this was his view of discipline. How much, in the retrospect, we admire a just ruler! And how completely, after the teachings of experience, we forgive the apparent severities! On March 1, 1861, Colonel Delafield gave place to Colonel A. H. Bowman, who held the superintendency from that time till near the close of the war. Bowman was from Pennsylvania. He was a dignified officer and had been put in charge of the original construction of Fort Sumter as early as 1838. With a high character and long, complete record

100

of service, he was a good man to succeed Delafield and to manage the academy during the war period.

Colonel Hardee's academy service as commandant of cadets expired September 8, 1860. A close friend of his family, I never ceased to be interested in his career. By his uniform courtesy he won the regard of all associates; junior officers and cadets appreciated this feature of his administration. By 1861 he had grown gray in service; he had given to the army his light infantry tactics; he had also won enviable distinction in the Mexican War, and probably no name was more familiar to the people at large than his.

January 31, 1861, the resignation of his army commission was tendered and accepted. Hardee's course in this matter produced quite a sensation at West Point. Lieutenant Colonel John F. Reynolds, of Pennsylvania, almost the first to fall at Gettysburg, succeeding Hardee at the academy, commanded the cadets till after my departure. His eminent loyalty to the Union, clearly in contrast with the sentiments expressed by Hardee, and his ardor in hastening forward from the academy the higher classes for junior officers, then in great demand at Washington, were ever remembered in his favor. Lieutenant S. B. Holabird, of the First Infantry, relieved Lieutenant Fry, the adjutant, and remained till May 1, 1861, when on promotion as captain and assistant quartermaster in the staff of the army, he left us to bear his part in coming events. Before his retirement Holabird reached the head of his corps.

Lieutenants John Gibbon and S. S. Carroll, both names now high on the roll of fame, filled one after the other the office of quartermaster at West Point. For a time Carroll and I, with our two families, lived under

101

one roof, dividing a pleasant cottage between us. For
the last two months, however, of my stay I had, by a
small accession of rank, attained a separate domicile.
Just before that, Carroll had a visit from Lieutenant
Fitzhugh Lee, the nephew of Robert E. Lee. How
sprightly, energetic, and full of fun he was! Secession
to him was fun—it would open up glorious possibili-
ties! He gave Carroll and myself lively accounts of
events in the South. Once, after speaking jocosely, as
was his habit, of the perturbed condition of the cotton
States, he stopped suddenly for a moment, and then
half seriously said: " Sprigg, those people of the South
are alive and in earnest, and Virginia (his State) will
soon follow their lead. The Union folks are apathetic
and half-hearted. A living dog is better than a dead
lion. You had better be up and doing or you will lose
your chances down South! You'll get no rank." His
talk, so characteristic, was more real than we dreamed.
He watched Virginia and followed her into the Confederacy. There were thirty-six officers of junior rank at
West Point in 1860 and 1861; twenty-four from Northern and twelve from Southern States. Their names
have since become familiar to all who know our war
history. Three of our eight professors were Southern
born. None of them left their post of duty, or veered
the least in loyalty to the Union. This is certainly a
good exhibit for our national school.

After the beginning of the year 1861 the causes of
excitement were on the increase. The simple fact of
Abraham Lincoln's election had been enough to inau-
gurate plenty of military operations in the South, such
as the capturing, by States, of forts poorly manned,
and of arsenals which had no guards to defend them.
Every new item of this sort had great interest for us,

for the evidences of an approaching collision on a large scale were multiplying. The story of Twiggs's surrender of United States troops to Texas, followed by details of imprisonment and paroling, reached us in the latter part of February. Twiggs's promises to allow the troops to go North were mostly broken. Six companies of the United States Infantry, including a few officers and men of other regiments, Lieutenant Colonel Reeve commanding, were obliged to give up to a Confederate commander, Earl Van Dorn, by May 9th.

The organizers of the secession movement soon succeeded "in firing the Southern heart." As we men from the North and South, at our post on the Hudson, looked anxiously into each other's faces, such indeed was the situation that we knew that civil war with its unknown horrors was at hand.

One morning, as officers and professors gathered near the lofty pillars under the stone archway of the old academy, there was rehearsed, one after another adding his own paper's version, the exaggerated accounts of the terrible handling that the Sixth Massachusetts Volunteers had had from a Baltimore mob. "Much blood shed! Some killed and many wounded, resulting in a complete break-up of the route to Washington and the shutting off of the capital from the North!" That was a brief of our gloomy news. Another morning the cloud lifted. There were better tidings. "Baltimore recaptured by General B. F. Butler!" Butler, even without General Scott's sanction, had appeared there in the night with enough men to seize and hold Federal Hill. From that fine position he commanded the city.

Another occasion (May 24th) brought us the wildest tales of our troops entering Virginia, and of the resistance at Alexandria. The new President's *protégé* and friend, young Colonel Ellsworth, had hauled down a hostile flag flying from the belfry of the Marshall House. The proprietor, Jackson, waylaying his descent, had shot him to death.

I recall, as if it were yesterday, a visit of an officer's wife to our house, about the time General Scott had ordered the first movement from Washington. She was from a cotton State and was outspoken for the Southern cause. She greatly deprecated this "forward" movement. Just before leaving our house, she said: " If it were not for those wretched Republicans and horrid abolitionists, we might have peace!"

I replied: " The Republicans who have now elected their president are not abolitionists, certainly not in your sense of that word. They only want to stop the extension of slavery."

" Ah, I tell you," she rejoined, " it is all the same thing! Why stop the extension of slavery? It shows that they are against us. It is all very plain."

I said: " Surely, it is wise to keep slavery outside the free States and the territories!"

The lady showed intense feeling, and shaking her finger at me, said excitedly: " If Mr. Lincoln has such sentiments as you express, sitting there in that chair, there'll be blood, sir, blood!"

Certainly, it was a great trial to Southern officers when the mails teemed with urgent epistles, calling upon them to resign their commissions, and no longer serve a Yankee government. " Come home!" said the appeals, " and join your fathers, your brothers, and your friends. Do not hesitate. No man of Southern blood can fight against his State! If you remain North you shall never darken our doors again."

104

At West Point as Instructor, 1857–61

At first our assistant surgeon, Dr. Hammond, of South Carolina, was much staggered. He would vehemently argue for the right of secession. Once he became quite incensed at me, who had long been his personal friend, because I spoke disparaging words of his " sovereign " State. When he was relieved and sent to another post, I was confident that he would resign and join his brother, an ex-governor in South Carolina, but he did not. That brother wrote him that being a medical man, and having only benevolent functions, he thought he could with honor remain in the federal army.

For a time in our social life there was a prevalent opposition to regular officers accepting commissions in the volunteers. Not only the Southern born but the Northern manifested the feeling. A letter, written by a Northern officer, of February 23, 1861, urging me to accept a professorship in North Carolina, uses these words: " As an officer of the army, I presume, of course, that you entertain no views on the peculiar institution which would be objectionable to a Southern community."

There arose quite an ebullition to disturb the ordinary sentiment, when Lieutenant A. McD. McCook accepted the colonelcy of an Ohio regiment of volunteers. A Kentucky officer, tall, dark, and strong, visiting our post at the time the report of McCook's action arrived, said loudly: " A West Point man who goes into the volunteers to fight against the South forgets every sentiment of honor! " When I confronted him and told him on the spot that I should probably become a volunteer officer, he became angry and denounced me, daring me ever to touch the soil of Kentucky. When we met again, I had passed, commanding volunteers, across that retaliatory soil, and my threatening friend had changed his manner to a submissive acquiescence.

Next after McCook, Gouverneur K. Warren, my co-instructor in mathematics, accepted the lieutenant colonelcy of the New York Duryea Zouaves. There was social criticism enough, but the promotion of Mc-Cook and Warren seemed to the other lieutenánts a wonderful advance. We had never met field officers who were not old and gray; yet, somehow, though the new rank was attractive, it did not look to us quite so much so when we had to give up our places in the regular army in order to join the volunteers. Our adjutant general at Washington, Lorenzo Thomas, for a time worked strenuously to prevent it. " They are needed in the army proper," he averred, " more than ever; we cannot spare them!" That idea was natural. Most regulars of advanced age so believed. As waters of different temperature put into a vessel soon reach a medium degree, so did people of various feelings and sentiments in the old army arrive at a moderate conservatism. " We belong to the whole nation, we do not want it divided; we propose to stand by it forever, but we do hate this civil strife; we will not be eager to enter the lists in such a conflict; certainly not merely for the sake of promotion. We do hope and pray that the differences will be settled without bloodshed."

Quite early in the spring I wrote to Governor Washburn, of Maine, and offered my services. His reply was unfavorable. Commissioned officers of regiments were all to be elected by the men. He, himself, had no power to choose. But the fact of the offer became known at Augusta. Not long afterwards, about the middle of May, a dispatch came to me from the Hon. James G. Blaine, then the youthful Speaker of the Maine House of Representatives. It read: " Will you, if elected, accept the colonelcy of the Kennebec Regiment?"

Over this dispatch Mrs. Howard and I had a conference. We thought it would be wiser to begin with a major's commission, so that I might be better prepared for a colonelcy when I came to it by promotion. Still, my heart began to swell with a growing ambition; for were not civilians without military knowledge taking regiments or even brigades? Surely, I was as well prepared as they! I hastened to Lieutenant Colonel Reynolds, the commandant of cadets, who was many years my senior and had seen service in various capacities, and asked him to tell me about a regimental command. Reynolds smiled at my ardor.

" Why," he asked, " what is the matter?"

" Oh, I've had the tender, or what amounts to it, of a Maine regiment. What answer would you give, colonel?"

" You'll accept, of course, Howard."

He then took up the army regulations and turned to the duties of regimental officers, folding down the leaves, and kindly explained a few things that a colonel should know.

" Surely, Howard, you know the drill and parades, and it will not take you long to get well into the harness."

Thus encouraged I telegraphed an affirmative answer. The news of my probable election and the rapid call for troops from Washington, as published in the press, decided me to anticipate official notification and so, having obtained a seven days' leave, I proposed to set out for Augusta. As soon, however, as it was plain to me that our grand old Government would need my

107

services, I gave up every other plan except as to the best way for me to contribute to the saving of her life. This decision I believed, as God has His plan in each human life, to be according to His will. In this faith I prepared to leave West Point.

PART II—THE CIVIL WAR

LIEUTENANT TO MAJOR GENERAL, AND IN COMMAND OF AN INDEPENDENT ARMY

CHAPTER VIII

THE cottage at West Point where with my family
I resided May 28, 1861, was a square two-story
building, a little back from the street. This street,
going south, passed the academy building and old
Cadets' Hospital, and ran along the brow of a steep
slope, parallel with the Hudson River. My cottage,
just below the hospital, had an eastern face toward the
river from which there was a pleasant outlook. The
luxurious foliage of the highlands was then at its best.
The cliffs, hills, and mountains on both banks of the
Hudson had already put on nature's prettiest summer
dress. If one entered our front hallway and glanced
into the parlor and up the stairway, he would say: " It
is a pleasant and comfortable home."

I came home that day after my morning lessons a
little later than usual. Before entering my front gate,
I raised my eyes and saw the picture of my little family framed in by the window. Home, family, comfort,
beauty, joy, love were crowded into an instant of
thought and feeling, as I sprang through the door and
quickly ascended the stairway.

I handed my wife the superintendent's paper grant-
ing me a short leave. " Nothing startling," I said, as
I noticed her surprise; " if I am chosen colonel of the
Kennebec Regiment, I wish to be on the ground to or-

111

ganize it." It was short notice, less than an hour for preparation, as the down train passed Garrison's, east of the Hudson, at 1.30 P.M.

My valise was soon packed, luncheon finished, and then came the moment of leave-taking, made a little harder by my wife's instinctive apprehension that I would not return to West Point. Her instinct, woman-like, was superior to my reasoning. In truth, I was not to come back! For an instant there was a momentary irresolution and a choking sensation filled my throat, but the farewell was cheerfully spoken and I was off.

My wife was patriotic, strong for the integrity of the Union, full of the heroic spirit, so when the crisis came, though so sudden and hard to bear, she said not one adverse word. I saw her watch me as I descended the slope toward the ferry landing, looked back, and waved my hat as I disappeared behind the ledge and trees. The swift train beyond the Hudson, emerging from the tunnel, caught me up, stopped three minutes, and then rushed on with increasing speed and noise.

Thus our young men left happy homes at their country's call; but the patient, heroic wives who stayed behind and waited, merit the fuller sympathy.

An army officer in New York City told me of my election to the colonelcy as an accomplished fact; so that I telegraphed to Blaine that I was *en route*, wrote a brief note to my home, and went on to Boston by the evening train. In the early morning I walked through the crooked streets of Boston from the Worcester Station to the Revere House, breakfasted there, caught the 7.30 train on the Boston & Maine, and sped off to arrive at Augusta before five the same afternoon. Here I received Mr. Blaine's reply as follows:

112

OLIVER OTIS HOWARD, COLONEL THIRD MAINE REGIMENT
UNITED STATES VOLUNTEERS, 1861.

Colonel of the Third Maine Regiment

Augusta, 29th of May, 1861.

My Dear Howard: You were chosen to the command of the Third Regiment yesterday and public opinion is entirely unanimous in favor of having you accept the position. You will be at once notified of your election officially. The regiment is enlisted for three years, and will be called into service at once. You must hold yourself ready to come at a moment's notice. I understand the Lieutenant Colonel is an admirable military man, one that will be both efficient and agreeable.

Truly yours, in great haste,

[Signed]   Blaine.

This letter did not reach me at West Point. As soon as I found that I was chosen to the colonelcy, instead of asking for an enabling lengthy leave of absence, I tendered a resignation of my army commision. Washington officials of the War Department were still obstructing such leaves, and ordnance officers were particularly wanted at arsenals. But the resignations of Southern seceding officers were promptly accepted.

When my resignation was also accepted with a batch of others and published in the newspapers, many old acquaintances, curiously enough, thought I had joined the rebellion. I was not out of service at all, for it was five days after I received my commission and took the new regiment that I ceased to be an officer of the Ordnance Department.

I made the Augusta House my temporary headquarters. It was on the north side of State Street and had a long porch in front, with a balcony above it. I found the porch and balcony very convenient for meeting the officers and friends of the regiment. At this hotel my brother, Charles Henry Howard, a Bangor theological student, met me, shortly after my arrival, to offer himself for enlistment.

113

Autobiography of Gen. O. O. Howard

Israel Washburn was Governor of Maine. He had a large, strong face, full of resolute purpose, and habitually covered his eyes with glasses for nearsightedness, so that he did not prepossess a stranger on first approach; but the instant the introduction had passed a wonderful animation seized him and changed the whole man. He was at that time replete with patriotic enthusiasm and energy, and soon held a foremost place among the war governors of his time.

The next morning after my arrival in Augusta, the governor was early in his office at the State House. He had hardly thrown aside his light overcoat and taken his chair when a young man with a brisk, businesslike air opened the door and entered without ceremony. He paid no attention to the governor's jocose welcome; but, opening his large eyes to their full, kept his mind steadily upon the matter in hand. He said:

"You know, governor, I recommended to you and to the Third Regiment a young man from the regular army, Oliver O. Howard, a lieutenant, teaching at West Point."

"Oh, yes. He belongs to Maine—to Leeds; was born there. He was elected. Will he accept?"

"Howard is already on hand," answered the governor's visitor, "and I will bring him up and introduce him, if you are at leisure."

"Certainly! Glad he has come so soon," answered Washburn. "Have him come up."

This energetic visitor was James G. Blaine. One could hardly find a more striking character. His figure was good—nearly six feet and well proportioned; his hair, what you could see of it under his soft hat pushed far back, was a darkish brown. It showed the disorder due to sundry thrusts of the fingers. His

114

coat, a little long, was partially buttoned. This, with the collar, shirt front, and necktie, had the negligee air of a dress never thought of after the first adjustment. His head was a model in size and shape, with a forehead high and broad, and he had, as you would anticipate in a strong face, a large nose. But the distinguishing feature of his face was that pair of dark-gray eyes, very full and bright. He wore no beard, had a slight lisp in speech with a clear, penetrating nasal tone. He excelled even the nervous Washburn in rapid utterance. Nobody in the Maine House of Representatives, where he had been for two years and of which he was now the Speaker, could match him in debate. He was, as an opponent, sharp, fearless, aggressive, and uncompromising; he always had given in wordy conflicts, as village editor and as debater in public assemblies, blow for blow with ever-increasing momentum. Yet from his consummate management he had already become popular. Such was Blaine at thirty years of age.

When I was presented the governor arose quickly, took my right hand in both of his and shook it warmly. "Many congratulations, my young friend. Your regiment is already here—across the way. You must hasten and help us to get it into shape. At first you will find 'the boys' a little rough, but we've got you a first-rate adjutant, haven't we, Blaine?"

"I think, governor, you will have to let the colonel choose his adjutant and organize his staff himself," answered Blaine, smiling. That reply was heplful to me, and Washburn rejoined:

"Well, well; all right," adding pleasantly: "Introduce Burt to the colonel. I guess they'll agree. Don't forget."

"Be sure, Governor Washburn," I said, "I shall always respect your wishes and we will soon be ready for the front.".

"Just so, just so. How I like the true ring. We will put down this rebellion in short order with this sort of spirit; eh, Blaine?" Thus Washburn ran on. Blaine laughed as he quietly assured the governor that he was too sanguine. "If you had come from a place as near the border as I did, you would not emphasize short order; not much! My mind is fully prepared for a long siege."

"As God wills," said the governor, rising. "Now let us go down and introduce Colonel Howard to 'the boys.'"

I was sure that Mr. Washburn felt satisfied with my election. His first three years' regiment—a thousand strong—made up of his friends and neighbors, was to be commanded by one who had received a military education, and who had at least some army experience.

Slender of build, and at the time pale and thin, I did not seem to those who casually met me to have the necessary toughness, but for reasons of his own, perhaps owing to his nearsightedness, Washburn gave me immediate confidence.

We three then left the governor's room, descended the broad steps to the east, crossed State Street, and proceeded along a gravel path to about the center of a grovelike park. This was a public lot which extended along the street for some distance and then east toward the Kennebec an eighth of a mile. A portion of that beautiful inclosure was alloted to my regiment. In fact, it already had possession. The choicest of everything belonged to the men at that time. They had new clothes (a gray uniform), new guns, new tents, new equipments, and new flags, and were, as I saw, encamped amid beautiful shrubbery, sweet-scented flowers, and blossoming trees. But one glance showed me that the camp itself was in disorder. A thousand recruits were there under captains and lieutenants who themselves were new to the business; here and there older men, women and children were mingled in groups with the soldiers. Parents had come to see their sons before they set out for the war. Young wives and sweethearts were there; but notwithstanding the seriousness of the occasion, there was more gala excitement than solemnity. Many soldiers were even jubilant; some had been drinking and some were swearing.

"Oh, pshaw, father! Don't be gloomy; I shan't be gone more'n two months."

"Come, mother, don't be alarmed; this will be a short trip."

"Hurrah, hurrah! Down with the saucy curs! We'll make short work of this business; only let's be off!"

Such scraps of conversation caught our ears as we passed near the groups. At one place a scene more pathetic reminded me of home. A wife with a child in her arms stood by a man in new uniform and was shedding tears while trying to hear her husband's kindly directions and hopeful predictions.

Quickly the people gathered near the stout governor; but he was too short of stature to see more than those near at hand, so noticing something elevated (an overturned half-hogshead) upon which he could stand, Washburn stepped on it and began speaking in his cheery way.

117

Some soldiers in a loud voice called: "Cheers for our governor!" A large number responded in strong, manly tones.

"Thank you, thank you, boys; I have brought you somebody you will like to see. Come up here, Colonel Howard. This is your new colonel."

All eyes turned steadily toward me as soon as I had mounted the rostrum and was standing beside the governor; but the cheers called for were noticeably faint. How young, how slender the new colonel appeared; hardly the man to be placed over strong, hardy fellows whose frames were already well knit and toughened by work. In spite of their vote two days before, a reaction had set in—it was evidently not quite the welcome thing for these free spirits to be put under anticipated West Point discipline. Some of the captains who had been to see me at the Augusta House the night before were already somewhat disaffected. They said: "Under Tucker, the other candidate for colonel, we could have had a good time, but this solemn Howard will keep us at arm's length." Blaine continued to befriend me. He told them that they would need men like me if ever called to fight. "In time, I assure you, you'll not be sorry that you chose him."

I attempted an address, but had spoken only a few words when a remarkable silence hushed the entire assemblage; a new idea appeared to have entered their minds and become prominent: I pleaded *for work in preparation for war*, and not a few months of holiday entertainment, and hurrah boys to frighten and disperse a Southern rabble by bluster; after which to enjoy a quick return to our homes.

Good men and women were glad for this evident change of front, and murmured around me: "God bless the young man and give him health and strength."

I had hoped that the officers of the regiment would elect my brother Rowland, a Congregational minister, chaplain. It would have been a great comfort to have had his companionship and counsel, but the Rev. Andrew J. Church, of the Methodist Episcopal Church, was preferred. Later Rowland went to the front as an agent of the Christian Commission. My disappointment was lessened by my younger brother's enlistment and detail as regimental clerk. This brother, Charles H. Howard, obtained his first commission as second lieutenant in the Sixty-first New York, was with me on staff duty till 1865, and received deserved promotion from grade to grade till he became a lieutenant colonel and inspector general. He was later made colonel of the One Hundred and Twenty-eighth colored regiment and was finally brevetted brigadier general for gallant and meritorious conduct during the war.

The proper form and order of an encampment were soon instituted and all the staff officers, commissioned and noncommissioned, appointed. Sergeant Edwin Burt, suggested by the governor, was made adjutant. Military knowledge and experience were then of great service. Burt, in time, by worthy promotion, became a lieutenant colonel and lost his life, May 6, 1864, in the battle of the Wilderness.

William D. Haley, of Bath, filled two offices, regimental quartermaster and commissary, and Dr. G. S. Palmer, of Gardiner, that of surgeon. One of the noncommissioned staff, the commissary sergeant, Joseph S. Smith, of Bath, became, in time, General Sedgwick's brigade division and corps commissary with the rank

of colonel. The field officers were Lieutenant Colonel
Isaac N. Tucker and Major Henry G. Staples. The former, who turned out to have no aptitude for military
command, resigned during the first year and Staples
took his place. Captain Charles A. L. Sampson succeeded Tucker as major. A very worthy lieutenant,
James H. Tallman, followed Haley on his leaving the
service the first year as regimental quartermaster.
His efficiency gained him afterwards promotion in the
regular army. The administrative functions of my
regiment were thus fully provided for, even though the
officers designated had had no experience. Some essential drilling was all I attempted at Augusta, just
enough to enable me to move the regiment in a body
and to load and fire with some degree of precision.

The call from Washington soon reached our governor; my regiment must be ready to go forward by
June 5th. The time was too short and my duties too
engrossing even to warrant visiting my parents at
Leeds, though but twenty miles distant. I, therefore,
sent my brother to bring my stepfather and my mother
to the city. But they had anticipated me. Fearing
from a rumor the sudden departure of the regiment,
they had under the unusual circumstances traveled on
Sunday and come all the way that day to relatives in
Hallowell, three miles distant from our camp. Here
we had a family meeting.

The morning of June 5th was beautiful. The
sun shone from a cloudless sky; the fruit trees and
the luxurious lilacs were in full bloom; the maples
in every part of Augusta were thick with leaves as rich
and charming as fresh green could make them. Very
early the city was astir; soon it was out of doors. The
dresses of women and children furnished every variety

of coloring, and little by little the people grouped themselves along the slope to the Kennebec River. Bright-buttoned uniforms were noticeable among them. The groups, varying in size, were in gardens, on hillsides, and upon porches, front steps, balconies, and all convenient housetops. All eyes were turned toward the railway, which ran southward not far from the river bank. The cars could easily be seen by the people. They were loaded inside and out, and always surrounded by a dense crowd of lookers-on.

Opposite the State House, at the outer edge of the multitude, I noticed a single group. The father, past middle life, stood watching as the men were placing tents and other baggage upon freight cars. Near him was a son talking hopefully to his mother: " Keep up heart, mother, and look as much as you can on the bright side."

" Oh, yes, my son, it is easy to talk, but it is hard——"

She did not finish the sentence, but after a few moments and tears, commended him to the keeping of the Heavenly Father and urged him not to forget Him or home.

Finally, the whistles blew significantly and the engine bells began to ring. There were many last embraces, many sobbing mothers, wives, and dear ones; then streams of bright uniforms rushed down the slopes to the trains.

Slowly these trains moved out of Augusta. Heads were thrust out of car windows; and the tops of rail-coaches were covered with men, sitting and standing. Before the trains had disappeared, the regimental band struck up a national air. But there was no responsive cheering from the cars. Hats and handkerchiefs were waved, and here and there a small national flag shaken out, as if to suggest to the waiting people the object of our departure.

Who can forget his last look at that multitude on the hillside—the swift motion of waving handkerchiefs, flags, and outstretched hands! A curve in the track shut off the view; and thus departed this precions, typical freight of war.

At Hallowell, where we tarried a few minutes, my brother Charles and I parted with our mother. Then and ever after I sympathized with soldiers who left true, loving, watching hearts at home. But the relief from oppressive sentiment was found in absorbing duties and active work.

CHAPTER IX

THE varying scenes which interested the soldiers and the people during that memorable journey were too abundant for record. At railroad stations in Maine, on the approach and departure of our trains, there was abundant cheering and words of encouragement. However, here and there were discordant cries. Few, indeed, were the villages where no voice of opposition was raised. But, later in the war, in the free States after the wounding and the death of fathers, brothers, and sons, our sensitive, afflicted home people would not tolerate what they called traitorous talk. They went so far as to frown upon any vigorous young men who clung to the home roof, and found means to compel blatant offenders to hush their utterances, and shake out to the breeze some semblance of the old flag. This conduct was imperious; it was earnest; it had its counterpart in the South; it meant war.

As we came whistling into the large depot at Brunswick, where Bowdoin College is located, professors and students, forgetting their wonted respectful distance and distinction, mingled together in the same eager crowd, and added manly vigor to the voices of enthusiastic lads who were crowning the fences and gravel-cars and other sightly places. Unexpected tears of interest, warm hand-pressures, and " God speed you, my

123

son," revealed to some former students, now soldiers, tenderness of heart not before dreamed of among those gray-haired instructors.

At Portland, Maine's largest city, we met a marked demonstration. Food, drink, and flowers were brought to the cars and freely offered, but we could not delay, though the people asked to extend a more formal welcome.

At Boston, early in the afternoon, a company of guards in spotless uniform and with wondrous perfection of drill paraded before our soldiers in their somber gray and escorted them through the eddies and whirlpools of city people, along the winding streets and out into the Common. Bunker Hill, Breed's Hill, the Old South Church, and other ancient sentinels, which had observed the beginnings of our liberty, looked solemnly and silently upon us as we passed. Surely, many of us would die before the boastful threat of Robert Toombs to count his slaves on Bunker Hill should be carried out. Boston Common! How beautiful, as we marched in, was its green, undulating surface; how pretty the lawns and little lakes; how grateful and refreshing the shade this hot June day.

The governor, John A. Andrew, of large heart and brain, who with his staff had come out from the State House to meet us, gave us a welcome in well-chosen words; but the hospitable multitude excelled on that occasion. The choicest supper was spread upon long tables, which were stretched out so as to barricade our way. My thousand men were never better fed or served, because mothers and daughters of Massachusetts were ministering to them. Our enthusiasm under such cheer and amid such surroundings underwent no abatement. All spoke to us in a language plainer and

124

deeper than words: " Go, fight for your flag, and free the land."

From my boyhood the sight of a large steamer has been grand to me, and in my eyes the *Bay State*, at Fall River, exceeded all others. That night, June 5th, it took on the thousand soldiers, and they seemed to make little impression on the vast passenger space. This superb transport ferried us the length of Long Island Sound as it, or its sister ships, had ferried thousands before us.

A committee of a New York association called the " Sons of Maine " met our steamer at the pier on North River. Unfortunately for us, it was a stormy day and the rain poured incessantly. In ordinary times there would have been little stir in New York City on such an arrival, particularly in the mud and slush of most unpropitious weather; but then the excitement ran high; nothing could dampen the patriotic fervor of the people, and crowds besides the " Sons of Maine " came to see us land. R. P. Buck, Esq., a native of Bucksport, was a fine-looking, well-dressed merchant, and the chairman of the committee. He took me by the arm and, led by the committee, regardless of moist clothes and wet feet, preceded by a military and police escort, the regiment marched *via* Battery Place and up Broadway to the White Street city armory. Twenty years after our walk in the middle of Broadway I dedicated a book [1] to my conductor in these words: " Whose heart beats with true loyalty to his country and to the Lord, his Saviour. From the time when he with other friends welcomed my regiment when en route to the field to the city of New York till to-day he has extended to me the tender offices of friendship and affection."

[1] Count Agénor de Gasparin. Translated from the French of Thomas Borel.

After our men had entered the drill hall of the armory they unslung their knapsacks and arranged them near the wall for seats. As soon as there was order the " Sons of Maine," by their committee, gave notice that they wished to present a flag to the regiment. Stewart L. Woodford, the youthful statesman, whose wife was a daughter of Maine, was selected to make the presentation speech. There was in it a mingling of seriousness and humor characteristic of the orator. Standing where all could see him, Woodford said: " I expected to present this standard to you in the Park. I am somewhat surprised that soldiers of Maine should not have faced the storm, for as soldiers you should have learned to keep your powder dry, and as citizens of a State that has given the temperance law, you ought not to be afraid of God's cold water.

" Each mother has given to her boy in your ranks that fittest pledge of a mother's love—her Bible. Each dear one has given some pledge that speaks of softer and sweeter hours. Your brethren in this hour of battle would give you a strong man's gift—your country's flag. Its blended stripes shall stream above you with protection. It is the flag of history. Those thirteen stripes tell the story of the colonial struggle, of the days of '76. They speak of the wilderness savage, of old Independence Hall, of Valley Forge and Yorktown. Those stars tell the story of our nation's growth; how it has come from weakness to strength, from thirteen States to thirty-four, until the gleam that shines at sunrise over the forests of Maine crimsons the sunset's dying beams on the golden sands of California. Let not the story of the flag be folded down and lost forever. . . .

" We give this flag to you, and with it we give our

prayers, and not ours alone; but as the loved home circle gathers, far in the Pine Tree State, gray-haired fathers and loved mothers will speak in prayer the name of their boy." Turning to me, he said: "Sir, in behalf of the 'Sons of Maine' I give you this flag; guard it as a woman guards her honor; as children keep the ashes of their father. That flag shall float in triumph on your avenging march, as those steel fingers point the way through Baltimore to Sumter. That flag shall hover with more than a mother's care over your head. We hear to-day above the sound of the conflict the voice of the archangel crying, 'Victory is on the side of liberty; victory is on the side of law.' With unbroken ranks may your command march beneath its folds. God bless you! Farewell!"

I thanked the donors for the flag, saying: "I was born in the East, but I was educated by my country. I know no section; I know no party; I never did. I know only my country to love it, and my God who is over my country. We go forth to battle and we go in defense of righteousness and liberty, civil and religious. We go strong in muscle, strong in heart, strong in soul, because we are right. I have endeavored to live in all good conscience before God and I go forth to battle without flinching, because the same God that has given His Spirit to direct me has shown me that our cause is righteous; and I could not be better placed than I am now, because He has given me the warm hearts of as fine a regiment as America has produced."

I then called for cheers for New York; for the Union; for the Constitution and the President of the United States. The response was given with tremendous effect, every man springing to his feet the instant the call was made.

127

A few encouraging words were spoken by Rev. Roswell G. Hitchcock, then a leading divine in the city; after which Dexter Hawkins, Esq., a fellow-graduate of Bowdoin, and then a lawyer of New York, in the name of the "Sons of Maine" invited the commissioned officers to dine with them at the Astor House. The remainder of the regiment dined at the armory.

Rev. L. C. Lockwood, on behalf of a generous lady and the Young Men's Christian Association of New York, presented to the regiment 250 Soldier's Scripture Text-books and 200 Patriotic Song-books. Those books often relieved the monotony of army service, and the songs enlivened tired groups around many a camp fire.

At that armory, before our hospitable entertainers had set out with the officers for their dinner, I met with a mishap which somewhat marred my comfort. While I was standing on the limber of a gun carriage, using it for an elevated platform in speaking and giving commands, some one accidentally knocked out the prop from under the pole. The sudden shock caused me to lose my balance and spring to the floor. I alighted on my feet, but attached to my belt was my heavy saber, which fell, striking my left foot with great force. My great toe nail was crushed and has troubled me ever since. This was my first wound in the war.

My friend, Mr. Buck, has since told this incident of the Astor House dinner: "When at the close of the menu we had risen, and with our wineglasses in hand were about to pledge the young colonel in a patriotic sentiment, he seized a glass of water and said: 'I join you in a drink of cold water, the only beverage fit for a soldier.' You should have seen," Mr. Buck added,

" how we all hustled around to get our glasses of water ! "

Surely, my conduct did not appear very gracious, but I was eager to keep strong drink of any kind from the regiment, and knew that I must set an example to the officers. I did not dream that our hosts would thus follow my lead.

My wife and children had come down from West Point. They joined me at the hotel and after dinner bade me and my regiment good-by as the ferryboat to New Jersey left the New York slip, many men of the regiment courteously uncovering in their honor and waving them a farewell.

Philadelphia gave its entertainment. The rain was over. We received a delightful supper between eight and ten ; abundance of food on tables set in squares. Ladies clad in white and adorned with flowers, with gentle voices, made us feel that we were already heroes, when with quickness and grace they moved within and without the squares to replenish our plates or fill our cups with steaming coffee. Loyal men and women breathed upon us a patriotic spirit which it then seemed no danger would ever cause to abate.

After the bloody passage of the Sixth Massachusetts through Baltimore a few days before our arrival in that city, the succeeding troops from the north had been conveyed to Washington in a roundabout way *via* Annapolis, thus avoiding the riotous mobs. My regiment was among the first to resume the direct route. In order to be able to protect ourselves in that city, I had ordered the men supplied with ten rounds apiece of ball cartridges.

A handsome police escort met the incoming train, reported to me as I left my coach, and were placed where they could clear the way for my column, which must march from station to station, a distance of about two miles. As soon as I had walked to a central place in the depot yard with a view to seeing my troops properly drawn up in line, a few persons, approaching slowly, came up behind me and, taking my hand, pressed it warmly.

A large crowd were waiting and interestedly watched our disembarkation. Every face in the promiscuous crowd which I saw had a look of apprehension or smothered passion. We might, like our comrades of Massachusetts, have trouble _en route._

To be prepared was my part. The line being formed facing me, I ordered " Load with cartridges, load!" wheeled into a column of platoons after the old fashion and started the march, following the city escort. We were then self-confident—ready for anything that might occur. The places of business were closed, giving a gloomy effect. No flags of any description were flying. All people appeared under some fear or repression. They were silent, yet curious and observing. We made the march, however, without disturbance, entered cars again at the Baltimore & Ohio Depot on Camden Street, and after moderate delay were on the way to Washington. While the baggage was in process of transfer I was invited to dine with a Union man at his house. I found there my host and a few chosen friends who were in sympathy with us. As soon as the doors were closed, everyone breathed more freely and heartily spoke his sentiments. With these men, already Unionism had become an intense passion and, like Maccabeus of old, they had a holy hatred, very pronounced, of individual enemies of the Government. They declared that the bloody riot which had stained their streets with blood was not the cause, as claimed, but simply the occasion of the rebellious conduct of prominent city and State officials. " Be on your guard, colonel," they urged, " against the seeming friendship and pretended loyalty of smiling villains." Matters just then, not only in Baltimore, but in many other parts of Maryland, were dark and uncertain. It was a critical period. Families were dividing and old friends at feud.

These things being so, it was a little strange that the ominous silence on our arrival had not been broken and our bold march through the flagless city interrupted. I believe that the possession of Federal Hill by Butler's soldiers and our own loaded muskets had much to do with the quietude of our passage. From this time on, Baltimore communication was never again broken.

The evening of June 7th, as we steamed into the ample Baltimore & Ohio Depot at Washington, we felt that our eventful journey was over. However proud and independent the individual soldier might feel, he found at once that he could not pick up his personal baggage and go straight to a hotel. An officer of Colonel Mansfield's staff with our own regimental quartermaster met us and led the way to a vacant building near by on Pennsylvania Avenue. What at some subsequent dates would have been counted luxury did not seem so then—a bare floor, a chairless room without table or lights was but a cold reception, a depressing welcome to their beloved capital, for whose preservation they had been ready to fight to the death. The contrast to the previous hearty, patriotic receptions was so great as to bring on a general attack of homesickness. Feeling for them the next morning as one would for a homesick youth just arrived at college, and knowing the need of removing at any cost a universal depression, I consulted with my commissary and arranged to give the entire command a breakfast at Willard's for fifty cents a man. Just think of it, to feed a whole regiment at a hotel! My army friends did laugh, and I had to confess my lack of wisdom according to ordinary reasoning, for I thus became personally responsible for the large amount. But after a spirited correspondence the State finally settled the account.

I reported at an early hour on June 8th to Colonel Joseph K. F. Mansfield, Inspector General of the Army, commanding the Department of Washington. He was already frosted with age and long service. Probably from his own Christian character no officer of the army then could have inspired me with more reverence than he. At that time Mansfield appeared troubled and almost crushed by an overwhelming amount of detail thrust upon him; but after two hours' delay he assigned me my camp on Meridian Hill.

CHAPTER X

CAMPING IN WASHINGTON; IN COMMAND OF A BRIGADE

ON June 8th, the day our veteran commander, General Winfield Scott, penned his famous letter to old General Patterson favoring his projected capture of Harper's Ferry, my new regiment was marching along Pennsylvania Avenue and Fourteenth Street to Meridian Hill. When we began the march the heat was intense. The men were loaded down with their knapsacks, haversacks, and cartridge boxes. Friends at home and along our route had been so generous that much underclothing, books, and keepsakes had been stowed away by the men, so that the weight for each was extra heavy. Again, these old-pattern knapsacks sagged, bound the arms, hurt the shoulders, and wearied the muscles of our young soldiers. Many a brave-hearted youth gave up, sat down by the way, or dropped out of ranks for water or rest and that before the end of the first three miles of *bona fide* marching. When about half way on the Fourteenth Street stretch a sudden storm arose, attended by wind, fierce lightning, and a pouring rain. The storm was at its height as the regiment began the last ascent, and then, somewhat quieter, continued till dark. About the time the rain set in one poor fellow left the ranks and undertook to get over a fence; he pulled his loaded musket after him with the muzzle toward him. As the hammer struck a rail or stone an explosion followed, inflicting upon him a desperate, disabling wound—and yet so far from any battlefield! How fruitless now to his vision appeared his ardent patriotism; how dim all anticipated glory! Thus it was with many another who had left home full of life, setting forth with fiery eyes and glowing cheeks, only to be arrested by a premature wound or prostrated by camp fever. Thus that short five-mile march was the beginning of the hardships and experiences of real war.

Tell me, soldiers, you who have bivouacked on the Bad Lands of the Missouri or endured the severities of winter in the Rocky Mountains, did anything quite equal the first stormy night under canvas? To arrive on new ground, muddy and sticky; to work in wet clothes; to put up tents, soaked, dirty, and heavy; to be where a stick of wood is precious and fuel is begrudged you—where it is a crime to burn a fence rail; then to worry out a long night without sleep for fear of a fatal cold; every veteran has had somewhere such an experience. The Kennebec men endured the trial the first night on Meridian Hill. President Sampson and other friends from Columbian College near by offered to many of us hospitality which is still gratefully remembered. Colonel Charles D. Jameson with the Second Maine was encamped on our flank; he, his officers, and men took compassion on our forlorn condition, and gave all who were not otherwise provided for an ample supper, including the soldiers' hot coffee. Jameson's regiment having preceded us a few days, had already comfortable tents and a general preparedness for storms. They housed us all for one night.

The beautiful June day which succeeded that night

set everything to rights. Tents were pitched in proper order and the strictest of camp regulations instituted. Here on Meridian Hill, in keeping with the lot of many another army officer, my popularity both on the spot and in many homes of the Kennebec Valley, where letters from camp found their way, greatly suffered. At first I granted passes freely, but finding many violations of them, I was obliged to stop them entirely.

One day in solemn conclave a delegation of soldiers came to my tent to reason with me and to remonstrate. Their complaints were many and profound; but they may be condensed into a sentence: "Why make the innocent suffer for the guilty?" It was extremely difficult for an independent freeman to see why he should not go when he pleased and have an interview with Generals Mansfield, Lorenzo Thomas, or Winfield Scott. Famous men were in Washington. It would be an opportunity lost not to see them in their official chairs. There was also their own President, Abraham Lincoln, for whose election many of them had contended in the political campaign of 1860; and there was the White House; could not every citizen avail himself of the poor privilege of just one visit? Furthermore, think of the Capitol, glorious and immense, though still without its crowning Goddess of Liberty. How was it possible to be so near and yet be allowed only a distant glimpse? Surely, the colonel would give abundant passes to the good and true? But I could not. They believed I would not. The regiment must be drilled, disciplined, and made ready for war. Ours was not a holiday excursion. The petitioners departed answered but not convinced.

Two West Point lieutenants, Buell and McQuesten,

were sent to me to give the elementary instruction, or, in military phrase, " to set the men up." These young officers added to the severities. Once, when I had been cadet officer of the day at West Point during a cadet disturbance which I could not quell, I myself was punished by the superintendent. Thus the responsible innocent suffered for the irresponsible guilty. Substitutive penalties in military affairs are expedient. By them men learn to govern their fellows. I now found this a very useful military doctrine, but not popular with volunteers—more tolerable, however, after a few battles, when they saw what havoc want of discipline produced.

What a military school was that on Meridian Hill! In bright memory I see them now—the men and the officers of my regiment before sickness and death had broken in—the major, the surgeon, the captains and lieutenants, and the entire staff; I recall the faces. The hard drill was the real beginning of our repute. Washington came at sunset in carriages to witness our evening parade. I had these men in but one battle, but they had a great history, especially after Colonel Moses Lakeman, one of my captains, succeeded Staples as colonel. Being called the " Fighting Colonel," he developed the energies of his regiment till it took high rank in Sickles's corps. It gave any flank strength to find the Third Maine there. Its presence made a rear guard confident, but its own chief pride in campaign or battle was to be in the lead. The officers very soon looked back to that exacting first colonel who insisted on close discipline and much drill, and forgave his severity. But at first there was considerable chafing; my brother, still a private in the regiment, on June 29th wrote to a friend: " We had a good deal of excitement

136

the night of taking the oath; fifty or sixty men refused at first, but after a few words of explanation they rallied under the colors at the command of Colonel Howard."

That June 29th I was made to sympathize with the poor fellows upon whom a radical change of life had brought illness. Suddenly, without previous symptom or warning, I suffered from an attack of something like cholera. So rapid was my decline under it that for a time our good surgeon, Dr. Palmer, had little hope of arresting the disease; but my brother's devotion, the firmness and skill of my doctor, and the care given me by the wife of Captain Sampson, with the blessing of God saved me at death's door. Then, to complete my good fortune, just as I began convalescing, the mother of my friend, Lieutenant S. S. Carroll, took me in her carriage to her home in Washington. Her gentle nursing gave me just those things which would nourish and strengthen, and soon restored me to the field and to duty. Her generous husband and herself always made their house a home to me. To my comfort the surgeon after that incisive attack congratulated me and himself on my solid constitution. " More recuperative energy than I have ever elsewhere met," he said. Later, I learned that President Lincoln kindly called twice at my tent and inquired for me while I was unconscious.

Washington in June and to the middle of July, under the immediate administration of Colonel Mansfield, was a scattered camp. Regiments crowned every height; officers in uniform thronged the streets and crowded the hotels. There appeared to the looker-on great confusion; not yet any regular, well-appointed force. Everybody talked; newspapers published and sometimes magnified idle rumors; they made and un-made reputations in a day. No one seemed to know what was to be done or what could be done. Alexandria, over the Potomac, was occupied by our troops; the new Confederate flag, unfolded to the breeze on a Virginia hill, waved its stars and bars in plain sight of the Capitol, and thus boldly challenged our rulers to a conflict which was destined either to wreck or establish our Union. State governors came on to Washington with their regiments; prominent citizens hastened thither with their proposals; avaricious dealers were on hand to make their fortunes. The White House, the departments, the hotels, and all public buildings were densely crowded. Had that capital been Paris, there would have been a speedy revolution, and, indeed, in the words of Carlyle, it did seem for a time that "if somebody did not do something soon things would do themselves satisfactory to nobody."

At every turn when I visited the city I met acquaintances or was introduced to strangers who afterwards became distinguished — Governor Fenton, of New York, quiet, watchful, self-poised; Governor Curtin, of Pennsylvania, with his tall form, ready wit, and tender, benevolent soul; Senator Morgan, of New York, of giant proportions, large purse, and larger heart; Senator Harris, of the same State, noble in bearing and in character; Secretary Seward, dignified and distant to young men, sanguine of our speedy success; Governor Sprague, of Rhode Island, very young, and putting youthful life into his well-equipped regiments; his colonel, Burnside, in uniform, handsome as a picture; Colonel A. McD. McCook, with the First Ohio Regiment, never fuller of happy humor, ready for anything that might occur; and Colonel Daniel Butterfield, commanding the Twelfth New York, then encamped in Franklin Square, himself the best dressed, the most self-contained, calm, and ambitious. We had occasional glimpses of General Irwin McDowell. For years I had heard and seen his name connected with the orders from General Scott, and was surprised to find him so tall and of such full build. His habitual demeanor now was that of one self-absorbed and distant. He was the subject at that time of constant observation and remark, for it was believed that he would soon command all our movable forces on the Potomac. Many voices around Mr. Lincoln made themselves heard, but all were not in his support. His cabinet, however, gave pretty general satisfaction. Chase, of the Treasury, with practical brain, could make and distribute the money, provided he had the handsome, sanguine, able banker, Jay Cooke, to help him. Montgomery Blair, the postmaster-general, with his political acumen, could coöperate with his brother, General F. P. Blair, in Missouri. The Blairs were watched with confident interest. Simon Cameron, in the War Department, a secretary, wealthy, experienced, and wise—how could the President have a better adviser than he? Most venerable of the Cabinet was Secretary Wells, in charge of the navy portfolio. It did us young men good to look upon him and upon General Scott because of their imperturbable faces. We needed solid men of age rather than ardent leaders.

The first great excitement was from the outside. During the afternoon of June 11th the news of General Benjamin F. Butler's attempt to capture Little and Big Bethel came to us. Butler ordered a night march with the hope of surprising a small intrenched force at Big Bethel. It was to be a combined movement of three detachments—one from Fortress Monroe, one from Hampton, and the other from Newport News. Brigadier General Pierce, of Massachusetts, an officer without experience, was placed over the field command. Colonel Abram Duryea, with his Fifth New York (Duryea Zouaves), starting at midnight, led the way from Hamptom, beyond the point of junction with the Newport News road. Colonel Bendix, with a New York regiment of Germans, a small detachment of New Englanders, and a section of a regular battery under Lieutenant John T. Greble, came next from Newport News to the junction. Bendix, considering the uncertainties of night work, went into ambush near the crossroads. Some two hours after Duryea had passed the junction, General Pierce, escorted by the Third New York, came up by the same road that Duryea had followed. Bendix mistook this force for the enemy's cavalry and opened fire. In the resulting skirmish with each other some were killed and many wounded. The air filled with the rattle of musketry created for a time a panic, and of course the secrecy of the expedition was over. At last all of our men passed Little Bethel and were before the small fort, which was fairly well manned with Confederate infantry and a few field guns. My friend and classmate, John T. Greble, while effectively firing his cannon against the fort at short range, was instantly killed. We had been next-door neighbors at West Point and had long lived in affectionate intimacy, so this blow was most afflicting to me.

He was the first regular army officer to fall in the Civil War, and was immediately officially recorded as a brevet colonel. Though he had not this grateful recognition in life, yet his patriotic and worthy family appreciate and cherish the record.

Camping in Washington

I wrote home: " Poor John Greble's death struck me like a thunderbolt. It seems to have been a disastrous fight under incompetent leaders."

But now in the retrospect one hardly casts blame. Experience and the habit of working together would have hindered the panic at the junction. The famous Magruder and D. H. Hill were on the other side in this combat. The victory then gave them joy and confidence—extravagant, indeed, but thus it was in both armies early in the war. Modesty and mutual respect appeared in reports and dispatches only later.

Before leaving Augusta Mr. Blaine and I were talking of the army to be organized from the volunteers. He remarked: " You, Howard, will be the first brigadier from Maine." Of course the proposition to me, accustomed only to wrinkled captains and white-headed field officers, appeared visionary.

Later, July 4th, I answered another friend who made the same suggestion: " I am as high as I desire. What could I effect in a higher position? I do not think there is any likelihood at present of taking me from my regiment."

Yet, three days later, I received a note from the War Department directing me to select three regiments in addition to my own to constitute a brigade of which I as the senior colonel was to take command and conduct them to Alexandria.

On July 6th at dawn I had had reveille; our men had promptly loaded the wagons, but the quartermaster did not get draught animals to us from the city till ten o'clock. That waiting indicated want of system and discipline. At last, proudly we marched from Meridian Hill back to Pennsylvania Avenue and down Sixth Street to the dock, the regimental band playing

141

national airs. Soldiers stepped out together with heads high, hopes strong, and hearts beating courageously.

After a brief halt the regiment crossed by steamer to Alexandria. Colonel S. P. Heintzelman, of the Seventeenth Regular Infantry, had been designated our division commander, with headquarters in Alexandria. He brought a good record from the Mexican War, and was in 1861 a hardy, fearless, energetic character, which our undisciplined levies then especially needed. He had a frank way of expressing the exact truth whether it hurt or not.

As my full regiment, of which I was proud, was marching up the main street, I caught sight of Colonel Heintzelman, who had come out of his office and was standing near a street corner which I was to pass. I brought the command to a carry-arms, but did not halt and fix bayonets as I would have done for a formal review. In this order we went past him, while he critically noticed every fault. I went up to him, hoping for a compliment, but heard a nasal speech: " Colonel, you have a fine regiment; they march well and give promise for the future, but you are not well drilled—poor officers, but good-looking men! " He evidently enjoyed my discomfiture, and would have no explanation.

Alexandria was more gloomy than Baltimore. The pavements were rough and broken; cobblestones in piles alternated with mudholes and pitfalls. Most residences were closed and empty and beautiful homes deserted; no business was transacted except what the army brought. Those who had fled and those now coming from over the Potomac were like locusts. They destroyed every green herb and even ate up the hedges and fences. Grass, foliage, and flowers disappeared before army movements.

Five miles to the Washington dock and three more to camp on the Alexandria side, eight in all, with the load each man carried, made labor enough for the first trial. We watched southward from the vicinity of R. F. Roberts's farm and had for a single brigade a wide front to protect.

As soon as I received the War Department note, making me a brigade commander, I visited, selected, and brought over to my vicinity from their several camps near Washington three other regiments—the Fourth Maine, Colonel Hiram G. Berry; the Fifth Maine, Colonel Mark H. Dunnell, and the Second Vermont, Colonel Henry Whiting commanding. The latter was a graduate of the Military Academy. My lieutenant colonel was absent, so Major Staples passed to the head of the Third Maine on my temporary promotion. Notwithstanding the usual depletions of new regiments, my command was at this time above three thousand strong. McDowell soon sent me forward as far as Mrs. Scott's farm, sometimes called "Bush Hill," four miles from Alexandria. The Maine regiments held the country to the south of the Centreville Pike, and Whiting's Vermonters had a handsome position in a field to the north of it.

About that time there was much camp criticism of McDowell, who had in charge the army of occupation officially called "the Department of Northeast Virginia." The accusers said that he had too much tenderness toward the enemies' property. Regular officers were berated generally in the soldier gossip and in the newspapers for using up the soldiers in guarding such property. This conduct, however, did not proceed, as charged, from Southern sympathy. McDowell and his associates wished to prevent the demoralization of the soldiers, for to take property *ad libitum* would soon overturn all order and leave no basis of rightdoing. Heintzelman's instruction just after the accession of my brigade to his division is a specimen of the prevailing restriction:

HEADQUARTERS THIRD DIVISION, ALEXANDRIA,
July 10, 1861.

Colonel Howard, Commanding Third Brigade.

SIR: The bearer of this note, R. F. Roberts, states that privates of the Fourth and Fifth Maine regiments have been committing depredations on his property, stealing potatoes, etc. The general commanding wishes you to investigate the matter and put a stop at once to all such proceedings. If the men can be identified, punish them severely.

Very respectfully,
CHAUNCEY MCKEEVER,
Assistant Adjutant General.

Our soldiers, through the servants and escaping slaves, always claimed that they knew the old residents who were disloyal better than their generals, and they had firmly adopted the theory that the spoils of all enemies belonged to them—particularly such reprisals as potatoes, onions, and other vegetables. They advocated the seizure of cattle, sheep, fowls, and preserved meats, and found great need for fence rails before their claim was admitted by the authorities. The wonder is that our men were not more demoralized than they were by our subsequent living on the country and foraging at will.

Near the position of the Fifth Maine below the turnpike and facing toward the enemy, who was at Manassas Junction, with outposts at Sangster's and

Camping in Washington

Fairfax Station, was a crossroad. The regiment had there a picket guard, the point being an important one and the environs much darkened by thick trees. A captain commanded this guard. One night the tramp of horses was heard. In an instant the whole guard was in readiness, and one may imagine how the hearts of new soldiers throbbed as they listened to the fast-approaching sounds. Three bold riders soon appeared, moving at a trot, one in advance. The outside sentinel called: " Who comes there? " The soldierly answer gave confidence: " Union officer and two men."

Dressed in our uniform, they correctly answered every question put to them. The captain spoke a pleasant word and was about to let them pass when it occurred to him to be a little extra cautious on account of a rumor of spies passing the lines. He said: " Very well, gentlemen; you may be all right, but I will take you to the senior officer of my guard." Turning to the first man, he said: " Please, sir, give me your gun." The stranger, taken by surprise, cried out: " My gun? " then, recovering, he whirled his horse and with a sharp exclamation gave him the spurs. The captain instantly ordered: " Fire! " The stranger wavered in his saddle and then fell dead to the ground, while his two friends escaped through the thicket. They had not approached so near the guard as their leader. The leader, as his papers revealed, was a young man from Mississippi. Bold and energetic, he had been chosen to go back and forth from Fairfax to Alexandria. This was by no means his first trip. He tried the experiment once too often. It is a singular custom of war that the bravest become scouts and spies, and if unsuccessful are stigmatized with dishonor.

CHAPTER XI

TO organize and mobilize the Army of Northeastern Virginia, McDowell had constituted five divisions: Tyler's, Hunter's, Heintzelman's, Dixon S. Miles's, and Runyon's. Our division had the left from the Centreville Pike southeastward to the Potomac; Runyon's kept in or near Alexandria as a reserve; while the other divisions ranged northward to beyond Georgetown, covering a frontage of more than ten miles. McDowell had for mounted troops an escort of United States cavalry not to exceed five hundred.

With a good body of horse and abundant reliefs of slaves used to hard work, Beauregard, even before the arrival of the Army of the Shenandoah, was surely well prepared with his " effectives " of 21,823 soldiers and 29 cannon to sustain a good defensive battle against the Union column of 28,568 men and 49 cannon.

Centreville was in 1861 an inconsiderable village with but one street north and south, the buildings mainly on the west side scattered along a ridge. The road from Centreville to Manassas Junction followed the trend of this ridge southward and crossed Bull Run three miles distant at Mitchell's Ford. The Warrenton Turnpike, coursing from east to west through the village, crossed Bull Run about four miles west of it at Stone Bridge. The country in the valleys of

146

Battle of Bull Run

Bull Run and its tributaries was for the most part woodland. The current of Bull Run was not rapid, but the banks were abrupt, often rocky and precipitous, so that it could not readily be crossed except at the bridges and fords. The higher ground afforded quiet slopes and plateaus, but everywhere so many trees had been allowed to grow that the farms were like glades of more or less expanse in the midst of a forest. There were no prominent points for observation, so that the commanding generals were obliged to work out their plans by maps and sketches.

Beauregard, with his staff, fort, depot of supplies, force of workmen, and necessary reserves, posted himself at Manassas; the right of his army, Ewing's brigade, at Union Mills; at McLean's Ford, Jones's brigade; at Blackburn's Ford, Longstreet's; just above Mitchell's Ford, Bonham's; at Lewis' Ford, Coke's; at Stone Bridge, the crossing of the Warrenton Pike, Evans's demibrigade of a regiment and a half, which formed the left of the Confederate army proper; Early's brigade of four regiments was drawn up in rear of Longstreet and Jones as a reserve. The above brigades, together with some seven other regiments and companies not brigaded, constituted Beauregard's " Army of the Potomac."

Radford's cavalry brigade was keeping watch along the front and south of Union Mills, and Stuart, after his arrival from the Shenandoah, scouted beyond Evans's position on the Confederate left.

McDowell, for the sake of contracting his lines, and gathering his regiments under their several commanders, ordered a short march, setting out from the Potomac on July 16th and sending them forward to several small places in Virginia not far apart. This march was duly made and Heintzelman caused our brigades to pass the Accotink and go to the Pohick. When I came to the Accotink I found many men of the preceding brigade sitting down and taking off their shoes—not to wade the shallow stream, but for fear they might slip off the narrow bridge which was made of two logs placed side by side, and so wet their shoes and socks. Regiment after regiment had been crossing in this way by file, so that each brigade before mine had taken full two hours to pass a stream not more than twenty yards wide and the water nowhere above their knees. This delayed my crossing till night. My men were somewhat incensed because I made them close up and march straight through the ford. They surely would not have been so fresh and happy the next morning if they had been three hours later than they were in getting into camp. In such small things as this West Point officers appeared to be too severe with new troops. Remembering Professor Mahan's rule: "Not to imperil the success of a campaign from fear of wetting the soldiers' feet," they doubtless showed indignation and scolded regimental officers for wasting important time in crossing shallow streams.

I wrote home from that first camp that two serious accidents had occurred to us, two men having shot themselves, so unused even then were our young soldiers to handling rifles. In consequence of hearing much profanity, I wished our men had more regard for the Lord; we might then expect His blessing.

Fulfilling our orders for July 17th, every command came up abreast of Fairfax Court House. Colonel Franklin and I encamped our brigades near each other upon a hillside. That night we reclined before the same map spread on the ground near a camp fire and

148

studied the orders for the next day which we had just received. Colonel Willcox's brigade had been in advance and had branched off southward toward the railroad and Fairfax Station.

" On our coming the enemy fled without a shot. We captured a sergeant, a corporal, and nine men belonging to the First Alabama Regiment."

This Confederate outpost at Fairfax Station had had two regiments as a guard, an Alabama and a Louisiana. Willcox had approached them from an unexpected quarter.

The morning of the 18th Franklin and I heard again from McDowell. Each column had found some obstructions—felled trees, extra-sized breastworks at the court house, and equally strong outworks at the railway station. The Confederates retreated before each column; they did not draw in their pickets, most of whom fell into our hands; four of our men of Miles's division were wounded. To this news McDowell added:

" I am distressed to have to report excesses by our troops. The excitement of the men found vent in burning and pillaging, which distressed us all greatly." Thus in general a responsible soul in an approaching crisis is grieved at the wrongdoing of his agents. Yet, notwithstanding considerable straggling, foolish delays at streams, carelessness with firearms, burning and pillaging on first news of success, we had accomplished this first stage of approach to our enemy as well as General Scott could have expected.

McDowell's instructions for the third march were few and comprehensive: Dixon Miles's division to Centreville; Hunter to get as near Centreville as he could and have water; while Heintzelman was to move up to the Little Rocky Run on the road, hence to Centreville. A postscript gave zest to his message to Tyler, who was in front of Miles: "Observe well the roads to Bull Run and to Warrenton. . . . Do not bring on an engagement, but keep up the impression that we are moving on Manassas."

When that postscript was penned, McDowell had just changed his purpose. Till then it had been his plan to move on Manassas by a rapid push from his left, but his engineers found the roads of approach "too narrow and crooked for a large body to move over and the distance around (southward) too great to admit of it with any safety."

During the 18th, as our men tramped along, a discouraging rumor ran down the column that Tyler was defeated. Though McDowell did not intend so much in his instructions, Tyler understood that he was to make toward Manassas a reconnoissance in force. It was difficult to do anything else with our fighting Colonel Richardson in front. It was so quiet when Tyler with Richardson neared Blackburn's Ford that they could not detect with glasses that Longstreet was there with his batteries and five infantry regiments and Early close behind with four more, yet such was the case.

Tyler naturally ordered forward a battery and supported it by Richardson's brigade. A few shots from the Union battery brought a battery response from the Confederates; and Richardson's supporting fire obtained quick and spiteful rifle retorts. One regiment, getting too far forward, was attacked and driven back. Richardson, now full of fire, begged of Tyler to charge with other troops and carry the enemy's position. Tyler refused; for he had reconnoitered and had found a strong force. In doing so he

150

had lost six lives and had twenty-six men disabled by wounds. His instructions were plain: "Do not bring on an engagement"; so Tyler was obliged to stop the fight. Is was a small affair, but it gave the *morale* to Beauregard. Later in the war such a skirmish would have passed with scarcely a remark.

The Confederate commander, General Johnston, had eluded Patterson, passed on to Piedmont, and then transported his infantry on the cars, sending them to Manassas, part at a time. He himself came on with the first trainload, reaching Beauregard Saturday, July 20th. His artillery, escorted by Stuart's cavalry, had marched. The last brigades, it is true, and the marching column did not get to the field of Bull Run till the afternoon of the 21st, but all came soon enough to participate in the battle.

After his arrival, though he had been modest about it, giving all credit to Beauregard, Johnston, being senior in rank, took the actual command and saved the day. He had, more than any other Confederate leader, a decided genius for war.

Of Johnston's army, Bee's brigade on arrival was placed near Coke's, and Jackson's (the sobriquet of "Stonewall" to the commander began here) was stationed midway between Ball's and Mitchell's fords to help Bonham. Holmes's brigade, coming up from Aquia Creek, was sent to reënforce the right. While other points thus received aid, the Confederate left near the Stone Bridge remained slender and weak.

Beauregard had a plan for the offensive which Johnston approved. It was to move out from his right and attack McDowell on that remarkable Sunday (July 21st) before Patterson could join him.

By Saturday night all the Union divisions except Runyon's at Alexandria were grouped around Centreville. McDowell, too, had his plan. Saturday night (July 20th), at his unpretentious Centreville headquarters, he assembled his division and brigade commanders. His tent having no floor, he spread his map on the ground and explained with care the proposed movements for the morrow. He had a well-conceived order of battle. In his talk the names Tyler, Dixon Miles, Hunter, and Heintzelman each represented a body of troops: "Tyler, you hold the lower fords of Bull Run and the Stone Bridge, making proper demonstrations; Miles's division will be behind you at Centreville for a reserve. Hunter, you go over Cub Run along the Warrenton Pike, then take country road and move up to Sudley Church, or rather to the ford there, turn to the left, cross Bull Run, and move down; when the next ford is reached Heintzelman will cross there and follow you. I hope to seize Gainesville on the Manassas Gap Railroad before Johnston's men get there."

McDowell did not then know that this wary Confederate was already at Manassas with half of his force and to have enough finally to more than match him in the engagement. Still, McDowell outweighed his opponent in artillery.

That evening before our first battle was a memorable one. I assembled my four regiments for the usual parade—then we had them closed in mass and all the men uncovered their heads while the God of battles was entreated for guidance, for shielding in the battle, and for care of those so precious in our far-away homes. Every soldier of my command seemed thoughtful and reverent that night.

Tyler drew his column out of camp at 3 A.M. Sun-

day. Hunter and Heintzelman were equally prompt.
But the three divisions became badly intermixed in the
dim light, and could not be moved in the cross directions like three blocks of regulars. In fact, the three
brigades of Tyler did not clear the turning point on the
Warrenton Pike till half-past five; so Hunter waited
two weary hours for Tyler to move out of his way, and
the impatient Heintzelman stood for an hour longer
with his advance at the Warrenton Pike for Hunter's
men to pass. My fretted brigade was the rear of this
slow-moving column and waited with its head at the
turnpike till the sun was an hour high.

The fatigue, coupled with the excitement always
existing at such a time, weakened many a strong man.
All this bad management—what a good staff should
see beforehand and provide against—kept Hunter's
troops back. Instead of beginning his attack at daylight, Hunter was not in position across the Sudley
Ford till after nine o'clock. Though naturally excited,
the leading brigades were at first cheerful and hearty.
The men, after getting started, went swinging along
singing "John Brown's Body" with a wonderful volume of sound. But they were soon affected by the sun,
then extremely hot, and the want of sleep troubled
them still more. All these new circumstances of war
nerved the men to a tension that could not last. Before the end of the second mile many fell out and sat
or lay down by the roadside sick and faint.

McDowell in the morning made a slight change of
plan which added to the weariness of Heintzelman's
men. He forbade us to make the short cut, and instructed us to follow Hunter all the seven miles by
Sudley Ford. In person he detained my brigade at
a blacksmith shop not more than a mile beyond Cub

Run after we had turned away from the Warrenton Pike toward the Sudley Springs. Mine was thus made a special reserve for Hunter or for Tyler as the exigencies of the conflict might demand. Here, then, with the thick forest in front, within sound of the battlefield, my Maine and Vermont men, naturally with some apprehension, waited from eight o'clock in the morning till afternoon. I cannot forget how I was affected by the sounds of the musketry and the roar of the cannon as I stood near my horse ready to mount at the first call from McDowell; for a few moments weakness seemed to overcome me and I felt a sense of shame on account of it. Then I lifted my soul and my heart and cried: "O God! enable me to do my duty." From that time the singular feeling left me and never returned.

Early in the morning we had seen McDowell, his staff, and escort pass us toward Sudley Springs. They presented a fine appearance as they trotted off, working their way through Willcox's and Franklin's brigades, which filled the road. On, on they went to the head of Hunter's command, then just arrived at Sudley Church. Burnside's handsome Rhode Island brigade, Hunter's advance, which had covered his front with skirmishers, was then with the remainder of the division taking a rest.

Burnside deployed under the eye of McDowell, and his front swept on, guiding itself by the Sudley and Manassas wagon road down the gentle slopes toward the valley of Young's Branch.

Evans, the quick-witted Confederate commander with that demibrigade at the Stone Bridge, began to suspect that Schenck and Sherman, the advance of Tyler, notwithstanding their bustle and noise, were not earnest in their threatened assault; for they rattled

154

away with their musketry, but did no more. Evans first sent a regiment up the Bull Run toward Burnside and then very soon changed his whole front to the left and pushed over toward the Manassas and Sudley Springs road in front of Burnside's skirmishers; he posted his men so as to face north, covering them as well as he could by uneven ground and trees, but his numbers were few—not a thousand men.

McDowell, on the high ground behind Burnside, not far from Sudley's Ford, took his post and had a fair view of the field, for that was the largest opening among those woody farms. The country in his sight made a handsome picture with its rolling, variegated features sweeping off toward Manassas. Here McDowell saw the skirmishers of both armies begin their noisy work and a few minutes later the main lines rapidly firing, while the field batteries whirled into place and commenced their more terrifying discharges.

At 9.15 Evans's Confederates opened a vigorous fire, which caused Burnside's brigade to halt in confusion. Then McDowell, through his staff, hastened Andrew Porter's brigade to Burnside's support.

Johnston and Beauregard before this, by eight o'clock, were together on a commanding hill south of Mitchell's Ford. Their signal officer detected our crossing at Sudley's Ford about nine. Immediately Bee with his brigade, Hampton with his legion, and Jackson were ordered to the assailed left. Bee, the nearest to Evans, spurred on by the firing, reached him first and took up that choice position, strong as a fort, near the Henry house. He located there a battery and supported it by his large brigade. But Evans was already across the valley northward and calling loudly for nearer help. Bee thereupon forwarded the most of

155

his force to Evans's support. But before an hour all the Confederates in that quarter were driven back by our men to the Henry house, because Heintzelman's two brigades, close upon Hunter, had become actively engaged and the Union troops from Stone Bridge had worked their way to Evans's new right. Bee's Confederates, running to the rear, could not quite halt or be halted at the Henry house, though Hampton's legion was covering their retreat. They were still going back when that indomitable leader, Jackson, being under orders and movement for another place, got news of Bee's trouble; he marched at once by the sound of battle to his relief. Several Confederate batteries were put close to the Henry house and supported by Jackson's infantry. Under the strong shelter of Jackson, Bee rallied his men. This occurred about 11.30 A.M., at which time Jackson called for cavalry to extend and protect his left flank. For Stuart's promptness in doing this Jackson highly commended him, as also for his successful charges against the national forces.

While their orders were being carried at a run, Johnston and Beauregard sped the four intervening miles from their commanding hill to the Henry house. There Johnston's presence under fire and example in carrying forward personally a regimental flag had the happiest effect on the spirit of his troops. After this important work and reënforcement, reluctantly leaving Beauregard in immediate command of the line of battle, Johnston went to the Lewis house, farther back and more central. Here he established his headquarters. From that point he could see the approaches beyond Bull Run, particularly those to the Stone Bridge, and he could from that point watch the maneuvers and movements of his own troops. Thus early in the fight, and constantly to the end, Joseph E. Johnston had an active supervision.

On the Union side, which promised so well in the first onset, misfortunes began to multiply. Hunter was severely wounded and left the field, cannon were captured from us, batteries that had been well managed were put too far in front of their infantry supports and lost their horses; several regiments, broken by the fighting, were intermingled, appearing like flocks and herds to be covering the slopes and the valley without order or organization. In the midst of this confusion McDowell sent his engineer officer, Captain A. W. Whipple, for my brigade. He was to lead it straight to the battlefield; but Whipple, not knowing any cross route, guided us by Sudley's Ford, six miles around instead of three across. The immediate need of my troops was so great that McDowell said: "Have them move in double time." Whipple gave the instructions. We began the march in that way, but the heat and fatigue of long waiting had already done its work. Many fell out of ranks; blankets, haversacks, and even canteens were dropped, so that those who persevered kept nothing but arms and ammunition; the pace was diminished, but that did not long avail to remedy the exhaustion. Overcome by their efforts, more and more left the column and lined the roadside. When we crossed the ford, at least one half of my men were absent.

At that point some facetious staff officer tried to hasten our march, crying: "You better hurry and get in if you want to have any fun." Here, looking forward to the high ground, I saw McDowell and his small escort a few hundred yards off. To my left and nearer

I saw Burnside's men, who had come back from the field with their muskets gleaming in the sunshine. They had some appearance of formation and were resting on their arms. I noticed other troops more scattered; ambulances in long columns leaving the field with the wounded — General Hunter was in one of them; there were men with broken arms; faces with bandages stained with blood; bodies pierced; many were walking or limping to the rear; meanwhile shells were shrieking and breaking in the heated air. I was sorry, indeed, that those left of my men had to pass that ordeal.

It was about 3 P.M. Away over toward the Warrenton Pike and by the Henry house there was still a fitful rattling of small arms and a continuous roar of heavy guns. "Send Howard to the right to support Ricketts's battery." Captain J. B. Fry, of McDowell's staff, brought me the word and led the way to the right, well across Young's Branch to a hill not far from the Dogan house. In the little ravine north of this hill I formed my two brigade lines, the Second Vermont and Fourth Maine in the front, and the Third and Fifth Maine in the second line. When forming, I so stationed myself, mounted, that the men, marching by twos, should pass me. I closely observed them. Most were pale and thoughtful. Many looked up into my face and smiled. As soon as it was ready the first line swept up the slope, through a sprinkling of trees, out into an open space on high ground. The six guns of Ricketts's battery which had fought there were already disabled or lost, and Captain Ricketts wounded and captured. One lieutenant, Douglas Ramsey, was killed. Another lieutenant, Edmund Kirby, covered with blood, on a wounded horse was hurrying along

158

saving a caisson. My first line passed him quickly, and as soon as the Second Vermont gained the crest of the hill, scattered hostile skirmishers being close ahead, the order to fire was given. The Fourth Maine, delayed a little by the thicket, came up abreast of the Vermonters on the right and commenced firing. An enemy's battery toward our front and some musketry shots with no enemy plainly in sight caused the first annoyance. Soon another battery off to our right coming into position increased the danger. And, worse than the batteries, showers of musket balls from the wood, two hundred yards away, made warm work for new men; but those unhit stood well for a time, or when disturbed by artillery shots, rallied till they had delivered from fifteen to twenty rounds per man. We had found no battery to support but were thrust into an engagement against Confederate infantry and artillery.

After that first line had been formed and was hard at work, I returned through the thicket to the valley behind us and brought up the second line, composed of a remnant of the Fifth Maine and a larger portion of the Third, intending to give the first line a rest. A part of the Fifth, in consequence of a cannon shot striking its flank and a rush of our own retreating cavalry, had been broken up and was gone. Our new line did not fully relieve the former; the Fourth Maine remained in position, the few of the Fifth going beyond the Fourth to the extreme right. The Second Vermont was ordered to withdraw and form a reserve. It was a hot place. Every hostile battery shot produced confusion, and as a rule our enemy could not be seen.

Soon the breakages were beyond repair; my order for part of the front line to retire to reform was understood for the whole. The major of the Fourth Maine asked anxiously: " Did you order us to retreat?" I shook my head, so he tried to stop his men. The colonel of the Fifth, exhausted by an attack of illness, said that he could do no more. Many officers labored to keep their men together, but I saw could effect nothing under fire. At last I ordered all to fall back to the valley and reform behind the thicket. Our men at the start moving back slowly soon broke up their company formations and continued to retire, not at first in a panicky manner, but steadily, each according to his own sweet will.

Before many minutes, however, it was evident that a panic had seized all the troops within sight. Some experienced veteran officers, like Heintzelman, entreated and commanded their subordinates, by turns, to rally their men; but nothing could stop the drift and eddies of the masses that were faster and faster flowing toward the rear. A final Confederate fire just before this retreat came upon our right flank when on the hill. Near there were the bodies of Zouaves conspicuous from their red uniform among the trees, who had fallen early in the day. That flank fire was from General E. Kirby Smith's Confederate brigade, which had come from the cars to that last battle scene, supported on his right by General Early. Some of our men had glimpses of bright bayonets a few hundred yards away above the low bushes. In front of them rode one officer on a white horse. At first he seemed alone. He turned and gave a command, but at the instant was shot and fell to the ground, though his men came forward, firing as they came. This was probably General Smith, who fell near that place wounded. One cannon shot striking among our men hit Alonzo Stin-

160

son, of the Fifth Maine. His wound was mortal, his arm being broken and his side crushed. His brother, Harry, then a private, afterwards my aid-de-camp, who became a lieutenant colonel before the war closed, bravely stayed on the field with his brother and was taken prisoner by the advancing Confederates.

Captain Heath, of the Third Maine, who, promoted subsequently to lieutenant colonel and fell in the battle of Gaines Mills, walked for some time by my horse and shed tears as he talked to me: " My men will not stay together, Colonel, they will not obey me," he said. Other brave officers pleaded and threatened. Surgeons staying back pointed to their wounded and cried: "For God's sake, stop; don't leave us!" Nothing could at that time reach and influence the fleeing crowds except panicky cries like: " The enemy is upon us! We shall all be taken!" These cries gave increase to confusion and speed to flight. Curiously enough, instead of taking a short road to Centreville, the unreasoning multitude went back the long seven-mile route, exposing themselves every moment to death or capture.

After the complete break-up, just before the re-crossing of Bull Run, Heintzelman, with his wounded arm in a sling, rode up and down and made a last effort to restore order. He sharply reprimanded every officer he encountered. He swore at me. From time to time I renewed my attempts. My brother, C. H. Howard, if he saw me relax for a moment, sang out: "Oh, do try again!" Part of the Fourteenth New York from Brooklyn rallied north of Bull Run and were moving on in fine shape. "See them," said my brother; "let us try to form like that!" So we were trying, gathering a few, but in vain. One foolish cry behind a team of horses thundering along the road was: "The black horse cavalry are upon us!" This sent the Brooklyn men and all others in disorder into the neighboring woods. Then I stopped all efforts, but sent out this message and kept repeating it to every Maine and Vermont man within reach: "To the old camp at Centreville. Rally at the Centreville camp."

No organization was effected before we reached that camp. There a good part of my brigade assembled and we remained in camp about one hour. Word was then brought me that our division and McDowell's entire army were retreating toward Washington, covered by Dixon Miles's fresh troops.

It was some small satisfaction to me to reorganize and to march at the head of my brigade again in good order, even though it were in retreat. We halted at Fairfax Court House and lay on our arms till morning. Following the universal example, I continued the march at daylight toward the Potomac. Four miles out, near Clermont, we were met by trains of cars and taken to Alexandria.

The next day, by means of strong effort, on my own motion I led three regiments of my brigade back westward four miles along the Alexandria and Centreville Pike to a good position near Mrs. Scott's farm. The other regiment, the Fifth Maine, having lost all of its blankets and being destitute of other needed supplies, I left temporarily in Alexandria. At last that was supplied and rejoined its brigade. The brigade thereafter faithfully guarded the approaches to Alexandria through many sore and dark days of discouragement, privation, and sickness, till McClellan, finally beginning to rebrigade and reorganize the army, ordered us to retire to a position nearer the Potomac.

Battle of Bull Run

At the battle of Bull Run heavy losses were inflicted in the brief time we were able to hold our ground—50 killed, 115 wounded, and 180 missing. We had among them two officers killed and seven wounded—total loss, 345. Smith's (or Elzey's) Confederate loss was 28 killed and 108 wounded; Early's, 24 killed and 122 wounded. Total killed and wounded in both brigades, 279.

McDowell's entire Union loss was 481 officers and men killed, 1,011 wounded, and 1,216 missing. Beauregard's and Johnston's entire Confederate loss was 307 killed, 1,582 wounded, and 13 missing.

It was at least two weeks after our Bull Run panic before much reliance could be placed on our troops. In Alexandria the second night we put the men under shelter in the empty houses. A dreadful rainstorm had set in after the battle. The rain poured down in torrents and flooded the roads and the streets of the city.

And now came the most trying period of the war to all patriotic hearts. The terrible discontent day by day was aggravated and continued among the men. They distrusted their officers, high and low, many of them pleaded to go home, some mutinied, some deserted, some worthless officers only encouraged the malcontents, while others feared them. Letters complaining of ill usage filled the mails; the supplies for a time were short; spoiled clothing could not be immediately replaced; blankets and equipments were not forthcoming to fill the want; food was scarce and often poor, bread being moldy and meat insufficient. Counter complaints attended with bitter charges came to us from the homes far away. The military authority was insufficient speedily to rectify all these evils. Officers and men rushed into Washington and thronged the hotels, boarding houses, and public offices with a saucy, idle, vagabond crowd. In many regiments even the arms were abused or allowed to become unserviceable from rust. But little by little the quartermaster general—the worthy, diligent, and able General Meigs —arranged to so supply every want in clothing and tentage as soon to relieve every cause of grumbling, and in like manner the commissary general, George Gibson, before long gave us plenty of new bread and fresh meat, so that the men became more contented and hopeful. And commanders in the field took the utmost pains to reëstablish and maintain discipline.

Congress voted 500,000 more men to help us, and McClellan, conspicuous, with the reputation of successful generalship in West Virginia, was speedily called to the command of the departments of Washington and of Northeastern Virginia.

I heard General Sherman once say when he had listened to a severe criticism of Patterson, McDowell, and other early leaders, that we must not be too critical and hard upon them, for we were green in those days and we all have to learn by experience. We were then taught many lessons—the indispensable need of organization, of proper commanders, drill, and discipline; how little things like waiting or overhaste in marching or unloading the men certainly forestall defeat; how essential it is somehow to keep the men who fight in confidence and in heart; how and when to bring up the supports and reserves and use them to the best advantage.

One thing which affected us much was the saying so often heard that day: "It is Sunday! The attacking party on the Sabbath is sure of defeat!" Whether

164

this be the superstition or the religion of a people, wise men will respect it. To violate the Sabbath weakens the soldiers who come from our churches and Sunday schools. With what a beautiful spirit General McClellan subsequently met this religious feeling in a superb order soon after issued: "The major general commanding desires and requests that in future there may be a more perfect respect for the Sabbath on the part of his command. We are fighting in a holy cause and shall endeavor to deserve the benign favor of the Creator. One day's rest in seven is necessary to men and animals. More than this, the observance of the holy day of the God of mercy and of battles is our sacred duty."

CHAPTER XII

ON July 25th Major General George B. McClellan took command of the combined departments of Washington and Northeastern Virginia, and November 1st succeeded the venerable General Winfield Scott as the commander of all the armies of the United States. McClellan's name became familiar to every household in the land. In addition to his active, high command and an exalted rank his name was made still more conspicuous in that he stood as a candidate for the Presidency in 1864.

Indeed, McClellan holds no small place in the history of his country. The story of the Peninsular Campaign of 1862 could not be told without making him the central figure from the organization of the Army of the Potomac till the sad withdrawal of its forces after the bloody battle of Malvern Hill.

My first sight of McClellan was in 1850, when I was a cadet at West Point. He had then but recently returned from Mexico, where he had gained two brevets of honor. He was popular and handsome and a captain of engineers, and if there was one commissioned officer more than another who had universal notice among the young gentlemen of the academy it was he, himself a young man, a staff officer of a scientific turn who had been in several battles and had played every-

166

where a distinguished part. Eleven years later, after his arrival in Washington, July 23, 1861, an occasion brought me, while standing amid a vast multitude of other observers, a fresh glimpse of McClellan. He was now a major general and fittingly mounted. His record, from a brilliant campaign in West Virginia, and the urgent demand of the Administration for the ablest military man to lift us up from the valley of our existing humiliation, instantly brought this officer to the knowledge and scrutiny of the Government and the people.

As he rode past me that day with his proud staff, many of whom I recognized, his person and bearing made an indelible impression upon my memory. I saw a man five feet eight in height, with a good figure, muscular and closely knit, square shoulders, shapely head, and fine face ruddy with health; he had withal a quiet and reserved manner and showed vigor in his motions.

I partook of the common enthusiasm and hope, and my heart, if not my lips, joined the loud acclaim which that day saluted his deportment. Though McClellan never drew me to him, his intimacies being with those nearer his academic graduation, I have uniformly cherished the belief that he was a pure man, loyal to truth, to honor, and to his country.

A month later I again saw McClellan near the troops that I was commanding. He spoke to me briefly as he finished his visit, and won me, as he did other junior commanders, by his cordial manner.

His popularity, which had come almost of itself, was thus deepened and made permanent throughout the army by his showing on all occasions a marked courtesy. A general who has gained the hearts of his soldiers has only to plan well and execute well to bring abundant success, but there is one drawback—his opponent may be equally well equipped in heart, plan, and purpose.

The first thing to be done by McClellan, on the heels of Bull Run, was to make an army. Our Congress had authorized the call for 500,000 more volunteers. It immediately fell to McClellan to receive, organize, equip, drill, and discipline the new levies which were flocking into Washington from the north and west, and prepare them for the field.

The Washington mobs still existed and were growing worse. They were made up largely from discontented regiments contributing to the disorderly mass, tenfold larger after the panic of Bull Run.

McClellan instituted three remedial measures: *First*, an order from the War Department, which organized boards of examination. Volunteer officers were to be brought before them to ascertain their fitness for the command they exercised. General Henry W. Slocum and I were for some time on one of these boards. Slocum at first demurred. He thought it hard for prominent citizens recently commissioned who had generously spent their time and money to raise regiments not to be permitted to reap some benefit for their labor and sacrifice. It did seem a little cruel to examine them in army regulations and tactics! But the orders required *that*, and so we fell to work and had one officer after another brought before us. It proved a good move. While a few worthy men not sufficiently acquainted with their new business were sent home, a host of idlers and triflers were dismissed or compelled to resign.

The *second*, and a most important measure, was a thorough system of inspection of men and arms, carrying it through relentlessly. I suffered from this, for while in command of the brigade I left the care of the Third Maine to the regimental commander and was severely condemned for the condition of the arms of "his own regiment" by an inspecting officer from army headquarters.

The *third* measure of relief was the inauguration of an effective provost marshal's department. General Andrew Porter set his machinery in motion and in a remarkably short time cleared the streets of Washington and Georgetown of all the vagrant soldiery who had daily congregated in those cities but had no proper business there. He issued not only a permit system, but so revised and controlled the passports across our lines as, at least for a time, to cause murmurers and traitors to fly from the District of Columbia or keep still. McClellan also made another wholesome regulation. He placed near Washington in provisional brigades the bulk of the newer regiments, keeping them there in camps under special discipline and drill before sending them to the front. The people behind us were always in haste, and the administration felt their quick pulsation; not so McClellan. Nobody ever saw him in haste.

Not long after Bull Run the brigades were broken up and mine with the rest, so with some disappointment I returned to my regiment and was encamped near Arlington engaged in furnishing working parties for the construction of the fortifications about Washington. Here I was under General Sedgwick. No one of his command will forget his quiet, watchful discipline and his fatherly management. An unexpected visit on 'August 8th from McDowell escorting Prince Jerome Napoleon through our camps had a cheering feature for me. Just before the general with his cavalcade rode away he turned to me and spoke of the orders of McClellan which had dissolved my brigade. He said: " Colonel Howard, that action is not final; you shall not suffer nor lose your brigade." The remark had its fruition on September 3, 1861, when I received my commission of brigadier general of volunteers. For several weeks thereafter I had, however, that unhappy experience of waiting for orders. Restless, talking with my adjutant, walking to and fro, reading the papers, conning over some books, and going over the regulations, or at orderly hours sitting in the anteroom of General Marcy, father-in-law and chief of staff to McClellan—the newly fledged brigadier feared that he never would be recognized again or trusted with a command. I suspected jealousy on the part of rivals who were near the throne. I was ashamed to go home and chagrined to remain unassigned.

But the change came. My first assignment was to another brigade, receiving, drilling, and forwarding new regiments under the supervision of General Silas Casey. We were sent to Bladensburg and encamped near the notorious dueling ground where members of Congress had formerly resorted to offer their blood for their honor's sake. The Sixty-first New York, Fifth New Hampshire, the Forty-fifth New York, the Eighty-first Pennsylvania, and Fourth Rhode Island took part under my command in one great review held on the public grounds east of the Capitol. McClellan was the conspicuous reviewing officer and Casey led the division. At first some slight mistakes very much disturbed our silver-haired division commander. He cried out despairingly: " Oh, oh, what a fizzle!" Still,

LIVER O. HOWARD, BRIGADIER GENERAL UNITED STATES VOLUNTEERS, 1861,
WITH HIS ADJUTANT GENERAL, FREDERICK D. SEWALL.

a little extra effort on the part of our active aids-de-camp put all matters to rights and we passed in a creditable review.

How necessary was that period of preparation to the new army! McClellan brought to bear upon it the conservatism of an engineer. He gathered around him a large staff, personal and administrative, which from time to time he caused to be announced to the army. Gradually he constructed, with immense labor, on both sides of the Potomac, a grand system of fortifications which environed the District of Columbia. They soon gave to the eye of every observer, military or not, the precise rallying points for times of attack; they were when manned a safe defense of the nation's capital.

The capital thus owed to McClellan not a little of its safety in his cleansing it of idlers and of traitors, in his strong army, and in his well-chosen and thoroughly constructed defenses.

The batteries of artillery and the infantry regiments, as soon as they emerged from the provisional state, were stationed around the new forts wherever convenient camping places could be found, at first under canvas alone; but when cold weather approached the men made themselves comfortable huts of logs, using their tentage for securing height and roofing. What veteran will ever forget the white-topped villages on every hill, patriotic and gay under their own flags, which seemed in perpetual motion? Together they formed a city of over 100,000 souls. The larger proportion constituting the main body was on the Virginia side of the Potomac, but no other fronts were neglected; for example, as we have seen, Casey's division looking to the east was on the Bladensburg road; Hooker's facing the south was kept below the eastern

171

branch; while Wadsworth's, north and east, scattered here and there, crowned a score of important heights. Some of the forts were named for distinguished officers who had already fallen in the war, like Lyon and Greble.

McClellan's purpose in delaying the corps formation is indicated in a single sentence: "I did not desire to form them until the army had been for some little time in the field, in order to enable the general officers first to acquire the requisite experience as division commanders on active service, and that I might be able to decide from actual trial who were the best fitted to exercise these important commands." This care and deliberation were characteristic.

It was not till March, 1862, that the corps formation was introduced, and then the President himself initiated it by his own orders.

The division commanders whose names, thanks to Bull Run and sundry reviews, had become familiar to the army were advanced in position but not in grade— our highest grade, except by special Act of Congress, was that of major general. McDowell, Sumner, Heintzelman, Keyes, and Banks were the first five army corps commanders. A few days later Banks's command was differently designated and a fifth corps was given to Fitz John Porter, a sixth to Franklin.

McDowell had for division commanders at first Franklin, McCall, and King; Sumner—Richardson, Sedgwick, and Blenker. Heintzelman's division commanders were Fitz John Porter, Hooker, and Hamilton; Keyes's were Couch, W. F. Smith, and Casey; and Banks's, Williams and Shields.

But I am anticipating the order of events. Possibly the Army of the Potomac thus formed and located might have remained sheltered along the Virginia Heights free from trials by combat or battle during the important time of incubation and growth had it not been for the Confederates. General Johnston at Centreville, Va., though disposed himself to stand mainly on the defensive, still had a teasing way of letting loose certain of his restless subordinates, such as Ashby, Stuart, Barksdale, and Evans.

While, during the fall of 1861, I was working away as a sort of school general at Bladensburg and vicinity and serving on those depleting boards and on several tedious courts-martial, there were several collisions which the enemy provoked or our troops brought on by foraging movements. For example, Stuart, my classmate, made his way to Loudon County, Va., about August 1st, and pushed out detachments here and there in the rudest way; one showed itself near "The Point of Rocks," south of the Potomac, just below Harper's Ferry, which was then but poorly garrisoned. A part of the Twenty-eighth New York, under Captain W. W. Bush, by a ford near at hand boldly crossed to the Virginia shore, where a lively skirmish ensued. Bush drove off the Confederate cavalry, inflicted a small loss in killed and wounded, captured twenty horses and came back with a number of prisoners.

At one period near the middle of October the daily journals were full of "Munson's Hill." That prominence could be seen by observers looking westward from Arlington Heights and from other points about Washington. The Confederates had occupied this famous ground between the two armies and kept flying from the hilltop their new banner so unwelcome to Union gazers. Reference to this audacious flag pointed

the speech of many a brave orator that fall while criti-
cising the slowness of McClellan. Munson's Hill
armed the " On-to-Richmond " press with pithy paragraphs. But suddenly and unexpectedly the Confederates withdrew from Munson's Hill and our cavalry
pickets found there only mock intrenchments and
" Quaker guns "—i. e., logs cut and daubed with black
paint to imitate cannon. The natural query was:
" What will our enemy do next? " To ascertain this,
reconnoissances were undertaken.

The divisions of McCall and W. F. Smith marched
out westward on October 19th. McCall, farthest
south, bearing off northwesterly, passed through the
village of Dranesville, and finding no enemy kept on
five or six miles beyond toward Leesburg. He delayed
his return march from time to time to enable his staff
to gather local knowledge and make sketches of the
country. A telegram to McClellan from Darnestown
the next morning said: " The signal station on ' Sugar
Loaf' telegraphs that the enemy have moved away
from Leesburg." Upon receiving this message Mc-
Clellan caused to be telegraphed to General Stone, at
Poolsville, Md. (upper Potomac) : " General McCall
occupied Dranesville yesterday and is still there; will
send out heavy reconnoissances to-day in all directions
from that point. . . . Keep a good lookout upon Leesburg to see if this movement has the effect to drive
them away. Perhaps a slight demonstration on your
part would have the effect to move them."

This simple telegram was the primary cause of the
battle of Ball's Bluff—and the death of Colonel Baker.

Being in the District of Columbia at the time of the
Ball's Bluff disaster, I realized how deeply people
there were affected by it. The President had known

Baker well, for he had but recently, under patriotic impulse, gone from the Senate Chamber to the field. President, Congress, and people felt bereaved by his death. When the colonel's body arrived in Washington, I became one of the pallbearers.

Baker, though acting as a brigadier general, was the colonel of the Seventy-first Pennsylvania. Rev. Byron Sunderland, a Presbyterian pastor, preached his funeral sermon. Baker's brother and son were present. One of his officers fell in a swoon during the exercises. To the cemetery, a distance of three miles, I rode with General Denver, of California. Senator Henry Wilson was one of the pallbearers; this occasion afforded me my first introduction to him. An immense unsympathetic crowd followed to see the military procession. Nobody evinced sorrow—very few even raised their hats as we passed.

The Washington crowd, however, was no sample of our patriotic citizens. The passions, appetites, and sins of the great small men who had run the Government upon the rocks had left their impress on Washington, and the military had called in its train its usual motley brood of followers—such was the mixed multitude which followed the noble and generous Baker without emotion to his tomb. The wail in Massachusetts and Pennsylvania over the excessive and bootless losses at Ball's Bluff followed. To Senator Wilson and myself that funeral was deeply saddening. The evening shadows were thickening as we placed Baker in his last resting place.

Had General Stone's plans leading to this battle succeeded, he would have been praised for his energy and enterprise. The arrest and punishment which he underwent on account of his defeat, without having a chance for a proper trial and without an opportunity to recover the confidence of the army, afford an extraordinary episode of injustice shown a good and able man.

At our homes the people were becoming vexed and impatient to have the war work so slow. While the bulk of the secession multitude were already in the war the majority of Union men were not yet at the front and a sort of apathy pervaded the armies in the field. I verily believed that they would not shake it off till their communications had been cut and the life of the defending hosts put in imminent peril. I wrote: "We have the numbers in the field, but the spirit and enthusiasm is at home. We want it here. God will help us when we stop self-seeking and money-making. When the pressure of want and deep sorrow is upon us, then will we turn to the Lord and cry unto Him; then will we grasp the means and go forth in His strength." This was my feeling in the presence of selfish and disloyal Washington talk and under the shadow of the Ball's Bluff calamity.

Ball's Bluff was the last affair in our vicinity of any considerable importance during that period of formation. But the delay and waiting were so long that not only our loyal friends became suspicious that something was wrong at headquarters, but the disloyalty in the neighborhood of the armies and, in fact, everywhere, became bold and vexatious.

Mr. Lincoln wanted something done on the lower Potomac or against Johnston's communications, but touching all plans for movement he still deferred to the judgment and respected the reticence of his popular army commander.

An affair at last came that relieved the monotony

of my own life and made me feel as if I was accomplishing something. As the November elections approached, certain hot-headed secessionists of Maryland were working hard to carry the State. Violent men began to intimidate the more quiet Union voters, and in the lower counties Confederate soldiers were crossing the Potomac in uniform to influence the polls. This gave to my troops for that month of November a "political campaign."

The 3d of the month, Saturday, receiving word from General Casey, I rode to Washington in a heavy and continuous rain and went to his headquarters. He instructed me to march my brigade forthwith to the southern part of Maryland, placing troops in Prince George and Calvert counties. For further specific instructions Casey sent me to General Marcy, McClellan's chief of staff. I was told that after my arrival in lower Maryland I must consult with Union men, coöperate with them, and do all in my power to prevent any obstruction of the polls. As it was very stormy I secured for personal use some waterproof clothing and returned to Bladensburg to hasten our preparation. By Sunday morning the weather had cleared but the eastern branch which flowed between our camp and Bladensburg had risen so much that it was over fifty yards across, and the ford, usually shallow, was deep.

When with my staff I undertook to cross, our horses lost their footing and had to swim, and all of the riders received more or less of a wetting. By planking the ties of the railroad bridge we quickly had a dry crossing for the men, but a squadron of cavalry sent me for the expedition and the supply wagons were obliged to worry through the ford; we had special contrivances to raise our ammunition and hard bread

177

above the water.[1] Our Sunday march, muddy and difficult, was fourteen miles and we bivouacked in a grove
at Centreville, Md. The troops, new to marching, were
weary enough to sleep. Some of them, however, before morning had wakened and made havoc of a
widow's fence. I put an officer of the Fourth Rhode
Island, who was on guard, under arrest and obtained
from the officers whose men had helped themselves to
rails a sufficient contribution to pay the widow for her
loss. There was no more burning of fences on that
expedition, but there was murmuring at my severity.
I sent companies on Monday to Upper Marlboro, to
Nottingham, Queen Anne, and Piscataway. Upper
Marlboro we found a very pretty village three miles
from the Patuxent River, having a courthouse, taverns, and churches. Here were several secessionists
who were giving much trouble, but finding there also
several excellent Union men I left Colonel Miller to
aid them in keeping the peace. With my cavalry
squadron I marched on to the Patuxent, the bridge
across which had been carried away by the freshet. In
two hours the bridge was made passable and we
crossed over, completing our projected expedition at
dark, and camping upon the large and beautiful estate
of Mr. Thomas J. Graham. His generous hospitality
could not have been excelled. Neither my officers nor
myself ever forgot the joyous welcome and kind treatment from host and hostess, for Mrs. Graham joined
her husband in the entertainment. My surgeon, Dr.
Palmer, Adjutant General Sewall, and I remained with
these good people for three days. It gave us a breath
of home. I had managed so promptly to distribute my

[1] The "contrivances" were cross-planks placed above the wagon-beds
and also deep empty boxes.

troops that there was not a voting precinct in Prince George or Calvert counties that was not occupied by my men on Wednesday, the day of election. On Thursday the scattered detachments were gathered, and on Friday and Saturday marched back to their respective camping grounds near Washington.

We had made some arrests. Mr. Sollers, at Prince Frederick, a former congressman, showed a violent disposition, threatening to kill any Union man he could reach and striking right and left with a bowie knife. He and four others were put under guard. On Friday morning Mr. Sollers was very ill, but as his excessive excitement was over I took his promise to report at Washington and released him. The others I let go upon their taking the oath of allegiance. Only one Confederate soldier in uniform was picked up; he was kept for exchange. General Casey's happy approval, commending my brigade and myself for our faithfulness and promptitude, gave me much pleasure, and McClellan's recognition of the work so quickly done, which owing to the storm he had thought hardly possible, awakened a strong hope that I would soon go to the front, taking with me instead of sending the regiments I had last drilled. That crossing of swollen streams, making long marches through clayey mud, bivouacking without canvas, disciplining the men on friendly soil, and giving officers something of importance to do, were, indeed, conducive to their contentment, to useful experience together, to comradeship, and in brief to all the needed preparations for grander trials in the coming events which were most consonant to our hearts.

CHAPTER XIII

THE first time that General E. V. Sumner's name made any considerable impression upon me was in connection with our new President's quick and secret journey from Harrisburg to Washington just before his first inauguration. There was for the time great excitement on the subject. Mr. Lincoln had left his home in Illinois on February 11, 1861. He experienced nothing harmful—only an ovation all the way. The people at halting places thronged to see him and insisted on speeches from him. He passed from Philadelphia to Harrisburg on February 23d, and addressed the Legislature there assembled. Being weary after his continued receptions, speeches, and excitement, he went to the Jones house and retired to his apartments for needed rest. It was given out publicly that he would not leave Harrisburg till the next morning, but Mr. W. F. Seward, son of William H. Seward, suddenly arrived from Washington and promptly conveyed to Mr. Lincoln the startling information from Senator Seward and General Scott, that he was to be assassinated in Baltimore while *en route* to Washington. The story, which from subsequent testimony, positive and direct, was fully substantiated, was at the time hardly credited by Mr. Lincoln himself, yet there appeared to most of his advisers who were present

180

such imminent danger and such vast interests at stake that his friends became importunate, urging him to start at once so as to pass through Baltimore many hours before the advertised time. He took this course, but with evident reluctance.

At that time Colonel E. V. Sumner and Major David Hunter were among Mr. Lincoln's many reliable friends—a sort of voluntary escort. Sumner protested. He was vehement. "What! the President elect of the United States make a secret and strategic approach to his own capital? Shall he skulk in such a manner as that proposed? No! Let an army, with artillery to sound his salvos, escort him publicly through the rebel throng!" This incident indicates the indomitable spirit of Sumner, always exhibited from the time of his entry into the United States service as a lieutenant at twenty-three years of age in 1819, till his death at Syracuse, N. Y., in 1863. The old army was replete with anecdotes illustrating his individuality. He was remarkable for two military virtues: an exact obedience to orders and a rigid enforcement of discipline. If two methods were presented, one direct and the other indirect, he always chose the direct; if two courses opened, the one doubtful and leading to safety, the other dangerous and heroic, he was sure to choose the heroic at whatever cost. Joseph E. Johnston when a subordinate was once under Sumner's command. Johnston, with other officers, was required to attend reveille every morning. On one occasion he had some slight indisposition which the early rising aggravated, so he asked Surgeon Cuyler to excuse him from that exercise. Sumner interposed at once: "He must then go wholly on the sick report." Once again, at a frontier garrison which Sumner commanded, he himself had a severe attack of indigestion, caused from drinking some alkaline water that he could not avoid. He was much weakened, and the officers, sure of what students would call " an absence " at the next reveille, congratulated each other upon the antici- pated rest to be had without discovery and punish- ment. But lo! Sumner next morning was in his place, the first man on the ground!

At the time of Colonel Sumner's early intimacy with President Lincoln, he was colonel of the First regular cavalry. He had gained distinction in the Mexican War and had obtained therefore the reward of two brevets. He had, however, been obliged before the war for the Union to play a part in Kansas not to his liking: for his orders had required him to dis- perse the free-state legislature. Still, whatever were his private sympathies or political sentiments, he did not hesitate to obey. It was then a compensative sat- isfaction to be sent under the new administration with which he was in accord to command the Department of California. General Twiggs's defection and dismissal gave Sumner a brigadiership. His California work was made remarkable by his rallying the Union ele- ment and frightening disunionists. Prominent seces- sionists he caused to be arrested; and some to be ap- prehended outside of California while they were *en route* via Panama toward the Gulf States. Such was the war-worn, loyal Sumner who arrived in Washing- ton the last of November, 1861. McClellan immediately assigned him to duty, expecting just then some active campaigning. Sumner was to choose his division from the provisional forces. He naturally advised with Casey, the commander of all the provisional organiza- tions. It was my good fortune to have won General

Casey's favorable opinion. He commended me for industry and energy. Those were the qualities for Sumner: he selected my brigade, French's, and later that of Thomas Francis Meagher.

I was delighted at the change, for I did not like the rear, however important the work might be, and none probably was more important than the preparing of regiment after regiment for service. One cannot always fathom or reveal his motives, but I know that I was eager for the advance and greatly enjoyed the prospect of serving under the redoubtable Sumner. I was ordered to report in writing to my new division commander. This I did. Sumner's first order to me was characteristic. He looked over the large map which embodied the position of the Army of the Potomac from Harper's Ferry to Aquia Creek, and stretched forward to take in the supposed position of the entire Confederate army in our front. He saw a place called Springfield out a few miles in front of Alexandria, on the Orange and Alexandria railroad. That being on the portion of the front he was to occupy, he at once sent my brigade there. This was too bold an order for our then defensive methods. It might stir up a hornet's nest. But feeling the exhilaration of a new enterprise, I pushed out promptly to comply with my instructions. I had reached the place —a mere railway station with no houses near—with two regiments and was quietly waiting for the other two of the brigade and for the baggage train, when Lieutenant Sam S. Sumner, a son and aid of the general, rode up in apparent haste and said: " The general made a mistake; it is not intended by his orders that we should push out so far." Empty cars quickly appeared to take us back to 'Alexandria. Sumner had

183

halted my wagon train there and caused it to wait while the remainder of my brigade encamped on the Leesburg Turnpike. On our arrival I housed for the night the men with me in the sheds and engine houses of the Alexandria railway depot. Sumner was in some house outside of the city. It was already evening. Taking two colonels with me, I made my way to the old city hotel. After supper I set out with one of them in the darkness and rainstorm to find General Sumner. We had hired a single team, but the horse was so broken down that he could scarcely walk. He soon ran into a post and fell, breaking his harness and rolling the carriage, the colonel, and myself into the mud!

Our search after several trials being unsuccessful, we postponed further effort till daylight, then we found the general at a farmhouse far out on the Leesburg Pike. This was my first meeting with the veteran commander. He had on a dark-blue blouse and light-blue uniform trousers and wore a rough flannel shirt. Shoulder straps with the star on each shoulder marked his rank of brigadier general, while a bright cravat beneath his rolling shirt collar relieved the monotony of his dress.

As he stood there before me, a tall, spare, muscular frame, I beheld a firm, dignified man; but his eye was so kindly and his smile so attractive that all embarrassment between us was banished at the first interview. After breakfast the general took me with him to select a proper position for his division. My brigade, the First, as I was the ranking brigade commander, was placed on the right north of the Pike, French's on the south, and Meagher's back toward the city. My camp was on Mr. Richards's farm. A charming grove of trees was behind the brigade, to the south of which were established my headquarters. The land had a light soil, was rolling, and easily drained. Back of us, farther off in plain sight, on a height was the well-known Fairfax Seminary.

Sumner, in honor of the Pacific Department which he had so recently left, called his new field home and environment "Camp California." More than ten thousand souls there formed a city and spent three months encamped in military order. French's was slightly in echelon with my brigade and arranged back and south of a house of Mr. Watkins, while Sumner himself occupied a Sibley tent near the house. Meagher's men were held some distance to the rear and opposite the center. Sumner had also near at hand the Eighth Illinois Cavalry and a six-gun battery of light artillery. We habitually kept one infantry regiment and a small detachment of cavalry on picket duty as far forward as Edsall's Hill, and kept the remainder at drill. Who of my brigade does not recall those lively trials over the sand knolls, too often through snow and mud, those skirmishes and passing the defiles so remorselessly repeated?

Mr. Richards, the householder, lived about two hundred yards in front of our right. He was afflicted with asthma—a trouble that usually increased under provocation. He would wheeze, laugh, cry, and stammer, as he good-naturedly tried to describe to me the work of the New Hampshire axmen while cutting down his beautiful and extensive grove. It was not long before his entire wood had been felled and carried off to block up and underpin the canvas tents or to be stored up somewhere for fuel.

"Why, general, ha! ha!" he wheezed, "the trees just lie down, ha! ha! ha! as Colonel Cross's folks look at 'em!" And, indeed, those New Hampshire men were expert woodmen.

Notwithstanding the burden of war there was much that was pleasant in our camp that winter. Friends visited friends; the Germans had their holidays and rifle shootings; the Irish brigade their hurdle races and their lively hospitalities. An enormous mail went out and came in daily. But there was a sad side. At times our hospitals were crowded with patients, because measles followed by typhoid fever, in virulence like the plagues of Egypt, ran through all McClellan's army and decimated our regiments.

Off and on for information we probed the spaces between our own and the enemy's lines, sometimes to catch spies and those who harbored them, and sometimes daringly to gather forage and provisions, but, indeed, we wished to be doing something in the line of enterprise as a preparation for the active work to which we all looked forward expectantly for the spring. Our bold, strict, straightforward, hospitable division general and his son and aid, Lieutenant S. S. Sumner, who combined his father's frankness, bravery, and impulse, and his mother's social amenities, with the gifted and genial adjutant general, Major J. H. Taylor, and Lieutenant Lawrence Kip, an aid well practiced in the ways of polite society, always welcomed us to headquarters, pleasant to visit and worthy to imitate.

General W. H. French, who commanded the next brigade, the Second, was a man advanced in years, who had graduated at West Point seventeen years before me. He had a mind of unusual quickness, well replenished by a long experience in his profession. French somehow was able to take more men into action and have less stragglers than any of his parallel commanders.

Among our colonels were Zook, who was killed at Gettysburg; Brooke, who, steadily advancing, attained the rank of major general in the regular army; Barlow, of the Sixty-first New York, who, by wounds received in several engagements went again and again to death's door but lived through a most distinguished career of work and promotion to exercise eminent civil functions after the war, and Miller, who fell in our first great battle.

My brother, Lieutenant C. H. Howard, and Lieutenant Nelson A. Miles were then my aids. Sumner, noticing his conduct in action, used to say of Miles: "That officer will get promoted or get killed." F. D. Sewall, for many months my industrious adjutant general, took the colonelcy of the Nineteenth Maine, and my able judge advocate, E. Whittlesey, at last accepted the colonelcy of another regiment. The acting brigade commissary, George W. Balloch, then a lieutenant in the Fifth New Hampshire, adhered to his staff department and was a colonel and chief commissary of a corps before the conflict ended.

To comprehend McClellan's responsibility and action after he came to Washington, we must call to mind the fact that he did not simply command the Army of the Potomac, which he had succeeded in organizing out of the chaos and confusion of the Bull Run panic, but till March 11, 1862, he had his eye upon the whole field of operations and was endeavoring to direct all our armies which were face to face with the insurgents. It never appeared fair to McClellan to bind him by stringent orders and then at last demand that he follow a changing public sentiment. It is like removing by fire process the temper from steel and then expecting from it the old elasticity.

In a letter dated November 7, 1861, McClellan indicates the will of the Executive at that time: " I know that I express the feelings and opinions of the President when I say that we are fighting only to preserve the integrity of the Union and the constitutional authority of the general Government."

We perceive at once from the following note to Buell the inference which came to McClellan from the President's known attitude—an inference doubtless strengthened by his own conservative feelings and convictions: " The military problem would be a simple one if it could be separated from political influences. Such is not the case. Were the population among which you are to operate wholly or generally hostile, it is probable that Nashville would be your first and principal objective point. It so happens that a large majority of the people of Eastern Tennessee are in favor of the Union." For this reason Buell was made to stand on the defensive all along the line toward Nashville, and directed to throw the mass of his forces into Eastern Tennessee by way of Walker's and Cumberland gaps, if possible reaching Knoxville. This was to enable the loyal to rise, a thing Mr. Lincoln greatly desired, and to break up all rail communications between Eastern Virginia and the Mississippi.

Another letter of November 12th reveals McClellan's purpose more clearly. " As far as military necessity will permit, religiously respect the constitutional rights of all. . . . Be careful so to treat the unarmed inhabitants as to contract, not widen, the breach existing between us and the rebels. It should be our constant aim to make it apparent to all that their property, their comfort, and their personal safety will be best preserved by adhering to the cause of the Union." Remember that that word "property" in McClellan's mind was meant to include the slaves.

Similar instructions went from him to Halleck, in Missouri, who was further ordered to mass his troops on or near the Mississippi, "prepared for such ulterior operations" as the public interests might demand.

General T. W. Sherman with a detachment was at the same time dispatched against Savannah and the coast below. The original plan was: to gain Fort Sumter and hold Charleston. But for a time that plan was postponed.

After New Orleans and its approaches had been secured by Butler, McClellan contemplated a combined army and navy attack on Mobile. His idea of "essential approaches" to New Orleans embraced Baton Rouge, La., and Jackson, Miss.

Burnside received his instructions to first attack Roanoke Island, its defenses and adjacent coast points.

These positive instructions given by McClellan and to a reasonable extent carried out, during the spring of 1862, show his activity of mind and good broad planning. The protection of the possessions of the disloyal, especially of the slave property, was doubtless an unwise insistence, but it originated in the great heart of Mr. Lincoln, who hoped almost against hope to win the secessionists back without going to dire extremities, and earnestly desired to please all *Union* slaveholders. McClellan was simply the soldier front of this view, a conscientious exponent of the policy.

I had reason to remember Burnside's going forth, for he was permitted to take with his other troops to North Carolina my Fourth Rhode Island Regiment.

On January 3d Colonel Isaac P. Rodman came to my tent at one o'clock in the morning, showing a dispatch which directed him to report immediately at Annapolis. He was an excellent officer and a great gain to Burnside. He died from wounds received in the battle of Antietam. The Fourth Rhode Island had as chaplain an Episcopal clergyman, Rev. E. B. Flanders, much esteemed in our brigade. He was as efficient in the field as he had been in his home parish. I find an old letter in which my aid writes that I scarcely slept the night after I received that order. This was foolish, indeed, but it indicates how much I was attached to that regiment. One good soldier, Private McDonald, being on detail as my orderly, remained with me till his death in Georgia during the campaign of 1864. When the news of Burnside's attack reached us from Roanoke and thirty-five men were reported killed, I was as anxious as a father to hear of the safety of those who had gone out from my command.

On January 4th, taking an aid with me, I hastened, as was then the custom when things went wrong, to Washington for redress. I found the venerable General Casey sitting in full uniform at the head of a court-martial. His uniform looked very bright and clean to me coming from camp.

Moving a chair close to General Casey I appealed to him to get me another regiment and one as well drilled as possible. After listening to my whispered argument he said: " Oh, I will give you a good selection. You had better take the Sixty-fourth New York —Colonel Parker." So very soon the Sixty-fourth New York came to fill the vacancy left by the Fourth Rhode Island.

At that time General Sumner was in Washington.

Just before this visit he had met with a serious accident and had gone to Washington, where he could receive better nursing than was possible in camp. Sumner was riding one day and crossing some fields not far from headquarters, when his horse stepped into a blind post hole and fell, throwing the general forward to the ground. Injury was done to his shoulder and lungs. He remounted his horse and rode back to camp with difficulty; lame and suffering as he was he sat up in his saddle, as was his custom. When he neared the camp he crossed the sentinel's post and the sentinel saluted. He not only became erect in his posture regardless of the pain, but carefully and politely returned the soldier's courtesy. God preserve to our people the remembrance of such a man!

I found the general in Washington convalescing, and he welcomed the messages of sympathy from his division. I was anxious for his return and coveted the anticipated advantages to be derived from his long and varied experience, always remembering his pronounced loyalty, ardent patriotism, and prompt action.

We have seen that military operations were influenced very much in the interest of slavery by purely political considerations. Plans were modified by the endeavor not so much to conquer an enemy under arms, as to restore the Union or preserve the Union wherever slaveholders existed and showed themselves loyal to the United States. Conquer the insurgents, of course, but hurt those behind them as little as possible! Save them from themselves and save the country!

Certainly the problem presented could not be thus solved, because the Confederates themselves were otherwise determined. Neither in the political nor

191

military arena did they so show themselves to us.
They were too heated to consider or comprehend such
high principles of action. They said everywhere
where the echo of their voices could reach: " Come on,
we defy you! We are in earnest. We mean war! We
have struck for independence!"

Their leaders were too ardent, too determined, too
well prepared in plan and purpose to accept any sort
of compromise. They had no patience whatever with
the Unionists and half Unionists among themselves.
And, indeed, we ought from every military conception
to have accepted this gage of combat as much as possible, as did Grant, Sherman, Thomas, and Sheridan
at later dates. But we must remember that in January, 1862, the country had not yet so decided, and our
Eastern forces were far behind the Western in the
wish to free the slaves. It is for this reason that so
many veteran soldiers, and among them those who
were even then loyal to humanity, maintained that Mc-
Clellan was doing his simple duty and could not be
censured for the politico-military course which he at
that time was obliged to pursue.

In order to prevent the ever-present hostile espio-
nage from probing and revealing his plan, McClellan
carefully guarded his lips. None of us could guess just
what our army would attempt. But Johnston, our
enemy at Centreville, Va., was shrewder than those
who came in daily contact with our young chief. The
sudden movement of Hooker's division down the east
bank of the Potomac to a point opposite Dumfries, ostensibly to prevent hostile agents from passing back
and forth with news and goods, was by him correctly
interpreted.

He justly reasoned: once behind the Rappahannock the Confederate army will be in place to meet either of the five possible moves of McClellan: 1st, the direct by the Orange and Alexandria Railway; 2d, the one via Aquia Creek and Fredericksburg; 3d, that via Urbana, McClellan's favorite project; 4th, via the Virginia Peninsula, and 5th, to ascend the south bank of the James. At Centreville he was only in position to meet the first or second. That move of a division to a point opposite Dumfries meant the Urbana route for McClellan and so no time was to be lost, because Johnston knew that our preparations in the way of transports were already far advanced. Johnston commenced his rearward movement the day before the publication, not of McClellan's Urbana design, but of the orders for more preliminary work which for the safety of Washington was insisted on by the Administration. To satisfy, if possible, the impatience of the people and doubtless excited himself by so many delays, Abraham Lincoln ordered on March 8th: " That the Army and Navy coöperate in an immediate effort to capture the enemy's batteries on the Potomac between Washington and the Chesapeake Bay." This, too, Johnston seems to have anticipated. His abandonment of Centreville was completed by the close of the 9th and his action in this was known on my front that same day. Disagreements now began to set in between the President, a large party faction urging him, and McClellan, in which several general officers took sides and bore a part. As a result of many councils, not McClellan's favorite Urbana project, but his second choice, the peninsular plan, was after a time chosen for the Army of the Potomac and very soon thereafter McClellan's command was reduced to that army. Probably the President thought that to be quite enough now that McClellan was to take the field and be constantly away from the capital.

General Sumner had sufficiently recovered from his hurt to admit of his riding, and he had come back to his division, but he left his Sibley tent to sleep for a time in Mr. Watkins's house. The evening of March 3d I was writing a home letter when I received a note from Sumner asking me as soon as convenient to come over to his quarters. I hastened to the interview, which resulted in my taking three regiments the next day to protect the bridge builders at Accotink Run, six miles ahead, on the Orange & Alexandria Railroad. I went as far as Fairfax Station, driving the Confederate pickets before me. That movement on March 4th and the bridge building, which did not deceive Johnston nor arrest his preparations for leaving Centreville, but rather quickened them, set the ball in motion. A brigade, E. Kirby Smith's, stationed at Fairfax and vicinity, retired as I advanced and soon after joined the main Confederate army at Manassas Junction.

The news, a few days later, came: "Centreville is evacuated." It startled and disappointed everybody at Washington. The peninsular plan now quickly came to the front. Quartermasters, commissaries, naval officers, commanders of steamers and army sutlers were stimulated and warmed into busy life. Everybody, great and small, had some mysterious and unusual thing to do. At last for a brief time fretting ceased, for there was a definiteness of purpose; there was activity; there was motion. The army so long "quiet on the Potomac" was going somewhere and was promising to do something, and, indeed, all parties except the grumblers, the faint-hearted, and a few secession wives and mothers who never could see why their husbands and sons should fight for the " Federal " Government, were far happier than they had been for six months because they were now full of hope for a victory and then a speedy return in joy. It is good for us that we cannot trump up all the consequences to the atoms we jostle and displace. Sorrow, sickness, wounds, and a harvest of death were ahead, but nobody but our farseeing President had then caught the glimpse of a fatal symptom spot. On April 9th he wrote to McClellan:

" I always insisted that going down to the bay in search of a field instead of fighting at or near Manassas, was only shifting and not surmounting a difficulty; that we should find the same enemy and the same or equal intrenchments at either place." Mr. Lincoln instinctively felt that the true objective all the time was not Richmond but Johnston's army.

After we had finished the bridge building across the Accotink we had returned to Camp California and settled back into our old ways of living, so that the news of the actual evacuation of Centreville stirred us up as it did the rest of the army. The night of March 9th, after the news came, I had lain down and slept a while, when, Sumner being again in Washington on some temporary duty, a dispatch came to me to move the whole division at six o'clock the next morning. It was already near midnight. I went at once to Sumner's headquarters at Mr. Watkins's house, called together the brigade commanders and handed them the order of march. We worked all night and set out in good trim at the appointed hour, but had hardly gained the road when Sumner returned and assumed command of his moving column.

That day, March 10th, Sumner gave his men, unaccustomed to marching, a hard trial of seventeen miles. "What's seventeen miles," he asked at evening, "for a soldier?" It had rained—poured—most of the time. I had commanded my brigade and also the advance guard. The mud was first slippery and then deep; the weather was chilly and damp, making the rests uncomfortable and the night worse, as we were without canvas shelter, yet owing to previous discipline there was none of the Bull Run straggling. Sumner's division, made up of the three brigades, and the Eighth Illinois Cavalry, with Clarke's and Frank's six-gun batteries of artillery, continued its march the 11th, and kept on to Manassas Junction and beyond. The Confederate cavalry leader, J. E. B. Stuart, watched our advancing forces, retiring from knoll to knoll, from grove to grove, as we pressed on. That cavalry was Johnston's rear guard, when his army was in motion southward, and became his outpost and picketing force as soon as Johnston halted. Sumner stopped his general movement at Warrenton Junction, thirteen miles south of Manassas. Now he had two divisions, because Blenker's, made up mostly of Germans, had joined him at Manassas.

In spite of McClellan's objection, Mr. Lincoln had caused him to organize his Potomac force into army corps. McClellan complied on March 13th, so that Sumner, during his first march, came into command of the Second Corps. I. B. Richardson was appointed commander of our division, John Sedgwick and Louis Blenker of the other two. The actual change of commanders was effected while we were tramping the Virginia mud, and by small fires drying sundry spots large enough to sleep on.

General E. V. Sumner and My First Reconnoissance

The main body of McClellan's army, which had started up like a suddenly awakened dreamer and pushed out in pursuit of Johnston with more than twenty-five miles the start, ceased advancing and moved back to the vicinity of Alexandria, March 15th. Sumner with two of his divisions was left at Warrenton Junction till other Union troops not of the Army of the Potomac should be sent forward to relieve him. McClellan desired Sumner to make a strong reconnoissance forward as far as the Rappahannock River, and the latter gave me a detachment for that purpose made up of my brigade, some regiments from French's brigade, Hazzard's battery, and the Eighth Illinois Cavalry. I was greatly pleased that I had been selected for this expedition, and I worked a whole night to make the needed preparations.

In the morning General French told Sumner that he ran too great a risk, that my detachment by going so far from support would be captured, and surely that it was not wise to let one like me, with so little experience, go with raw troops so far away from the corps as the Rappahannock. Sumner called me in and said that he feared to let me make the reconnoissance. Instantly I begged him to try me. I showed my night work, my preparation, and my safe plan, and said: " General, you will never regret having trusted me."

Suddenly, with that fierce determination which we always saw him have in battle, he said: " Go! go! " And I am sure I let no moments waste in setting off. All day, March 29th, covered with a good infantry skirmish line, and scouting broadly with our cavalry, I marched my regiment steadily forward by these means and by the occasional use of the battery from

197

hill to hill driving my old friend's (Stuart's) forces beyond the Rappahannock.

My personal friend, Captain George W. Hazzard, commanding the battery, greatly aided in accomplishing the purposes of the expedition. For a while Hazzard had been the colonel of an Indiana regiment, but he left it alleging that the tender-hearted Indiana mothers had banished him because of the hardness of his discipline. It inspired our men greatly to see with what lightning rapidity his six guns flew into action and fired under his quick, confident commands.

After the work of the day had been done and we saw the smoking Rappahannock Bridge, I went into camp with great care, facing different ways upon the top of a thickly wooded height. I was told that the venturesome Stuart during the night came over the river and made a personal examination, and that he afterwards said Howard had taken such a position and so posted his troops that he decided not to attack him. On my return Sumner met me with the gladness of a father.

As the Maryland " political campaign " had gained me General Casey's confidence, so this reconnoissance and successful skirmishing for nine miles, small affair though it was, had gained for me the hearty good will of General Sumner.

By trying to do thoroughly the lesser things intrusted to me, I find they have proved stepping-stones to something more important.

CHAPTER XIV

IN order to leave McClellan's army free to act General Banks was to come from West Virginia and command a fifth corps with which to cover Washington. He was to give up Sedgwick's fine division to complete Sumner's corps. While matters were being planned and were not yet half executed, Stonewall Jackson, always our marplot, struck one of Banks's divisions near Winchester. Fortunately, General Shields, the division commander, with his arm shattered in the beginning of the battle, succeeded in holding Jackson at bay, and after a terrific conflict forced him up the Shenandoah Valley. But the battle itself served to call back to West Virginia General A. S. Williams's division, which belonged to Banks and was already *en route* to Manassas with orders to relieve our troops, that we might go back to Alexandria and follow our comrades via the Chesapeake to the Virginia Peninsula.

Banks himself with his Fifth Corps never did succeed in making that contemplated Centreville and Manassas march to cover Washington. But provisional troops from Washington were at last sent out to replace ours, watch against Confederate raids in that quarter, and secure the Manassas field as a shield to the capital.

199

Autobiography of Gen. O. O. Howard

Stonewall Jackson's interruption of well-conceived and well-ordered proposals caused such apprehension on all sides that the President gave the following order, which I have always wished he had not been worried into issuing:

ADJUTANT GENERAL'S OFFICE, April 3, 1862.
To General George B. McClellan, etc.

By the direction of the President, General McDowell's army corps has been detached from under your immediate command and the general is ordered to report to the secretary of war. Letter by mail.

L. THOMAS,
[Signed.] *Adjutant General.*

To McDowell he wrote:

While cooperating with General McClellan, you obey his orders, except that you are to judge, and are not to allow your force to be disposed otherwise than so as to give the greatest protection to this capital.

This came from the President's anxiety for the protection of Washington. He could, however, have secured precisely that same protection by giving his instructions directly to McClellan. Mr. Lincoln evidently had begun to distrust McClellan; if so, it was not wisdom to keep him in command and at the same time plainly show distrust by telling a corps commander to obey his orders or not, according to that commander's judgment.

I am not surprised at McClellan's grievous complaint. " I may confess," he said, " to have been shocked at this order which, with that of 'the 31st *ultimo*, removed nearly 60,000 men from my command and reduced my force by more than one-third after its task had been assigned, its operations planned, and its

200

fighting begun. . . . It compelled the adoption of another, a different and a less effective plan of campaign." To this statement his officers agreed and still agree. It was a heavy blow, and with one constituted like McClellan it was so crippling and disappointing as to render subsequent operations on his part less brilliant and decisive.

What paralyzed his arm most was this want of confidence on the part of the President and his advisers, and the growing opposition to him everywhere for political reasons. Think of the antislavery views of Stanton and Chase; of the growing antislavery sentiments of the congressional committee on the conduct of war; think of the number of generals like Fremont, Butler, Banks, Hunter, and others in everyday correspondence with the Cabinet, whose convictions were already strong that the slaves should be set free; think, too, of the Republican press constantly becoming more and more of the same opinion, and the masses of the people really leading the press. McClellan's friends in the army had often offended the Northern press. In his name radical antislavery correspondents had been expelled from the army. An incident affecting the popular Hutchinson family shows some of the conditions that existed. Because they had been singing a song which ended with:

> What whets the knife
> For the Union's life?
> Hark to the answer:
> Slavery! Slavery!

an order of McClellan was issued recalling the permit given to them to sing in camp; and their pass to cross the Potomac was annulled.

Autobiography of Gen. O. O. Howard

On April 1, 1862, the country was divided in sentiment touching the political policy henceforth to be pursued, the majority evidently inclining to the belief that " the Union as it was " could never be restored.

It is not under these circumstances at all unaccountable that Mr. Lincoln's faith in McClellan should have been gradually undermined. McClellan had begun his work when the preservation of slavery was accepted as necessary and, naturally conservative, it was next to impossible for him to modify or abandon an opinion once formed.

Thus McClellan, a soldier of conservative tendencies, promising sincerely to prevent, if possible, the dissolution of the Union, and to preserve or restore that Union as it was before the war, became now, the moment the abolition of slavery as a war measure or otherwise entered as a watchword, the great name around which to rally all the political forces opposed to the party in power.

On the contrary, Lincoln, moving with his party, naturally kept with his political household, while the Republicans gradually passed from their "nonextension " principles to their final stand against all human enslavement. McClellan was, and continued to be, a war Democrat. Lincoln at heart detested slavery and became an emancipator. He personally liked McClellan, but he began to see, prior to Johnston's retreat, that McClellan must gain victories and gain them quickly, or as President he would be forced by an imperious public sentiment to choose another chief. He practically began this (March 11th) by relieving McClellan from the command of all other armies besides that of the Potomac.

The Peninsular Campaign Begun

While he longed for his success on the peninsula, he did not dare to risk Fremont in the Mountain Department, Banks in West Virginia, or Wadsworth in the District of Columbia, without giving to each sufficient force to make the defense of the capital secure. And in addition it seemed to him imperative to detach McDowell, put him directly under the Secretary of War, and hold him and his corps for a time at Falmouth and Fredericksburg.

Could McClellan instinctively have comprehended all this, he doubtless would have been chary of his entreaties and beseechings for more force, would have masked the Confederate troops near Yorktown with a good division, and pushed the remainder of his army rapidly up the left bank of the York River before Johnston's arrival and before his enemy's reënforcement. That was McClellan's opportunity.

On April 1st in all the land satisfactory results were not wanting. The Confederacy had been pushed into narrower limits along its whole northern frontier and along the Mississippi, and important Atlantic and Gulf Coast positions had been captured.

In the face of many disasters to the Confederate cause there was much discouragement at Richmond. On March 30th General Robert E. Lee was put in command of all the Confederate armies, but was not expected to go into the field himself. This left General Joseph E. Johnston to command only in our front on the peninsula.

A letter from Richmond said: "The President (Davis) took an affectionate leave of him (Johnston) the other day; and General Lee held his hand a long time and admonished him to take care of his life. There was no necessity for him to endanger it as had

203

just been done by the brave Albert Sydney Johnston, at Shiloh, whose fall is now universally lamented."

This gallant Confederate commander, once away from Richmond in the turmoil of battle, fogot that affectionate warning.

Here, then, we have McClellan and Johnston, each set apart to manipulate a single army—the one the Army of the Potomac and the other the Army of Northern Virginia — no wider range and view demanded of them than a single field of operation and the two contending armies.

As McClellan stepped ashore near Fortress Monroe the afternoon of April 2d, Admiral Goldsboro was out in Hampton Roads with his fleet; the entrance to York River was then clear enough of foes, but a terrible soreness was afflicting that naval squadron. There was a waning confidence in wooden vessels! Only a few days back the long-dreaded Confederate ironclad, the *Merrimac*, had come like a gigantic, all-powerful monster and destroyed the *Congress* and the *Cumberland* and disabled the *Minnesota* and sent a large percentage of our naval force to the bottom. *Nothing but that little shapeless Monitor*, providentially arriving the day after that one-sided, hopeless, bloody battle, was between the fleet and utter destruction. The monster *Merrimac* had not only faced and defied our navy with the contempt of a Goliath and slain her stalwart sons without the hope of redress, but had humbled and conquered the old-fashioned and well-merited naval pride with which our brave officers and men had regarded their well-manned and well-armed ships. The *Monitor* thus far was thought to have succeeded only in worrying the gigantic enemy and causing a temporary withdrawal. Nobody then believed it the final contest. Of course, Admiral Goldsboro and his men bravely stayed in Hampton Roads, ready to die there if need be; but McClellan could not get that strong, constant, energetic, sanguine help for Yorktown that Grant had had from Commodore Foote's fleet at Fort Henry, or that was subsequently rendered the army by Admirals Porter and Farragut on the Mississippi and at Mobile.

Johnston had two forces to watch—McDowell on the Fredericksburg line of approach to Richmond and McClellan landing at Ship Point near Fortress Monroe. The Confederate general Magruder, having Johnston's advance troops, had seized and fortified the line of the Warwick and made that swampy stream the meeting point of the two great armies. Magruder's force numbered somewhere between 10,000 and 17,000 effectives at the time our advance touched his outposts. It must have been contemplated by both Lee and Johnston in the outset to force the principal expected battle to grounds near Richmond, because at Yorktown or Williamsburg the left of their position was already completely turned by McDowell's corps. They doubtless did not base their plans on a Washington scare, and so could not count upon McDowell's being suddenly anchored back there at the Rappahannock. Undoubtedly, Magruder's energy and enterprise did secure a longer delay at the Warwick and near Yorktown than was intended or dreamed of by his seniors. This accounts for his receiving no reënforcement before he began his retreat.

The country below the Warwick, which, indeed, guards all the ground from river to river, from Yorktown to the James, was low, flat, and wooded with thickets difficult to penetrate. The natural stream

205

heading near Yorktown was narrow, but had been widened by artificial means, having several dams recently made. Wyman's and Lee's dams were there before Magruder came. The banks, gentle and swampy, covered with dense fringes of thickets and small trees, were, for the most part, impassable, easily defended, and remarkably uncertain to the assailant as to what force he would have to encounter should he assault. At Gloucester Point across the York River from Yorktown and also on the James River Magruder had good field works and had thoroughly manned them. The remainder of the Warwick stretch he held by detached bodies at the dams and other points to be reënforced at need by movable columns. The dense, impassable forest shores enabled him to do this handsome defensive work without detection.

There were on our side but two roads at all practicable as approaches to the Warwick: the one near the east shore and parallel with the direction of the York, running by Howard's Bridge straight to the village of Yorktown, and the other near the James via Horse Bridge and Warwick Court House to Lee's Mill. The country roads coursing hither and thither from one small farm to another were never reliable. Fair to the eye at first, with the rain and the travel of heavy trains, the crust, like rotten ice, gave way, and then horses, mules, and wagons dropped through into sticky mud or quicksands.

Magruder had his Confederates on the north shore of the Warwick, and McClellan, with at least 50,000 men of all arms, was working his way toward the obstructions, hoping to reach Yorktown on one highway and pass far beyond it on the other to the Williamsburg "Halfway House."

The Peninsular Campaign Begun

My brigade in Richardson's division, Sumner's corps, at last turned back from Warrenton Junction toward Alexandria, Va. We had been four weeks during the stormy March weather in the field without our tents. The men's shoes were spoiled by tramping long distances in slippery, cloggy mud with the constant wetting and drying, and their clothing was much soiled and rent, so we were hoping to halt somewhere long enough to refit. At Bristow Station, a place subsequently renowned, welcome home letters found their way to our bivouac for the night. They added their cheer to the supper and the camp fire.

The next day, April 3, 1862, we marched over ground already more familiar than the farms and meadows of my native town—Manassas, Bull Run, Sangster's, Fairfax, and Springfield. The excessive weight originally carried by the men was reduced to a minimum. My men did not straggle. At a rout step they smoked and chatted with each other, keeping well closed up and never relaxing their swinging, easy gait. Now and then for relief they lifted the musket from one shoulder to the other. Now and then somebody struck up a song with a chorus and all joined in the singing. It was a pleasure to see the men cross a fordable stream—frequent in that part of Virginia. They waded creeks fifty feet wide. Sometimes, to forestall grumbling and set an example, I dismounted and walked ahead to the farther bank. The regimental bands played during the passage and the soldiers, without elongating the column, marched straight through the waters. In crossing Broad Run the water was high and came up to our hips.

We reached Alexandria on April 4th, three days after McClellan's departure for Fortress Monroe.

The transports were already on hand, so that we could not stay to refit as I had hoped, but marched at once on board. Here our division commander, General Richardson, for the first time joined his division. He was a large, fleshy man, generally careless in his attire and toilet; an officer who knew him said: " He is inclined to lie abed in the morning." I soon, however, learned to prize him for his pluck and energy that came out in battle and on an active campaign. In the fight he was a capital leader, very cool and self-possessed.

The greater part of my brigade found good accommodations on the *Spaulding*, a transport ship where our men could be well distributed and find the rest they coveted. They were much interested to see for the first time the lower Potomac and catch a glimpse of Mount Vernon as we steamed down the broadening river. Personally, having been much wearied with the care and movement of the troops, I did enjoy that short voyage. The rest was sweet and more precious when that night, after all but the sentinels and a few officers were asleep, I sat down with pen and paper to think of home. It had been almost a year of absence from the precious little group there! A startling question not so restful closed my revery: When shall I see them again?

Saturday evening, April 5th, brought us to the place of debarkation and I sent two regiments ashore. This was Ship Point intended just then for the main depot of supplies for the army. A dim twilight survey of this landing and the vicinity was my first introduction to the Virginia peninsula. The landscape in the fading light appeared delightful—small openings amid variegated forests generally level, and the roads smooth and promising. A few days later I recorded: The ground is almost all quicksand. I have worked my brigade very hard, making roads and bridges, loading and unloading barges and wagons filled with commissary and quartermaster's stores.

We took up our first camp a little to the south of the landing in a pretty grove, making my own headquarters at Mr. Pomphrey's house. Mr. Pomphrey passed for a poor man, yet he owned 200 acres of land, 15 slaves, and had a wife quite as much a slave, as the others, to the pipe which she incessantly smoked.

One never saw more grateful people than Mr. Pomphrey and his wife when I proposed to make his house my headquarters. He said with a sigh of relief: "I shall sleep to-night!" Their wilderness had been suddenly transformed into a strange city where soldiers, wagoners, negroes, and camp followers were constantly coming night and day, rummaging and often seizing what they could lay their hands upon. I could not help thinking how my own mother would feel to have her cows shot, her chickens killed, the eggs stolen, and the cellar robbed of an entire winter's supply. Such was the work of some characters who—hard to discover and control near that thickly populated landing—mingled with us.

General McClellan paid us a visit on April 9th, making a brief stay at my headquarters, and a longer one at Richardson's.

There my first knowledge of a difference between him and our much-loved President dawned upon me. His aid-de-camp, Colonel Colburn, complained bitterly to me of the action of the President in taking away over 50,000 troops which had been promised to McClellan. Of course, Mr. Lincoln's promise had been contingent upon the safety of the capital, but at that time I did not know of the contingency and so could make no reply.

I heard McClellan, during this visit, remark to another officer that he found Yorktown a very strong place. He said: "It cannot be carried without a partial siege."

He examined carefully our temporary wharves, structures, and roadways along the shore. He talked very much to the point with our quartermaster in charge and with others; while doing this he partook of a luncheon and indulged in a smoke at Richardson's headquarters; then, with the small staff which had accompanied him, rode away toward Yorktown. I trusted McClellan and sympathized with his disappointments, but had misgivings when I heard the words, " a partial siege at Yorktown! "

For a short time while we were waiting for men and material that belonged to our division to come by other steamers than the *Spaulding*, the days were mainly spent in constructing a " log road " from Ship Point to Yorktown. Indeed, after the first cold and drenching rain, we discovered that that whole vicinage was underlaid with " sinking sand." We constantly beheld whole fields of poor, struggling mules more than half buried in front of heavy wagons with wheels sunken to the hubs. All the roads, which on our arrival had been beautiful and smooth, without rut or stone, had become miry and treacherous. We were toiling on with the vigor of men who knew how to work and were making commendable progress with our corduroying when, on April 16th, the order came to proceed at once to Yorktown and join our corps. Before the close of the 17th all the brigades of Sumner's command were together in " Camp Winfield Scott." This force, usually from this time designated by its number " the Second Corps," was not far from the center of the general line and pretty well back.

My private notes made after our arrival at York-town indicate a considerable impatience on my part because of the slowness of the army. The reasons given for so much delay seemed insufficient. A siege party was working on our right indicating circumvallation and regular approaches, and a detachment of our men were throwing up breastworks near the middle of our front line, as though we might have to resist an attack from Magruder.

The morning of April 24th I rode to McClellan's headquarters to pay my respects to him and to some of his staff. The grandeur of that staff greatly impressed me. I had a long talk with my old friend Colonel Kingsbury, chief of ordnance in the field. He said in parting: " General McClellan wishes to get all his batteries in readiness before he opens fire. If our friends could realize the kind of country they are in they would not be impatient." Thus Kingsbury gently rebuked my impatience.

In the afternoon of the same day I went to the extreme left of McClellan's lines and followed the War-wick River in that neighborhood as far as I could on horseback, along its swampy border and impenetrable thickets, and visited Generals Erasmus D. Keyes, Silas Casey, and other acquaintances who were stationed near that flank. During my ride we were crossing a narrow ravine in the midst of which was a sluggish, muddy stream. Lieutenant Nelson A. Miles, my aid-de-camp, rode up and, though usually ardent, wisely checked his horse. Believing I could easily clear the stream at a bound I let my active horse, "Charlie," have the reins. He sprang forward but was unable to make the leap—the ground at the starting point not being firm enough; in fact, the whole bank before and beneath him gave way and we sank to his shoulders in the yielding mud. I scrambled off as best I could and left "Charlie" to himself. After some floundering and a few plunges he managed to catch the firm ground. My own mishap saved the remainder of the party from a mud bath.

Warwick Court House consisted of a small, brick schoolhouse, a building for the court, a jail of less size, and one other fair structure, probably intended for a store. Near at hand was a dilapidated dwelling house. These made up the little village which occupied one clearing. The intervale lands in the neighborhood at that season of springtime were beautiful. Apple and peach trees were in blossom, the grass was a bright green, and all the trees were putting forth their leaves.

CHAPTER XV

FROM April 17 to May 4, 1862, my brigade did not change its camp and was employed by detachments in constructions for siege operations, such as fascines—long bundles of rods or twigs—or gabions—tall baskets without bottoms—for use in lining the openings or embrasures of earthworks through which cannon were to be fired. The men of the division not otherwise employed did picket and guard duty, and were exercised daily in company, regimental, and brigade drills.

In order to be as familiar as possible with the places where I might have to take my command into action, I visited in turn the various portions of our front. On April 26th, after I had set large detachments from my brigade at work and had seen them diligently constructing fascines and gabions, I rode over to the York River in order to examine the water batteries. From that locality the Confederate fort on Gloucester Point across the river was in plain sight, and we could also see the enemy's water battery on the Yorktown side. From our position to the opposite shore the distance was two miles. Five of the guns in our Battery No. 1 were one hundred pounders, Parrott muzzle-loading rifles, and two two hundred pounders, Parrott. They were mounted on wrought-iron

213

carriages which appeared so slender as to be in danger of being broken by a single recoil. Other batteries had ten-, twenty-, and thirty-pounder Parrott and four and one-half-inch guns in place ready for work. Others had eight- and ten-inch mortars. The next morning I continued my visits and found near the center of our position—directly in front of Sumner's corps— with a field battery having epaulements for six guns, my friend Lieutenant Edmund Kirby in charge; he had just recovered from a serious attack of typhoid fever.

My next ride for information was made May 1st. It was along the front and to examine our first parallel, which was a trench twelve feet wide and three feet deep, the dirt being thrown toward the enemy. All along the parallel were openings in the embankment for batteries of siege guns. This trench was parallel to the enemy's works and 1,500 yards from them. Accompanied by my brother and aid, Lieutenant Howard, I continued back of the parallel eastward as far as the York River, and we took a good look at the waiting gunboats, some of which had come up the river to coöperate in the siege. We looked at each other and inquired: "How soon shall we do something?"

From day to day we read and wrote letters and had plenty of time to visit each other, as well as to study the slowly growing constructions. Occasionally the enemy would toss a shell over to our side, and now and then roll a ball of iron along our road with motion too swift to touch. A skirmish somewhere on the front line occasionally came off, and sometimes we were startled into abnormal activity by a false alarm; but on the whole we had a long and peaceful sojourn near Yorktown.

The Battle of Williamsburg

Near the end of "the siege of Yorktown," Franklin's division was permitted to come to us from McDowell, and, remaining on transports, was waiting for the great bombardment before commencing to perform its appointed rôle. But the great bombardment never came.

Sunday morning, May 4th, all at my headquarters had attended to ordinary military duties. Before breakfast I invited to my tent Captain Sewall, my adjutant general, Lieutenant Howard, Lieutenant Balloch, Orderly McDonald, an English manservant, and Charley Weis, a messenger whose sobriquet was "Bony." We read that chapter of Daniel which tells the story of Shadrach, Meshach, and Abednego passing through the fiery furnace unscathed. Then followed, from one of the officers present, an earnest petition to the Lord of Hosts for protection, guidance, and blessing. As soon as breakfast was over I commenced a letter to Mrs. Howard, and, writing rapidly, had finished about two pages, when suddenly, without completing the sentence, I jotted down: "Yorktown is abandoned and our troops are marching in." I added a little later: "I am now, quarter before eight A.M., under marching orders. Thank Him who doeth all things well."

It was Sumner's entire corps which had received orders of march. Besides the two divisions, Richardson's and Sedgwick's, Sumner's corps still included the Eighth Illinois Cavalry. Our division artillery had four batteries—twenty-four guns. Thus far no change had been made in the entire division, except the transfer of the cavalry to corps headquarters.

From our location south of Yorktown in the rear of all, we were naturally long delayed in taking up the

215

march toward Williamsburg, for the only through
routes, already almost impassable after the Confederate columns had waded through them, were thronged
with cavalry and the corps of Heintzelman and Keyes.
We held ourselves in readiness, impatiently waiting all
day the 4th. McClellan's first plan, made known later
in the day, designated our division with Sedgwick's
and Fitz-John Porter's as the reserve, either to go to
Williamsburg, if imperatively needed, or to follow
Franklin's division on transports up the York River
and support him in his work, or take and hold a
landing on the same side of the river twenty-five
miles above. To carry out this plan, early on Monday,
the 5th, Sedgwick's and our division broke camp and
marched to the immediate neighborhood of Yorktown.
Here we bivouacked and completed all our preparations for close work—rations in the haversacks and
ammunition on the person of each soldier.

Owing to McClellan's siege operations, General
Johnston determined to withdraw his Confederate
forces just before the destructive bombardment should
begin. His retreat toward Richmond was ordered and
carried steadily forward. Stuart's cavalry curtained
the moving forces on the Yorktown-Williamsburg
road, and also on the Lee's Mill and Williamsburg
road, the two roads leading up the peninsula.

Critics accuse us in the Army of the Potomac of not
being early risers, and not being keen to catch the first
evidences of evacuation. It is, indeed, a just charge
against McClellan's information bureau; the want of
information did enable Johnston to gain a coveted advantage during the first day of his difficult retreat. It
was good generalship on his part to so blind McClellan
as to his purpose. The withdrawal of the enemy, how-

ever, was discovered at dawn almost simultaneously at several points of the front. Heintzelman, in front of Yorktown, seeing fires reflected in the sky and hearing explosions which sounded like a skirmish, had himself taken up in a balloon to make sure of the cause before ordering a general advance, and saw the destruction of magazines, and our pickets unopposed sweeping over the works which had been so formidable. Hancock, then a brigade commander, was notified also at dawn by two negroes that the enemy had gone.

McClellan, taken thus by surprise, needed time to think and time to interpret Johnston's design. It might be a ruse. So he put Fitz-John Porter's division in the Confederate works to hold them against a possible return. He got Franklin with his fine body of fresh men ready to send in transports up the York, with reserves to follow, and naval gunboats to aid.

The orders to Heintzelman and Keyes were: "Draw in your guards, pickets, and outposts and replenish everything for a march."

Between the Warwick and Williamsburg was a belt of country in breadth from nine to thirteen miles. It was a country of swamps, tangled forests, and small farms here and there, like glades in the woods, connected by wretched lanes. There were only two roads from our front, and one of them the Lee's Mill road, which was connected occasionally with the other, the Yorktown road; and it took watching and tacking to keep off the main thoroughfare from Yorktown to Williamsburg and yet travel toward the latter town. The men marching in the night and rain, on account of the effort required to lift their feet, heavy with adhesive mud, never exceeded one mile an hour. Our people during that march, short as it appears, were like flocks of children playing at blindman's buff. They wandered right and left; they ran into each other; they reached out tentatively for obstacles and gained ground slowly with extreme fatigue.

There were other troubles. When our infantry began its march a warning came along our military telegraph line that everybody should look out for " buried bombs." Torpedoes had been buried in the ground along the paths and roads which led to the Confederate works. Some were also found near wells and springs of water, a few in some flour barrels and sacks in the telegraph office, and one or more near a magazine.

There was with us at Yorktown a young man by the name of D. B. Lathrop, from Springfield, Ohio. He was the son of a widow, and had been, before the war, studying for the ministry. When the war broke out, wishing to do something helpful to the Union cause, he joined that hard-worked and useful body, the telegraph corps. Mr. Lathrop was attached to General Heintzelman's headquarters. As soon as Yorktown was opened, following the wires he hurried to the telegraph office. He sat down at the operator's table and touched the instrument. Instantly an explosion of a percussion shell took place and young Lathrop was mortally wounded.

A little later in the day when Davidson's brigade was about to cross the Warwick at Lee's Mill, Colonel E. C. Mason, of the Seventh Maine, receiving word concerning Lathrop, whom he knew, and fearing torpedoes, went himself in advance of his column on the road beyond the dam. As he was walking slowly he crushed a percussion cap. Brushing away the dirt, he discovered the red wax at the top of the buried shell.

Providentially for Mason, only the cap exploded. The colonel then called for volunteers. Upon their hands and knees they crept along and succeeded in uncovering more than a dozen shells. In the approaches to the Yorktown works the torpedoes were usually arranged with a narrow board, upon which a soldier's or horse's tread would effect an explosion. Several horses and men among the first passing troops were killed or wounded by them. McClellan soon set several Confederate prisoners of war to ferret them out.

During Sunday General Stoneman with our cavalry and horse artillery worked his way forward, having small combats with Confederate cavalry under Stuart. Nothing very discouraging checked him, or any of our cavalry detachments, from a steady advance till he came upon the Williamsburg outworks. About a mile and a half from Williamsburg a considerable work called Fort Magruder was located so as to obstruct both the roads of which I have spoken. Fort Magruder had on its right and left several small redoubts, and the whole front was an open field for several hundred yards, except for the slashing of trees and other artificial obstructions.

Stuart had been pressed so hard that the Confederate commander of the rear guard called back into the woods a division of infantry and considerable artillery. As soon as Stoneman's men with a battery of artillery swept into the spaces before these formidable works, they encountered all along their front a terrific fire of both infantry and artillery. Stoneman, thus suddenly repelled, fell back a short distance and called for help, having suffered the loss of some forty men, one piece of artillery, and three caissons, which had sunk deeply in the mud, and the horses of which were nearly all killed or wounded by the prompt Confederate fire.

This partial success determined our enemy to remain a while longer and take advantage of this well-selected checking position. He might possibly overwhelm a part of McClellan's forces before the remainder could wade through the ever-deepening mud to its relief, for the rain had poured down all the day; and, indeed, Johnston needed more time to secure a reasonably safe retreat.

Sumner, being sent forward Sunday morning by McClellan to take care of everything at the front, heard the firing at Williamsburg. He hastened infantry from the heads of columns of both the other corps to Stoneman's support, and at evening, himself being cut off by a sudden Confederate sally, passed the night with one of the brigade commanders. No aids or orderlies from Heintzelman or Keyes could find him. In fact, Heintzelman, judging from his own instructions, thought himself to be in command. General Keyes, leading Casey's and Couch's divisions, had for himself a similar impression. Heintzelman's head of column under Hooker, now nearest to the James River, had been the first to respond to Stoneman's call for help. Early in the morning of Monday the three not very harmonious corps commanders succeeded in getting together.

After ambitious contention, Sumner's rank was yielded to and his plan to turn the Confederates by our right agreed upon. Heintzelman set out for the left of our line, but was much delayed by ignorant guides. At last he reached Hooker. Hooker had worked up close to the redoubts the night before with deployed lines. The instructions which had come to him were to support Stoneman and harass the enemy, and, if possible, cut off his retreat. Baldy Smith's division he knew was on his right, and other troops in plenty somewhere near. These circumstances were to " Fighting Joe Hooker " just those for winning laurels by a successful assault.

Exactly contrary to Sumner's plan Hooker, already on the ground by daylight, commenced a regular attack on the Confederate right at about 7.30. A fierce and noisy struggle went on there all day. Longstreet came back and brought more troops. Hooker's men, reserves and all, pushed in, and were nearly exhausted, when, about 4 P.M., Phil Kearny managed to get up his division. Hooker's division was at last relieved by Kearny's and fell back to be a reserve. Hooker's soldiers deserved this rest, for they had faced Fort Magruder and those strong redoubts well manned and actively firing for nine hours. Kearny's men charged and cleared the outside point of woods, carried some rifle pits, and silenced troublesome light batteries, so that Kearny declared: " The victory is ours! " His men bivouacked where they had fought.

Thus the battle went on contrary to all planning, working along from left to right. While the operations just recounted were progressing under Heintzelman's eyes, Sumner and Keyes were trying to bring order out of confusion on the right of our line and back to the rear on the Yorktown road.

A passageway across a stream and through the woods around the Confederate left flank having been discovered, Hancock's brigade, somewhat reënforced, was selected to make a turning movement, and its commander fought with it a brilliant and successful engagement against Early, who was badly wounded in this action. Hancock's victorious troops bivouacked on the field in a heavy rain. When this was going on beyond our extreme right, the enemy made strong counter attacks along the Yorktown road from the flanks of Fort Magruder. In resisting these attacks our men from New York and Pennsylvania received a heavy fire, and left many a poor fellow dead or dying upon a plowed field and among the felled timber which protected the fort. The whole conduct of this battle created among our generals so much dissatisfaction, bickering, and complaint that McClellan was induced about three o'clock in the afternoon to come to the front. The fighting was all over when he reached Sumner's headquarters. He gathered what news he could from different points and sent to Washington a dispatch which put Hancock far in advance of all other participants in the engagement.

He thought that General Johnston intended to fight a general battle at that point and that his own troops were outnumbered; so he at once ordered Sedgwick's and Richardson's divisions to march from Yorktown to Williamsburg.

Just before sunset that Monday evening, May 5th, my brigade received its marching orders. The rain still continued to pour down. We set out as quickly as possible, my brigade following that of General French. I was obliged to march my men through a narrow roadway across the Yorktown works; the clay mud, which stuck to the men's feet in lumps or masses, was from eight to ten inches in depth. Horses, wagons, mules, and footmen were coming and going both ways and often meeting in the narrow passage. As my brigade passed I remained for some time at the Yorktown sally port. The bits of board attached to torpedoes

The Battle of Williamsburg

had not all been removed, but little flags were placed as a warning of the presence of explosives. Some of us became hoarse calling to the soldiers not to move to the right or left, and not to step on the boards where the small flags were seen. It was dark before I got my brigade past Yorktown.

Almost the entire night was spent in struggling forward. I tried to walk now and then to rest my horse, and for quite a time to allow an officer who was taken suddenly ill to ride, but I found it necessary to hold on by the halter to keep on my feet. Our men straggled dreadfully that night, but as soon as the day dawned they worked their way on to the command. We had finally bivouacked for the night in a rough-plowed field till dawn. My adjutant general, a thin man, gloomily placed his hips between two rails; for myself, with crotchets I constructed a wooden horse, fastened one end of a piece of canvas over it, and pulled the other end along the ground near to my cheerful fire, and lay down against the canvas for a short, sweet rest.

At last we were halted not far from the battlefield. With a few officers I went to the bloody ground. The Confederates had departed in the night. The open muddy soil and the thickets were still strewn with the swollen dead, whose faces were generally toward the sky. I saw, as I moved along, a little headboard to mark the place of a Union soldier. His form and his face were carefully covered by a blanket. Near him was another in gray clothing left without care. In my heart I wished that he also had been covered. They seemed to be resting together in peace. I thought: " May God hasten us to the close of such a war! " This yearning was deepened by my visits to the hospitals filled with poor sufferers from both armies. United in

223

pain and forced imprisonment, Confederate and Union soldiers there were at peace. But, receiving orders from General Richardson, I myself quickly returned from that gloomy region to my brigade and hurried it back to Yorktown, to wait there for transports which would enable us to follow Franklin up the York River to West Point.

I have seen that, of the two armies, the Confederate brought into action at Williamsburg about ten thousand, and our army from twelve to thirteen thousand. Our aggregate loss, 2,239, was very large, as the troops in general fought against prepared works. The Confederate loss was from 1,300 to 1,500 men.

Before and after the first battle of Bull Run it will be remembered that I was associated with General Franklin; he and I each commanded a brigade in Heintzelman's division. His associates always respected his ability and had confidence in his judgment. Franklin's division, composed of infantry and artillery, after its arrival had been disembarked on May 3d, at Cheeseman's Landing near Ship Point, with a view to take part in the proposed assault of Yorktown. The morning of the 4th, as soon as McClellan knew of the Confederate withdrawal, he instructed Franklin to reembark and take his division to Yorktown. Franklin commenced the work at once, finishing the reëmbarking, as quickly as it could be done, about one o'clock of the 5th. The difficulties of reëmbarking, owing to the weather, to the loading of supplies, and the putting on board of the artillery carriages and other impedimenta, much of which had to be hoisted from rafts, were greater than anybody had estimated. At any rate, there was no unnecessary delay. Proceeding to Yorktown, Franklin received further orders and was ready the same evening to continue on to West Point accompanied by a naval convoy. The naval commander declined to start, owing to the increasing darkness and the danger of navigation during a furious storm. Therefore, the flotilla only left at daybreak on the 6th. Arriving at West Point, the disembarking was begun and the vicinity reconnoitered at three o'clock, but the landing of the artillery was not completed till the morning of the 7th. Canal boats, which were aground by the bank, were used as wharves.

General Johnston suspected, on account of the fewness of our troops marshaled against him at Williamsburg, that McClellan was sending a flotilla up the York River, to seize a landing place in the vicinity of West Point, and attack from it the flank of his retreating army. The evening of Tuesday, the 6th, General G. W. Smith, commanding the Confederate reserve, had Whiting's division not far from Barhamsville, opposite West Point, and three miles away. He reported to his chief, General Johnston, that a large body of United States troops had debarked from transports at Eltham's Landing, a little above him, and were occupying not only the open spaces, but a thick wood stretching from the landing to the New Kent wagon road. As this menaced Johnston's line of march he instructed Smith to dislodge our troops. This work Smith directed General Whiting to do. Franklin had put his troops into position as they landed. His flanks were protected by the gunboats, which were at hand, to shell the woods beyond. Each flank rested on swampy creeks running into the river. Besides, he possessed himself, as far as his small force could do so, of the encircling woods. General H. W. Slocum commanded Franklin's left wing, while General John

Newton, a loyal Virginian, commanded the right. Whiting, to cover Johnston's army in retreat, bivouacked in a line of battle facing Franklin, but did not attack that evening, as Franklin's troops appeared to be in a position hard to reach. He hoped to attack him as he moved out, but as Franklin did not advance Whiting attacked him furiously in position the next morning, the 7th, at ten o'clock. Franklin, however, in a three hours' conflict secured his landing, which was his object, and not, as Johnston feared, to attack him in flank during his retreat. West Point, the place where the Pamunkey and Mattapony unite to form the York River, and which is the terminus of the Richmond Railway, was now set apart for our new base of operations.

Slowly and steadily through the abounding mud, or by water from Yorktown, the army worked its way to Franklin's neighborhood, while General Johnston, with scarcely any further molestation, was suffered to draw in his forces to the vicinity of the Confederate capital.

CHAPTER XVI

THE BATTLE OF FAIR OAKS

B^Y May 16, 1862, McClellan's force was reorganized so as to give to each of his corps commanders two divisions. We moved toward Richmond from our new depot at White House in this order: Porter with the Fifth Corps, Franklin with the Sixth, Sumner with the Second, Keyes with the Fourth, and Heintzelman with the Third. Our first move was to the Chickahominy, a stream flowing from right to left across our line of advance. At first, Heintzelman and Keyes bivouacked near Bottom's Bridge; Sumner's corps, to which I belonged, a few miles up stream; Franklin not far from New Bridge, and Porter near Mechanicsville. Meanwhile the main body of our cavalry, well out, guarded our right and rear with a view to clear the way to McDowell's force, then in front of Fredericksburg, and protect our large depot at the White House and the railroad line from that point to the army.

Porter, with a slight reënforcement to his corps, moved out from our right and fought the successful small battle of Hanover Court House, May 27th, and returned to Mechanicsville. McClellan had placed his own headquarters not far from Franklin, at Gaines Mills. A small detachment of cavalry had reconnoitered through the White Oak Swamp and up the south bank of the Chickahominy to Seven Pines and the Fair

Oaks Station, five or six miles from Richmond, and had reported the ground clear of any considerable hostile force. On May 23d, four days prior to Porter's movement, Keyes, and later, the 25th, Heintzelman, had passed over Bottom's Bridge.

McClellan did not like to have his principal supplies dependent on the York River and the railway from the White House landing, and, further, he already meditated working over to the James River to thus secure by the help of the navy a safer base and, as he thought, a better approach to Richmond. He had now over 120,000 men, but his estimate of his enemy on data obtained by his information bureau exceeded that number, so very naturally he wanted on the spot McDowell's entire corps which had been promised. With McDowell present he could move his army so as to draw his supplies from the James at once. Without him and with instructions to coöperate with him, far off on his right, he could not do so. McClellan therefore sent only two corps over the Chickahominy instead of moving there with his whole force. This was called a river, but ordinarily it was no more than a creek with low banks, between which water and swamp varied in width from two to three hundred feet. McClellan and his officers deprecated this division of his army even by so small a river, but it appeared a necessity and they sought to make amends for it by building bridges. Sumner's corps built two, one of which was constructed of large logs by the Fifth New Hampshire of my brigade. General Sumner, seeing the water rising from the rains and hoping to hasten the work, gave the men a barrel of whisky—at the same time answering my objection to its use by saying: "Yes, general, you are right, but it is like pitch on fire which gets speed out of an engine though it burns out the boiler." The two structures were named Sumner's upper and Sumner's lower bridge. Our engineers farther up, when the south bank had been seized by us, repaired the old bridges and threw across others till the Chickahominy appeared but a slight obstruction.

On May 25th Casey's division of Keyes's corps moved forward to Seven Pines, a "crossroads" on the main pike from Williamsburg to Richmond, where the "nine-mile road" comes from New Bridge into that highway. Keyes, being ordered to hold Fair Oaks Railway station in advance of that position, moved again the 29th, placing Naglee's brigade in advance and bringing up Casey's other two brigades, Wessells's and Palmer's, in support, with pickets out in front of all.

Here Casey's division, really too far forward for safety, fortified as well as it could with the time and implements at hand.

Keyes at first intrenched his other division, Couch's, near Savage Station, but a little later brought it up to the vicinity of Seven Pines and there camped it as a second line to Casey facing toward Richmond. Field works were being constructed to cover every approach, particularly the nine-mile road, which, coming from the New Bridge, was joined by a road from Richmond at the Old Tavern. Couch's division, as a reserved line, was arranged to hold the Seven Pines crossroads. His brigades were Peck's, Abercrombie's, and Devens's. The entire corps of Keyes on the ground did not exceed 12,000 men, who stretched forward for more than two miles and, though partially intrenched, were not within very easy support of each other in case of attack by a larger force.

On May 29th and 30th Confederate reconnoissances were made against Keyes's corps in order to ascertain the position and strength of our troops in that vicinity.

Heintzelman, when he had crossed the river with his corps, had moved Hooker's division to the neighborhood of White Oak Swamp Bridge, three miles due south of Bottom's Bridge, and Kearny's division forward on the Richmond road about half as far, stopping it a little short of Savage Railway Station. Heintzelman in his own corps had for duty at the first symptoms of battle about 20,000 men. He was the ranking officer and in command of all the troops south of the Chickahominy. The Eighth Pennsylvania and part of the Eighth Illinois Cavalry were present to watch the flanks of Couch and Casey, but not able to do much in such a thickly wooded region. Casey evidently felt the weakness of his force, for when the Confederate reconnoissance occurred on the 30th he sent at once to Keyes for help. Peck's brigade was placed on his left during that alarm.

Now came during that night a most terrific storm; the rain fell in torrents and it was accompanied by high winds. It was difficult to keep our tents standing and in that peculiarly soft soil the mud deepened and the discomforts were beyond description, so that the soldiers in every camp had little rest while the storm continued. The arms and ammunition were not improved by the pouring rain, though in these respects one side suffered no more than the other. But for some reason those who stand on the defensive are more subject to discouragement and apprehension than those who are in movement.

General Johnston, the Confederate commander, had a few days before planned a combined attack against our troops north of the Chickahominy, similar to that which the Confederates made a month later, but military reasons caused him to change his purpose.

After his reconnoissance of the 30th he was ready to strike on the south bank. The Chickahominy, during the fearful succession of storm bursts, had risen and spread rapidly over all the low ground till the stream had become a broad river.

What could be more favorable to his plan? True, the Confederate artillery might be hindered by the water and soft soil, but seemingly Keyes's corps of the Union army was now isolated and Johnston had in hand five strong divisions. McClellan could reënforce but slowly from the north of the river, for already some of the bridges had been carried away and the others would not long be safe to cross.

The Confederate order of attack was: Hill to concentrate on the Williamsburg road and suddenly, vigorously assail with his division Keyes in front; Hill to be supported by Longstreet, who was to have the direction of all operations from the Williamsburg road to the Confederate right, and whose own division was to follow Hill; Huger's division, starting early, was to move rapidly by the Charles City road, which was southward nearer the James River, and come up in rear of Keyes's position. G. W. Smith with his own and McLane's divisions was intrusted with a double duty to serve as a general reserve and be ready to reënforce Longstreet down the nine-mile road, and also to watch the New Bridge and all other approaches of our corps from the Chickahominy.

Longstreet, despairing of Huger's coöperation, about 12.30 P.M. ordered D. H. Hill to commence the

231

assault. Hill's strong division sprang forward in the road and on both sides of it with lines far overlapping Casey's front. They crowded forward with slight skirmishing, and at first with but few pieces of artillery and with as little noise as possible, hoping for a surprise.

The capture that morning of Lieutenant Washington, one of Johnston's aids, in front of the Union line, and his conduct after capture had satisfied Casey that an attack from some direction was about to be made. After that, General Casey increased his diligence, striving to finish his redoubts and intrenchments and extend his abatis. Large numbers of men were working with spades and axes when not long after noon two hostile shells cut the air and burst in their neighborhood. Thus Casey was warned and in a few minutes his line of skirmishers, with a fresh regiment in immediate support, became engaged.

The assault was so abrupt and overwhelming that but little resistance was made by those in advance of the main line. The pickets and regiment just sent forward, leaving the dead and badly wounded, were quickly swept away by their advancing enemy. They assailed the center and both wings and had sufficient numbers to whip around the flanks.

When Casey found his unfinished trenches too weak and his fighting force too small to hold back Hill's brigades, his artillery and his musketry making but faint impression, he ordered a bayonet charge by four regiments. General Naglee led the charge and succeeded in pressing all the Confederates in sight in the direct front back across the open space to the edge of the woods. That was, however, but a momentary respite; for from those woods Naglee's men received a

232

fire that they could not stand and quickly ran back to their intrenched lines.

Many of Casey's troops being new levies, after they had once had their ranks broken, scattered off to the rear, falling back even beyond Couch's position. Still, most of them preserved a show of order and were subsequently brought up by their officers as far as Seven Pines to renew the struggle.

Hill, while he attacked with three brigades in front, sent Rains with his brigade to work around Casey's left. He went under cover of the marshy forest, turned, and came up behind Casey's intrenchments. He thus had a large brigade enfilading our lines and pelting the backs of our soldiers. After losing heavily and inflicting a great loss upon his assailants Casey ordered the abandonment of that front. Our new regiments, which had fought hard till now, broke up badly in the retreat. A regiment from Peck's brigade, sent forward from the left of Couch, delayed Rains sufficiently to enable Casey's men to retire without destruction. Casey passed Couch and gathered up all the remnants he could behind him at Seven Pines.

The line of rifle pits in front of Seven Pines could not long be held by Couch's division—because Couch had first to reënforce Casey and then by the orders of his corps commander he was obliged to extend too much, even as far as he could reach along the nine-mile road. That line of three brigades, Abercrombie's, Devens's, and Peck's, crossed the railroad near Fair Oaks Station. The contest at Couch's new position was at times as fierce as at Casey's, and the line with little or no cover for the defenders was kept till after four o'clock.

As soon as the assailants recovered their breath

and were reasonably reorganized by their leaders, they made another vigorous push to complete the destruction of Keyes's corps.

While all this fury of battle was in progress—and over two hours of it had passed—by some extraordinary circumstance Heintzelman, whom McClellan looked to as the veritable commander of all the forces on the Richmond side of the Chickahominy and whose headquarters were near Savage Station, received no word of the hostile attack, until too late to help Casey. At last he was on his way battleward, storming at criminal stragglers and hurrying forward Kearny's division.

With such a battlefield won, with much food, and eight captured cannon and hundreds of prisoners in hand, no wonder there was confidence and enthusiasm in Longstreet's ranks. General Johnston and G. W. Smith at their junction of roads on the Confederate left, had failed to hear the musketry till after 4 P.M., and were at last informed by a returning messenger. Then they moved straight on toward the battlefield. It was a time for a great success which might bring Confederate independence.

Phil Kearny, following his instructions literally, sent Birney's small brigade to the railway, which took post far back of the staggering line of battle.

After Birney had gone Kearny heard of Casey's retreat and Couch's danger, and received Heintzelman's order for the other brigade with him. Passing through throngs of fugitives he joined Berry at the head of the brigade on the Richmond road and urged the utmost haste. He also sent to Bottom's Bridge for Jameson's brigade left there as a guard.

He now came up to Seven Pines with his head of

column in an incredibly short time. The impulsive Kearny found Keyes and Casey together. Couch was with Abercrombie over the railway toward the Chickahominy. Kearny quickly took in the situation; the zigzag rifle trench sheltering crowded men, and the open space in front, from beyond which the Confederate riflemen were firing from both the felled and standing timber. Kearny eagerly asked: "Where is your greatest need?" Casey, cheered by the newcomers, said: "Kearny, if you will regain our late camp the day will still be ours." Kearny just then had only the Third Michigan up. The men moved forward with alacrity; they ran over the open space into the timber and began a contest as determined as that of their foes, "heedless," said their general, "of the shell and ball that rained upon them." But even when Berry's three other regiments had joined the fiercely fighting line Kearny found that after all his promptness he could effect but little. He gained some ground, then lost it, backing off in fairly good order toward the White Oak Swamp and Hooker, stoutly disputing the ground as he retired.

About the time of Kearny's arrival, Hill's and Longstreet's divisions of Confederates with some reenforcements from their reserves, having four brigade fronts abreast, stretching from the swamps of White Oak to and beyond Abercrombie at the railroad, more than a mile of breadth, came surging on with cheering and musketry, the charge made the more formidable by the rapid use of our captured cannon turned against our irregular masses herded together at Seven Pines.

It did not take many minutes to break our very attenuated opposing lines. Couch saw the blackness of the storm as it filled the air with fury and speed. Upon the break in what remained of his division he swung off a few regiments of his right, including Abercrombie's brigade, till they were well north of the railroad and parallel to it, and then retired slowly toward Sumner's upper bridge. In the edge of the wood he made a firm stand to check any hostile advance in that direction. As a thundercloud approaches, but stops at a river and passes harmlessly away, giving but a gentle sprinkling, so did this cloud of insurgents approach Couch and his men, touch the woods, and pass on along the railway beyond him. But this portion of Couch's division was thus hopelessly cut off from the rest of its corps.

Meanwhile, Kearny, finding a safe road via the saw mill back of his line, hastened his men to the rear in that way till he reached the defenses at Savage Station which had been constructed originally by General Couch. To this strong place were gathered all the regiments of Keyes except Couch's detachment, and all of Heintzelman's corps including Hooker, now arrived from White Oak Swamp.

Longstreet's forces, exhausted by six hours' fighting, could get no farther. But he knew that for him heavy reënforcements were at hand. Five fresh brigades were partly behind him and partly on his left, extending beyond the Fair Oaks railway station.

As the fresh Confederate troops were coming on cheering and confident there came from their left front, toward the Chickahominy, a sudden check. Some guns of a Union battery opened a cross fire. It was not safe to ignore them and their support. Smith ordered them to be taken at once. Two Confederate brigades attempted that. Then others already somewhat ahead turned back and joined in the attack. Smith became impatient. He went to the railroad to discover what was the matter. The firing grew worse. No such stubborn resistance should come from that quarter. While Smith, and later, Johnston, are examining this flank interruption, I will explain its cause.

Sumner's corps, we know, lay along the Chickahominy, opposite the battlefield. An order from McClellan restraining him from moving without permission was received by Sumner that morning. We heard the first fitful sound from Casey's guns, and before one o'clock we knew that a hard battle was going on. Sumner at once asked, by telegraph, permission to cross the river. He walked up and down like a caged lion. McClellan first telegraphed him to be ready. He was ready. But to save delay he sent Sedgwick's division with three batteries to his upper bridge and our division to the lower. The order to cross came at last at 2.30 P.M. As Sumner with Sedgwick approached, a part of the upper bridge rose with the water, starting to float off with the current. It was difficult to keep the green logs in place by ropes and withes; great cracks appeared. The engineer officer met Sumner and remonstrated: "General Sumner, you cannot cross this bridge!"

" Can't cross this bridge! I can, sir; I will, sir!"

" Don't you see the approaches are breaking up and the logs displaced? It is impossible!"

"Impossible! Sir, I tell you I *can* cross. I am ordered."

The orders had come and that ended the matter with Sumner.

When men and horses were once on the bridge they pressed down the logs and accomplished the task more easily than the engineer had believed possible. Beyond the bridge the water was sometimes up to the thighs of Sedgwick's men. Our lower bridge was worse. As soon as French's brigade had crossed, the bridge began to break so much that Richardson turned my brigade, followed by Meagher's, to the upper one. The water was now deeper on the flats and the mud was well stirred up from the bottom.

Kirby's battery of six light twelve-pounder smoothbore brass guns, following Sedgwick's leading brigade, had found the road a veritable quagmire. By unlimbering at times and using the prolonges, the cannoneers being up to their waists in water, at 4.45 P.M. three pieces with one caisson were landed on harder ground and put in place for action. A little later came two or more, and the sixth gun was at last dragged out by an abundance of men. Our other batteries were too late for the action.

Couch had sent to Sumner for help, and of his emotion, as he saw our troops approaching, he has made this record: " I felt that God was with us and victory ours! "

We found this command, four regiments and a battery, astride a country road leading from Fair Oaks Station via Mr. Courtney's and Dr. Kent's houses to the meadow near our bridges, and holding on persistently against the fire of flankers of Smith's Confederate column. Of Sedgwick's leading brigade under General Gorman, Sully's regiment, the First Minnesota, went to the right to secure that flank and the other three to the left of Couch's line. Kirby's guns, as fast as they arrived, and two guns under Lieutenant Fagan, of a Pennsylvania battery on the ground, went into action at once, facing toward Fair Oaks,

i. e., in front of the left of Couch's line with their own right at the corner of a grove; behind this grove Couch's infantry line extended. Sedgwick's second brigade, W. W. Burns in command, was formed in reserve and the two regiments present of the third brigade, General Dana commanding, extended the front farther to the left from the flank of Gorman.

Soon the firing was tremendous. This was the interruption—the check to the advance of the Confederate left—which came to them so suddenly. Then there was a brief pause, when General Whiting with his own, Pettigrew's, and Hampton's brigades faced to the left and attacked our troops in line of battle from the nine-mile road. They advanced straight toward Sumner, firing as they came and shouting.

Our infantry returned the fire in volleys, while the artillery discharges were continued with extraordinary rapidity and accuracy. This fearful fire stopped that first Confederate advance.

Failing in the attempt directly upon the battery, the Confederates tried to reach it through the woods on its right. But limbers brought up ammunition from the caissons buried in the mud of the swamp and returned for more. Each discharge buried the guns, trails and all, to the axles in the soft soil. Yet, by the help of infantry men standing in rear, the pieces on the left of battery were carried forward and the front changed to the right to meet the Confederates' flank move as they emerged from the woods, and bring upon their front a tremendous fire of canister.

At the same time the infantry on the left of the battery, under Sumner's personal direction, was advanced, and charged the right of the Confederates as they came on. Two guns only could be soon enough extricated from the mud to follow up the enemy's retreat.

At the same time a fourth Confederate brigade, Hatton's, was put in, and in the woods advanced to within a few yards of the Union line, but made no impression.

Thus, all Smith's wing of the Confederate army that night within reach as reënforcements for Longstreet, except Hood's brigade, was diverted, and in this engagement of an hour and a half lost 1,283 men, including the brigade commanders, Hampton and Pettigrew, seriously wounded; the latter was left unconscious on the field and captured, and General Hatton killed.

About sunset General Johnston himself was struck from his horse, severely wounded by a fragment of a shell, and carried from the field. The command of the entire Confederate army then devolved on General G. W. Smith; the defeat of his troops by Sumner did not soften the responsibility of the morrow.

Our change from the lower to the upper bridge and the difficulties of the march brought my brigade to the battlefield nearly two hours after Sumner's and Sedgwick's timely arrival.

As we approached the front a thick mist was setting in and a dark, cloudy sky was over our heads, so that it was not easy at twenty yards to distinguish a man from a horse. The heavy firing was over. As soon as Sedgwick's advance had pushed the enemy back beyond Fair Oaks Station, Lieutenant Nelson A. Miles, whom I had sent on ahead, returned from the battle, meeting me near the edge of a swampy opening over which the Confederates had charged and been swept back by the countercharge.

240

Miles, guiding us, remarked: "General, you had better dismount and lead your horses, for the dead and wounded are here."

A peculiar feeling crept over me as I put my feet on the soft ground and followed the young officer. Some stretchers were in motion. A few friends were searching for faces they hoped not to find. There were cries of delirium, calls of the helpless, the silence of the slain, and the hum of distant voices in the advancing brigade, with an intermittent rattle of musketry, the neighing of horses, and the shriller prolonged calls of the team mules, and soon the moving of lanterns guiding the bearers of the wounded to the busy surgeons: all these things made a weird impression and a desire to be freed from following in the wake of the ravages of war.

I remember that the call of one poor fellow was insistent. He repeatedly cried: "Oh, sir! Kind sir! Come to me!" I walked over to where he lay and asked: "What regiment do you belong to?"

He answered: "The Fifth Mississippi."

I then said: "What do you want?"

He replied: "Oh, I am cold!"

I knew it was from the approach of death, but noticing that he had a blanket over him I said: "You have a good warm blanket over you."

He looked toward it and said gently: "Yes, some kind gentleman from Massachusetts spread his blanket over me, but, sir, I'm still cold."

A Massachusetts soldier had given his only blanket to a wounded man—a wounded enemy.

We silently passed on to our allotted lines. I pondered over my instructions, prepared orders for others, and then, with mingled hope and apprehension

241

and conscious trust in God, lay down to dream of home. Only one of my regiments (the Fifth New Hampshire) was called to the front that evening. The Confederate and Union men were so mixed up by the conflict at dark that they often during the night unwittingly walked into the wrong camp. It had been a costly day to us, but the left wing of our army was not destroyed, and the Confederate casualties were as many as ours. We waited for the morrow to renew the strife, believing that we had come to a decisive battle, maybe the last great struggle of the war.

The sudden check by Sumner and the desperate wounds of Johnston had produced an astounding effect upon the Confederates. At 4 p.m. they were confident, jubilant; at dark they had lost their head and confusion reigned.

General Smith, regarding the morrow, directed General Longstreet to push his successes of the previous day as far as practicable, pivoting his movement upon the position of General Whiting on his left. Whiting was to make a diversion, and in extreme case to hold at all hazards the junction of the New Bridge and nine-mile road.

That point was so far back that Smith's orders practically meant that Longstreet alone was to finish the battle. Longstreet, though reënforced, had a hard task, especially under his pivotal orders. He did not and could not do else but hold on a while and finally withdraw.

On the morning of June 1st matters had shaped themselves fairly well for us. From right to left in a bend, concave toward Smith and Longstreet, were the divisions of Sedgwick, Richardson, Kearny, and Hooker. Sumner's troops were at the extreme right, parallel to the nine-mile road. The Union line then ran along the railway, and finally crossing the railway and turnpike it continued on by the strong works near Savage Station to White Oak Swamp.

Of our division, on Sedgwick's left, French's brigade of four regiments was the front line, my Fifth New Hampshire still covering the whole front as a picket guard. The remainder of my brigade (the Sixty-fourth New York, Colonel Parker; Sixty-first New York, Colonel Barlow; and the Eighty-first Pennsylvania, Colonel Miller) formed a second line a few hundred yards back.

General Meagher's brigade of three regiments made a third line, and Hazzard's, Frank's, and Petit's batteries, belonging to the division, were located on convenient knolls near the front. Thus at dawn we stood ready for work.

As soon as it was light the Fifth New Hampshire, under Colonel Cross, advanced slowly till it had seized the woods beyond the railroad near Fair Oaks Station. Hazzard quickly found a favorable place for the batteries, whence by a cross fire he commanded all the open spaces, over which the enemy would have to approach us. The guns and battery men were shielded by epaulements hurriedly thrown up.

The first noisy collision of this Sunday morning was about five o'clock; it became a smart reveille to all; first, a brisk skirmish, a few bullets whizzing through the tree tops. Colonel Cross had every man ready. The artillery officers with good field glasses were watching. There was always a strange thrill of interest at such a time. The movement was, however, only a Confederate reconnoissance. The reconnoiterers were hunting for the Fair Oaks Railroad Station, which, unknown to them, had changed occupants. For a brief period their cavalry and infantry showed in the openings along our front, but everywhere found themselves met by Cross's skirmishers, whose steady firing, supported by the rapid cross fire of our batteries, drove them beyond range.

This event increased our caution. Too long an interval between French and Birney, of Kearny's division, was reported—only pickets connecting. French then gained ground to the left, thinning his ranks and taking greater distance from Sedgwick. Still he could not reach far enough, so by Richardson's order I sent Colonel Miller with the Eighty-first Pennsylvania. Miller promptly deployed his men and moved forward till abreast of Colonel Brooke, who commanded French's left regiment. The reason for not connecting with Birney's brigade, now under command of Colonel Ward, was that it was much farther back from the enemy than French expected to find it, and the underbrush was too thick to see very far.

Sumner was now the senior officer south of the Chickahominy, but in command of his own corps only, and Heintzelman commanded his part of the line. The commander of the whole battle was McClellan at his headquarters several miles away. The day's work resulted in spasmodic activities at several points of our front, and no general aggressive movement even after the Confederate partial attacks had been repulsed.

The Fifth New Hampshire was relieved from the skirmish line and placed in reserve. There were but a few minutes to wait. Upon French's left front there came a Confederate attack with two deployed brigade fronts, Armstead's and Pickett's. They moved at a quick walk and, owing to prevalence of the woodland, drew wonderfully near before they were discovered. Along the whole of our front line they opened a heavy rolling fire of musketry within fifty yards. French's men instantly returned the fire, and the contest for over an hour was as severe as any in the war.

At this time Miller, of my brigade, who, as we have seen, was to the left of French, saw through the trees the coming troops. He gave the word "Ready!" when some officer near him said: "No, no, colonel, they are our men!" Probably thinking them detached from Ward, Miller in his strong voice commanded: "Recover arms!" and called out: "Who are you?" They cried: "Virginians!" and instantly fired a volley which killed Colonel Miller and so many of his men that the regiment lost its continuity. A captain, Robert M. Lee, Jr., sprang upon a stump near at hand and rallied six companies. At once I sent Lieutenant N. A. Miles to look up the other four. He soon found them and brought them together at the railroad where there was an open space, and then led them again into action.

It was at this period of the conflict that Richardson sent to me to fill the interval made worse by the loss of Miller. I brought the two regiments into line at the railroad—the Sixty-first on the right and the Sixty-fourth to its left.

Just as we were ready to advance, the enemy's fire began to meet us, cutting through the trees. My brown horse was wounded through the shoulder, and I had to dismount and wait for another. Turning toward the men, I saw that some had been hit and others were leaving their ranks. This was their first experience under fire. I cried out with all my might: "Lie down!" Every man dropped to the ground; then my staff and the field officers aided me in sheltering the men by forming line behind the railroad embankment, but we could not fire yet without the danger of pouring shot into French's line.

In five minutes I had mounted my large gray horse, my brother riding my third and only other one, a beautiful " zebra." In order to encourage the men in a forward movement I placed myself, mounted, in front of the Sixty-fourth New York, and my aid, Lieutenant Charles H. Howard, in front of the Sixty-first. Every officer was directed to repeat each command. I ordered: " Forward! " and then " March! " I could hear the echo of these words and, as I started, the Sixty-fourth followed me with a glad shout up the slope and through the woods; the Sixty-first followed my brother at the same time. We moved forward finely, taking many prisoners as we went and gaining ground leftward, until we came abreast of French's division.

Before reaching French's line I was wounded through the right forearm by a small Mississippi rifle ball. Lieutenant Howard just then ran to me on foot and said that the zebra horse was killed. He took a handkerchief, bound up my arm, and then ran back to the Sixty-first.

As the impulse was favorable to a charge I decided to go on farther, and, asking Brooke's regiment on French's left to lie down, called again: " Forward! " And on we went, pushing back the enemy and breaking through his nearest line. We pressed our way over uneven ground to the neighborhood of the crossroads at Seven Pines, where our men the day before had left their tents standing. Behind those tents was found a stronger force of Confederates, kneeling and firing.

246

We approached within thirty or forty yards and, halting on as favorable ground as possible, promptly and efficiently returned their fire.

When at last we halted near the standing tents and I had passed to the rear of the line which was rapidly firing, my gray had his left foreleg broken and, though I was not then aware of it, I had been wounded again, my right elbow having been shattered by a rifle shot. Lieutenant Howard was missing.

Lieutenant William McIntyre, of the Sixty-fourth, seeing the condition of my horse, seized me, and put me in a sheltered place on the ground. I heard him say: "General, you shall not be killed." McIntyre himself was slain near that spot, giving his life for mine. The bullets were just then raining upon our men, who without flinching were firing back. As a faintness warned me, I called to Colonel Barlow, who was not far away, to take command. He answered me in a clear, cool voice: "Shall I take command of the whole brigade, sir?" I replied: "No, only of this portion." It would have broken Cross's heart to have forgotten even at such a time his seniority, and the colonel of the Sixty-fourth was also Barlow's senior, but he had failed in the necessary physical strength that day.

Barlow took command and stood his ground until Brooke, to whom I spoke on my way to the rear, brought up his line. After a little further conflict in that vicinity the Confederates gave way and along our division front the victory was complete.

Meanwhile, to the eastward the enemy passing through the thickets beyond my left flank crossed the railroad, encountering only such slight opposition as the remnants of the Eighty-first Pennsylvania under

Lee and Miles could administer, caught sight of the right of Ward's brigade and opened upon them a brisk fusillade. Ward threw back the right of my old regiment, the Third Maine, and moved his other regiments so as to come forward in echelon. He began by firing volleys, then inclining more to the right charged furiously. This was done at the same time Lieutenant Howard and I were leading our two regiments into the *mêlée*. Ward's vigorous onset cleared that important quarter of the pressing enemy.

To the left of Ward came Hooker, his front making a right angle with the railroad. He was ready for his part. His advance on account of thickets and swamps was slow but positive.

Thus our division and portions of two others were brought into the Sunday battle. Finally, from the right of Richardson to the left of Hooker had been made a general advance, and the whole obscure and dreadful field of both days compassed by our men. Why was not that Confederate retreat followed up and the fruits of victory secured? After weighing with care the many reasons which our commanding general has left recorded for not at this time pushing forward his whole strength, I still think that his headquarters were too far away, and that just then and there he lost a great opportunity.

General French's medical director, Surgeon Gabriel Grant, close up to the troops, was operating under fire [1] beside a large stump. He there bound up my arm. I found my brother shot through the thigh, just able to limp along by using his empty scabbard for a cane. He had a fox-skin robe, which had been on his saddle, thrown across his free arm.

[1] For this, Dr. G. Grant received the Congress Medal of Honor.

" Why weary yourself, Charlie, with that robe? " I asked.

" To cover me up if I should have to stop," he smilingly answered.

Dr. Grant dressed his leg and provided him with a stretcher. I preferred to walk. *En route* I encountered a soldier among the wounded with his fingers broken and bleeding. He cried out with pain. Seeing me he drew near with sympathy. " You are worse off than I," he said, and putting his arm around me he let me share his strength. We wounded wanderers at last found Courtney's house, a half mile or more. north of the Fair Oaks Station.

Dr. Hammond, my personal friend, met me near the house, saw the blood, touched my arm, and said with feeling: " General, your arm is broken." The last ball had passed through the elbow joint and crushed the bones into small fragments. He led me to a negro hut, large enough only for a double bed. Here I lay down, alarming an aged negro couple who feared at first that some of us might discover and seize hidden treasure which was in that bed.

My brigade surgeon, Dr. Palmer, and several others soon stood by my bedside in consultation. At last Dr. Palmer, with serious face, kindly told me that my arm had better come off. " All right, go ahead," I said. " Happy to lose only my arm."

" Not before 5 P.M., general."

" Why not? "

" Reaction must set in."

So I had to wait six hours. I had received the sec-one wound about half-past ten. I had reached the Courtney house about eleven, and in some weakness and discomfort occupied the negro cabin till the hour appointed. At that time Dr. Palmer came with four stout soldiers and a significant stretcher. They placed me thereon, and the doctor put around the arm close to the shoulder the tourniquet, screwing it tighter and tighter above the wound. They then bore me to the amputating room, a place a little grewsome withal from arms, legs, and hands not yet all carried off, and poor fellows with anxious eyes waiting their turn.

On the long table I was nicely bolstered; Dr. Grant, who had come from the front, relieved the too-tight tourniquet. A mixture of chloroform and gas was administered and I slept quietly. Dr. Palmer amputated the arm above the elbow. When I awoke I was surprised to find the heavy burden was gone, but was content and thankful.

CHAPTER XVII

THE next morning, June 2, 1862, my brother and I set out on leave with surgeon's certificate of disability. To Fair Oaks Station I rode beside the driver of the ambulance, while Lieutenant Howard, Capt. A. P. Fisk, and others reclined inside.

At the station I had hardly reached the ground when General Philip Kearny rode up with his staff. They dismounted and stood near us, while Kearny and I grasped hands. He had lost his left arm in Mexico. To console me he said in a gentle voice: " General, I am sorry for you; but you must not mind it; the ladies will not think the less of you!" I laughed as I glanced at our two hands of the same size and replied: " There is one thing that we can do, general, we can buy our gloves together!"

He answered, with a smile: " Sure enough!" But we did not, for I never met him again. He was killed at Chantilly. That evening I was near by but did not see him.

All the passengers in our freight car, which left Fair Oaks for the White House landing that day, save Captain F. D. Sewall, my adjutant general, were suffering from wounds. Some were standing, some sitting, but the majority were lying or reclining upon straw which covered the floor of the car. From one of

251

the latter I received a pleasant smile and a word of recognition. It was Capt. A. P. Fisk, the adjutant general of French's brigade, who greeted me. His surgeon, having examined his most painful wound near the knee joint, at first feared to leave his leg unamputated, but the captain and he finally decided to take the risk. Every tilt or jar of the rough car gave him intense pain; still his cheerfulness, showing itself in sprightly conversation, never forsook him. He also constantly cheered others around him who were gloomy and despondent.

The roadbed was in bad condition and the freight peculiarly sensitive, so that from compassion the conductor moved us at a snail's pace. With pain from bruised nerves and loss of blood I found it difficult to endure the shaking of the car and be as cheery as my brother and Captain Fisk. The trial lasted three hours, and I was glad enough to catch a glimpse of the steamer *Nelly Baker*, which was to transport us from the White House landing down the York River. It took but a few minutes to get us on board. Here were plenty of medicines and other supplies. Three or four ladies, serving as nurses, gave the wounded men their quick attention and care.

As soon as I could get ink and pen, I made my first effort at writing with my left hand. The letter is still preserved and fairly legible, the letters having the backward slant. To this is added Lieutenant Howard's postscript, which ends: " There is for me only a flesh wound in the thigh."

Only a flesh wound, it is true; but so severe as to necessitate the use of a stretcher to carry him from place to place. It was a more troublesome wound than mine and required more time for healing.

Second Battle of Bull Run

Twelve years before, while a cadet at West Point, I had had a severe wound in the head, made by a fall while exercising in the gymnasium; a hard attack of erysipelas followed. Surgeon Cuyler, of Georgia, attended me there. No mother could have been more faithful and gentle than he during the period of my suffering. The same good physician, as we neared Fortress Monroe, came on board our steamer, dressed our wounds, and prescribed a proper diet. He begged my brother and myself to remain with him until we were stronger, but the home fever had seized me and nothing short of compulsion could then detain us.

Several little children were playing about the steamer and now and then dodged in and out of the room where the wounded officers were sitting. When I noticed them, they began their happy play with me. The nurses, fearing injury, endeavored to remove them, but the other wounded joined me in a protest. It was a great comfort to be not only rid of the scenes of carnage but able to mingle again with the joys of childhood. Many there knew that their own little ones were waiting hopefully, though anxiously, for their return.

We had a rough experience after our arrival in Baltimore. Thrust into a hack, the lieutenant and I were driven swiftly two or three miles over the cobblestones from the wharf to the railroad station. In great distress I clung to the side of the carriage, made springs of my knees, and thus found a little relief from the jar. My brother could get no such respite, so the agony he endured was excessive.

On our arrival in New York, Wednesday afternoon, we were taken directly to the Astor House, considerably exhausted and remained a night and a day. We received the most motherly attention from Mrs. Stetson, the wife of the proprietor. Would that every bruised soldier had fallen into such kind hands!

From New York we went directly to Lewiston, Me., meeting on the steamer and the cars, in the cities and villages wherever we passed, every demonstration of sympathy and affection. Our condition suggested to other hearts what had happened or might happen to some beloved relative or friend still on the field of strife.

At last, arriving at Lewiston station, the whole population appeared to have turned out to greet us. We were not suffered to cross the river into Auburn, and meet my little family after more than a year's separation, till words of welcome and appreciation had been spoken and acknowledged. Then the desired relief from such patriotic love came and we hastened to the hotel in Auburn where my wife and children were.

Sweet, indeed, was the rest of a few subsequent days when we enjoyed the nursing and comforts of home.

My confinement to my room was brief—not over three days. Ten days after our arrival, accompanied by my friend Dr. Wiggin, later a surgeon in the Twenty-first Maine, I visited Portland and participated in a State religious convention, where I gave two public addresses.

After speaking in Livermore on July 4th, in descending a flight of steps I slipped and fell. I tried to catch support with the hand which did not exist and so thrust the stump of my amputated arm into the ground, making the hurt from the fall very severe; it would have been worse, except for a sole-leather protection. I felt for my comrades on the peninsula who were worse wounded and suffering. For I had sympathy, tender nursing, and gentle voices at hand, and they often had not.

The people in Maine were restless and anxious. What has the army effected? What does it purpose to do? When will this dreadful war end? Is McClellan the man for us? These were the questions that met me at the convention. At that time I warmly espoused the cause of McClellan and resented every criticism as an aspersion. I entertained and expressed the strong hope that he would yet lead us to victory. At the same time I fully believed that slavery must go to the wall before the end.

The speeches which I made at that large Portland meeting were the beginning of a canvass of Maine for filling the State quota of volunteers. Governor Washburn entreated me to aid him in this matter, as the enlistments just then were too slow to supply the men who were needed. I went over the State, my wife going with me, visited the principal cities and villages, and often made two addresses a day, urging my countrymen to fill up the ranks. My speech in substance was: "Our fathers, with their blood, procured for us this beautiful heritage. Men now seek to destroy it. Come, fellow citizens, regardless of party, go back with me and fight for its preservation."

The quota of Maine was filled, and after an absence of two months and twenty days I returned to the field in time to participate in the closing operations of the second Bull Run campaign.

Military affairs during the summer of 1862, particularly the second battle of Bull Run, fought August 29th and 30th, excited virulent controversies which only subsided with the death of the participants. The ferment was by no means confined to the field.

Autobiography of Gen. O. O. Howard

By the help of his secret service bureau and his own strong will, Mr. Stanton, the Secretary of War, from the time he took the department, began to turn and overturn with a view to eliminate every disloyal element. As the abolition sentiment, constantly growing in the country, was evidently beginning to dominate public affairs, Mr. Stanton, penetrated with new convictions, hastened to leadership. We need only to follow him in the Cabinet, in Congress, in the committees of inquiry, and in every branch of military administration to account for a disturbing influence which had for some time been perceptible in military operations. This influence, more than Mr. Lincoln's apprehensions, kept up small armies, as Wadsworth's in defense of Washington, Fremont's toward the Ohio, Banks's and Shields's in the valley, and McDowell's at Fredericksburg—a division of forces that resulted in the defeat of them all, and perhaps, as McClellan claimed, in his own discomfiture on the peninsula. McClellan's Seven Days' Battles, in which he had repulsed the enemy each time, and yet changed his base to the James River, and his final retreat, all took place while I was absent from the army.

The administration now made a shift of policy. John Pope was brought from the Mississippi Valley and made the peer of McClellan, commanding all the armies above named except his. Halleck, under whom Grant, Pope, and others had won laurels in the Mississippi Valley, was called to Washington and assigned to duty as general-in-chief.

After this, Abraham Lincoln, endeavoring to follow, not lead, a changing public conviction, often lowered his head under the weight of heavy care. Once he said in his peculiar humorous sadness, when a case of plain justice to a soldier was hindered at the War Department: "We'll try; but, you see, I haven't much influence with this administration!"

He many times, however, took control when he was convinced that he ought to act.

After reaching Harrison's Landing, McClellan entreated to remain there, be reënforced, and go back again toward Richmond. The President at first favored this course. Pope, on his arrival from the West, had strongly opposed the change of base to the James. He predicted that every chance of mutual support would thus be lost to our Eastern armies. Concerning the Confederates, he said: "The loss of Richmond would be trifling, while the loss of Washington to us would be conclusive or nearly so in its results on this war!" This was before the Seven Days battling. After the retreat, Pope was more courteous to McClellan. He wrote him, seeking concert of action, and promised to carry out his wishes with all the means at his command.

It was a touch of human nature for McClellan to reply with reserve and some coldness; partisanship *pro* and *con* ran high at that time.

Halleck came to Washington ostensibly to make the Eastern armies cease maneuvering and fight. He determined that Pope should begin direct operations against Richmond; that McClellan, when brought back by water from the peninsula, should strongly reënforce him. Pope was to be bold, so as to free McClellan from pressure, and enable him to speedily transport his army to the Potomac. This McClellan did.

Pope promptly concentrated, bringing Fremont's army under Franz Sigel to Sperryville, Ricketts's division of McDowell's corps to Waterloo Bridge, and

Banks's command to Little Washington. His cavalry under General Hatch was kept well out toward the Rapidan. Pope's aggregate was then about 40,000 and well located for his undertaking.

Hearing that Stonewall Jackson was already crossing the Rapidan at different points, Pope ordered everything he could get to Culpeper. He would have hastened his army to the foothills of the Bull Run Range, that he might make a descent upon his foe, choosing his own time, but his orders from Halleck obliged him to protect the lower fords of the Rappahannock. Halleck thus insisted on his covering two independent bases: Falmouth, opposite Fredericksburg, and also Washington. It was a grave mistake. Pope's order of the 7th to Sigel to join him at once was not immediately obeyed. Pope says: " To my surprise I received, after night on the 8th, a note from General Sigel dated at Sperryville at half-past six o'clock that afternoon, asking me by what road he could march to Culpeper. As there was but one road, and that a broad stone turnpike, I was at a loss to understand how Sigel could entertain any doubt as to his road." Because of Sigel's delay Pope did not have his corps for the next day's battle. Another annoyance ruffled his temper. He sent Banks forward toward Cedar Mountain with all his force to join his own retiring cavalry and check the advancing foe. Banks was ordered to halt in a strong position designated, and send out his skirmish line and notify Pope. Ricketts's division was put at a crossroad in rear of Banks, with a view to help him in case of need.

But, strange to say, Banks, on approach of Stonewall Jackson, left his strong position, advanced two miles, and assailed the Confederates in a vigorous

258

manner. He had to cross open fields and was obliged to attack Jackson, who was just moving into a fine position for defense. The terrible struggle that resulted continued for an hour and a half. Against Jackson's leading divisions Banks was successful; but A. P. Hill's arriving drove Banks's men back little by little to the strong position which he had left. Ricketts's troops, ordered up by Pope, were only in time to prevent a retreat. Banks's defense was that a staff officer of General Pope had brought him subsequent instructions to attack at once as soon as the enemy came in sight. Pope's loss in this battle of Cedar Mountain was heavy: 1,759 killed and wounded, 622 missing. The Confederates' total loss was 1,314. Jackson gained a victory, though not as complete as he had hoped. Without renewing the conflict, he backed off slowly to the Rapidan. Jackson's advance had been for the purpose of defeating the portion of Pope's army reported isolated at Culpeper Court House.

A few days after this battle, Lee discovered our transports running from the James to Aquia Creek. Burnside with his command back from North Carolina was already at Fredericksburg.

Lee organized his troops into two wings—Longstreet to command the right, Jackson the left, and Stuart the cavalry, Lee himself taking the field in person. This force numbered between fifty and sixty thousand. Lee moved toward Pope, at first directly. Pope now had all of McDowell's corps and part of Burnside's. The rest of the latter was retained to guard the lower fords of the Rappahannock.

As soon as Lee began to advance in earnest, Pope drew back to the north side of the Rappahannock; placing Banks to keep his center near the railroad crossing. McDowell was designated to hold the left and lower crossings, and Sigel the right and upper, while the active cavalry now under Buford and Bayard took care of Pope's extreme right flank.

After a few skirmishes Lee began a turning operation. On August 22d, the day I reached Philadelphia on my way back to the army, Lee sent Stonewall Jackson, preceded by Stuart's cavalry, up the Rappahannock as far as Sulphur Springs, well beyond Pope's power to defend. Lee then, with Longstreet, followed slowly.

In the face of this strategic move, Pope decided to retire from the Rappahannock, but Halleck interposed and directed Pope to stay where he was two days longer and *he* would take care of his right, for was not McClellan's army coming in its strength? There was, fortunately for Pope, an unexpected help. Early's brigade only had crossed the river when a storm struck that up-country. The mountain streams poured in so rapidly that all fords were rendered unsafe and all bridges carried away.

Next, Pope aimed a blow at Early, Jackson's advance; but swollen streams delayed his eager march, so that Early, by Jackson's help, made a rough bridge and got back before the blow fell.

Lee gained some advantage during that freshet; he kept most of his troops quiet, cool, and resting, knowing that the streams in twenty-four hours would run down and be fordable.

Had Halleck allowed Pope to retire at once behind Warrenton, to meet there the reënforcements from McClellan, the problem of the campaign would have been of easier solution. But Lee's next move gave a sad lesson to Halleck. First came another of Stuart's raids. On August 23d, when I reached Washington, his cavalry was close by at Catlett's Station and our communications with Pope cut off. Stuart captured provisions, and carried off Pope's important orders. He then returned to Lee, the way he had come, with the detail of our plans in his possession. Lee acted quickly, making a bold move like that of Grant at Vicksburg, having on the face of it but few reasons in its favor. He ordered Stonewall Jackson, on August 25th, to cross the Rappahannock above Waterloo; move around Pope's right flank; strike the railroad in the rear; while Longstreet must divert his attention in front and be ready to follow.

Jackson made the march with great celerity, Stuart ahead and working his way to Gainesville, on the Manassas Gap railroad, and keeping the eyes of our cavalry upon himself. Jackson was at Salem the first night, and, bursting through Thoroughfare Gap, joined Stuart, and appeared on our railroad at Bristoe Station just after dark the next day. Without considering the fatigue of his troops, that night he sent Trimble's brigade with cavalry, ten miles up the railroad, to seize Manassas Junction. Very early the next morning Jackson himself was there with everything except Ewell's division—left at Bristoe for a guard against a rebound from any Union force below. The Manassas garrison, abundance of artillery, small arms, ammunition, and quantities of food fell at once into his hands. Our railroad guards and a Union brigade were driven back toward Alexandria, and Stuart's force continued on even to Burke's Station.

While Jackson thus delayed near Manassas, feasting on captured stores and destroying what he could not carry away, Ewell, at Bristoe, was not having so comfortable work. For Heintzelman's, with Hooker's and Kearny's divisions, coming from McClellan before Jackson's arrival at Bristoe, had passed beyond there by rail; and on the evening of the 25th they had been dumped down at Warrenton Junction. Porter's corps, too, marching west from Aquia Creek, was approaching the same point.

The instant Pope had found Jackson in his rear and upon his communications he turned his whole command north. His left, under McDowell, he sent to Gainesville; his center, under Heintzelman, to Greenwich, a few miles south of Gainesville, while he himself, leaving Hooker in command of the right, rushed on to reëstablish his connections with Washington. Sigel's corps was attached to McDowell, while Reno replaced Hooker with Heintzelman. That arrangement made Porter's approaching corps a strong reserve.

The afternoon of August 27th Hooker came upon Ewell's division at Bristoe. On sight, these veterans— veterans on both sides—had a sharp battle. Ewell was dislodged with a loss of 300 men and some of his *materiel*. But as he retired northward he burned the bridge over Broad Run and tore up the railroad track. While Hooker's men were restoring the bridge, Ewell made a rapid march and joined Jackson at Manassas.

In spite of the confusion here and there and the anxiety at Washington on the evening of August 27th matters could have hardly been better for Pope. There was the best ground for belief at his headquarters that Jackson and Longstreet were far asunder, and that Pope with at least 50,000 men would fall upon Jackson and defeat him.

Pope's sanguine heart was filled with joy at that

prospect. But how soon the change! The night of the 27th news came that A. P. Hill's division and part of Jackson's wing had got north of Centreville, and that Stuart had gone from Burke's Station also north to Fairfax Court House; true, Jackson himself with a few troops lingered at Manassas, but Pope believed that his adversary would try to escape him by passing over the mountains at Aldie Gap and turn back in the great valley beyond to join Longstreet. That was not, however, Jackson's purpose, but Pope under this misconception rashly issued a new set of orders.

With his Manassas force Jackson quickly moved to a strong position several miles west of Centreville, slightly north of Groveton. He placed his men behind a railroad cut; his line faced south and stretched off eastward to our old Sudley Spring crossing of Bull Run. How easy now for A. P. Hill to dillydally about Centreville, till our forces should rush that way via Manassas and touch his outposts, and then slip off via the upper crossings of Bull Run, and close in on Jackson in his new position. That ruse showed Jackson's generalship. He was adroitly giving Lee and Longstreet time to get near him before battle.

Phil Kearny's division, passing to the north of Manassas, soon skirmished with A. P. Hill's rear guard, while the latter was drawing off toward Sudley Springs and Jackson. Naturally, Kearny was not able to bring him to battle. King's division, of McDowell's corps, coming toward Centreville from Gainesville along the Warrenton Pike, unexpectedly encountered just at evening Confederate troops. A combat resulted. Gibbon's brigade, of King's division, supported by Doubleday's, with remarkable persistency resisted these assailants, the Confederates at once having attacked this intruding division. There was heavy loss on both sides. Ewell and Taliaferro were badly wounded, the former losing a leg. King's command remained two hours after the conflict and then went to Manassas. The end of this remarkable day found Pope with his headquarters at Centreville. He now saw plainly that he had been outgeneraled, having misinterpreted Jackson's purpose; in fact, he had helped Stonewall Jackson to concentrate his brigades, where Longstreet might join him.

Now, for Pope to get back his army from Centreville, from Manassas, and from wherever the night of the 28th found his hurrying troops, was not easy. It caused, indeed, much countermarching. Many men, short of food and ammunition and overfatigued with going from place to place on errands which they did not understand, had become discouraged.

But Pope resolutely gave new orders: the morning of August 29th, Heintzelman was turned again westward from Centreville; he led three divisions under Hooker, Kearny, and Reno toward Gainesville. Sigel's corps, on the Sudley road, south of Groveton, was faced northward and pushed forward toward Stonewall Jackson. McDowell with King's and Ricketts's divisions and Porter's corps was also ordered to come up to the left of Sigel.

Sigel deployed his troops as early as 5 A.M. and moved carefully and steadily forward. Soon a stubborn resistance came from Jackson's chosen position. It was a hard battle that day, begun differently from the first battle of Bull Run, but not far from that point. Sigel put in the divisions of Schurz, Schenck, Milroy, and Reynolds, and kept on firing and gaining ground till noon, when the ardent Kearny arrived.

Second Battle of Bull Run

By two o'clock Hooker and Reno also were on the ground.

Pope coming up rearranged the battle front; he placed Kearny's troops on his right, Reynolds's on his left, with Hooker's and Reno's at the center, and then made a reserve. There was irregular fighting till about 4.30, when a desperate attack was made. Kearny and Hooker got nearer and nearer, firing and advancing, till it appeared as though the railway cut and embankment of Jackson would certainly be taken by their repeated charges.

McDowell and Porter, quite early, marching from the east had come upon a stubborn skirmish line; the former left Porter to watch this resistance, whatever it was, and bore off with King's and Ricketts's divisions to the right and formed a solid junction with Pope's front.

Judging from Pope's orders of 4.30 P.M., he did expect Porter to attack Jackson's right. However, according to the weight of testimony now extant, Longstreet's large command had already joined Jackson's right when the order of Pope to General Porter was issued.

Owing to all the unhappy circumstances of this and the day previous, August 29th ended this prolonged contest in a drawn battle.

During the anxious night which ensued, from various circumstances which influenced the mind of a commander, Pope received the impression that Lee was retiring; but, strange to tell, Lee and Pope were both preparing to advance and take the offensive.

Porter's command was at last drawn forward to the main army, and on the 30th his men went into action, side by side, with the rest. It was a stormy fight, bad enough for us, because Stuart and Longstreet were able to envelop Pope's left flank, and they pressed our army back to the same old ground of the first Bull Run. There was a constant change of front; our best troops held woods, ravines, knolls, and buildings with unwonted tenacity. But we were undoubtedly defeated; at dark Lee held the fields which were covered with the dead and wounded; yet our lines were not broken up, and we still stuck to the Warrenton Pike. During the darkness of the night, by using that highway and such other roads south as he wished, Pope slowly drew back his command to the heights of Centreville.

During these exciting operations I was an observer from different places. August 23d I went in the afternoon to Halleck's private dwelling in Washington, and waited half an hour for him to finish his nap. At last he stood in the doorway of his reception room, and, looking at me sternly, as if I had committed some grave offense, said: " Do you want to see me officially, sir?" Being taken aback by his manner I stammered: "Partly officially and partly not." "Well, sir, what is it?"

With no little vexation I told him that I had been wounded at Fair Oaks, but was now sufficiently recovered for duty, and that I wished to find my command. Without relaxing his coldness or offering me the least civility he replied: " The adjutant general will tell you that, sir." I bowed and said: " Good day, sir," and instantly left his house. I was afterwards assured that this uncalled-for treatment was not intended for insult or discipline, but was rather the way Halleck behaved after great perplexity and trial.

By August 27th I had found my way to Sumner's corps, then at Falmouth. Stern as he was by nature and habit, he received me kindly; gave me a seat at his mess table, and Colonel Taylor, his adjutant general, surrendered to me his own bed for the night.

My old brigade gave me every demonstration of affection; but thinking that I would never return to the army, Sumner had caused General Caldwell to be assigned to it. He quickly offered me another brigade in Sedgwick's division. General Burns, its commander, wounded at Savage Station, was away, and I was put in his place. It was the " California brigade " of Colonel Baker, who fell at Ball's Bluff.

On the 28th Sumner's corps was moved up to 'Alexandria and went into camp in front of that city near the Centreville Pike, where we had early news of Jackson's raid and shared the capital's excitement over that event.

Toward the evening of the 29th, when so many of our comrades were falling on the plains of Manassas, General Halleck ordered our corps to march to a place four or five miles above to Chain Bridge, on the Potomac, to anticipate a raid of Stuart.

We made all possible speed, but were hardly there when peremptory orders sent us back in haste to Alexandria, and then, at last, out to Centreville. By forced marches, moving night and day, and following Franklin's corps as soon as we reached the Pike, we arrived on the heights at noon of the 31st. We met Pope's overworked army there and, fatigued as we were, cheered our companions by our comparative freshness. Just to the north of the other troops, between there and the supposed position of Lee, we went into bivouac.

To my satisfaction I was selected the next morning

to conduct a reconnoissance in force still farther north, to find if Lee were there and report. Besides my brigade I had some cavalry. Covered with a good body of skirmishers, we marched rapidly till we aroused Lee's pickets. They gave way; then we came in sight of his skirmishers, who opened fire upon us at once. When we had pressed them more closely we succeeded in drawing the fire of their noisy batteries. My purpose was now gained, and I fell back slowly and steadily to my place in the general lines. We had found that Lee's army, or a part of it, was out on the Little River Turnpike between Aldie and Fairfax Court House. On that pike, somewhat east of the point to which I had pushed out, was the small hamlet of Chantilly. While I was reconnoitering, Stonewall Jackson, cautiously feeling his way eastward to gain Pope's rear and cut his communications near Fairfax Court House, was advancing his command along that same turnpike. But this time Pope, having troops enough, had sent a wing in the same direction and so was ready to check the enterprising general.

Near a crossroad was an abrupt knoll named Ox Hill. This hill with a considerable ravine in front of it was already occupied by our troops, Reno's and Stevens's divisions, with Phil Kearny's near at hand. Hooker's had passed beyond, nearer to Fairfax. When, toward evening, Jackson came near Ox Hill, as usual, he promptly put his men into line of battle, and pushed forward. On our side Reno's division on the left held its ground and repelled every charge; General Stevens did the same for a while and then his soldiers began to give way, and he himself was killed. Then Reno's flank was uncovered and his right regiments had to break back. It was at this trying epoch of this battle that Kearny sprang to the rescue. Birney's brigade he caused to replace Stevens's troops, and the battle was renewed with fierce energy, while a heavy chilling rain poured down upon the combatants. Kearny, to see what more could be done at the right of Birney, as he had often done before, instead of sending another, rode his horse straight out toward his right front beyond his own men. He encountered Confederates. They fired upon him and he was instantly killed. Thus passed from the stage of action in that brief combat at Chantilly two officers of great ability and energy—Philip Kearny and Isaac I. Stevens. It was a serious loss to the Union cause.

Jackson was forced to halt, and Pope's line of communication became his line of withdrawal. Pope, doubtless with much chagrin, formed his retreating column, and marched back to the Potomac, retiring within the ample fortifications of our capital.

I had command of the rear guard; of that one of these columns which fell back toward the Chain Bridge. General Sumner gave me a detachment of all arms to do the work assigned. Who will forget the straggling, the mud, the rain, the terrible panic and loss of life from random firing, and the hopeless feeling—almost despair—of that dreadful night march! After passing Fairfax Court House we were not molested by the Confederates, yet the variety of experience of that march gave me lessons of great value for all my subsequent career. A most important one was to have, as I then had, a cool, courageous, and self-reliant officer, like Colonel Alfred Sully, in command of the last regiment. Another lesson was, in order successfully to cover a retreat in the night, a degree of discipline for cavalry, infantry, and artillery is required beyond that needed at any other time. A third, which is always necessary, but there impressed me as indispensable, was for the rear-guard commander to have a well-instructed, reliable, indefatigable staff.

CHAPTER XVIII

THE BATTLE OF SOUTH MOUNTAIN

COULD the reader have seen with Mr. Lincoln's eyes—sad, earnest, deep, penetrating as they were—the condition of the Republic on September 2d and 3d, when the Union army with broken ranks and haggard looks came straggling and discouraged to the protection of the encircling forts of Washington, he would have realized the crisis. Divisions in council—envy and accusation among military leaders, unsatisfied ambition struggling for the ascendency—waves of terror gathering force as they rolled from Washington through Maryland and Pennsylvania northward—a triumphant, hostile army, well organized, well officered, and great in numbers, under a chief of acknowledged character and ability, within twenty miles of the capital—these served to blow the crackling embers, and fan the consuming flame.

But Abraham Lincoln, who cried to God for strength, was equal to this emergency. He brought Halleck over to his mind. He checked the secret and open work of his ministers which he deemed too abrupt; he silenced the croakings of the war committees of Congress; he stirred all truly loyal hearts by cogent appeals to send forward men and money; he buried his personal preferences and called back McClellan, his former though fretful lieutenant. from the position of

271

helplessness and semidisgrace to which he had recently
been consigned by having his army turned over to
Pope piecemeal. He gave McClellan command of all
the scattered forces then in and around the District
of Columbia. A vein of confidence in McClellan as a
safe leader ran through the forces—in fact, just the
commander for that tumultous epoch, and Mr. Lincoln's good judgment was sustained by the army.

McClellan accepted the trust without remonstrance
and without condition, and at once went to work. He
refitted and reorganized, moving each division with
caution by short marches northward; and this time he
made proper provision for the defense of Washington.
Slowness was wise then.

It gave proper supplies. It arranged order, which
soon replaced an unparalleled confusion and brought
cheerfulness and hopefulness to us all. Hooker became commander of McDowell's old First Corps.
Sumner retained the Second. One division of the
Fourth Corps was present under Couch. Porter still
had the Fifth, and Franklin the Sixth. The Ninth was
commanded by General Cox after Reno's death. The
Twelfth Corps was commanded by General Mansfield;
the cavalry by Alfred Pleasonton.

After Chantilly, Lee, whom we left in force not far
from Centreville, after one day's delay for rest and re-
fitting, marched to Leesburg, near the Potomac, in
Northwestern Virginia. He was beginning an invasion of Maryland and Pennsylvania, for he could there
obtain more supplies than Virginia, denuded by the
war, could furnish. Such a movement also transferred
the theater of the war beyond the borders of the Confederacy. Confederate hopes were based on Maryland. Would not a victory on her soil aid her down-

272

trodden and oppressed people to set themselves forever free from Northern domination?

By September 7th the Confederate army had crossed the Potomac above us at different fords between Poolesville and Point of Rocks and bivouacked in the neighborhood of Frederick City, Md. The Confederate political leaders were disappointed with Maryland. It was too late for a few fire eaters to carry by storm the hearts of the Union Marylanders. So Lee, though in a slave State abundant in resources, with here and there a sympathizing family, found himself virtually in a land of lukewarm attachments to his cause. But few recruits joined him. The Confederate currency was not willingly received as money. The stars and bars flying over some of the public buildings gave the people no satisfaction. General Lee, though aided and encouraged by a few secession citizens, soon ceased his futile efforts, and gave his attention to the military problems before him.

Harper's Ferry, with an outpost at Martinsburg, eighteen miles to the west, was commanded by a veteran Union officer of the regular army, Colonel Dixon S. Miles. He had under his authority about 13,000 men, including artillery and cavalry, while General Julius White had a small force at Martinsburg.

The Confederates, after crossing the Potomac, below Harper's Ferry, had completely turned Miles's position. McClellan then asked Halleck to have Miles move from Harper's Ferry up the Cumberland Valley. Halleck being unwilling, for he had much wrongheadedness concerning that historic place, McClellan then requested the withdrawal of Miles to Maryland Heights; but even this was denied him.

At this time the Potomac, between Harper's Ferry

and Maryland Heights, was not too deep to ford. The country is rugged, and the Shenandoah entering the Potomac there from the south makes with it a right angle. The two rivers after confluence break through the mountain chain and roll on eastward. Between this increased torrent and the Shenandoah are Loudon Heights. Crossing from the Maryland side the village of Harper's Ferry is on a lower level than any of its environment. The old armory and its dependencies were already in 1862 in ruins, and there was little else there. A well-pronounced ridge called Bolivar Heights, two miles out toward the southwest, extended from the upper Potomac to the Shenandoah. To an unpracticed eye these heights signified a line of defense. Colonel Dixon Miles, not realizing how completely Loudon and Maryland Heights commanded every nook and corner of his position, remained at Harper's Ferry to defend it.

By September 12th our Army of the Potomac, well in hand, had worked its way northward to Frederick City.

Lee, after he was north of the Potomac, had pushed off westward, crossing the Catoctin Range, seizing and occupying the passes of the South Mountain, with the intention to take Harper's Ferry in reverse and pick up the garrison of Martinsburg, that he might have via the Shenandoah clear communications with Richmond, and gain the prestige of these small victories, while he was making ready to defeat McClellan's large army. All the while this rich region of Maryland gave him abundant supplies of animals and flour. From the mountain passes Stuart's cavalry was watching our slow and steady approach.

On the 13th inference and conjecture became a certainty. D. H. Hill lost one copy of Lee's order of march and it was brought to McClellan. That order sent Stonewall Jackson west from Frederick City, through Middletown, to recross the Potomac near Sharpsburg,, choke the Baltimore & Ohio Railroad, capture Julius White at Martinsburg, and then close in on Harper's Ferry, and be sure not to permit the Union troops of Colonel Miles to escape west or north. McLaws, adding Anderson's division to his own, was to branch off southward from the Middletown road and, keeping north of the Potomac, hasten to seize and hold Maryland Heights, and thus to do his part in capturing Harper's Ferry; while Longstreet would halt at Boonsboro, west of South Mountain, and delay our westward march. To make assurance doubly sure Lee sent Walker's division to hurry south to Cheek's Ford, cross the Potomac there, and turn back by Lovettsville, Va., and seize Loudon Heights. Lee kept the new division of D. H. Hill for his rear guard, to be gradually drawn in till it should join Longstreet at Boonsboro.

These instructions of the Confederate leader were plain. They were dated September 9th, and their execution began the morning of the 10th. Three days and a part of another passed before McClellan had in his hand the hostile plan; he was three days too late for its prevention; yet if our troops at Harper's Ferry could make a reasonably successful defense, two important things might follow: First, Lee might be caught, as was McClellan on the Chickahominy, with an army worse divided, and be overwhelmed in detail; and second, the Harper's Ferry force might be saved.

This view of the situation became current among us; the hope of officers and men was an inspiration as

275

our columns marched off. The soldiers pressed forward eager to fulfill their new instructions.

Stonewall Jackson, having good roads, quickly led his noted marchers from Middletown to Williamsport, and September 11th crossed the Potomac into Virginia. Getting wind of this, General White during that night withdrew from Martinsburg to Harper's Ferry, but did not assume command over Dixon Miles. Early on the 13th Jackson encamped just beyond the range of Bolivar Heights, near the village of Halltown, in full view of Miles's skirmishers.

Our Colonel Ford, of the Thirty-third Ohio, with a brigade was across the river on Maryland Heights. McLaws drove in Ford's farthest outpost the evening of the 11th, and on the 13th deployed his command for severer battle.

Colonel Ford gave up, with practically no fight at all, the vital point—the very citadel of Harper's Ferry —spiked his four cannon, and crossed the river to swell the force already there. His alleged excuse was that his own regiment refused to fight.

The Confederate division under Walker had performed its part. The morning of the 13th found them at the base of Loudon Heights; a few hours later cannon, supported by sufficient infantry, had crowned that convenient mountain. Before night Walker had concerted with McLaws and closed up every eastward escape on the Potomac.

At sunset of the 13th Miles's garrison was completely invested. The whole story of the defense is a sad one—more than 13,000 of as good troops as we had were forced to surrender.

One would have thought that any army officer, one even as feeble as Dixons Miles, would have placed his strongest garrison on Maryland Heights and defended it to the last extremity; and, indeed, while he ventured to remain at Harper's Ferry, how could he have failed to fortify Loudon Mountain and hold its summit and nearer base? Had this been done there would have been some reason for facing Jackson along the Bolivar Ridge.

Sunday evening my friend and classmate, Colonel B. F. Davis, had obtained Colonel Miles's permission, and with 1,500 Union cavalry forded the Potomac and passed off northward. He captured some of Longstreet's wagons on the Maryland shore, made a few prisoners, and, avoiding the Confederate columns, joined McClellan, the 16th, at Antietam.

The Army of the Potomac was still *en route* westward toward Lee. On September 13th McClellan simplified his organization. The right wing was assigned to Burnside, the left to Franklin, and the center to Sumner. Burnside had two corps — Hooker's and Reno's; Franklin two—his own and Porter's; Sumner two—his own and Mansfield's. As each corps commander had three divisions, except Mansfield and Porter, who had two each, there were sixteen divisions, giving forty-seven brigades of infantry, the brigades averaging 1,800 strong.

Our cavalry division then counted five brigades of cavalry and four batteries. We had, all told, some forty batteries of artillery generally distributed to the divisions for care and support in action.

Franklin with the left wing was sent from his camp south of Frederick City, the 14th, past Burkittsville, and on through Crampton Pass into Pleasant Valley, aiming for Maryland Heights. Three requirements were named: To gain the pass, cut off, destroy or capture McLaws's command and relieve Miles. "I ask of you," McClellan added, "at this important moment all your intellect and the utmost captivity that a general can exercise."

Skirmishing began with the enemy before reaching Burkittsville, and Franklin's men swept on, driving the Confederate pickets up the mountain defile until his advance came upon a force of Confederate artillery well posted.

General Howell Cobb, of Georgia, was left back by McLaws to defend this defile. It was a strong position; but Franklin came on with vigor and carried the first position by storm.

Cobb and his main force fell back, ran hastily to the top of the ridge, and there made another stand.

Our men after rectifying their lines followed on over rough ground on both sides of the narrow road till they approached the summit. The crest was soon carried and Franklin warmly congratulated his men for their sturdiness. He took one piece of artillery and three Confederate flags. Of our men 110 were killed and 420 wounded, while Franklin buried 150 Confederate dead and held 300 as his prisoners.

Franklin camped in Pleasant Valley the night of September 14th, only five miles from Maryland Heights. Had that position not been deserted, Franklin could have drawn off the garrison at Harper's Ferry from the grasp of Jackson. Of course, Franklin was disappointed by Miles's surrender and McClellan chagrined, yet they had done their best.

In our march to attack Lee's divided forces my small brigade belonged to the center in Sedgwick's division. We pushed our way northward a few miles up the valley just east of the South Mountain, and skirmished with Stuart's watching force, backing up our own cavalry in that direction.

Meanwhile, Burnside's wing, followed by the remainder of Sumner's forces, hurried straight forward to Turner's Gap on the direct road from Frederick to Hagerstown. This part of the South Mountain is a mountain indeed, much wooded, very rugged, and steep. The National road leads from one side straight up through the natural depression, which is named Turner's Gap. A road to the right, called the old Hagerstown road, after leading to the north, comes back into the National road at the summit. Another highway crosses the mountain a mile or so to the south of the National road, and is called the old Sharpsburg road. Should we ascend by the one to the right of the turnpike, we would wind around a spur and find a small valley between this spur and the main ridge. This valley was occupied by the enemy. The Confederates found a crossroad near the crest. Along this crossroad D. H. Hill arranged his brigades. Both to the north and south of the National road fine locations for cannon were selected and occupied by him. Some were placed so as to sweep a high point well to the north, rather too commanding to admit of possession by an enemy. This, a sort of peak, every engineer called the key of the position. From it two distinct mountain crests coursed off southward for a mile or more with hardly a break. These crests protected the little summit valley and D. H. Hill's Confederates held them.

The evening of the 13th Pleasonton followed Stuart to the mouth of the gap. Feeling instinctively that the Confederates would occupy and defend such a defile he dismounted half of his men and sent them up the *old* Hagerstown road. They were soon stopped by a heavy fire. That night Pleasonton contented himself with reconnoissances for information. Early, the 14th, Burnside having sent him an infantry brigade he so located a battery as to cover an advance, and sent the brigade up the National road. It had just started when Cox, the division commander, arrived with another brigade and pushed it on to help the other. They made a lodgment near the top of the mountain to the left of the National road. General Cox now brought up artillery and two brigades to the points gained, when Garland's successor commanding that part of the Confederate field undertook by desperate charging and rapid firing to regain the important crest. But he could not. During the first part of the engagement when our men cleared the crest and made the first break, General Garland lost his life. D. H. Hill denounced that success of Cox as a failure, because it did not secure the extensive crossroad behind him, and he gave the credit of its defense to Garland, alleging that " this brilliant service cost us the life of that grand, accomplished, Christian soldier."

The battle thus far had consumed five hours; there came then, as is usual, a mutual cessation from strife —a sort of tacit understanding that there would be some artillery practice and skirmishing only while each party was getting ready to renew the conflict.

Meanwhile, Rosser had come to replace Garland, and several Confederate brigades had been brought up and located for a rush forward, or for an effectual defense.

On our side Reno's division had closed up to Willcox's, Sturgis's, and Rodman's divisions.

The men of the South, possessed of American grit, were wont to exhibit all the *elan* of the French in action. They were ready sooner than Reno and charged furiously upon our strengthened line, aiming their heaviest blows against our right, upon which they had brought to bear plenty of cannon. Though not at first prepared to go forward, Reno's men stood firmly to their line of defense. At last, not being satisfied with this, though volley had met volley, and cannon answered cannon, Reno ordered his whole line to advance. These orders were instantly obeyed and the forward movement started with enthusiasm. Our charge, however, was checked here and there by countercharges, the Confederates putting forward desperate efforts to break and hold back the advancing line. After all, at dark, it seemed but a drawn battle to those in immediate contention on this front. While examining his new line, General Jesse L. Reno was killed. Reno was one of our ablest and most promising commanders. D. H. Hill's comment, considering his passion, was a compliment, when he said: " The Yankees lost on their side General Reno, a renegade Virginian, who was killed by a happy shot from the Twenty-third North Carolina."

As Reno was never a secessionist, and as he was always true to the flag of his country, to which several times he swore allegiance, no stretch of language could truthfully brand him as a deserter. He was a true man, like such other Virginians as Craighill, Robert Williams, John Newton, George H. Thomas, and Farragut.

The most decisive work was on another front. Hooker was at the head of his corps. McClellan in person gave him orders on the field to press up the old Hagerstown road to the right and make a diversion in aid of Reno's attack. That movement was undertaken

281

without delay. Hooker's corps took on this formation: Meade's division to the right, Hatch's to the left; Ricketts's in the center a little back in reserve.

Pleasonton sent two regiments of cavalry to watch the flanks. Naturally expecting slow progress from Reno, Hooker thought the best diversion would be an immediate assault on whatever was before or near him.

The high peak before named, the key of the field, did not appear to be strongly occupied by Confederates; there was a battery discovered and thin lines to sweep the height, but that was all that was apparent. So Meade and Hatch with their deployed lines went forward as fast as men could in climbing such a rough mountain. They soon encountered an enemy; probably at first there were but three opposing brigades and a few pieces of artillery, but the resistance increased. It was a rugged place where the Confederates could and did take advantage of every obstacle to disable or hold back Hooker's soldiers.

Longstreet, hastening up from Boonsboro, was ascending the mountain about this time. His brigades, as they came to the western crest, weary though they were from the march, were rushed into position and into hot battle; but our Ricketts dispatched thither a brigade which, by a prompt change of front, stopped that danger, while Meade had the satisfaction of crowning the desired peak. That key was taken and batteries drawn up before sundown. To cover the guns by barricades and arrange them to enfilade the two crests, artillerymen were not slow to accomplish. They saw at once that they had a plunging fire upon the little mountain valley.

Meade had the summit peak, but lest it be retaken, Hatch, to his left, struggled over the uneven ground through the forest, fighting his way forward. He was so hard pressed that Hooker sent him a brigade from Ricketts to thicken his lines. This help came when most needed; but while Hatch during the rain of bullets was riding along and encouraging his soldiers to charge and take a fence line held by the enemy, he himself was severely wounded by a shot from behind that fence. Doubleday then took Hatch's place while the firing was still frequent and troublesome. He tried a ruse: he caused his men to cease firing. The Confederates, thinking they had cleared their front, sprang forward a few paces to receive from Doubleday's ambush a sweeping volley—this broke up their alignments and they were chased back from the battle ground. The woods which Meade and Doubleday had fought through, the minor combats continuing in the darkness of the night, resounded with the cries of wounded and dying men; while the many dead, especially on Hatch's route, at dawn of the next day, showed the severity of the struggle.

Burnside had detached General John Gibbon from Hooker to keep up a connection with Reno, but near night Gibbon was sent up the National road. He kept a battery in the road well forward. The Confederates from their crest began to fire as they got glimpses of this bold move both upon the brigade and the battery. But Gibbon's men by strengthening their skirmishers and steadily moving on pushed everything before them; they ran from tree to tree, or rock to rock, till the battery thus covered by them had worked ahead enough to be effective. Then Gibbon's battery began its discharges straight upon the Confederate guns, which had hitherto annoyed his march. By its effective help the battery aided the regiments abreast of it to stretch out into lines as good and regular as the ragged, rocky slope would permit. The men, taking a fresh impulse, clambered up over the rocks, driving their enemies—two regiments of them—from woods, crags, and stone fences. The two Confederate regiments were then helped by three more, and our men were clogged for a time. But Gibbon in the end secured the gorge and slept on his battlefield.

I came to the scene of the conflict near the close of the contest. The triumph was evident and welcome, but much tempered by our severe losses and by the presence of the wounded men who with fortitude were suppressing the evidences of pain. Burnside was riding around among his troops. They generally looked pleased and hopeful, but very weary. They did not cheer.

About midnight Hill and Longstreet had drawn off their commands, leaving their dead and severely wounded in our hands. The Confederates had here the advantage of position, of course. We put more men than they into action. We lost 325 killed and 1,403 wounded and 85 missing. The Confederate loss was about the same as ours in killed and wounded. We took 1,500 prisoners. In spite of the Harper's Ferry disaster our army took heart again, on account of our victory in the battle of South Mountain, and reposed confidence in McClellan.

The spot where Reno fell is marked by a stone monument, erected to his memory by Daniel Wise. Friends and foes in that beautiful mountain valley fell asleep together. Would that they awake in the likeness of the Man of Peace!

Very early in the morning of the 15th our division passed the troops of Reno and Hooker, and pressed forward down the western slopes of South Mountain, through Boonsboro in pursuit.

As we descended the mountain road thus early, I could see little puffs of smoke from many rifles and sudden clouds rolling up from cannon, yet, strange to say, could hear no sound. The air was very clear, and the distance greater than it appeared. Our own division's advance brigade and Pleasonton's cavalry were skirmishing with Lee's rear guard.

CHAPTER XIX

THE two columns of the Army of the Potomac, fighting their way through Turner's Gap and Crampton Pass and pressing their pursuit of Lee, debouched into the valley west of the mountains; one appeared at Boonsboro and the other southward at Rohrersville. The stretch of valley from Boonsboro to the Potomac is named the Antietam Valley, because the Antietam, a small river which runs near Hagerstown and a little east of Sharpsburg, enters the Potomac a few miles below. The general course of this crooked stream is south.

September 15th, the day after the defeat at Turner's Gap, Lee rapidly gathered his material and troops upon the peninsula which is formed by the Antietam and the Potomac. The bends of the Potomac cause the intercepted space to be broadened here and there, yet, higher upstream, the neck of the peninsula is scarcely two miles across. The country around Sharpsburg is fertile and beautiful and afforded Lee special advantages as a position in which to halt and stand on the defensive till he could gather in his several scattered columns.

A main road, the Sharpsburg Pike, coming across the Potomac at Shepherdstown where there was a good ford, ran northeast through Sharpsburg, crossed the Antietam by a stone bridge, and kept on through Boonsboro. Another, the Hagerstown Pike, divided the peninsula by a north and south trend. One other important highway divided the southeast angle of the other two bisecting roads; from Sharpsburg, as an apex, this road crossed the Antietam at Burnside's bridge and forked when it reached higher ground; the upper fork led to Rohrersville and the other ran south into the Harper's Ferry road. A few miles above the regular crossing was a zigzag country road —sometimes named " the diagonal." It intersected the Antietam at Newkirk and passed from pike to pike.

As the Antietam River, from Newkirk to its mouth, had steep banks and scarcely any practicable fords, it was to Lee just the obstacle he needed to cover his front.

He located D. H. Hill and Longstreet on the right and left of the main pike, while he sent off Hood's division to the left. The convenient curves of the Potomac would protect his flanks as soon as he had men enough to fill the space. At first he did not have more than 25,000 men on the ground; but with considerable artillery he was able to so arrange his batteries as to defend the bridges and cover all approaches from the Antietam to Sharpsburg. In fact, he had a surplus of cannon and so sent an artillery reserve across the Potomac to protect the fords in his rear. He found for his use in that uneven country rocky heights, favorable ravines, deep-cut roads, abundant fences of rail and stone, buildings, and well-located strips of woodland.

Dunker Chapel was near a hotly contested spot, being equidistant from Newkirk Bridge, the Potomac upper bend, and Sharpsburg. It was quite enveloped

287

by a small forest that stretched off for a half mile toward the Potomac. People called this forest "the Dunker Woods." No prize of chivalry was ever more desperately contended for than this locality. East of the Hagerstown Pike, and still farther north near Dunbar's Mills, was a large, open grove called "the East Woods." That grove was the left of Lee's first temporary line.

McClellan, seeing that Franklin was detained by McLaws, who, having now the impregnable Maryland Heights, was able to avoid battle, ordered Franklin to Antietam. McLaws, quick to notice Franklin's departure, crossed the Potomac twice and reached Lee at Sharpsburg at the same hour that Franklin reported to McClellan.

The column to which I belonged pushed forward its head as rapidly as possible from Boonsboro to the east bank of the Antietam. During that first day, September 15th, only two divisions, Richardson's and Sykes's, drew sufficiently near to receive the enemy's fire.

Eager as McClellan was to engage Lee before Jackson and other detachments could get back to him, Lee's bold attitude and evident preparation forced him to wait, to reconnoiter and get up force enough to attack. Putting together the sickness and discouragements that followed our second Bull Run and the Harper's Ferry disaster, nobody will wonder that our army had many stragglers between Washington and the Antietam. Even our moderate successes at South Mountain produced much additional weariness and wilfulness with some indifference and slowness on the part of certain officers holding important commands. These suggestions account for unusual delays in the marches

288

which McClellan had ordered, as well as for the comparatively small force assembled as late as the morning of the 16th to take the offensive. McClellan had hoped for a prompt attack on overtaking Lee, certainly by nine o'clock of the 16th. But, coming forward himself to the front, he did not order an immediate assault. He could not at first get Burnside with his left wing to understand or execute what he wished. His own information was too incomplete. He had word that Jackson was already returned to Lee, so that there was no longer need of precipitation. Later, he found that McLaws did not join the main army till the morning of the 17th, Anderson's division afterwards; and A. P. Hill's, left at Harper's Ferry to finish the work there, was still later on the ground. From want of previous knowledge and from a natural desire that Franklin and Couch should close up to swell his numbers, McClellan delayed action till late in the afternoon of the 16th.

Hooker's corps, Mansfield's in support, and then Sumner's, were destined for the right column. Burnside's command, consisting of four divisions with plenty of artillery to help him, was given the work of storming the lower stone bridge which now bears his name. Porter's or Franklin's troops, or such as could be brought up in time from Pleasant Valley, were to be held in hand for necessary reënforcement or for the direct central thrust, whenever that should become practicable.

The first movement in the way of executing the plan had to begin in plain sight of our watching foes. They understood it from the start. About 4 P.M. Hooker's divisions, having previously worked far up the Antietam, passed over that stream by a bridge and ford west

289

of Keedysville, crossings having been early secured and held for them by our cavalry. General Hooker led his corps, evidently with a hope of completely turning Lee's left, far away past Dunbar Mills. Doubleday's division was in advance. He had proceeded, perhaps, a couple of miles from the bridge and ford north-westerly when the enemy's skirmishers opened fire. Hooker at once faced his command to the left and deployed his lines. The Pennsylvania reserves under Meade formed the center, Doubleday's to the right, and Ricketts's division to the left of Meade.

Hood's division of Confederates with assisting batteries held the " East Woods " and was *vis-a-vis* to Hooker. D. H. Hill extended Hood's line down toward the Antietam. Jackson's two divisions, Lawton's and J. R. Jones's, were by this time holding the " West Woods " about Dunker Church. Stuart with cavalry and considerable artillery was farther west than Hood.

Without hesitation the Pennsylvania reserves pressed the enemy and opened a brisk fusillade which was returned with equal spirit. There was considerable musketry that evening and some artillery exchanges with apparent success to Hooker. About ten, Jackson, finding Hood's men overweary and hungry from a long fast, sent him two brigades and put in some fresh artillery, rectifying the lines as well as it could be done in the darkness of the night.

Hooker, sleepless at such a time, rearranged his batteries and their supports and had everything in order for an advance at the first glimmer of daylight.

Mansfield's supporting corps crossed the Antietam where Hooker did, but encamped through the night more than a mile in his rear; while our corps (Sumner's), intended also for the support of Hooker, was still far off near McClellan's center, bivouacking by the Boonsboro and Sharpsburg Turnpike and all the time within the reach of a disturbing artillery fire.

One fact quite impressed me there the evening of the 16th. General Sedgwick, always a warm friend of McClellan, and I were standing together and examining by help of our glasses Lee's position beyond the river, when an officer in charge of McClellan's headquarters' baggage train led his column of wagons to a pleasant spot on the slope, just behind us, in full view of our whole division. The enemy sent a few bursting shells into his neighborhood. This officer, much disturbed, quickly countermarched his train and hurried it off far out of range to the rear. It was done amid the jokes and laughter of our men. Sedgwick, seeing the move, shook his head and said solemnly: " I am sorry to see that ! "

McClellan himself did not go back that night; but the men thought that he did. Some of his staff never could understand how easily in times of danger the *morale* of an army may be injured.

For September 17th Sumner's orders were for him to *be ready to march* from camp one hour before daylight. We were ready on time, but McClellan's order of execution failed to reach us till 7.20 and then it embraced but two divisions, Sedgwick's and French's, Richardson's being detained to await Franklin's arrival. Immediately our division (Sedgwick's) moved off in good order to the upper crossings of the Antietam, marching at the rate of at least three miles an hour.

As soon as we had crossed the small river, by Sumner's arrangement we moved on in three parallel columns about seventy-five yards apart, Dana's brigade in the middle, mine to the right, and Gorman's to the left.

We pulled on rapidly in this shape till we came in sight of the Dunbar Mills and our columns extended through the "East Woods." Here every column faced to the left, making three brigade lines parallel to each other with Gorman's in front and mine in rear. We formed in an open space in which was a cornfield.

Promptly at the break of day the battle had begun. Hooker's six batteries had started a roar resounding like thunder, being answered by a quick though not so noisy response, which, but for the return projectiles, would have passed for an echo of Hooker's guns. Then, hoping that his cannon had sufficiently opened the way, Hooker had each division commander advance. Doubleday, the first, astride of the Hagerstown Turnpike, pressed forward in the grove as far as the crossroad. But at once he encountered a heavy fire from both artillery and infantry as if it had been all fixed for them. They did as troops usually do, delayed, stopped, and returned fire for fire with rapidity.

Meade, who had the heaviest force before him the night before, succeeded in making more progress than Doubleday, firing and advancing slowly.

Ricketts's division, supporting the batteries to the left of it and materially aided by their fire, gained even more ground than Meade. But soon there was surging to and fro. The forces engaged on the two sides were about equal, and the losses of men, killed and wounded in Hooker's corps, were startling. Ricketts's division alone exceeded a thousand, while Gibbon's small brigade counted nearly four hundred. The

Confederate losses were equally heavy, but our men did not then know that.

The depletion was so great that when there was at last not enough infantry to guard his battery, Gibbon ordered it to limber to the rear and retire. Soon he followed with his infantry on account of reduction of numbers and want of ammunition.

Hooker, however, persisted as usual, and, contrary to his first design, kept swinging to his own left and pressing forward. It had the effect to dislodge Jackson and D. H. Hill from their first line, and at last to force them through the cornfields and open spaces into the "West Woods."

In this severe work General Starke, having the "Stonewall" division, and Colonel Douglass, leading Lawton's brigade, were killed. Lawton himself and Walker, brigade commanders, were sadly wounded. At least half of the men whom Lawton and Hays led into battle were disabled. Trimble's brigade suffered nearly as much. All the regimental commanders, excepting two, were killed or wounded.

This is enough to indicate the nature and severity of the struggle for those vital points, the "East" and the "West Woods." About the time Ricketts's enterprise succeeded in seizing the edge of the woods near Dunker Church, Jackson brought in a fresh division and located it in those "West Woods." It was harder for Ricketts's men, for they had no such help. Stuart, the Confederate cavalry commander, had his batteries ready, and the instant Hooker's soldiers came into the open field brought a hurtful plunging fire to bear upon them.

There is no marvel in the fact that Hooker's fine divisions were already much broken before emerging into the open, and now were fearfully handled and must soon have gone to pieces; but just then, though too late for better results, the supports came on in time to prevent anything worse. Just as Hooker's opponents were taking the offensive and about to make a charge Mansfield, whom Hooker had urgently called for, appeared on the ground with his corps. It was then between seven and eight o'clock. Mansfield at first only reënforced Hooker's lines and enabled him to recover a portion of his front that he had lately lost; but the troops went forward only to come back again. Then the old general resolved to make a bold attack. He formed in semicircular order with Greene's division on the left and Williams's on the right. A brisk forward march was made like Hooker's of the early morning and met similar obstinacy. But under that impulsion the Confederates were forced to retire; they were losing heavily, and even Stonewall Jackson's command was driven beyond the Dunker Church, but the gallant Mansfield, with his snowy white hair, while urging his troops in that charge, fell from his horse mortally wounded.

About that period of the battle Lee, seeing little likelihood of McClellan's left under Burnside doing him much damage, almost stripped that quarter of troops. In fact, he left there only D. R. Jones and Toombs with thin lines and rushed the rest forward to his center and left. The distances were not great and the roads were good. In fact, the entire Confederate line did not exceed three miles in length and so curved on the upper flank as to be easily cared for. Hood, thus reënforced, now rested, and D. H. Hill, having all his available troops with the advance, made a strong charge against Mansfield's corps, which was not in good condition for defense, and which was at best but weakly supported by Hooker's tired and broken divisions.

This Confederate move, backed by the fresh troops and batteries well located to sweep our lines, soon succeeded in breaking up and disorganizing the whole front. The greater portion of our men of the two corps fell back to the "East Woods" or northward to a grove on the Hagerstown Turnpike. Hooker, badly wounded, had left the field; and the two division commanders, Hartsuff and Crawford, were disabled. What an hour before were fine regiments now appeared in the edge of the woods and behind trees like squads irregularly firing toward the enemy. The batteries that came with Mansfield's corps were left almost alone, yet, unsupported, had checked that last Confederate charge and prevented the enemy from crossing the open ground between the "East" and "West Woods."

General George S. Greene, a tenacious officer, had, with a part of his division, clung to the "West Woods" at a projection, and kept up for a time an effective firing.

This was the condition of affairs in that portion of the battlefield on our arrival. I saw abundant evidence of the preceding conflict, surely not very encouraging to men just coming upon the field. Too many were busying themselves in carrying their wounded comrades to the rear. Sumner sent a staff officer to find the places where Hooker's corps was to be found. He came upon General Ricketts, the only officer of rank left there, who declared that he couldn't raise 300 men of his corps for further work. While at nine o'clock Sumner with our division was preparing to take his turn in the battle, Lee, as we have seen, had already sent troops to watch him.

Without waiting for French's division, not yet near, or Richardson's, still at the distant bivouac, with an extraordinary confidence in our column of brigades and caring nothing for flanks, Sumner, with his gray hair streaming in the wind, rode to the leading brigade and ordered the advance. We broke through the cornfield; we charged over the open space and across the turnpike and forward well into the " West Woods " till Gorman's line encountered the enemy's sharp musketry fire. Then all halted. Our three lines, each in two ranks, were so near together that a rifle bullet would often cross them all and disable five or six men at a time. While Gorman's brigade was receiving and returning shots, the waiting brigades, Dana's and mine, naturally sought to protect themselves by taking advantage of the rocks, trees, and hollows, or by the old plan of lying down. While I could hear the whizzing of the balls, the woods being thick thereabouts, I could see no enemy. The first intimation which I had that neither Greene's division, which had held the projection of the woods, nor French's was covering our left flank, came from a visit of Sumner himself. He approached from the rear riding rapidly, having but two or three horsemen with him. The noise of the firing was confusing. He was without his hat and with his arms outstretched motioned violently. His orders were not then intelligible; but I judged that Sedgwick's left had been turned and immediately sent the necessary orders to protect my flank by changing the front of my brigade to the left. Those nearer to the general than I were confident that he said: " Howard, you must get out of here," or " Howard, you must face about! "

The Battle of Antietam

With troops that I had commanded longer I could have changed front, whatever Sumner said; but here, quicker than I can write the words, my men faced about and took the back track. Dana's line soon followed mine and then Gorman's. When we reached the open ground Sumner himself and every other officer of courage and nerve were exerting themselves to the utmost to rally the men, turn them back, and make head against the advancing enemy. But it was simply impossible till we had traversed those cleared fields; for we now had the enemy's infantry and artillery in rear and on our flank against our broken brigades, pelting us with their rapid and deadly volleys. That three-line advance had run Sedgwick's division into a trap well set and baited. Greene's spare command, hanging as we have seen to a projection or fragment of the "West Woods," was the bait, and Hill's brigades, already making for Greene, completely passed our left and sprung the trap. Sumner, too late, discovered Hill's effort. Sedgwick and Dana, badly wounded, left the field. The Second Division Second Corps then fell to me. It had good troops. Though losing heavily in our futile effort to change front before D. H. Hill, the division was speedily re-formed in the edge of the "East Woods" and gave a firm support to the numerous batteries which now fired again with wonderful rapidity and effect. We prevented all further disaster except the loss for the third time that day of those mysterious "West Woods."

I have a further picture. It is of a ravine in the "West Woods," where my own staff and that of General Burns sat upon their horses near me, just in rear of my waiting line, when the round shot were crashing through the trees and shells exploding rapidly over our heads, while the hissing rifle balls, swift as the wind, cut the leaves and branches like hail, and whizzed uncomfortably near our ears. Astonishing to tell, though exposed for an hour to a close musketry fire, though aids and orderlies were coming and going amid the shots, seemingly as thick as hail, not one individual of this group was hit.

Captain E. Whittlesey had taken the place of F. D. Sewall, then colonel of the Nineteenth Maine, as adjutant general of the brigade. He and my brother, Lieutenant Howard, badly wounded at Fair Oaks, had rejoined after the command left Washington. It was the first time I had seen Whittlesey under fire. He reminded me, as I observed him, of General Sykes, who, in action, never moved a muscle. The effect of this imperturbability on the part of a commander was wholesome. With a less stern countenance, but an equally strong will, Whittlesey was to me from that time the kind of help I needed in battle. Lieutenant Howard also, if he detected the least lack of coolness in me, would say quietly: "Aren't you a little excited?" This was enough to suppress any momentary nervousness.

The worst thing which resulted from our retreat that day was the effect upon General Sumner himself. He concluded that if such troops as composed Hooker's corps and Sedgwick's division could be so easily beaten any other vigorous effort in that part of the field would be useless.

Franklin's corps arrived from Pleasant Valley and reported to McClellan at 10 A.M. That was all, except Couch's attached division which Franklin had dispatched to Maryland Heights, which came to us the morning of the 18th.

The Battle of Antietam

Franklin soon sent his leading division under W. F. Smith to aid Sedgwick, but, like all other supports in this ill-managed battle, it was a little too late. The trap had been sprung already and we had been forced back from the "West Woods." Smith, to guard the batteries, deployed Hancock's brigade to our left. Hancock separated the protecting batteries and put regiments between them. I sent a regiment, the Twentieth Massachusetts, to help him support his right battery. The Confederates fired upon these new arrivals and were answered by the batteries. They ventured no farther, nor did we. General Smith sent Irwin's brigade to prolong Hancock's line leftward, while Sumner took Smith's other brigade to watch his extreme right, being apprehensive of some hostile countermove from that direction.

French, as we have seen, was not in sight when Sedgwick went into action. He formed his parallel columns as we did. Instead of keeping on in our track, when about a mile behind us he faced to the left and marched off toward that part of the enemy's position. He directed his march obliquely toward Roulette's house, making a large angle with Sedgwick's direction. He doubtless thought Greene occupied more space and would move to the front with us—a natural mistake. But a big gap was left. It took four or five batteries, besides Hancock's and Irwin's elongated lines, to fill the interval.

French's division marched briskly, driving in hostile skirmishers and engaging first heavy guns in chosen spots and then thicker musketry. The diagonal road which cuts both pikes and passes in front of Roulette's house is what the officers called the "sunken road." D. H. Hill filled a part of it with Confederate brigades; standing behind them were several batteries and the brigades of Rodes and Anderson in support. It was a well-chosen position for defense. Some of these troops had fought near Dunker's Church and had run back there after Sedgwick's discomfiture. Colonel Weber, commanding French's leading brigade to my left, now monopolized the fight. Soon his left was turned, while his front was hotly assailed. Kimball, seeing this, rushed his men up to clear Weber's exposed left and drove back the Confederate flankers, but they immediately ran to cover in the "sunken road" and there successfully defied his nearer approach. The hard contest here, varying in intensity from moment to moment, lasted three full hours and our men found quite impossible a decisive forward movement in that place.

French had upward of 2,000 men near there put *hors de combat.* Irwin's brigade of Smith's division, near Hancock, made one charge in the afternoon and went into those "West Woods," but then experienced the same trouble as the rest of us—it was striking in the dark; they also were forced to retreat.

Richardson's division after the arrival of Franklin was sent by McClellan to join our corps. After crossing the Antietam, Richardson directed his march on the Piper house, taking his cue from French's field, and soon was breasting the same deep roadway farther to the left. He did not attempt our formation but placed Meagher's brigade and Caldwell's abreast, Caldwell's on the left and Brooke's brigade considerably in the rear to watch his flanks. Thus he moved into close action. Once the Confederates were moving between Richardson and French, for there was free space enough. Brooke caught the glimmer of their rifles and

300

sent to his right a regiment to meet and stop them at the right moment.

Cross of the Fifth New Hampshire, aided by the Eighty-first Pennsylvania, did a like handsome thing for Caldwell's left flank. Cross in this successful move made a run for higher ground, while Brooke generously sent forward enough of his brigade to keep up Cross's connection with his proper front line. In these impulsive thrusts of subordinates, almost without orders, a part of that horrid " sunken road " was captured and passed, and Piper's house reached at last and held. Francis C. Barlow was given that day two regiments— the Sixty-first and Sixty-fourth New York. By quick maneuvering he caught and captured 300 prisoners in the deep road. General Richardson was mortally wounded near that place.

There was not much infantry engagement on our part of the field after one o'clock, but the artillery was unceasing all along the lines. Hancock was quickly sent to command Richardson's division. For one more trial Slocum's division under Franklin's instructions formed lines of attack. They made ready for another desperate charge through those " West Woods " and up to the Dunker Church. But Sumner just then hurried one of its brigades to the right and thus created a delay. In a few minutes after this Sumner took a fuller responsibility and ordered Franklin out again to attempt to carry those fatal woods.

Sumner shortly after this order to Franklin had planned a general advance. His adjutant general and aids had distributed the order to four corps, what were left of them, and had cavalry ready to help. All were to start simultaneously at a given signal. All were waiting—but there was an unexpected halt. Sumner

301

consulted with McClellan, and then concluded not to risk the offensive again, and so the work for September 17th for our center and right was substantially closed. Sumner's purpose and McClellan's plan for the early morning of this day, to have Hooker, Mansfield, Sumner, and, finally, Franklin go into battle in echelon by division from right to left as far as possible, was wise. We have seen how the scheme was marred simply in the execution. Hooker was exhausted before Mansfield began. Mansfield was displaced and had fallen when Sedgwick went singly into battle. I, replacing Sedgwick, was back on the defensive when French entered the lists far off to my left; while, in conjunction with French, Richardson alone touched the right spot at the right time. Franklin and the batteries were only in time and place to prevent disaster. Simultaneous action of divisions with a strong reserve would have won that portion of the field, but there was no simultaneous action.

Down by the Burnside bridge was a rise of ground on our side. The enemy there, after Lee had arranged his defense, consisted in the main of D. R. Jones's division and Toombs's brigade in support of abundant artillery. The guns, well placed, swept the road and other approaches. All the country behind them and to their left was favorable to prompt reënforcement. On our bank Burnside's officers of artillery posted a battery of twenty-pounder Parrotts and another of smaller guns, covering the highest knoll, hoping for unusual execution. Crook's brigade of Scammon's division stretched upstream to the right, with Sturgis's division formed in his rear. Rodman's division, with Hugh Ewing's brigade behind it, extended down the Antietam. Pleasonton, commanding and supporting by cavalry several batteries, together with Sykes's division of Porter's corps, held all the ground between Burnside and Richardson. Our Willcox's division and the reserve artillery were kept back for emergencies. There was only the Ninth Corps on the left. Burnside with Hooker away simply commanded Cox. The Ninth Corps that day had virtually two heads, Burnside and Cox. At 7 A.M. of the 17th McClellan ordered Burnside to prepare to assault and take the bridge, but, when ready, to wait for his word. The troops were put in place. Every good spot was occupied by favoring cannon. McClellan at eight o'clock sent the *word*. Why, nobody knows, but Burnside, standing with Cox, did not receive the order till nine o'clock. He then directed Cox to execute it. Cox went to the front to watch for results, and in person set Crook's brigade, backed up by Sturgis's division, to charge and see if they could not force a crossing. Two columns of four abreast were to rush over under the raking fire and then divide right and left. Meanwhile Rodman's division, forcing the ford below, must charge Toombs's Confederates out from behind a stone wall.

Crook got ready, covered his front with skirmishers, and pushed for the river, reaching it above the bridge. The fire of cannon and musketry from beyond was so worrisome that his men halted and that assault failed.

Next, after some delay, Cox tried Sturgis's division. The Sixth New Hampshire and the Second Maryland were each put into column. They charged, but the enemy's sweeping fire broke them up.

The Fifty-first New York and Fifty-first Pennsylvania were next arranged for a forlorn hope. To help

303

them one of our batteries tried fast firing. It created smoke and noise and sent screeching shells to occupy Confederate attention, while the rush was made. At last a part of our men were over.

Following this lead the troops of Sturgis and Crook passed the bridge, and driving the enemy back formed with speed in good order on the west bank.

Rodman had been led off by false or ignorant guides down the Antietam. After search and experiment he discovered a ford, successfully made his crossing and came up on the other bank as ordered. The daring work was done, but it had taken four good hours to accomplish it, so it was already one o'clock. The hard contest all along our line northward was then substantially over; thus Lee was able to reënforce against Cox, and further, A. P. Hill's Confederate division, *en route* from Harper's Ferry, was not far from Sharpsburg.

Again, as if to favor Lee, Burnside had further delay. The excessive firing before and after crossing the Antietam had exhausted the ammunition of the leading division, so that Burnside had to send over Willcox's command to make replacement, which consumed another precious hour. Considering that the Confederate D. R. Jones had kept rifle shots and shells flying against Cox's lines, it was a difficult business, after so long halting, to form and send forward attacking and charging brigades.

As soon as ready, urged by repeated orders brought by McClellan's staff officers and forwarded by Burnside from his rise of ground, Cox went forward. Willcox and Crook, carrying Jones's front, made for the village; but Rodman, to the left, was delayed by Toombs; and Cox had to meet a strong reenforcement of A. P. Hill's corps, which had just arrived.

Sturgis, however, seized a hostile battery and marched on through the town, while Crook was giving him good support. A victory seemed already gained, but it was not secure. Rodman's check, of course, created separation and weakness in Cox's corps. At that very juncture, A. P. Hill deployed more and more of his strong force before Sturgis and Crook and commenced firing and advancing rapidly. He first recaptured the Confederate battery just taken, and caused Cox's right to leave the village and the important vantage ground he had so happily obtained. Rodman's division was in this way doubly checkmated, and he, one of our best New England men, once under my command with the Fourth Rhode Island, was slain. His troops, thus defeated, fell back in haste.

Nearer the river Cox took up a strong defensive position, re-formed his corps, and prevented further disaster.

Lee's generalship at Antietam could not be surpassed; but while McClellan's plans were excellent, the tactical execution was bad. Had all of the right column been on the spot where the work was to begin, Sumner, seizing Stuart's heights by the Potomac, could have accomplished the purpose of his heart—to drive everything before him through the village of Sharpsburg and on to Burnside's front. Of course, Burnside's move should have been vigorous and simultaneous with attacks on the right. McClellan so intended. We had, however, a technical victory, for Lee withdrew after one day's delay and recrossed the Potomac. Porter's corps, following closely, lost heavily at the Shepherdstown ford—so that every part of our army except Couch's division, which after its late arrival was only exposed to artillery fire, suffered great loss at the battle of Antietam.

Longstreet says that Antietam was " the bloodiest single day of fighting of the war." The Confederate loss in Maryland was 12,601; while ours at Antietam alone, including prisoners, was 12,410.

While, with a view to avoid their mistakes in the future, we may study the *faults* and *omissions* of the brave men who here contended for the life of the Republic, let us not blame them, for there were often cogent reasons—hindrances and drawbacks which after many years no one can remember.

CHAPTER XX

THE night of September 17th my headquarters were near the " East Woods." I slept on the ground under a large tree. Just as I lay down I saw several small groups stretched out and covered with blankets, face and all. They appeared like soldiers sleeping together, two and two, and three and three, as they often did. In the morning as the sun was rising and lighting up the treetops, I arose, and, noticing my companions still asleep, observed them more closely. Seeing that they were very still, I approached the nearest group, and found they were cold in death. The lot fell to my division, with some other troops, to remain behind on the sad field and assist in burying the dead. The most troublesome thing, and that which affected our health, was the atmosphere that arose from the swollen bodies of the dead horses. We tried the experiment of piling rails and loose limbs of trees upon them and setting the heap on fire. This, however, for a time, made matters worse, as the dreadful stench appeared to be only increased in volume, and there being no strong wind, it settled in the valley of the Antietam.

The 22d, our sad and sickening task being done, the men of my division moved out toward Harper's Ferry, and quickly took up the swinging gait as they tramped along the hard roadway. As is usually the case after a military funeral, the quick march soon restored the spirits of the men. We crossed the Potomac and encamped with the remainder of our army corps on Bolivar Heights.

The main purpose which McClellan now had in view was to recruit his army, fill up the depleted regiments and batteries, and gather from the country, far and near, a sufficient number of horses to replace those killed in battle and worn out in service. The discouragements and homesickness that had attacked us at one time on the peninsula and at another time at Falmouth, had suddenly fallen upon Lee's army during the campaign. But on the Opequon, the thousands of half-sick, straying men, strolling along from Sharpsburg to Richmond, had been cheered and refreshed by the numerous zealous secession families along their route, so that soon the tide set back, and these, together with those who had recuperated from their wounds on previous fields, some 20,000 altogether, returned to give new heart and vigor to Lee's army.

In answer to McClellan's joyful dispatch, announcing that Maryland was entirely freed from the presence of the enemy, Halleck replied coldly: " We are still left entirely in the dark in regard to your own movements and those of the enemy."

McClellan, deeply chagrined that Halleck had no praise for our achievements, yet dispatched to him in detail with feeling the urgent wants of his army.

While such controversies were going on, from the battle of Antietam till October 26th, the main body of the army was located between Harper's Ferry and the mouth of the Monocacy. McClellan's headquarters were near Berlin. During our interval of rest I remember to have been placed upon courts of inquiry and upon courts-martial. One very interesting court on which I served was that demanded by General Caldwell, my successor after my wound and absence.

We looked into all the charges of misconduct and could find really nothing against this worthy officer.

About the same time, October 1st, President Lincoln came to see us. He was received everywhere with satisfaction, and at times with marked enthusiasm, as he reviewed the troops. At Harper's Ferry I saw him and heard him relate a few of his characteristic anecdotes. He noticed a small engine run out from the bridge, through the village of Harper's Ferry, below the bluff, which gave a peculiarly shrill and mournful whistle as its shadow fled rapidly around a hill and passed out of sight. Mr. Lincoln inquired what was the name of that little engine. When told the name, alluding to the panic and terror at the time of John Brown's visit to Harper's Ferry, he said that, in honor of the Virginians of that day, it might well have been named " The Skeered Virginian." He admired the horsemanship of Captain Whittlesey, and when some one said, " That officer was lately a parson," he looked pleasantly after him as he galloped off to carry some order, and remarked, as if to himself, " Parson? He looks more like a cavalier." Thus humorously, and with seldom a smile on his sad face, he moved around among us.

On October 6, 1862, after his return to Washington, President Lincoln directed our army to cross into Virginia and give battle to the enemy while the roads were good. He thought, as he always had before, that we might move along east of the Blue Ridge, and he promised a reënforcement of 30,000 men, provided this be done.

I had returned to the field, to encounter extraordinary excitement, exposure, and hardship, too soon after losing my arm; for just after the President's review I was taken ill with a slow fever; and, under medical advice, I obtained a twenty-days' sick leave and left Harper's Ferry for home. But by the time I reached Philadelphia my fever abated and my appetite returned—in fact, I was so thoroughly convalescent that I was almost disposed to turn back to the army, yet, judging by the past few weeks, I concluded that there would be no movement; so, to gather further strength from the change and the journey, I made a brief visit to my family in Maine, and then hastened back to my post. I reached Harper's Ferry November 5, 1862, about ten o'clock at night. My brigade surgeon, Dr. Palmer, being left behind in charge of the sick and wounded, gave welcome to Captain Whittlesey and myself, and kept us for the night.

The army had gone. McClellan had decided to take President Lincoln's suggestion and move east of the Blue Ridge.

On the morning of the 6th, with a borrowed horse and an old ambulance, Whittlesey and I crossed the Shenandoah and pulled on with all the speed we could command after the army. We rode up the Catoctin Valley over an unguarded road. From the poor condition of our horse we had to be satisfied with thirty-five miles the first day. The next day, the 7th, getting an early start, we made Rectortown by 11 A.M. Owing to a severe snowstorm, that portion of the army near Rectortown and the general headquarters did not stir. Immediately upon my arrival I visited General Mc-

Clellan; found him and his adjutant general, Seth Williams, together in a comfortable tent. From them I received a cordial welcome. McClellan thought I must be a Jonah to bring such a storm and was half minded to order me back. He said that they were talking of me and were really glad to see me. I went thence to our corps, and was pleasantly welcomed by our new commander, General Couch, and very soon fell into the old place—the headquarters of the second division. Here, surrounded by my staff, I was in heart again, for it had been a great cross to arrive at Harper's Ferry and find the army several days ahead of me, and in the enemy's front, for the march had commenced the morning of October 26th. There had been slight changes in commanders—Couch having our corps (the Second) and Slocum the Twelfth; Sumner remaining in charge of the two. The Fifth and Sixth Corps retained the same chiefs, Porter and Franklin, each having been enlarged to three divisions. Willcox, taking the Ninth, had succeeded Reno (killed in battle), and John F. Reynolds had the First Corps in place of Hooker (wounded). These two (the First and Ninth) were still under Burnside's direction. The new troops promised from the defenses of the capital were commanded by Sigel, Heintzelman, and Bayard, the latter having only one division of cavalry. General Sumner's command was immediately divided. The Twelfth Corps was left behind to guard the fords of the Upper Potomac. When the army started, though the rain was falling in torrents, the main body, now brisk, hardy, and hopeful, had pressed on rapidly up the valley of the Catoctin, a valley situated between the Blue Ridge and the Bull Run range. Our corps, followed by the Fifth, had crossed the Shenandoah near its

311

mouth and passed directly into the little valley, which was to be the general route of the army. Pleasonton's cavalry was in advance, and occupied successively the gaps in the Blue Ridge. The different corps were kept within supporting distance of each other during the march, yet by the time the rear guard had crossed the Potomac, on November 2d, the head of column was already in the vicinity of Snicker's Gap. Mr. Lincoln's policy proved correct. General Lee, with Longstreet's wing, with very little cavalry, made a parallel march up the Shenandoah, so that by the time we had touched Snicker's Gap, two of the passes of the Blue Ridge farther up—Chester's and Thornton's—were even then in use by Lee passing the material and troops of the enemy to the vicinity of Culpeper.

Thus the army was quietly transferred to the vicinity of the Manassas Gap Railroad. Sigel's Eleventh Corps, and part of Heintzelman's, with Bayard's cavalry, had marched out from Washington and were holding Thoroughfare Gap, New Baltimore, and Warrenton Junction.

Reynolds's corps was at Warrenton, Willcox's at Waterloo; ours (the Second) at Rectortown, while Porter's and Franklin's were not far in the rear, toward Upperville—McClellan's headquarters being at Rectortown.

Whatever bold project was in Lee's or Jackson's mind, it certainly had been interrupted by McClellan's holding his main body so tenaciously west of the Bull Run range.

One may imagine my surprise and sincere regret when I heard, on arrival, that McClellan had been removed, and Burnside assigned to the command of the army.

312

The evening of the 6th, General Buckingham, an officer on duty in the War Office, had been made, by General Halleck and Secretary Stanton, the bearer of dispatches. Buckingham went during the 7th to Burnside to urge his acceptance of the command. Burnside at first made strenuous objections, claiming his pleasant relations with McClellan, and insisting on his own unfitness. But finding that McClellan would be relieved in any event, he finally, with considerable reluctance, yielded to Mr. Stanton's wish. The two then rode to Salem, and, taking the cars, were soon in Rectortown. Buckingham says: "About eleven o'clock we found him alone in his tent examining papers, and as we both entered together he received us in his kind and cordial manner."

Burnside betrayed more feeling than McClellan. The latter, after reading the dispatch, passed it to Burnside, and said simply: "You command the army."

In order to complete the concentration of the army in the vicinity of Warrentown, McClellan's orders, already prepared, were issued and executed. My command made a march of eight miles during November 8th; this brought us to the neighborhood of Warrenton, where we encamped in a ravine to shelter ourselves from a severe wind storm. The next morning I turned out my troops and drew them up beside the road to give a parting salute to General McClellan. He rode along the line, the tattered colors were lowered, the drums beat, and the men cheered him. Burnside rode quietly by his side. At my last interview McClellan said to me: "Burnside is a pure man and a man of integrity of purpose, and such a man can't go far astray."

One other remark I have preserved: "I have been

long enough in command of a large army to learn the utter insignificance of any man unless he depend on a Power above."

It is easy to see why the officers and soldiers were so much attached to McClellan.

Soon after this interview I met Burnside, who appeared sad and weary. He had been for two nights almost without sleep. He remarked in my presence that he had concluded to take the command of the army, but did not regard the subject as one for congratulation.

It is impossible to predict with certainty what a man will become under the weight of a new responsibility. Every officer of rank in our war doubtless had some thought beyond his immediate command, some plan of operations in mind based upon the circumstances of his surroundings; but the instant he had the whole authority put upon him he saw everything in a new light. His knowledge of the force to be used became more complete, and of the force to be opposed much enlarged; and the risks to be run presented themselves as practical questions, no longer as mere theories.

Thus when Burnside at Warrenton came to command the Army of the Potomac, then over 100,000 strong, his whole character appeared to undergo a change. A large, brave, prepossessing man, popular with his associates, he was accustomed to defer greatly to the judgment of his chosen friends.

When the proposal of command first met him he expressed a self-distrust and declined. Indeed, he was urged to shoulder the burden, and at last did so. When it became necessary to submit a plan of campaign to Washington without delay, he was forthwith astonish-

ingly decided. The obvious course mapped out by Mc-
Clellan would not do for him—he rejected that. He
then proposed ostensibly to maneuver toward Chester
Gap and Culpeper as McClellan had been doing, but
really to turn these maneuvers into feints. Under
their cover, behind the blind of sundry marchings,
skirmishes, and cavalry raids, he would transfer his
army straightway to Falmouth, cross the Rappahannock to Fredericksburg, seize the heights beyond, and
hold them preparatory to future movements. That
was Burnside's plan of campaign. Who could say
before the trial that it was not a good one?

To execute demanded prompt preparation. The
docks near the Potomac at Aquia Creek needed rebuilding, and the railway thence to Falmouth must be
repaired. Our pontoon bridges, left at Harper's Ferry
and Berlin, must be transferred to the Rappahannock.

Halleck, after a visit to Burnside, promised, if his
plan and method should be accepted, to look after
docks, railway, and pontoon bridges. He then returned to the President. Mr. Lincoln said: " Adopt
Burnside's plan; there is a chance of success if he
moves quickly."

Burnside unwisely left two most important things
to Halleck, one of which was vital: the repair of the
railway and *forwarding his pontoon train.* Unless he
could deceive Lee as to his intentions, the problem
would reduce itself simply to a race of the two armies
for the Fredericksburg Heights. Without the bridges,
unless by some singular providence the river should
be fordable at Falmouth on his arrival, a single day's
delay for the means of crossing would be fatal to Burnside's enterprise, however swiftly he might move his
columns.

315

On November 15, 1862, Burnside's march for Falmouth began. The right grand division of two corps under Sumner introduced the rapid movement. The first day, however, my division in the lead was permitted to make only thirteen miles, so necessary was it to get Sumner's command together and well in hand.

We were off early the next day, one division of our corps in the road and the other two abreast in the fields, mine on the left. The pioneers kept well ahead of the side columns to clear away the brush, cut the small trees, and throw down the fences. The road was dry and the weather fine.

Our march was to-day (Sunday, the 16th) more than the Hebrew Sabbath day's journey, for we made twenty miles and encamped at Spotted Tavern, only thirteen miles from Falmouth.

On the morrow our grand division, Sumner himself close to the front and full of his accustomed sanguine hope, pushed on to the Stafford Hills, and began to descend them near Falmouth, in plain sight of Fredericksburg. A small detachment of the enemy, with a few pieces of artillery, met our advance guard at the town and began firing upon us. A brigade of ours, with a single battery quickly ready, cleared the neighborhood. One solid shot from Fredericksburg opposite struck the wheel of an artillery carriage near me and broke it, but the fire from beyond the river was nervous and panicky, and the hostile defenders but few in number. Seeing our troops coming steadily on, the Confederates soon abandoned the shore line and fled, so that we quietly occupied the left bank and the town of Falmouth.

After the enemy's detachment had disappeared from our view behind the houses of Fredericksburg, one of Sumner's officers saw a steer start from the south side and wade slowly across to the north bank of the Rappahannock. The commander of the leading brigade, Colonel Brooke, whose attention was called to the fact, went to the animal and measured the height the water had reached on his side; it did not exceed three feet. This being reported to Sumner, he dispatched a letter to Burnside, asking permission to cross immediately and seize the heights beyond the city. Burnside answered: "Wait till I come." When he came forward and looked at the broad river, the rough river bed and swift current, he decided that the risk of crossing before his bridges were in sight would be too great. "No, Sumner," he said; "wait for the pontoons."

The bridges were not there, and not likely to be at Falmouth for several days; but the ford was practicable, the town and heights but weakly occupied, and the ability of Sumner's command fully equal to the enterprise. Forty thousand men could have crossed before dark on that Monday, made a strong bridgehead on the lower plane of the right bank and, intrenching Marye Heights beyond the city against Lee's approach, have had within twelve hours rejoisted and replanked the denuded railway piers for use for supply or reënforcement from the Falmouth side.

The left grand division (Franklin's) encamped a few miles north of us at Stafford Court House; while the center grand division (Hooker's) was halted eight miles above us. Hooker, not to be outdone by Sumner, soon entreated Burnside to allow him to cross the river near his own bivouac, that he might move down and seize the Fredericksburg Heights. This request was too late. We had had a heavy rain and the river was

317

rising rapidly. Still, Hooker's project would have been better than the one we adopted.

The inhabitants of the country were too zealous for Confederate success to leave Lee long in ignorance of Burnside's doings. Even the skillful pretensions of our cavalry did not deceive him. He had word at once of our starting. Stuart, turning Pleasonton's right, made a reconnoissance in force, which confirmed the previous intelligence that the Army of the Potomac had changed its base from Warrenton Junction to Aquia Creek. Before Stuart's assurance came to Lee, he had dispatched troops to Marye Heights and vicinity. Cavalry, artillery, and two divisions of infantry, under McLaws and Ransom, with Longstreet in chief command, were hurried forward, arriving on the 18th and 19th. They reoccupied and fortified the best Fredericksburg positions, and with no little anxiety as they beheld our extension and preparations, waited for the arrival of their main body.

The story of the moving of the bridge train from Harper's Ferry and Berlin to our front at Falmouth is a strange one. It seems to indicate, judging by the uncalled-for delays, the misunderstandings, changes of orders, and going into depot for repairs near Washington, the uncertainty as to the route to be chosen, and final inadequacy of the transportation provided, that Halleck himself was playing a part, and possibly hoping to get Burnside well into winter quarters without anybody being particularly to blame.

The detail which fretted Burnside would be amusing, were it not so serious a matter.

Major Spaulding, in charge of the large pontoon train, took up his bridges at Harper's Ferry and vicinity fairly well; arrived with them at Washington, the

MAJOR GENERAL HOWARD'S COMMISSION FROM PRESIDENT LINCOLN.

19th, and reported to his chief (of the engineers), General Woodbury. Woodbury put him off a day; the next day when he came to the office Woodbury told him he must see Halleck first; that conference sent Spaulding into depot and camp near Anacostia. Burnside, the 15th, called for his promised bridges by a telegram to Halleck; Spaulding then received an order to send one train by land and forty boats by water; the boats which went by water were sent off to Belle Plain, but without wagons or mules. They were there helpless ten miles away from Burnside. Major Spaulding at Anacostia at last secured sufficient transportation, and the 19th in the afternoon started from Washington. Now heavy rains began and his roads were fearful; he then wisely took waterways for the whole, and arrived at Belle Plain the 24th. He now moved up in good shape and was handsomely in camp at evening on November 25th, close by Burnside's headquarters.

As it required thirteen days to do a piece of work which could easily have been done in three days, it would be a marvelous stretch of charity to impute it to mere bungling.

Had Woodbury and Spaulding in the outset been properly instructed by Halleck, those bridges would have been near at hand the 17th on our arrival. Spaulding would have reported to Sumner at once and in less than an hour would have been pushing out his boats from our front.

Of course it was now plain enough to Burnside that his primary plan had been defeated. Goaded by his disappointment and spurred by the popular expectation that he had awakened by his prompt marches, Burnside decided to move down the river fourteen miles, surprise his enemy, and effect a crossing at that

319

point, but Lee was too vigilant for that, or, indeed, for any crossing without sharp resistance. Too many eyes from the opposite shore beheld our reconnoitering parties; and as soon as preparations for bridging began at any place a strong force was immediately on hand to dispute the passage. Seeing this, Burnside's second project was necessarily abandoned.

Then, suddenly, our general took a new thought. It was to do as most great generals in history had done — after getting up sufficient supplies for use, present and prospective, then move straight forward upon the enemy's works. The chances in all such hardy enterprises were better where there was no river to be crossed, and when the works to be assailed were not so hopelessly strong as were those upon the Fredericksburg Heights.

Lee, who could hardly before this have dreamed of our crossing in his direct front, must have smiled at our folly. Burnside chose three points for his pontoons—one in front of my division near the Lacy house; another farther down, opposite the lower part of the city, and a third a mile below.

As the time drew near for laying the bridges I ascended the Stafford Hills, where General Hunt had placed Burnside's numerous cannon so as to cover the bridge approaches. The Confederate lines, of which I had glimpses here and there, appeared to be drawn up in a semicircle along the Fredericksburg Heights. The heights touched the Rappahannock a mile above the city and, going back, extended with their knolls, woods, and slopes southward all along my front, leaving between them and the wide river, besides the city, much undulating open ground. The Marye Hill was about the middle of the curve. South of the Marye

Hill the ridge ended; thence there stretched farther southward a wooded space of lower ground; again another abrupt height, the highest part of which was named Prospect Hill; then the high land gradually sloped off to the Massaponax, a tributary of the Rappahannock which, running easterly, bounded Lee's position and covered his right flank. After taking a good look at this suggestive landscape, I wrote a friend December 10th: "Before you get this letter you will have the news of a battle. I try to rely on the Saviour in these trying hours. . . . I have no forebodings of disaster, but I know the desperate nature of our undertaking." I was unusually sad in the prospect of that battlefield, sad for my men and for my personal staff. Experience had already taught me its lessons.

There was already murmuring among the officers in general and they were not overcareful in what they said. Some spoke against the administration, and sharply condemned the change of commanders, and openly expressed distrust of Burnside. Scraps of this adverse talk came to his ears. The night of the Monday in which I was surveying Lee's semicircle, Burnside called to him a number of us subordinates, field and staff. He addressed a roomful with very pertinent and pointed remarks, saying substantially: "I have heard your criticisms, gentlemen, and your complaints. You know how reluctantly I assumed the responsibility of command. I was conscious of what I lacked; but still I have been placed here where I am and will do my best. I rely on God for wisdom and strength. Your duty is not to throw cold water, but to aid me loyally with your advice and hearty service. . . ."

In noting at the time this conference, I said concerning Burnside's address: "Solemn, noble, manly, and Christian were his remarks."

Burnside, thus pressed with the shafts of bitterness, having neither warm sympathy nor kindly advice, steeled himself to leave everything to the maze of battle and went on to prepare the way for the sacrifice.

Sumner's grand division broke camp and marched to convenient points for the bridges that were to lead into Fredericksburg, where the engineers proposed to push out the pontoons and plank them.

Hooker's grand division was held a little back of Sumner's for support; while Franklin moved his to the lower crossing.

At the early hour of three on the morning of December 11th, under the veil of a thick fog, the energetic engineer soldiers began their work. Some of our infantry under my eye was located close at hand to guard the working parties. The artillerymen on the heights behind me also contributed their portion as soon as they could see. One of Franklin's bridges was laid by 2.30 in the morning, and the other, close by, was finished at a later hour.

Our engineer battalion throwing out our bridge was not so successful. At about eight o'clock I detached Hall's whole brigade to assist it in every way possible. Putting in the boats one by one, the engineers had worked out their bridge about one-third of the way, when the fog thinned and the Confederate pickets, deeply intrenched on the other bank, began to fire upon our bridgemen with accuracy. The workers soon desisted, ran back, and abandoned their boats. Their officers commanded, went before them, and entreated, but all to no effect. There were just then few hopeful chances for bridgemen! Now the roar of our

artillery behind us became deafening. It poured shot
and shell by concentrated firing upon those Confederate pickets and upon the sharpshooters in the edge of
the town; but these active opponents were too well
covered in houses, cellars, behind walls and buildings,
and in deeply dug pits to be much disturbed. Neither
musketry nor artillery, abundant as they were, lessened the enemy's galling fire.

Burnside came to our front in the afternoon and,
noticing that the whole force in that vicinity was in
waiting, sent for Woodbury and Hunt. Woodbury
showed him the impossibility of getting any farther,
now that the fog had cleared away and that his bridgemen had no cover from Confederate riflemen. Hunt
mentioned the daring feat of crossing in separate
boats. Burnside said: " Let us do that." I selected
Hall's brigade of my division for the trial. The instant Colonel Hall in the presence of his men asked
who would go ahead in the precarious enterprise, Lieutenant Colonel Baxter and his entire regiment, the
Seventh Michigan, volunteered to fill the pontoons.
Woodbury undertook to get the boats in readiness, but
the poor workmen, unused to soldiering, made only
abortive attempts. Two or three would get hold of a
big boat and begin to move it, but as soon as a bullet
struck it in any part they would run back. Finally,
Baxter said that his men would put the boats into the
water. His soldiers did that at command, filled them
with men and shoved off so quickly that the enemy's
fire became fitful and uncertain. In going across the
river one man was killed and several wounded, including Baxter himself. For his bravery Baxter was made
a brigadier general.

As the boats struck the opposite shore the men disembarked without confusion and made a successful rush for the deep pits, trenches, and cellars. One company alone secured thirty-two prisoners.

The Seventh Michigan had hardly landed and seized the obstructions when the Nineteenth Massachusetts, by the same conveyance, followed in support—next, the Fifteenth Massachusetts and the Fifty-ninth New York in succession.

In this way brave soldiers made a bridgehead, and the engineer workmen, less nervous under such a screen from danger, soon finished their bridge across the Rappahannock.

My corps commander (Couch) next ordered me to take my entire division over and clear that part of the town near our advance of all Confederates, and so secure a safe transit for the remainder of our corps. Two regiments of Hall's and all of Owen's brigade crossed the bridge. With a small staff I went over with Owen. The hostile guns had found the range, so that shells burst uncomfortably near the moving column, but none on the bridge were hurt. A regimental band, to cheer us on, stood some fifty yards up river on the Falmouth side, and were just commencing to play when an explosive missile lodged in their midst. The bandsmen threw themselves upon their faces to avoid the immediate peril, and then ran to shelter. After that, our music was confined to cannon, musketry, and the shouts of the soldiers.

Hall pushed straight on; Owen rushed his men into the outskirts of the town to the left of Hall, while Sully reserved his brigade for the bridgehead nearer the river.

First, Hall's guide was killed; at the second street he met formidable resistance; he found persistency and exposure of his men necessary to root out his worrisome opponents; now darkness was approaching and he feared too much massing and begged me to stop the crossing on the bridge. This I declined to do, and so we kept in motion till my division was over. With shots to meet from roofs, corners, alleyways, and from every conceivable cover, and heavy losses, our division succeeded at last in gaining the third street parallel with the river, and in securing some prisoners. Here I halted for the night and had the pickets carefully established.

Fredericksburg had been much damaged by Sumner's bombardment, yet many people remained in the city. Men, women, and children who had spent the day in cellars now ran to us for protection. There was some rioting; some soldiers for sport dressed themselves fantastically in all sorts of apparel, and some gave themselves to plunder; but no instance of personal abuse or violence to noncombatants came to my ears. Several mothers and their children were sent to Falmouth for safety. A few men, as usual, found the wine cellars and became intoxicated.

As I was making a night inspection I came upon a very hilarious group. Some were playing upon musical instruments, while others embellished the music with singing and dancing. I remarked to one of the group that this was an unusual preparation for battle —the battle that all were expecting on the morrow. "Ah, general, let us sing and dance to-night; we will fight the better for it to-morrow!"

The city bridge below ours had an experience like our own. The Eighty-ninth New York of Hawkins's brigade bravely crossed in bateaux, surprised and captured the Confederate pickets. Hawkins followed up the Eighty-ninth with the rest of his regiments and cleared the lower part of the town.

Hall and I had our headquarters together in an old house which had been considerably knocked to pieces in the shelling. The situation was so peculiar that I did not sleep much. At three in the morning I went along the picket line. I found that the enemy had withdrawn from our immediate neighborhood. At dawn I had Owen and Sully enlarge our space. They opened like a fan till they had possession of the whole city and had their skirmishers beyond on the first ridge near the suburbs.

Thus far well. Sumner praised our action, giving us a handsome compliment for judicious dispositions, advancing steadily, sharp fighting, and success in driving back the Confederates so as to occupy and hold at daylight the entire town of Fredericksburg.

The remainder of Sumner's grand division (the Second and Ninth Corps) during December 12th crossed the river; the Second Corps held all the right half of the city, the Ninth the left, and connected with Franklin's grand division down river. Hooker's grand division kept that day to the Falmouth side for support and reënforcement.

During December 12th there was no actual battle; but there was considerable artillery practice and some brisk skirmishing.

CHAPTER XXI

IN the early morning of the 13th, about 3 A.M., I wrote a home letter for my children that is preserved:

"We are now in a house abandoned by Mr. Knox, and near the front line. One or two shells have passed clear through the house, but my room is in pretty good shape. Charles (Lieutenant Howard) is well and sleeping. So are Lieutenant Stinson, Captain Whittlesey, Lieutenants Steel and Atwood sleeping on the floor near me.

"I am sitting on this floor near a fireplace . . . writing on my lap, having an inkstand, candlestick, and paper on a large portfolio, with Tom, a little colored boy, holding up the outer edge. Tom drops to sleep now and then, when my candlestick with its light, and inkstand with its ink, slip down; but I wake Tom and it is soon all righted."

That very morning a little later a charming old lady saw my staff officers and myself at breakfast, and listened to the brief reading of Scripture and morning prayer. She seemed much moved. To a remark of hers I said that we should conquer in the end. She shook her head and rejoined with a look: "You will have a Stone wall to encounter, Hills to climb, and a Long street to tread before you can succeed." But, afterwards, seeing us depart with cheerfulness, like a

327

merchant going to business or a rested workman to his shop, as I said good morning, she replied: " Now I fear you more than ever, for I had understood that all of Lincoln's men were bad. What! So cheerful when going straight into battle?"

About eleven o'clock of December 11th Franklin reported to Burnside that the lower bridges were in readiness. The latter instructed him to keep his grand division where it then was for the present; but at four that afternoon he was directed to cross his whole command. The movement over the pontoons began. Before many men had reached the south shore Burnside changed his orders, sending over, only one brigade, Devens's, which deployed and held a position there as did Hawkins and I, a mile above.

On the 12th Franklin's two corps, Baldy Smith's and Reynolds's, completed their crossing before 1 P.M. Smith put out two divisions in line of battle, keeping one in the rear as a reserve; he then moved forward to the old Richmond road, which here was parallel with the river and a mile from it.

Reynolds formed his corps in the same style on Smith's left, but refused his line so that he made an angle, and rested his left on the Rappahannock.

Franklin for his entire grand division had far less opposition than we who were in the city. There was some skirmishing and random shots from Lee's artillery during this unfolding operation. Reynolds's front now looked directly toward the Massaponax, less than a mile away.

Thus Burnside's army faced that of Lee. During the 12th Burnside " visited the different commands with a view to determining as to future movements." During his visit to Franklin, Franklin strongly advised the use of his whole grand division of 30,000 men for assaulting the enemy's right, the assault to begin December 13th at daylight. Franklin asked, with a view to support, that two divisions of Hooker be sent him during the night. Burnside at that time appeared to favor this good advice. He promised as he left Franklin about dark to send his orders, whatever they might be, before midnight.

As the orders were not received at midnight, Franklin sent an aid-de-camp for them. The reply to the aid was that they would be ready soon and sent; but they did not reach Franklin until about seven o'clock of the 13th. Of course it was too late for an attack at dawn. The supporting divisions from Hooker never came, so that it is plain that Franklin's plan was not adopted. Strange as it may appear, Burnside was evidently relying on Sumner's grand division to make near the Marye Heights the main assault and so wanted Hooker's command held at the upper bridges to reënforce him.

Beck's Island is above the city. On the south shore, opposite this island, Dr. Taylor had his residence on high ground. The river road, running north, leaves the Rappahannock, opposite Beck's Island, and passes over Dr. Taylor's farm. Lee's left rested on this road. He crossed the heights thence southeasterly, one height being called Stanbury Hill; his lines next found a more level plateau named the Cemetery Hill; and then in order the Marye Heights, over which passed the Orange Court House road, perpendicular to the river, dividing Fredericksburg into halves. In the city it is Hanover Street.

Another roadway leaves the city three blocks lower, passes straight out parallel with the plank road till it comes to the higher ground, then, turning to the right, courses along beside the Marye Heights and, finally, goes off into the country southwesterly. This is the telegraph road. There was a connecting street near Marye Heights which went from the plank road to the telegraph road. This street and a part of the telegraph road had a bank wall, the roadbed being a few feet below the crest of the wall. It was a Confederate infantry outwork already prepared.

Near the city the canal which started from the river above Beck's Island and ran along the base of the heights, continuing in front of the deep cross street which I have described, served for the most part as the broad ditch of a fortification—an obstacle to our approach in itself. The lower part of the canal was more like the rough outlet of a creek. On Marye Heights, a little back from the street, were dug by the Confederates and their slaves double intrenchments with works in the form of redoubts on the summits behind them. The lower ground down river, as we have seen, was generally undulating, and wooded to a considerable extent. Lee had a new road constructed behind his lines so that his troops could be readily moved from one point to another. The strong point of his right was "Prospect Hill." Along the foot of this ran the Fredericksburg & Potomac Railroad which, from a point called Hamilton's Crossing, continues northward, parallel to the river, and enters the city on its south side. The old Richmond wagon road which Franklin had seized with his leading divisions was also parallel to the river and about halfway between it and the railway. These two roads each made a right angle with the Massaponax. Lee's permanent right flank was established upon the Massaponax so that the general form of his entire line was that of a sickle; the high ground forming the handle and the low ground occupied in front of the new road and over Prospect Hill and on to the bend of the Massaponax forming the blade, having the concave edge toward the Rappahannock.

Our own lines, more than half enveloped and facing Lee's peculiar formation, were straight and parallel with the river excepting Reynolds's corps, which on the extreme left faced almost south and was nearly at right angles with our main line.

The Fredericksburg plateau west and southwest of the city is divided into three parts by two streams, the Hazel and the Deep Run, each of which has numerous branches. Hazel Run enters the Rappahannock close to the city. One branch from behind Marye Heights affords an extended, sheltered position in its valley; the other stream, the Deep Run, drains the high ground about Prospect Hill and enters the Rappahannock some distance south of the city.

Before the arrival of Jackson, Longstreet had posted the troops, Anderson's division from Taylor's Hill eastward, to include the cemetery; Ransom's holding all the lines and works on Marye Heights; McLaws's division, coming next, covered all the low ground from Hazel Run to Harrison's place. Pickett, with his division's irregular formation, held some knolls from which he could sweep all the *terrain* between his front and Deep Run. Hood at first rested his left on the heights and extended his division as far as the Fredericksburg Railroad, in front of Prospect Hill, where were the notable " Walker Batteries." Stuart with his cavalry and some artillery watched the remainder of the front to the Massaponax.

331

As soon as Jackson's forces arrived the morning of December 13th, he put A. P. Hill's division into Hood's place, arranged so as to form substantially two lines, while Early's and Taliaferro's divisions made a third line. The division of D. H. Hill, being wearied with a night march, was placed farther back, as a general reserve. The general facing of Stonewall Jackson's concentrated command was toward the north and the northwest, overlooking every approach from the direction of Fredericksburg. Hood, as soon as relieved by Jackson, changed position to the north side of Deep Run and held his forces for use in any direction.

Longstreet, referring to the long front which he commanded, says: " In addition to the natural strength of the position, ditches, stone fences, and road cuts formed along different portions of the line, and parts of General McLaws's lines were farther strengthened by rifle trenches and abatis."

Burnside's orders to Franklin, which he received at so late an hour, were dated 5.50 A.M. General Hardie of his staff came to carry the message and remain with Franklin. Burnside now directed that the whole grand division be held for a rapid movement down the old Richmond road. Franklin was to send out at once a division to pass below Smithfield, to seize, if possible, the heights near Hamilton; crossing the Massaponax, the division to be well supported, and to keep open the line of retreat. Burnside informed Franklin that another column from Sumner's grand division would move up the plank road to its intersection with the telegraph road, where the troops were to divide and seize the heights on both sides of these roads. Burnside thought that holding the two heights with the one near Hamilton's Crossing would compel the Confederates to evacuate the whole ridge between these points. Burnside further said that Hooker's command would be in support at the bridges. The division of Franklin must move as soon as the fog lifted; the watchword for the battle to be given to every company was *Scott*. The special instructions to Sumner were dated at 6 A.M. First: Extend to Deep Run and connect with Franklin; push a second column of one division or more along the plank and telegraph roads with a view of seizing the heights in rear of the town. Sumner's movement was not to commence until further orders.

Hooker's instructions were dated at 7 A.M. Hooker was to place Butterfield's corps and Whipple's division so as to cross the river at a moment's notice, using the three upper bridges. These forces were to be in support of Sumner's grand division; the two remaining divisions of Stoneman's corps were to be in readiness to cross at the lower bridges in support of Franklin.

To obey his instructions Franklin chose the corps of John F. Reynolds, which was made up of three divisions: 1st, Doubleday's; 2d, Gibbon's; 3d, Meade's. Franklin believed, as anybody would, that this fine corps was sufficient to carry out the letter and spirit of Burnside's new order. Meade's division was taken for the assault, and was to be supported on its left by Doubleday and on its right by Gibbon. In order to give an additional confidence, two divisions of Stoneman's corps were brought up from the bridges and made a reserve to Reynolds.

Meade started southward as if to cross the Massaponax, moved seven or eight hundred yards, and then changed face squarely to the right, and directed his march upon the " heights " mentioned in his orders.

The point which was coveted near the Massaponax was also not far from Prospect Hill. It was, indeed, on Lee's new road and actually behind A. P. Hill's advance lines.

Meade kept on under increased artillery fire from right, left, and front, well across the old Richmond road. Here his men were delayed in destroying hedges and in constructing bridges for his artillery over the deep side ditches.

Meade had a column of two deployed brigades, followed by another in fours ready to deploy. His formation, to start with, had skirmishers and flankers in plenty. Having gone somewhat farther, a Confederate battery from Stuart's front opened a troublesome fire upon Meade's left. Soon Union artillery ran to the place and replied shot for shot. Then a heavy line of Confederate skirmishers sprang from the troublesome quarter. The brigade, in fours, faced that way, and by rapid firing cleared the field. As soon as Meade was rid of that left flank annoyance he advanced this third brigade to his left front and brought up three batteries to his advanced position.

Again his command moved forward to encounter more hostile cannon now coming from his left front. The three Union batteries were turned upon this new enemy, and in a short time had exploded two of the Confederate caissons and driven their battery men from their guns. Success at that time cheered Meade and the men of his division.

Meade was now near what appeared to be a gap in the Confederate lines. His men, under his orders, rushed forward, first over a cleared field, rapidly driving in the enemy's skirmishers; next succeeded in getting possession of a piece of woods which jutted out between him and the railroad, and soon his men cleared the whole front as far as that railroad. But in the neighborhood, taking advantage of embankments, ditches, and other cover, the Confederate soldiers in solid line were waiting for Meade's approach. Yet, with hardly delay enough to take breath, the leading Union brigade threw itself upon these strong lines, broke them up, and forced them back upon the heights. Having already passed A. P. Hill's front, Meade began to feel artillery and infantry fire from his right, so that while his first brigade sped onward the second brigade was delayed by changing front and meeting the new danger. But this was done.

Thus Meade worked his way along with delays and hard fighting with artillery and infantry to the left of him, to the right of him, and finally to the front. At one time Meade sent Lieutenant Dehon with instructions to the commander of the third brigade (our General Jackson) to capture an annoying battery. Dehon was killed just as he came to the commander and a few minutes later Jackson himself fell. It was a great loss, for our brave Jackson had, a few minutes before, seized the desired point for which Meade had been advancing and contending. The brigade, without its commander, subject to an increasing fire, gave back little by little and so lost its important hold. Meade took more than three hundred prisoners and many battle flags. When he most needed it he found small support on his right and none on his left, and there was none very close in his rear. Feeling that the opposition was too strong to be met by but one division, he began his retreat, which was executed under fire and without confusion.

When back as far as the edge of the woods near the

railroad, he found a brigade of Birney's division supporting some of his batteries, which gave him some relief.

Gibbon had separated from Meade while advancing in the woods. He had a sharp encounter of his own to meet and was now in position to succor, more thoroughly than Birney, Meade's breaking and retiring lines. Sinclair, who commanded Meade's first brigade, was badly wounded, and he lost in the action 22 officers and 496 men. The second brigade aggregated a loss of 22 officers and 718 men, while our Jackson's brigade suffered a loss of 28 officers and 525 men. Meade's artillery lost 5 officers and 25 men. These figures indicate the severity of the engagement.

General Gibbon, wounded during the day, had with his division done his utmost to give Meade a flank support. He faced a strip of woods strongly occupied by Pender's deployed lines. Gibbon endeavored to rush Taylor's brigade across an open field into the woods. The men got about halfway, when the Confederate artillery fire from different directions became so severe that the troops took cover by lying down behind a slight rise of ground. Now when Meade made his last advance, Gibbon, perceiving the effort, sent Taylor forward again. The Confederates were behind a railroad embankment to stop him. The other brigades of Gibbon's division came into line to the left of Taylor. The whole Union force in that quarter was at first repulsed; but now fully aroused, Gibbon gathered as many as he could from his reliable regiments and made a bayonet charge. This was done with tremendous energy and spirit, and the railway was taken with 180 prisoners. Gibbon, bleeding, was obliged to leave the front and Taylor succeeded to his command.

Battle of Fredericksburg

Doubleday, to the left of Meade, with his division had been occupied all day by the batteries of Walker and Stuart, who had other Confederates of all arms to support them. This occupation had prevented Meade from having any effective help upon his left flank, or any reënforcement from that division.

Meade retired after the hard day to the position from which he had set out in the morning.

The part which our grand division played in this battle affords a sorrowful picture. There is nothing to relieve its gloom but the excellent conduct of the troops under appalling circumstances.

Ransom, whose Confederate division divided the ground with that of McLaws, and held the deep suburban street and the telegraph road at the base of Marye Heights, uses strong language when he speaks of our successive efforts to get near his position on that deplorable day: " The Yankee line advanced with the utmost determination; moved, almost massed, to the charge heroically; met the withering fire of our Confederate artillery and small arms with wonderful stanchness! " Those attacks would not permit him to despise our courage or our hardihood.

So much for our *amour propre*. Burnside having heard from Franklin and from his own staff officer, Hardie, that Meade was gaining important advantage on Stonewall Jackson's front, thought that the fullness of time had come for Sumner to coöperate. He gave the old general the order for which he had been all the morning waiting: " Advance and attack! "

The Second Corps (Couch's), to which my division belonged, was to lead; to direct the main assault between the plank and the telegraph roads; to ascend the Marye Heights from that base; and break through the

337

Confederate lines, forcing the enemy back and capturing his batteries. It was a task easy to set but difficult even to begin.

General Sumner prescribed to Couch his favorite method: after covering the front with skirmishers, to get into action in a column of brigades. The simple way was for one brigade to form a long line two ranks deep, facing Marye Heights; follow that brigade by a second brigade line, leaving 150 yards' space between them; then send on the third brigade, preserving the same distance.

French's division thus formed was to have the advance; Hancock's to follow, and after Hancock's, my division was to complete the fighting column.

Close to the Second Corps on our left Willcox's Ninth Corps was instructed to move up abreast, to keep our left flank clear of any too enterprising Confederates, and to keep up connection with Franklin, occupying all the ground between Hazel and Deep Run. As we have seen, the Second and Ninth Corps were already over the Rappahannock. The instructions were clear and well understood. My division, having led in taking the town, must now fall to the rear, and let another have the post of honor.

Troops in regiments, brigades, divisions, or corps, after some service, show to some extent the characteristics of their commanders—their courage, steadfastness, self-reliance, or their impulsiveness, energy, and tenacity of purpose, and, of course, when such defects exist, the opposite qualities, nervousness and unreliability.

French, who was to lead, very soon gained an ascendency over all officers who were under him, and secured from them prompt obedience and hard work.

He was often imperious and impatient, but no one ever saw his troops, without stragglers, go into action without a thrill of admiration for him and his command.

A strong skirmish line was first organized. It consisted of three regiments—one by the flank in column of twos went quickly out Hanover Street, crossed the canal, and deployed to the left; the other two in similar order crossed the bridge in Princess Ann Street near the railway depot, and deployed to the right till their open line met the other. As soon as the columns had appeared at the bridge the Confederate batteries, whose guns were trained on the streets, opened a fearful discharge. Many of our men were killed or wounded before getting into line, but the remainder did not falter. They went into place at a run. The enemy's skirmish line now interposed its rapid fire. Our men set in motion those skirmishers and drove them, following them up for at least 400 yards, breaking down fences as they went forward, and traversing muddy ground till they struck an abrupt slope and lay down behind its crest. It was to them like a great rock in a weary land. It afforded such shelter from a terrible fire that the temptation was great to remain there while shells were bursting over their heads, round shot plowing the ground in their front, and musketry peppering every yard of the slopes beyond them.

The next brigade, Kimball's, let no time run to waste. It was drawn out in line on Caroline Street parallel with the river. Mason, who commanded the skirmishers, had just left Princess Ann Street when Kimball's brigade came on by the flank, passed the depot, crossed the canal bridge, and formed line of battle behind the skirmish line near the canal bank. The enemy's fire during these movements was murderous. Shells burst in their ranks, destroying many men at each shot; but there was no panic and no disorder. Gaps made by wounds and death were quickly filled by comrades of battle. The men at command now bounded forward and cleared the open space beneath increasing volleys till French's line of battle stretched from road to road.

Kimball's main line was at last not more than 600 yards from the perfectly protected Confederate brigade of General Cobb, which, with other men from Ransom's and McLaws's divisions, filled the deep roadway. The hostile skirmishers had been withdrawn. Every man in the roadway had loaded his rifle. The wall or the banks of fresh earth kept them from Kimball's sight. As our men moved up the gentle acclivity, who can describe what followed? More artillery than before was detected by the puffs of smoke, to the right, to the left, and all along the high ground. How rapid, how awful that series of discharges and those death-dealing missiles! Still this long, handsome line with bayonets fixed and flags flying were steadily moving forward without firing a shot. They overtook their own skirmishers and went on. The worst was yet to come. As soon as the Confederates' abandoned skirmish rifle pits were reached by our men, the waiting enemy, as if by a simultaneous impulse, gave them volleys of leaden hail which extended from the plank road to the east of Marye Heights, against which no line of men could move or stand. Kimball's rapid advance had secured a little hamlet whose straggling buildings gave some protection from the Confederate fire. There Kimball rested his right. As the line could not advance farther, the men covered themselves as well as they could by the buildings and incidents of the ground, with a purpose to hold what they had gained and wait for help. It was here that their commander fell with a severe wound in his thigh. The next brigade (**Andrews's**) having but three regiments, the fourth being in the skirmish line, followed in the same manner according to the order. At the depot and the canal it took its turn and received the same dreadful baptism of fire. It pushed on with the same experience over the muddy ground and up the slopes, and was stopped at about the same point of advance. All the colonels present were disabled by wounds, so that a lieutenant colonel (Marshall) came to command the brigade. The last of French's brigades having also but three regiments, Palmer commanding, was deployed in the street and then followed the same path as the others without different results. It appeared at the canal; crossing that, the Confederate cannon had attained the exact range of the passage, and Palmer commends the firmness and bravery of his troops in dashing across that barrier.

To our field glasses French's brave division had almost disappeared.

Hancock's division came next. He sent up two regiments to replace two of French's. It was a way of renewing ammunition, for it was next to impossible to carry it up and distribute it in the ordinary way. Zook's brigade led Hancock's division. He deployed at the canal, then advanced with great speed, so that many of his men gained points beyond former troops along the ridge and at the hamlet.

Some of French's men in rear sprang up and joined in the brisk movement. Still they failed to take the stone wall, although our dead were left within twenty-five paces of it.

Meagher's brigade line followed next and suffered like the preceding from the continuous and murderous discharges, but really gained nothing.

Caldwell commanded the next brigade. With great zest and spirit his men went forward and rushed to the front, but they accomplished no more than those who had preceded them. These had been my troops at Fair Oaks. Their loss on this Fredericksburg front was 62 commissioned officers and 932 enlisted men. The brigade commander was himself wounded. Colonel Cross, who subsequently commanded the brigade, was also wounded.

Colonel Nelson A. Miles, having been promoted, had left my staff and was commanding two regiments in this battle. He received, during the advance, a severe wound in the neck. Seated on a stretcher and holding the lips of the wound together, he pluckily had himself brought to me to show me where he thought I could put my troops into action to advantage so as to make some impression on the enemy's line. I had just before that taken my position on a prominent knoll, and had seen the havoc among the two divisions preceding mine. From the sunken roadway came an increasing storm, bullets flying swift and sure, dealing death and wounds to our brave fellows almost without a return fire.

All this the officers of my division fully apprehended, yet, without faltering, that division, in its turn, swept forward. Owen's brigade went first and Hall's next. I kept Sully's for a time in the edge of the town for a reserve, but was soon obliged to send forward one regiment after another as Hall and Owen called for help. My regiments began to fire when each in its turn reached the general line of battle, so that the rattle of musketry for hours was unceasing.

To help us Hazard's Rhode Island battery came up at a trot, crossed the canal, and unlimbered in the open ground in the rear of Owen's troops and for a time fired with wondrous rapidity. The battery lost so many men in a short time that it was ordered back. Frank's New York battery followed Hazard's example and endeavored by rapid fire to open the way to our infantry for a front attack. But our attempts were futile, as had been those of the other divisions. We continued, however, to make sundry experiments, hoping almost against hope to make a lodgment along the enemy's front.

At last Hooker's grand division made its appearance in our rear. Hooker, himself on the field where he could take in the situation, stationed with his field glass just north of the canal, sat quietly on his horse. I wondered that he was not shot. He pushed in Humphrey's excellent division in the same manner as the rest. As we ceased firing Humphrey made a charge, leading his men in person amid the leaden rain. They reached my front line and passed it a short distance, where they met a tremendous volley of artillery and musketry and, like all the others who had ventured near the base of Marye Heights, were broken up and forced back.

Some more efforts were put forth by Hooker's troops and by ours, but all in vain, until darkness put an end to the hopeless sacrifice.

My division being the last of the Second Corps to go under fire on this fatal day, remained up there in close proximity to the foe till far into the night, but at last fresh men from Hooker's command let us return to town, one brigade coming in as late as 2 A.M. the next day. The loss in my division aggregated 64 officers and 813 men.

All the aids-de-camp had an unusually hard time in this conflict. I had a feeling akin to terror when I sent an aid or mounted man to carry an order. Lieutenant H. M. Stinson, one of my aids, showed such fearlessness under musketry fire that several commanders noticed him and mentioned him in their reports; so they did Lieutenant A. J. Atwood of my staff. Once my brother and aid, Lieutenant Howard, leaving me with an order, was obliged to cross the most exposed street. On his return he exclaimed, as he rode up, " Oh, general, they fired a volley at me, but it passed over my head! "

The other corps (the Ninth) of our grand division was commanded by O. B. Willcox. Through Sumner, Willcox was required to give support to the Second Corps (Couch's) on his right hand and to the First Corps (Reynolds's) on his left. The word " support " is an uncertain one, and often a very unsatisfactory one in a battle. The front of the Ninth Corps extended from our flank to the left across Hazel to Deep Run. Sturgis's division left the city limits, came under a direct fire almost immediately from artillery and infantry, marched across a rough ascending slope, and attained a crest, a close position to the Confederates' sheltered line. The division remained there till after dark. Once the Confederates attempted to move out and turn one of Couch's divisions, when our Ferrero's brigade " drove them back to their cover of stone walls and rifle pits." Many valuable lives were lost in that sharp work.

Battle of Fredericksburg

At 3 P.M. W. W. Burns's division crossed Deep Run and tried at Franklin's request to give what help it could.

By four o'clock Willcox, while the fire was at its height, thought he might create some diversion for my men who were plainly seen from his point of observation, standing near their rough shelter or lying behind a slight rise in a crest of the upper slope. He advanced Getty's division from the shelter of the town. Each regiment set out by the flank, went forward, marched to open ground, and then deployed into brigade lines much as we had done; then rushed over a plowed field, across the railway cut, the old canal ditch and marshy ground. The brigade kept on under the usual artillery explosions till within close musketry range of the Confederate rifles. Then they underwent the same rough handling which our men met farther to the right earlier in the day. Getty's brigade was forced back to a poor sort of shelter near the canal. Willcox's losses aggregated 1,328 officers and men.

At first, Burnside, saddened by the repulse of his attacks in every part of his lines, planned another battle for the 14th. His heart naturally went out to the old Ninth Corps that he had but lately commanded.

Willcox brought back Burns's division from Franklin and prepared the Ninth Corps to make the next main assault. Positions for six batteries of artillery had been carefully selected to break the way for the first infantry charge and support it by strong cannon firing. But the order for a renewal of the strife was first suspended and later countermanded.

On the 14th, while matters were in suspense, I went up into a church tower with Couch, my corps commander, and had a plain view of all the slope where the severest losses of the preceding day had occurred. We looked clear up to the suburban street or deep roadway and saw the ground literally strewn with the blue uniforms of our dead.

Burnside closed this remarkable tragedy by deciding to move the night of December 15, 1862, his brave but beaten army to the north side of the Rappahannock. That work of removal was accomplished without further loss of men or material.

CHAPTER XXII

AFTER the battle of Fredericksburg we returned to the same encampments which we had left to cross the Rappahannock, and on January 27, 1863, orders from the President, dated the day before, placed our " Fighting Joe Hooker " in command of the army. Burnside, Sumner, and Franklin were relieved. For a few days General Couch went to take Sumner's place over the grand division. This gave me command of the Second Corps. But very soon, among the changes made by Hooker, the grand division organization was broken up, and I returned to the second division of the corps. It would have been very wise if Hooker had gone a step further in simplifying, and had consolidated his eight corps into four—three of infantry and artillery and one of cavalry, with its horse batteries.

Notwithstanding misgivings respecting General Hooker, whose California record had been ransacked, and whose private conduct had been canvassed, the army received him kindly. He had been a little hard, in his camp conferences, upon McClellan, and for poor Burnside he had shown no mercy.

My own feeling at that time was that of a want of confidence in the army itself. The ending of the peninsular work, the confusion at the termination of the second battle of Bull Run, the incompleteness of Antietam, and the fatal consequences of Fredericksburg did not make the horizon of our dawning future very luminous. We had suffered desertions by the thousands. I brought two commissioned officers about that time to trial for disloyal language, directed against the President and the general commanding. Mouths were stopped, but discontent had taken deep root. Hooker, however, by his prompt and energetic measures, soon changed the whole tone of the army for the better. Desertions were diminished, and outpost duty was systematized. The general showed himself frequently to his troops at reviews and inspections, and caused the construction of field works and intrenchments, which, with the drills, occupied the time and the minds of the soldiers. The cavalry became a corps, and Stoneman was put in command of it. The artillery reserve, given to General Hunt, was brought to a high degree of efficiency.

In truth, during February, March, and April, the old cheerful, hopeful, trustful spirit which had carried us through so many dark days, through so many bloody fields and trying defeats, returned to the Army of the Potomac; and Hooker's success as a division and corps commander was kept constantly in mind as an earnest of a grand future. As soon as General Sickles, who was then my junior in rank, was assigned to the Third Corps, feeling that I had been overlooked, I wrote a brief letter to General Hooker, asking to be assigned according to my rank. Immediately I was ordered to take command of the Eleventh Army Corps, which General Sigel had just left. I assumed command at Stafford Court House, where General Carl Schurz was in charge. My coming sent Schurz back to his division and Schimmelfennig back to his brigade. The corps was then, in round numbers, 13,000 strong. It had about 5,000 Germans and 8,000 Americans. Two divisions were under the German commanders, Von Steinwehr and Carl Schurz, and one under Devens. One of Devens's brigades was commanded by Colonel Von Gilsa, a German officer, who at drills and reviews made a fine soldierly appearance. Outwardly I met a cordial reception, but I soon found that my past record was not known here; that there was much complaint in the German language at the removal of Sigel, who merely wanted to have his command properly increased, and that I was not at first getting the earnest and loyal support of the entire command. But for me there was no turning back. I brought to the corps several tried officers: for example, General Barlow, to command one brigade in Von Steinwehr's division, and General Adelbert Ames to take a brigade. I had the command drilled and reviewed as much as could be done in a few weeks.

On April 8th the corps of Couch, Sickles, Meade, and Sedgwick were reviewed by President Lincoln, accompanied by General Hooker. There was a column of about 70,000 men, and it must have taken over two hours and a half for them to pass the President. It was the largest procession until the last review before President Andrew Johnson in 1865. Mrs. Lincoln came down from Washington, and the President's two sons were at the grand review. The smaller, Tad, rode a beautiful pony, and was noticeable for his ability to manage him.

On the 10th Mr. Lincoln came to review my corps. The German pioneers had fixed up my tent and its surroundings with everything that evergreens and trees could do to make them cheerful. Of all this Mr. Lincoln took special notice and expressed his admiration. My salute and review were satisfactory.

Up to April 25th General Hooker had managed to keep his plans in his own bosom. True, inferences were drawn by everybody from the partial movements that were made up and down the river. For example, April 13th, Stoneman, started up the Rappahannock with his cavalry corps, except Pleasonton's brigade, ostensibly to go to the Shenandoah Valley. It was my part to send Bushbeck's infantry brigade of Von Steinwehr's division in his support as far as Kelly's Ford. But the flooding rains again began, and had the effect of detaining the whole of Stoneman's force for some days in that neighborhood. Just what he was to do we did not then know.

April 21st, Doubleday, of Reynolds's (First) Corps, also started down the river, and went as far as Port Conway. He here made sundry demonstrations which indicated a purpose to try and effect a crossing. Colonel Henry A. Morrow with his Michigan regiment (Twenty-fourth) made another display near Port Royal. The Confederate commanders believed them to be but feints. These demonstrations had, however, the effect of causing Lee to send troops down the river to watch our proceedings. Jackson went thither in command.

On April 25th I was instructed to send knapsacks and other supplies to Bushbeck at Kelly's Ford, and to see that his men had on hand eight days' rations in knapsacks and haversacks. The instruction ended with this sentence: " I am directed to inform you confidentially, for your own information and not for publication, that your whole corps will probably move in that direction as early as Monday A.M."

Our army at that time numbered for duty about 130,000 — First Corps, Reynolds; Second, Couch; Third, Sickles; Fifth, Meade; Sixth, Sedgwick; Eleventh, Howard; Twelfth, Slocum; cavalry corps, Stoneman; reserve artillery, Hunt.

The Confederate army opposite numbered about 60,000: four divisions under Stonewall Jackson, two (Anderson's and McLaws's) acting separately, and Stuart's cavalry. General Pendleton brought the reserve artillery under one head. Anderson's and McLaws's belonged to Longstreet's corps, but the remainder over and above these two divisions was at this time absent from the Army of Northern Virginia. Lee's forces occupied the Fredericksburg Heights and guarded all approaches. His cavalry, with headquarters at Culpeper, watched his left flank from his position to the Shenandoah Valley.

The plan of operation determined upon by General Hooker, which began to be revealed to his corps commanders little by little in confidential notes, was, first, to send his whole cavalry corps, except one division, to raid around by our right upon Lee's communications; second, to make a crossing, a feint, and possibly an attack, by his left wing at and below Fredericksburg; third, to start the right wing up the Rappahannock to the upper fords, cross them, and push rapidly to and over the Rapidan via Chancellorsville to the heights near Banks's Ford; fourth, to follow up this movement with his center; to throw bridges across and below the mouth of the Rapidan at the United States Ford, or wherever convenient, and reënforce his right wing. The plan was well conceived, except the sending off of his entire cavalry force. But for that there is little doubt that, humanly speaking, Lee would have been defeated. Stoneman would have curtained our movements, occupied the attention of Stuart, guarded our right flank, and let General Hooker and his corps commanders know what maneuvers of Lee were in progress before the wilderness and its deceptive wilds had been reached. But at the outset we were divorced from this potential helpmate. Pleasonton's brigade, which was left to Hooker, was too small to subdivide, so that we were usually left to skirmishers, scouts, and reconnoissance from the infantry arm to ascertain what the enemy was about. From this one mistake arose a dozen others, which contributed to our final discomfiture.

The orders of April 27th made the left wing to consist of the First, Third, and Sixth Corps, Sedgwick to command.

According to instructions, Reynolds took his command (the First Corps) to the lower place, near Pollock's Mills Creek. The Sixth Corps undertook Franklin's old crossing just below the mouth of the Deep Run. With some little delay and after overcoming the enemy's pickets, Wadsworth's division of Reynolds's corps was firmly established on the other shore, and the remainder of that corps held at hand.

The Sixth Corps was equally successful, and Brooks's division, aided by a battery, held a stone bridgehead below Fredericksburg and kept the way open for his corps. The preliminaries to all this work —Hunt planting the helpful artillery and Benham bringing up his bridges, and the concentration of the troops—were thoroughly provided for and executed with secrecy and dispatch; yet General Lee's watchful assistants soon let him know what was going forward. He got ready for a possible attack, but when Wednesday passed away and then Thursday with no further effort on Sedgwick's part beyond the preparations which I have named, Lee rightly concluded that Hooker's main attack was not to be undertaken at that point. The right wing, which at the time most concerned me in these movements, was to be constituted from the Eleventh, Twelfth, and Fifth Corps.

Monday morning at 5.30, April 27th, my command left its camp near Brooke's Station, on the Aquia Creek Railroad, and took the most direct road by the way of Hartwood Church toward Kelly's Ford. We made a fair march (fourteen miles) the first day, and went into camp a little beyond that church. Everything was then in good order, the men in fine health and spirits, glad of any change which relieved the monotony and tedium of their winter quarters. Our orders were very strict to keep down the trains to the smallest number for ammunition and forage only. I found that on that march several of my subordinate commanders had been very careless in not carrying out these instructions to the letter. General Hooker and his staff passed my trains during the march, and said to me: " General Meade has done better than you." Of course I had issued the orders, but field officers would here and there slip in an extra wagon till there were many; for where were they to get their meals if ration wagons were all left behind? This condition I quickly corrected, but it was my first mortification in this campaign. Some of the American officers were as careless as some of the foreign in the matter of orders—glorious in eye service, but conscienceless when out of sight. Our main trains were parked not far from Banks's Ford. My corps was followed by Slocum's, and his by Meade's.

The next day (Tuesday) we were on the road by 4 A.M., and accomplished our march to the neighborhood of Kelly's Ford by four in the afternoon; trains as well as troops were closed up and all encamped by that early hour.

I had hastened on ahead of my command to visit General Hooker, who had transferred his headquarters to Morrisville, a hamlet some five or six miles north of Kelly's Ford. Here he received me pleasantly, gave specific instructions, and carefully explained his proposed plan of attack. After this interview I returned to my troops and began to execute my part. Captain Comstock, of the engineers, who had graduated from West Point in the class following mine, was on hand to lay a bridge, for this ford was too deep for practical use. By 6 P.M. the bridge was commenced. The bridge layers were detailed mainly from my corps. Four hundred of Bushbeck's brigade seized the boats, which they put together, put them into the stream, and pushed for the south bank. The enemy's pickets stopped to fire one wild volley and fled. There was then quick work. The bridge was done before ten o'clock and the crossing well covered by picket posts far out. Immediately I broke camp and took my command over the bridge. Colonel Kellogg, with the Seventeenth Pennsylvania Cavalry, reported to me for temporary duty. With his force we extended our outposts and patrolled the country around our new bivouac, but owing to the ignorance of our guides of the character of the country and to the pitchy darkness, the troops were not in position until near daylight. Still, as Slocum was now to lead the column, we had time for a short rest before resuming the march. Soon after getting upon the road to Germania Ford we could hear firing on Slocum's front, and before long shells began to burst over our heads and uncomfortably near to the marching men. Colonel Kellogg made some attempts to stop this; but as there were with the enemy two field pieces supported by cavalry, it proved too difficult a task. Just then a brigade of Stoneman's corps swept along southward in that neighborhood and rid us of the annoyance.

General Slocum had cleared the Rapidan, so that by eleven at night of this day (Wednesday, April 29th) my command began to cross the river. Slocum had here no bridge at first and could not wait for one. Part of his men, supporting each other and cheering, waded the current from shore to shore. The old bridge, however, was soon repaired and I used it. By four in the morning of Thursday my men were again in camp, except those with the train, including its guard.

On this day (Thursday) we did not delay for rest, but marched at seven o'clock, following Slocum, coming up abreast of his corps near Dowdall's tavern. As soon as my head of column came to this place—a small opening in the wilderness, within which are a few houses and a church—it was halted and I rode over to the Chancellor House, or Chancellorsville. Meade's command was already there. Here I met General Slocum, who was to give me instructions. His orders were to occupy the right, by Dowdall's tavern, resting my extreme right flank at a mill, marked as on Hunting Creek, or a tributary. He promised me to cover the whole ground from Chancellorsville to Dowdall's tavern. I went back at once and in person reconnoitered the right, riding through the woods and small glade-like openings. I could find no mill in that neighborhood, but I posted the command as directed, drawing back my right across the pike, and having considerable reserve. I had hardly got into position before I found three-quarters of a mile more of space between me and Slocum's nearest division, and I was obliged, to my sorrow, to use up most of my reserve to fill this vacancy. At this time, though there was an interval on my right, Pleasonton's cavalry, with some artillery, remained at the place where the Ely Ford road crosses Hunting Creek, and I sent him two companies of infantry for support; this, with such cavalry pickets as Pleasonton would naturally throw out on all the roads which led to him, afforded me a good outpost of warning to my right rear. But there was no cavalry placed on the Orange plank road, nor on the old turnpike, which near Dowdall's tavern passes off to the north of west, making a considerable angle with the plank road.

As soon as Meade had crossed the Rapidan, Anderson's two Confederate brigades were drawn back from the United States Ford; the bridges were immediately laid and all but Gibbon's division of the Second Corps (Couch's) came to join us at Chancellorsville. Sickles, too, with the Third, had been taken from Sedgwick and was (Thursday night) in bivouac near the United States Ford, just across the river.

General Hooker, with a portion of his staff, had already come up and taken his headquarters at Chancellorsville. Our troops had skirmished all along with Stuart's cavalry, and exchanged some shots with Anderson's division in front of Slocum's center and left, yet thus far everything had worked well. We had entered upon a vigorous offensive campaign. We had reached the enemy's vicinage, and were but a few miles from his left flank, with no natural or artificial obstruction in our way. Such was the situation Thursday evening.

Friday morning at dawn Sickles completed his march and joined us on the front line. He took post on my left, relieving some of Slocum's thin line and some of Steinwehr's, near Dowdall's tavern. I thus obtained Barlow's excellent brigade for my general corps reserve. These, with a few reserve batteries, were held in hand, in echelon, to cover my extreme right flank in case of such need.

Let us notice again, on that Thursday night, how favorable matters looked, when General Hooker was so jubilant and confident and full of the purpose of pushing on to the heights near Banks's Ford. He had then 50,000 men well concentrated at Chancellorsville and more within easy support. His left wing, under Sedgwick, had thus far occupied enough the attention of the Confederates to keep them in its front at Fredericksburg. It was not, then, strange that the sanguine Hooker caused to be issued and sent to us that night, to be read at our camp fires and to be published to our commands, as speedily as possible, a congratulatory order. (For full order, see Appendix.)

General Hooker intended to push for Lee's left flank and assail him there in position. Should Lee move upon Sedgwick with all the force which he could make available for that purpose, he would probably no more than get well at work before Hooker's right wing would be upon him.

The alternative for Lee was to leave as small a force in his works before Sedgwick as possible, with instructions to keep Sedgwick back, while he himself, with the main Confederate army, Napoleonlike, hurried to join Anderson beyond Salem Church, whose skirmish line boldly fronted Hooker's at Chancellorsville, and promptly gave battle. This plan had been matured from the first, and was already well understood by all the Confederate brigade and division commanders. Their brigades were large and corresponded very well to our divisions—for they made no mistake in consolidating their troops. However much of a disturbance or panic in the rear our cavalry under Stoneman was creating, Lee did not send his cavalry force under Stuart to try and head us off, but simply let his son, General W. H. F. Lee, with his small cavalry division, watch, follow, fight, or do whatever he could, while he retained Stuart with two-thirds of that corps with himself. His 1,800 cavalrymen, with some horse artillery, were never better employed.

Early's division of Stonewall Jackson's corps and Barksdale's brigade, with a part of the reserve artillery, to be commanded by Pendleton, were selected for the defense of the works in front of Sedgwick at Fredericksburg. Anderson already had in our front at Chancellorsville five infantry brigades, in all nearly 11,000 men. At midnight of Thursday, while we were sleeping near Chancellorsville, in that wilderness, McLaws's division joined Anderson with some 6,000 men. On Friday morning at dawn Stonewall Jackson (who was now at Fredericksburg) with all his command, except Early, followed McLaws. Jackson had three divisions, numbering about 26,000 men, besides 170 pieces of artillery. He reached Anderson's lines by eight o'clock Friday morning (May 1st) and, as was his wont, took command and prepared to advance. It was a goodly force—upward of 43,000 men of all arms, well organized, well drilled and disciplined, and under that best of Southern leaders, the redoubtable Stonewall Jackson. The troops fell into position on their arrival. McLaws went to the right of Anderson and put his forces on high ground in front of a country road which crosses from the river road to the "Old Mine" road. Anderson crossed the Old Mine road and the turnpike, while Jackson's men were upon the plank roadway and the new railway route. Owens's regiment of Confederate cavalry made the first reconnoissance, and by 11 A.M. this movement was followed up by other forces.

As revealed in his orders to Sedgwick Thursday evening, General Hooker's confident purpose still was to push on from Chancellorsville, drive back Anderson, and seize and occupy the high ground near Banks's Ford. But for the delay of Chancellorsville, as if that was our real destination, Hooker would have easily gained his point. Probably he waited first for Couch, and afterwards for Sickles. Still, after a personal scout of observation and examination of his front, Hooker issued his instructions for the execution of his proposed plan: First, Meade, using two divisions, was to take the river road and get to a designated position opposite Banks's Ford by 2 P.M.; second, Sykes, supported by Hancock from Couch's corps, was to take the same direction on the old Fredericksburg turnpike, move up abreast of Meade, both columns having deployed their skirmishers and lines so as to connect, and to fight any enemy that might be found there; third, Slocum, with the Twelfth Corps, was to march out on the plank road eastward to Tabernacle Church and mass his corps there. It was a point on the same general line as those to be attained by Meade and Sykes. I, with the Eleventh, was to follow Slocum and post my command a mile in rear of him. All these movements were so regulated as to be completed by two in the afternoon.

As a grand support to our whole wing, Sedgwick, below Fredericksburg, was directed to make a demonstration in force against the enemy's intrenchments at Hamilton's Crossing. This was ordered to be undertaken at 1 P.M. But Sedgwick did not get the orders till four hours later. As Hooker's chief of staff was at Falmouth, and had constant telegraphic communication with him, the wretched failures in the transmission of orders and messages between Chancellorsville and Fredericksburg have never been understood.

The other columns lost no time. They started out on their respective roads. True, there was some clogging at the Chancellorsville crossroads, for many troops passed that one point, and the result of this clogging was that Sykes got considerably ahead of Hancock, and Slocum's appearance at Tabernacle Church was delayed—still, Slocum came forward and I, with my corps, supported him. Meade reached his point in fine style, but did not succeed in connecting with Sykes on his right; neither did Slocum reach out far enough to touch Sykes's right flank. Yet very soon Hancock was on hand in his rear for support.

Both of the armies were now in rapid motion in comparatively open ground. Jackson had a shorter front than we, and produced unity by commanding the whole line. We had four detached columns—those of Meade, Sykes, Slocum, and French—feeling out experimentally for a line of connection beyond the ground already passed by Jackson; and our common commander unfortunately was not, like Jackson, at the front, where he could make the corrections now of vital importance. Meade's skirmishers occupied the heights in sight of the coveted Banks's Ford. Sykes beheld McLaws with deployed troops on the very hills he was directed to occupy. He did not hesitate an instant, but moved forward at double quick and attacked with all his might, driving back the brigades before him, and seized the strong position.

This position Sykes continued to hold. He was outflanked; but, with General Hancock close at hand, Sykes did not propose to retire nor fear to hold his ground. It was just the instant to reënforce him. Behind Hancock was all of Sickles's corps. But, to everybody's sorrow, our commander had *changed his mind* at that moment, and the orders of Hooker came to Sykes to return to Chancellorsville at once and take the old position. Slocum had encountered the brigades of Wright and Posey, but the action had hardly begun when the same orders came to him; the same also to Meade, as he was getting ready to give Sykes a strong support on his left. My command had gotten in readiness and gone out two miles, and a brigade of Sickles's had come to watch at Dowdall's toward the west, as French was doing toward the south at Todd's tavern. We all received the orders of retreat with astonishment: "Go back to the old position!"

It gave to our whole army the impression of a check, a failure, a defeat. It was a sudden change from a vigorous offensive to the defensive, into a position not good at all to resist a front attack, and one easily turned; for our right had no river or swamp or other natural obstacle on which to rest, and the whole position was enveloped in a vast and difficult forest, of which we knew little. Such maps of the roads as we had we subsequently found to be wholly incorrect.

During the confusion of the changes of troops at Dowdall's tavern some female members of a family there, taking a basket of provisions with them, escaped from our lines and informed some Confederate officer of the situation, carrying accurate information of how we occupied that position.

On the other hand, our retreat was counted a great victory for the Confederates. They gained the *morale* which we had lost. They became jubilant and were confident of our final defeat. Hooker in motion was a great lion in their way, but now he had decided to lie still, and they, anticipating his fatal spring, would creep upon him and slay him.

Had General Hooker been at the front with Sykes or with Hancock at the time of Sykes's attack, he would have seen that his ability to concentrate there was greater than he dreamed. Meade, Couch, and Slocum were already out of the forest and my corps was just emerging from it when he ordered us to retire.

The old position which we resumed was as follows: A stream called Mineral Spring Run, rising perhaps a half mile west of Chancellorsville, runs northeast and joins the Rappahannock at right angles. Meade stretched his command along the western crest of this run, and, resting his left not far from the Rappahannock, faced toward Fredericksburg. The whole of Meade's line ran through an unbroken forest; its extent was about three miles. Couch continued the line, but was obliged to bulge out for a half mile to cover the Chancellorsville house and knoll. Hancock's division of this corps made a right angle, the apex being on the old turnpike. French's division covered the space be-tween Hancock and Meade, being substantially in re-serve. Slocum's corps was next. Geary's and Will-iams's divisions, abreast of Hancock's foremost men, carried the line along some high ground to a second knoll, called Hazel Grove. Sickles, making an obtuse angle with Slocum's front, filled the space between Slocum's right flank and the small open field which embraces Dowdall's tavern. This he did with Birney's division; the remainder of his corps was in reserve, lo-cated between Dowdall's and Chancellorsville.

My own corps (the Eleventh) occupied the extreme right. As this position became subsequently of special interest, I will describe it. First, the old plank road and the old turnpike coming from the east are one and the same from Chancellorsville to and across Dowdall's opening; there the road forked, the plank continuing west, making an angle of some twenty degrees with the pike. North of the plank, in the Dowdall's opening, is the Wilderness Church; Hawkins's house is in the small gladelike space, about a quarter of a mile north of the church, and Dowdall's tavern, where Melzie Chancellor's family lived, was southeast of the church and also south of the main road. Here were my head-quarters and Steinwehr's before the battle of Sat-urday. The next opening to Dowdall's, westward, situated between the forks—i. e., between the plank road and the turnpike—was called Tally Farm. The highest ground was at Tally's, near the pike, and at Hawkins's house; there was only a small rise at Dow-dall's. These elevations were but slight, hardly as high as Hazel Grove or Chancellorsville. Except the small openings, the forest was continuous and nearly enveloping. Generally the trees were near together,

363

with abundant entanglements of undergrowth. Now, beginning with Sickles's right and facing south, General Steinwehr, commanding my second division, deployed two regiments of Bushbeck's brigade, some 100 yards, more or less, south of the plank road; the remainder of that brigade he deployed or held as a reserve north of the road—holding all of the ground to the Wilderness Church and to the forks of the roads. General Schurz, in charge of the 3d division, took up the line and carried it to a crossroad, and then, making a right angle, ran back along this crossroad to the turnpike, and thence farther, just south of and parallel with the pike. He kept about half of the brigades of Krzyzanowski and Schimmelfennig in reserve, holding his reserves in the Dowdall's opening north of the church. The next division (the first) under General Devens, was deployed in the extension of Schurz's line, first along the turnpike westward, with similar reserves. He drew back one brigade, Colonel Von Gilsa's, and a small part of another, nearly at right angles to the turnpike, and extended this line well out into the woods, facing it toward the northwest. There was a country road behind him, so that he could easily reënforce any part of his line. The artillery was distributed along the lines in favorable positions—two pieces near Devens's right, the remainder of Heckman's battery on Devens's left; Dilger's fine battery of six guns at the crossroads, and Wiedrich's four guns at Steinwehr's right and three at his left. Besides, I had three batteries in reserve. I had a line of intrenchments made off against the little church, extending across the opening into the woods, and facing toward our extreme right and rear. I put the reserve heavy guns in position there to protect that flank, and supported them by my general reserve of infantry, viz., Barlow's large brigade. My whole front was covered with rifle pits or barricades, constructed under the constant inspection of Major Hoffman, the chief engineer. Early Saturday (May 2d) General Hooker, with Colonel Comstock, his engineer officer, visited my corps and rode with me along my front line. He frequently exclaimed: " How strong! " and made no criticism. At one point a regiment was not deployed, and at another was an unfilled gap in the thick forest. Comstock advised me to keep these spaces filled, even if I had to shorten my front. I made the changes suggested. Further, the whole command was covered with a good line of skirmishers.

The first commotion in my front occurred Friday evening. It was apparently a force of infantry with a battery of artillery, sent by General Lee and moving along the lines from our left toward our right. The force went no farther than Schimmelfennig's brigade. He had marched out a battalion, had suddenly assailed the reconnoiterers, and driven them off.

During the next day frequent reconnoissances were made from my front. Individual scouts pushed out under the cover of the woods, and at one time a company of Pennsylvania cavalry undertook to patrol the various roads outward from the vicinity of my command.

During the morning of this Saturday it was evident to us that the enemy was doing something—most probably preparing for a general attack. Hancock's angle, or that between Slocum and Sickles, were most favorable points. I sent out my chief of staff more than once to see if my line was in shape and to order the command, through the division commanders, to keep on the alert. Once my staff officer, Major Whittlesey, rode over the entire picket line to see that the front was well covered with skirmishers. He went from the left to the extreme right and made his report. I speak of this to show what unusual precautions I took because of the forest and of the uncertainty of the enemy's movements. Doubtless other corps commanders did the same. The officers, during Saturday, frequently discussed the situation at my headquarters. Every iota of information which I received I sent at once by mounted orderlies to General Hooker. I did not think General Lee would be likely to move around our right, because our whole force was much larger than his. He had already been compelled to divide his army in order to hold back Sedgwick and come against us. He could not afford to divide again, for, should he attempt that, certainly Hooker would attack his separate bodies and conquer him in detail. So I reasoned, and so did others. Again, if my flank should be turned, it appeared plain, from the roads on our maps, that Lee would have to make a large detour. To withstand this, Reynolds's corps, recently come up from Falmouth, was on hand, besides the artillery and the reserves of the other corps stationed near Chancellorsville. Further, should an attack by any possibility reach us, Devens was to hold on as long as he could, using his reserves to support the points most threatened; Schurz was to hold his regiments that were free from the line, ready to protect the right flank. He preferred, he said, to hold them *en masse*, so as to charge in column. And last, as I have said, I put my reserve artillery in position and supported it by Barlow's men, facing the right, so that, should the troops of the right be dislodged, they could be drawn back beyond his line,

and still the fight continue till help came. Was not
Sickles's whole corps at hand? Would not he simply
face about and reënforce me? Once in the West, a
year later, with the Fourth Corps, I was situated in
the same manner, but by using all corps reserves and
reënforcements that I sent for, the enemy's brigades
were met in time and driven back with great loss.

General Lee says: " Early on the next morning of
the 2d (Saturday, May 2, 1863), General Jackson
marched by the Furnace and Brock's road; his movement being effectually covered by Fitz Lee's cavalry
under Stuart in person." This direction was nearly
parallel with our front line from east to west till, opposite Sickles, the road which Jackson took turned suddenly toward the south and kept on for several miles
away from us toward Spottsylvania. Then, intersecting a road running northwest, the column turned up
that one and kept on to the plank beyond, and massed
under the cover of the thick forest. This march took
nearly all day. General Lee, as he knew how to do,
with McLaws and Anderson, kept Meade, Couch, and
Slocum busy—and Sickles busier still near the Furnace as soon as Jackson's guns were heard.

There was a point at the Furnace clearing where
the moving troops of Jackson were seen by some of
Sickles's skirmishers. This was reported to Sickles,
and by him to General Hooker. A strong reconnoissance was made. Clark's battery, well supported, was
put in position, and fired upon the Confederate column.
This firing forced the enemy to abandon the road, and
the whole force appeared at first to retire rapidly
eastward and southward toward Spottsylvania.

The Twenty-third Georgia Regiment, left behind,
deployed toward Sickles to hold the corner where

the road changed direction. This resistance caused Sickles, with Hooker's consent, to send forward two and a half miles Birney's entire division, supporting it by other troops. This command worked along slowly through the woods, bridging streams, sending out Berdan's sharpshooters as skirmishers, and pressing forward. Considerable resistance was encountered, but the Twenty-third Georgia was, after a while, captured by the sharpshooters.

In brief, the circumstances seemed to warrant the conclusion that Lee was moving off—probably to Orange Court House—in retreat. Assuming this to be the case, Hooker directed Slocum to support Sickles's left, and I received orders by Captain Moore, of Hooker's staff, to support Sickles's right with my reserve troops, while he vigorously attacked the flank or rear of Stonewall Jackson.

As an attack in that direction was to be made by our troops and by those near me, and as my general reserve was taken away to support it, I deemed it of sufficient importance to go myself and see what further should be done. General Steinwehr accompanied me. We saw our men in position on the right of Sickles, over two miles south of us, but not finding the engagement very active in that quarter we hastened back to my headquarters at Dowdall's Clearing. We were again at the tavern. Our horses had been unsaddled for their evening meal. There was no news for me, except what the scouts brought and what General Devens had frequently reported, that Lee's column had been crossing the plank road obliquely between two and three miles ahead, and apparently aiming toward Orange Court House. Had I then been familiar with the routes as I am now I should have distrusted the conclusion. General Hooker, who had more sources of information than I, thought Lee was retreating. He so telegraphed to Sedgwick about the time of Sickles's attack. He ordered all the troops toward the Furnace in that belief. I had then the same conviction.

When Stonewall Jackson began his march, Anderson watched us closely. He reported: "At midday Sickles's corps, Birney's division, appeared in some force at the Furnace. Posey's brigade was sent to dislodge him and was soon engaged in a warm skirmish with him." This combat became so lively and Posey was so hard pressed that he called for help. Then Anderson took Wright's brigade from the line and sent it to the support of Posey. Further, Major Hardaway's artillery was added to that of Lieutenant Colonel Brown. Both of these large brigades of Posey and Wright with artillery were here, deployed in as long a line as possible; they fought by increasing their skirmishers till night, and intrenched as soon as they could.

This all shows that Hooker's attack upon Stonewall Jackson's flank at the Furnace was not really made. It was General Lee himself, who, during Jackson's wonderful march, by means of Anderson and McLaws and part of his artillery, took care of Sickles's whole line. Thus, Hooker's movement toward the Furnace carried away from my flank all immediate support to be expected from Barlow, Sickles, and Slocum; and, further, these troops were looking, moving, and fighting in an opposite direction. They were engaged, not as Hooker telegraphed, with Lee in full retreat, but with Lee himself staying behind after Jackson's departure. He was then controlling the smaller wing of his army. Lee took great risks as he did at Gaines's

Mill before Richmond, where 25,000 men only held in check the whole of McClellan's army, while he himself crossed the river and defeated Porter and all the supports that McClellan dared send him. This time Lee took the smaller force himself.

Stonewall Jackson continued his march until he ordered a temporary halt. At this halt Fitzhugh Lee, who from a wooded knoll had discovered my flank, returned to Jackson and asked him to go and see. The two generals then rode to the wooded knoll. Jackson took a good look at our right flank and then, without a word, went back and marched his command still farther, at least half a mile beyond the " Old Turnpike." The lines of battle were there formed about 4 P.M. The divisions were in line 100 yards apart. Should they preserve the order of arrangement indicated, Jackson's flank would be beyond our General Devens's waiting line of battle—beyond his right battery and Von Gilsa's supporting brigade. Still, with ten minutes' notice or fifteen minutes' hard fighting, Devens could have held or extended his line.

It was already six o'clock. Hearing the sound of a skirmish toward Devens's position, I mounted with my staff and rode toward a high ridge not far from my reserve batteries. With a little more than 8,000 men at hand and with no other troops now nearer than Chancellorsville, I heard the first murmuring of a coming storm—a little quick firing on the picket line, the wild rushing of frightened game into our very camps, and almost sooner than it can be told the bursting of thousands of Confederates through the almost impenetrable thickets of the wilderness and then the wilder, noisier conflict which ensued. It was a terrible gale! the rush, the rattle, the quick lightning from a hundred points at once; the roar, redoubled by echoes through the forest; the panic, the dead and dying in sight and the wounded straggling along; the frantic efforts of the brave and patriotic to stay the angry storm! One may live through and remember impressions of those fatal moments, but no pen or picture can catch and give the whole.

A few words of detail will make clearer to the reader the situation. General Dole said that at 5 P.M. the order was given the Confederates to advance. If his time was right it must have taken him an hour to work forward " through the very thick woods." He first encountered our skirmishers who were so obstinate that it required his main line to drive them back; then his men were " subjected to a very heavy musket fire, with grape, canister, and shell." Immediately his line assailed our barricades and intrenchments, drove our defenders off, and seized our batteries. Von Gilsa's Union brigade was supporting two guns; Dole's left regiment broke through the interval between Von Gilsa and the remainder of Devens's division, while Rodes's brigade faced Von Gilsa in front and so the greater part of Iverson's long line reached beyond Von Gilsa's position. Von Gilsa and the troops to his immediate left were quickly driven from their intrenchments, and they rolled along down Devens's line and created a panic in all that front. But there was another line to encounter after the first real resistance made by Devens's reserve regiments and part of Schurz's division, which was on a side hill in an open field east of Hawkins's house. Against this line the Confederates had come and succeeded in dislodging it, capturing one rifle gun; then they pushed on rapidly 300 yards more over an open field. During this movement they faced another severe fire from musketry and batteries on the crest of a hill which commanded their field of approach. Our infantry was there in considerable force and protected by rifle intrenchments. We had filled these intrenchments, which had been prepared for Barlow's brigade, with fragments of regiments and individual men in retreat, who had volunteered to stay and help.

In the outset of the conflict I instantly sent a staff officer (Colonel Asmussen) to see that all was right in the direction of the firing. After Colonel Asmussen left me I had proceeded some 200 yards toward my reserve batteries, when the louder firing reached my ears and I saw Von Gilsa's men running back from their position. Immediately I made an effort to change the front of part of Devens's and all of Schurz's division. The rush of the enemy made this impossible. To render matters worse for me personally my horse got crazy, like some of the panic-stricken men, and plunged and reared and left me on the ground. Of course, I was soon mounted, but this hindered and delayed my personal work.

Steinwehr, who was always at hand, at this juncture brought me two regiments. For a time the reserve artillery at that point fired steadily and did well. It took the Confederates twenty minutes to take that place. It was taken too soon, because the instant that the fire became severe our men, who were separate from their companies, ran back in panic and four cannon were captured, but some of the batteries were withdrawn in good order. Dilger's, for example, kept up its fire all along the Chancellorsville road. Behind the reserve batteries near Dowdall's tavern Steinwehr had his men spring over their breastworks and hold on, firing as soon as they could. One brigade of his (Bushbeck's) was kept quite entire and faced the enemy through the whole retreat.

Schimmelfennig's and a part of Krzyzanowski's brigades moved gradually back to the north of the plank road and into the eastern border of Dowdall's opening. They, too, kept up their fire. The whole center, as well as Devens's right, seem to have been seized with a blind indescribable panic. Several staff officers were near me and one of General Hooker's staff—Colonel Dickinson. We worked hard to stay the panic-stricken —officers as well as men.

" It's of no use," they would sing out. One colonel said: " I have done what I could! " and continued his flight. What artillery we kept was for a time well served, but we could only fight for time.

The next stand I attempted was at the forest's edge, but when that position was outflanked by Jackson, I rode back to the first high plateau to which we came on the Chancellorsville route. Here I met General Hiram G. Berry, of Maine. He said: " Well, general, where now?" I replied: " You take the right (north) of this road and I will take the left and try to defend it." All of my batteries were joined to others already there and placed on the brow of the plateau. I here brought all the troops of the Eleventh Corps which I could collect and faced them to the rear in support of the batteries. The enemy reached us with his fire. Some of our officers misbehaved even here, so much had our defeat disheartened them; but many were still resolute and helpful. Berry, of the Third Corps, put his men into line and marched off to hold back the advancing masses, till he fell mortally wounded. Pleasonton, returning from Hooker's Furnace movement, used his troops and some batteries effectively from the opening at Hazel Grove, southeast of Dowdall's, and succeeded in stopping some troops of Jackson's which were pursuing beyond our now left flank the fugitives who had taken that direction in their flight. Soon, with Berry's division, the cannon on our hill, Pleasonton's help and that of various other detachments swinging into a line perpendicular to the one thoroughfare—the plank road—we were able to check Jackson's advance.

What a roar of cannon pouring their volleys into the forest, now black with the growing night! It was in that forest that the brave, energetic, and successful Southern leader fell. Jackson's death was more injurious to the Confederate cause than would have been that of 10,000 other soldiers, so great was the confidence he had won, so deep was the reverence of citizen and soldier for his character and ability!

It has been customary to blame me and my corps for the disaster. The imputations of neglect to obey orders; of extraordinary self-confidence; of fanatical reliance upon the God of battles; of not sending out reconnoissances; of not intrenching; of not strengthening the right flank by keeping proper reserves; of having no pickets and skirmishers; of not sending information to General Hooker, etc., etc., are far from true. My command was by positive orders riveted to that position. Though constantly threatened and made aware of hostile columns in motion, yet the woods were so dense that Stonewall Jackson was able to mass a large force a few miles off, whose exact whereabouts neither patrols, reconnoissances, nor scouts ascertained. The enemy crossing the plank road, two and a half miles off, we all saw. So the turning at the Furnace was seen by hundreds of our people; but the interpretation of these movements was certainly wrong. Yet, wherein did we neglect any precaution? It will be found that Devens kept his subordinates constantly on the *qui vive*; so did Schurz. Their actions and mine were identical. The Eleventh Corps detained Jackson for over an hour; part of my force was away by Hooker's orders; part of each division fought hard, as our Confederate enemies clearly show; part of it became wild with panic, like the Belgians at Waterloo, like most of our troops at Bull Run, and the Confederates, the second day, at Fair Oaks.

I may leave the whole matter to the considerate judgment of my companions in arms, simply asserting that on the terrible day of May 2, 1863, I did all which could have been done by a corps commander in the presence of that panic of men largely caused by the overwhelming attack of Jackson's 26,000 men against my isolated corps of 8,000 without its reserve—thus outnumbering me 3 to 1.

There is always a theory in war which will forestall the imputation of blame to those who do not deserve it. It is to impute the credit of one's great defeat to his enemy. I think in our hearts, as we take a candid review of everything that took place under General Hooker in the blind wilderness country around Chancellorsville, we do, indeed, impute our primary defeat to the successful effort of Stonewall Jackson, and our other checks to General Robert E. Lee. Certainly those are wrong who claim that I had no skirmishers out at Chancellorsville, for every report shows that the whole front was covered with them, and they are wrong who declare that there were no scouts or reconnoissances—for scouts, both cavalry and infantry, were constantly sent out, some of whom reported back to Devens, to me, and to General Hooker. The reconnoissance made by Schimmelfennig's brigade was as bold and as effective as it could be in such a forest. Or again, that there were no intrenchments; for under Major Hoffman, the faithful engineer officer, the front and the batteries were fairly covered; and the woods, in places barricaded and obstructed, occupied by the right brigade of the corps, and afforded also a natural protection.

The extraordinary precaution of a cross intrenchment extending over the open ground and into the woods in rear of our right where were all the reserve artillery and Barlow's division to-support it, should not be forgotten. If there were any axes, picks, or shovels obtainable which were not used, then I was misinformed. The order from the commanding general addressed to General Slocum and myself jointly, cautioning me to look to my right flank, etc., must have been made prior to the visit of Generals Hooker and Comstock, for General Sickles's corps had already replaced General Slocum's on my left and certainly General Hooker would not have sent away all of Sickles's corps and all of my general reserve on the very day of the battle, if he had deemed those masses necessary for the strengthening of his right flank.

Neither the commander, the War Department, nor Congress ever saw fit, by any communication to me, to hold me accountable for the dislodgment of the Eleventh Corps at Chancellorsville. That General Hooker should have believed General Lee to have been in full retreat, as he telegraphed to Sedgwick, was not unnatural or confined to him alone; upon that theory the move he made of Sickles, Slocum, and Barlow during Saturday was not bad. And, indeed, my conduct in this battle was in no respect different from that in other engagements.

The Eleventh Corps was soon reorganized and marched to relieve the Fifth Corps, under General Meade, on our extreme left. Here it held an intrenched or barricaded line till the end of the Chancellorsville campaign.

For the operations of the next day; the work of Sedgwick's command at Fredericksburg; his fighting near and crossing the Rappahannock; the unjust aspersions cast upon him by pretentious writers; the grand council of war, where, mostly, the general officers voted to fight, and the final withdrawal, I wish to call attention to the good accounts of the Comte de Paris and to the more exhaustive handling of Chancellorsville by a brother officer—Major Theodore A. Dodge.

Chancellorsville was a dreadful field. The dead were strewn through forest and open farms. The wounded had often to wait for days before succor came. Sometimes it never came. One officer on my personal staff, Captain F. Dessaur, was killed while near me beside Barlow's intrenchments, endeavoring to rally the panic-stricken men. His young wife had besought him to resign and come home to Brooklyn, N. Y., before this battle commenced. He tendered his resignation, explaining the peculiar circumstances of the case. But we were before the enemy, and soon to be engaged in battle, so that I wrote my disapproval upon his application. Poor fellow, he was slain, and my heart was deeply pained at his loss and in sympathy with his stricken family. Dessaur is an example of that dreadful sacrifice made in the cause of our national unity and of human liberty.

CHAPTER XXIII

PROBABLY there was no gloomier period during our great war than the month which followed the disasters of Chancellorsville. Then I entered with fuller understanding into the meaning of " the valley of the shadow of death." On May 26, 1863, an officer, high in rank and claiming to be a warm personal friend, wrote me with great apparent frankness and urged me to leave the Eleventh Corps. I have his letter before me, in which occur these remarkable words: " The first thing they [the men, Germans and Americans] will do when placed in position will be to look behind them, and the accidental discharge of a musket in the rear will produce another panic, another disaster, another disgrace to yourself, to the troops, to all of us," etc.

I would not believe it; I courted another trial for the command other than that of the terrible Wilderness. I was then obliged to raise my eyes above the criticisms and well-meant advice of my companions in arms; I looked to the Great Shepherd for his care and guidance. As a result, in the end, nay, in the very campaign so soon to begin, my judgment was justified.

The feeling of the country at that time, North and South, was far from satisfactory to those patriots who had struggled the hardest and suffered the most.

Campaign of Gettysburg

The three months' and two years' men at the end of May were going home to be mustered out, making the army of Hooker some 25,000 less than that of Lee. The raid of Stoneman had been severe upon the cavalry horses; the terms of enlistment of many cavalrymen had expired; so that, when General Pleasonton, succeeding Stoneman, assumed command, our cavalry had been depleted at least one-third.

As to the outlook for the cause itself, when was it ever worse? I remember well the feelings displayed and the opinions entertained by our military men at General Hooker's council of war just before we returned from Chancellorsville. General Sickles, then the able commander of the Third Corps, was very frank. Though our army was still so strong, much of it as yet unhurt, and though the other general officers thought it wise to give the foe another trial before retiring, he said, substantially: " No! the last election went against the administration; the copperheads are gaining in strength; the enemies of the Republic everywhere are jubilant. It will not do to risk here the loss of this army. We have gone far enough. I do not speak as a military man from a military standpoint— you, gentlemen, are better fitted for that—but from my view of the political arena." We returned, as everybody knows, to the old camps. Then came the fever to go home, the terrible newspaper abuse of us all—sometimes of the officers and sometimes of the conduct of the soldiers. With it were the old animosities, envies, and jealousies, and the newly awakened ambitions. There was a constant rushing to Washington for the purpose of interviewing Halleck, Stanton, and Lincoln. The committee of Congress, sitting to look after the conduct of the war, had hosts of voluntary witnesses from the army, and the foundations were then laid for unusual fame, for extraordinary reputations. It is refreshing to-day to review the batch of wise plans and critical statements which were evolved, having been made after the events which they deplore.

We could gather little hope from the splendid condition of Lee's army. It had been reorganized. Its numerous brigades were grouped into divisions and the divisions into three army corps, and cavalry. Stonewall Jackson, it is true, was no more, but the three lieutenant generals—Longstreet, A. P. Hill, and Ewell—were not wanting in ability or experience. They were trusted by Lee and believed in by the troops and people.

J. E. B. Stuart was cut out for a cavalry leader. In perfect health, but thirty-two years of age, full of vigor and enterprise, with the usual ideas imbibed in Virginia concerning State Supremacy, Christian in thought and temperate by habit, no man could ride faster, endure more hardships, make a livelier charge, or be more hearty and cheerful while so engaged. A touch of vanity, which invited the smiles and applause of the fair maidens of Virginia, but added to the zest and ardor of Stuart's parades and achievements. He commanded Lee's cavalry corps — a well-organized body, of which he was justly proud.

It took each army some time to get its artillery into practical shape. It was sometimes attached to divisions and distributed here and there as might be required, but finally, General Lee gave to his artillery a form of organization; putting together, for one battery, four guns instead of six, the usual number, he constituted a battalion of sixteen pieces. He placed fifteen such battalions under the command of Pendleton, who, in his own arm, rivaled Stuart in energy and experience. Habitually, as I understand it, one artillery battalion was assigned to a division of infantry, making three to each corps. This placed six battalions in the reserve. Besides these guns there were thirty of light artillery or horse artillery attached to the cavalry. The total number of guns for Lee's service with his army in the field was then 270 pieces.

I am inclined to believe that Lee's aggregate in the outset reached the number which General Hooker gave it, by comparing several counts, viz., 80,000 men of all arms.

In the midst of our depression it was not deemed possible to cut out and cut down our reduced brigades and regiments. It might have destroyed our existing *morale*. And I think General Hooker, like McClellan, enjoyed maneuvering several independent bodies. At any rate, he had the awkward number of eight small corps, besides his artillery. John F. Reynolds commanded the First, Hancock the Second, Sickles the Third, Meade the Fifth, Sedgwick the Sixth, Howard the Eleventh, Slocum the Twelfth, and Pleasonton the cavalry; while Hunt had general charge of the artillery. We had then, in May, 1863, an average of about 11,000 in each infantry corps, in the neighborhood of 10,000 cavalry ready for the field and 4,000 artillery with 387 guns—making an effective force of about 102,000 of all arms. The armies thus organized stood on opposite sides of the Rappahannock.

Rumors had reached us soon after our defeat that the Confederate authorities proposed another effort to turn our flank, similar to that of the year before which ended in the battle of Antietam. General Hooker, however, seems to have had no valid evidence from his scouts till about May 28th, that Lee contemplated a movement. Even then, opposite our pickets everything appeared to be *in statu quo*. On June 5th I rode from my headquarters, then near Brooks's Station on the Aquia Creek Railway, to Hooker's headquarters, and, returning, made a note that the day before there was cannonading near Fredericksburg—a sort of a reconnoissance in force on our part, with an attempt to lay a bridge; that some brigades of the enemy were reported moving off, but that as soon as our troops began to show signs of making a crossing their brigades reappeared. It was the very afternoon of my ride to headquarters (June 5th) that the bridges were thrown over the Rappahannock, near Franklin's crossing. There was some resistance, but only by skirmishers. The same method was pursued as at the Fredericksburg battle, and the sending over soldiers in boats served to dislodge the enemy's pickets and secure the crossing.

Early June 6th, General Howe, of the Sixth Corps, moved his division to the enemy's side and made ready to advance, but orders from Halleck were so positive not to move over to attack in that quarter that it was impossible by a simple demonstration long to deceive Lee. At first, Lee did bring back some troops, put them in readiness to withstand Howe, and sent checking orders to other of his forces which were already *en route* toward the west. But very soon Howe's movement was plainly seen to be but a demonstration, and, so believing, General Lee went on to carry out his purpose.

Lee's forces had for some days been in motion. Stuart with his cavalry was watching the Rappahannock, with his headquarters not far from Culpeper;

Longstreet's corps was concentrated there, and Ewell *en route.* Lee himself started, after Howe's demonstration, for the same point. Culpeper was to be to him the point of a new departure. Besides Howe's reconnoissance, General Hooker determined to make another by cavalry supported by infantry. A scouting party had been organized. General Adelbert Ames, commanding an infantry brigade, departed to proceed up the Rappahannock and attack Stuart or intercept one of his raids. Underwood's regiment (Thirty-third Massachusetts) formed part of Ames's command. His wife and little daughter had just arrived in camp. But I was obliged to choose his regiment, deeming it the best fitted for the work to be done. I wrote June 10th: " An engagement is now in progress between our cavalry and that of General Stuart, not far from Culpeper. General Ames with his brigade must be there. I do hope this affair will be a success worth the mention. I understand that Stuart was completely surprised just as he was getting ready to go on some expedition to the north of us. Particulars of the engagement have not yet come to hand. One brigade of General Sedgwick's corps (Russell's) is also with Pleasonton, who now commands our cavalry. A division of the same corps is still across the river below Fredericksburg. Our own guns cover these troops, and they can stay there in safety as long as they please. Harry Stinson, my aid-de-camp, went with General Ames."

Stuart, having spent much time in putting his cavalry into excellent condition, had written General Lee entreating him to come and give it a review. On June 7th Lee joined him near Culpeper, when with a smile he said, as he pointed to Longstreet's corps, " Here I am with my friends, according to your invitation."

The next day, in the open country, not far from Brandy Station, upon ground well fitted for the purpose, Stuart caused his whole cavalry force to pass in review before his general-in-chief. It is said that Stuart, in such presence, was not content with a simple review, but drilled his brigades and exercised them in a sham fight, freely using his light artillery.

After these exercises, Stuart placed his headquarters upon a knoll called Fleetwood Hill, situated to the north of Brandy Station, and here followed the battle of Brandy Station between Stuart and Pleasonton, where the latter developed the fact that not only was Stuart's command in the neighborhood of Culpeper, but also an entire corps, and probably more of infantry; and, further, he had the captured plan of Lee's campaign in his possession. Therefore, Pleasonton now slowly withdrew across the Rappahannock, reaching the other side before dark and sending his important report to Hooker. He had lost, in killed, wounded, and missing, about 600 men, and also two pieces of artillery. Stuart's loss was fully equal to ours. This conflict, mainly a cavalry engagement, at the beginning of the campaign, hard as it seems to have been, was of decided advantage to our cavalry, for, under good leadership, it had been able to take the offensive and hold its own against equal if not superior numbers of the well-handled and enterprising Confederates. Ever after, during the campaign, the brigades of cavalry rivaled each other in desperate charges, and in often meeting and withstanding bodies of infantry that were undertaking to turn our flanks.

It now appears that General Hooker, after obtaining the information which he had desired from Pleasonton's reconnoissance, urged upon General Halleck and the President the wisdom of crossing the Rappahannock at Falmouth and striking Hill's corps with his whole force. He believed that this course would give him a successful battle, if Hill should wait for him on the Marye Heights; or, otherwise, at the worst, would force a return of Hill and a recall of all the Confederate forces intended for the invasion of Pennsylvania.

In my judgment there was at that time no possible success for our Republic except in a great victory to be gained by the Army of the Potomac; not in fighting for position, not for Richmond, but in encountering and defeating the confident Army of Northern Virginia.

What Mr. Lincoln evidently desired was that General Hooker should consider Lee's army as *the objective;* strike it in its weakest point; divide it and fight it in detail, if possible; but not ignore it.

Lee's movements in his northward march are not very plain to us, but just what they would be could not then be predicted. He used his lively cavalry as a curtain, supporting it by one corps; appearing here and there with it, as if moving on Washington or Baltimore, and thus drawing our whole attention to this work; while the remainder of the Confederates steadily kept on their way through Chester Gap, across the Shenandoah, down the valley of that river, and picked up our small armies which we always kept carefully separated and ready for Confederate consumption!

It was some time, and after reiteration, before I came to comprehend at West Point what our old Professor Mahan meant by " common sense." At last I defined it, " a state of mind the result of careful observation." There was certainly a want of this kind of common sense at the War Office in June, 1863.

There had already been given us several lessons in sight of the Shenandoah. Hooker was to cover Washington and Harper's Ferry, yet the troops at and beyond Harper's Ferry were not under his command.

On June 10th (the very next day after the bloody combat of Brandy Station) Stonewall Jackson's old corps, now under General Ewell, began its march from Culpeper into the Shenandoah Valley, and there defeated Milroy at Winchester.

The evening of June 17, 1863, I made this pencil note: " Goose Creek, near Leesburg.—The weather has been very hot and dry. We have marched as follows: twelve miles, nineteen, eighteen; rested two days, and then marched seventeen. I was a little feverish at Centreville, but am now quite recovered. This corps (the Eleventh) has marched in very orderly style and all my orders are obeyed with great alacrity. June 18, 1863.—Almost too hot for campaigning. I am waiting for orders. General headquarters (Hooker's) are thirty miles away just now, at Fairfax Court House. Charlie (Major C. H. Howard) is quite well, and so is Captain Stinson, aid-de-camp. Charlie has just at this time gone to General Reynolds's camp, and Captain Stinson to that of General Meade. I have a new officer on my staff—Captain Daniel Hall, additional aid-de-camp, formerly John P. Hale's private secretary—a very fine young man. He has been sick and I am afraid he will not stand the fatigue."

When in permanent camps our notes and letters were kept up with much regularity, but when the long marches began they became few and short. We first, setting out the next day after Ames's return from Brandy Station, came to Catlett's Station. General J. F. Reynolds was given a wing of the army, just then the right; it consisted of the First (his own corps), the Third (Sickles's), and the Eleventh (mine). When I was at Catlett's, the First was a little west of south of me at Bealton Station, and the Third Corps, which had begun its march on June 11th, was above the Rappahannock Station and near the famous Beverly Ford. These three bodies were facing Culpeper and in echelon. Should Lee attempt a close turn of our position, we could quietly form line facing southwest, or even to the north, and become at once the nucleus for the whole army.

Hooker obtained information that Ewell's entire corps had passed Sperryville. This news came during June 12th. He then hesitated not a moment, but issued the necessary orders to place his army farther north. We marched on the 14th to occupy Manassas Junction and Centreville, while three other corps—the Second, Sixth, and Twelfth—had set out the 13th, aiming for the neighborhood of Fairfax Court House; the Fifth (Meade's), which had been nearly opposite the United States Ford, on the Rappahannock, followed us toward Manassas, to reënforce Reynolds if the occasion should arise. It was there at Centreville that he remained two days, the 15th and 16th.

On June 17th Reynolds's wing, including the Fifth Corps, was pressed still farther northward and grouped substantially about Leesburg, while General Hooker's headquarters remained near Fairfax Court House. In this way it will be noticed that our wing— about one-fifth of the army — was first grouped in echelon facing south. The next move brought it in the same order facing west. The third move carried it to the northwest and uncovered the other corps, which were looking westward from positions nearer Washington. A division of cavalry under General Stahl, who had been scouting this region from Leesburg to Manassas, was released by the presence of an army and enabled to unite with Pleasonton and increase his force. Pleasonton with his cavalry had carefully watched the Rappahannock to its sources and then followed up the movements of Stuart and Longstreet, whose forces he usually kept in view at least by his scouting parties and outposts. Lee's rear corps, under A. P. Hill, left Fredericksburg as soon as Hooker's troops disappeared from his front, June 14th, and pushed on with great rapidity across the Rapidan, through Culpeper, Chester Gap, and Front Royal into the Shenandoah Valley, keeping upon Ewell's track. His peril was over. He had quickly placed two ranges of mountains, a river, Longstreet's infantry, and Stuart's cavalry between his command and our army. Longstreet, with his large and effective army corps, was designated to march down the eastern bank of the Shenandoah River as a cover to the other troops and *materiel* of Lee's army, while Stuart acted as a body of flankers to Longstreet, keeping upon the ridges or in the valleys nearer still to our command. Pleasonton and Stuart often came into contact.

The two armies were then (on June 17th) pretty well concentrated and much alike—Lee, in the Shenandoah Valley, with one corps (Longstreet's), and Stuart's cavalry near the crest of the Blue Ridge; Hooker, in the valley of the Potomac, between Lee and Washington, with one corps (the Fifth), and his cavalry (Pleasonton's) on the crest of the Blue Ridge Range. Stuart and Pleasonton were crossing the east and west road, and but few miles apart.

During that day (June 18, 1863), while the greater

388

part of the army was waiting to see just what Lee would attempt next, and when the weather was so warm in the Goose Creek Valley that I considered it too hot for campaigning; while aids and orderlies were skipping from corps to corps, with great difficulty and danger to life, through a country infested by Mosby's guerrillas, in order to keep us mutually informed and properly instructed, Pleasonton and Stuart were acting like two combatants playing and fencing with small swords. Neither wished to hasten a battle. Stuart took a stand at Middleburg. Pleasonton cautiously approached, skirmished, and moved as if to turn Stuart by the left. Stuart declined the close quarters, and fell back southward. But, as if a little ashamed of backing off, the early morning of the 19th found Stuart in a good defensive attitude west of Middleburg.

Pleasonton made a vigorous attack. For eight miles there was a running fight till Stuart had concentrated his forces on the last ridge at Ashby's Gap—the pass of the Blue Ridge. Here he saw the columns of Lee slowly in motion toward the north.

My pencil note dated June 22, 1863, indicated the position of the Army of the Potomac to be: the Eleventh Corps at Goose Creek, not far from Leesburg, Va.; the Fifth, still under General Meade, somewhere near Adlie. The Second Corps had been pushed out from Centreville to Thoroughfare Gap. The remainder of the army was not far from the Eleventh Corps. General Hooker was endeavoring to get from Halleck and Stanton another fair-sized corps. It was to be a coöperating force, to move up rapidly on the eastern side of the Potomac. It could check cavalry raids like those of Jenkins, who, having preceded

Ewell in Pennsylvania, had gathered horses, cattle, and other supplies from Chambersburg and its neighborhood, securing them from the fleeing and terrified inhabitants. This corps should be strong enough to meet and hold back any small or sizable body of the enemy's infantry, should Lee decide to send Early, Rodes, or even Ewell across the Potomac into Cumberland Valley with a view of scattering the troops, so as to live on the country and bring together and send to him much-coveted and much-needed contributions of food for his large command. But for some reason there was at Washington a want of confidence in General Hooker. Troops which were promised for this purpose were never sent; some which had been ordered and had set out for the rendezvous were stopped by Heintzelman's or Halleck's subordinates. Schenck furnished a few—a single brigade—under Colonel Lockwood; but these were insufficient for the avowed purpose, and what was worse to Hooker than the withholding was the manner in which it was done. Hooker was, at that time, suffered to be overridden by subordinate commanders, whom, to his chagrin, his seniors in authority sustained.

On June 24th we were still at Goose Creek. The day before, my brother, the Rev. R. B. Howard, a member of the celebrated Christian Commission, reached our camp after a ride of forty-five miles and some little exposure to "bushwhackers." The word "bushwhackers" comprehended scouts, spies, and all partisan insurgents who were never really made part of the Confederate army. They penetrated our lines in spite of every precaution, picked off our aids and messengers on their swift journeyings from corps to corps, and circulated every sort of false story that might be made use of to mislead us. In this Goose Creek region we were much annoyed by them. It was near here that Mosby with his peculiar force of guerrillas came near capturing me. In a small thicket which had grown up not far from the road a part of Mosby's men were concealed. They saw horsemen approaching, at first at a slow pace, but we outnumbered them, so their leader decided not to attack. I was glad of that decision, for I had then simply orderlies, servants, and spare horses, with but few armed soldiers.

The Confederate Corps Commander Ewell, as early as June 20th, withdrew from Winchester and marched on above Harper's Ferry. Edward Johnson's division crossed the Potomac at Sharpsburg and encamped on our old battlefield of Antietam; Rodes's division went on to Hagerstown; but Jubal Early's division was detained on the western bank of the river. This disposition of the enemy's leading corps when reported to Hooker puzzled him, as it did the War Department. What was Lee, after all, intending to do? This occasioned the singular multiplicity and sudden changes of orders. For example, on the 24th, the Eleventh Corps was first ordered to proceed to Sandy Hook, just below Harper's Ferry; next, before setting out, it was to cross the Potomac instead, at Edwards' Ferry, and report from that place to the headquarters of the army; next, to cross over there and push at once for Harper's Ferry. Soon after General Hooker directed me to go into camp on the right bank of the Potomac, and before that was fulfilled the orders were again changed to pass to the left bank of the river and guard the bridges. Surely somebody was nervous!

At last, on this same day, General Tyler, who was still the commander at Maryland Heights, gave General Hooker some definite information: that *Longstreet was crossing* the Potomac at Shepherdstown. In a letter, which must have been sent before Tyler's dispatch came, General Hooker explains to General Halleck briefly his thoughts and plans. He says that Ewell is already over the Potomac; that he shall endeavor, without being observed by Lee, to send a corps or two to Harper's Ferry, with a view to sever Ewell from the remainder of Lee's army. This he would attempt in case Ewell should make a protracted sojourn with his Pennsylvania neighbors.

Of course, Tyler's report about Longstreet changed all this. It was now too late to cut off Ewell—too late to think of dividing Lee's army by way of Harper's Ferry. It was evident also that Lee proposed to put his whole force east of the Potomac. Washington and Baltimore would be passed, and Harrisburg menaced.

My instructions the morning of June 25th became clear and positive: "Send a staff officer to General Reynolds to report to him; move your command in the direction of Middletown instead of Sandy Hook." Reynolds still commanded the wing, viz., the First, Third, and Eleventh Corps, and was ordered to seize the passes of South Mountain, and thus confine the Confederate general "to one line of invasion." I do not suppose this reason thus given amounted to much. If Lee had taken several lines of invasion he would have divided his forces and enabled us the better to strike him in detail; but, indeed, it was a wise move of Hooker to thus threaten Lee's line of communication, while he completely covered and protected his own. Of course, had he pressed on hard and close in that quarter, Lee would have been forced to stop all invasion and turn his attention constantly and completely to his adversary. Middletown was quickly reached; Harper's Ferry (or rather the Maryland Heights) was held, and the lower passes of the South Mountain were within our grasp.

In one day the army could at last be concentrated in that vicinity, because our wing under Reynolds had been followed up by the other corps. Slocum, with the Twelfth Corps, having crossed at Edwards' Ferry the 26th, had moved rapidly toward Harper's Ferry. The other three, with the artillery reserve, hastening over the Potomac the same day—for there were two good pontoon bridges for their use—moved up to Frederick and vicinity. Thus the Army of the Potomac was the morning of June 27th well in hand, in good condition, and rather better located for the offensive or the offensive-defensive operations than the year before under McClellan, when it approached the field of Antietam in about the same locality. Hooker had gone off to Harper's Ferry to see if it was feasible to begin a movement from his left. He had asked for Tyler's command near there. He now proposed the abandonment of Harper's Ferry as a garrison or station after the stores should be withdrawn. He could not afford to hold the works in that neighborhood at the expense of losing the services of 11,000 men, just then changed to General French. Halleck rejoined, in substance, that Harper's Ferry had always been deemed of great importance, and that he could not consent to its abandonment.

Hooker then sent this famous dispatch: " My original instructions were to cover Harper's Ferry and Washington. I have now imposed upon me in addition an enemy in my front of more than my numbers. I beg to be understood, respectfully, but firmly, that I am unable to comply with these conditions with the means at my disposal, and I earnestly request that I may be relieved at once from the position I occupy."

As if at once abandoning his own plan, General Hooker, after sending this dispatch, sent the Twelfth Corps to Frederick and went there himself. The next day, June 28th, General Hardie, a staff officer from the War Department, arrived at Frederick with the formal orders which relieved General Hooker of his command, and appointed in his place the commander of the Fifth Corps, General George G. Meade.

A comrade feels less and less inclined to criticise with any severity Hooker's intended work. There were jealousies; there were ambitions; there was discontent, and often insubordination in our army. General Hooker had formerly severely criticised McClellan. He had accounted for his own want of success at his own first attempt at supreme command by blaming others. Reactions would come. McClellan's friends and many others somehow impressed our large-hearted and frank-spoken President with the feeling that Hooker was not fully trusted in the army; so he wrote him at the outset of this campaign, June 14th: " I have some painful intimations that some of your corps and division commanders are not giving you their entire confidence."

From facts in my possession I am sure that this was a mild statement of the case, and I think it more of a reflection upon those who manifested the distrust than upon Hooker. But now, taking everything into account, I believe that, ill-timed as it seemed, the change of commanders was a good thing—especially good for that unexplainable something called the " *morale* of the army."

Campaign of Gettysburg

Lee and his officers did not rejoice when they learned that the able, upright, and well-reputed Meade had succeeded Hooker.

As soon as Meade took command of the Army of the Potomac he exhibited a mind of his own, and immediately changed the plan of our march. My corps (the Eleventh) turned at once from Middletown, Md., to Frederick, arriving there on the evening of June 28th. The army was at this time concentrated around this pretty little city. As soon as I reached the town I went at once to headquarters full of excitement and interest, awakened by the sudden changes that were taking place.

I had known Meade before the war, having met him and traveled with him on our northern lakes when he was on engineering duty in that region, and I had seen him frequently after the outbreak of hostilities. But he seemed different at Frederick. He was excited. His coat was off, for those June days were very warm. As I entered his tent, he extended his hand, and said:

"How are you, Howard?"

He demurred at any congratulation. He looked tall and spare, weary, and a little flushed, but I knew him to be a good, honest soldier, and gathered confidence and hope from his thoughtful face. To him I appeared but a lad, for he had graduated in 1835 at the Military Academy, nineteen years before me. He had served in the artillery among the Indians; in the Topographical Engineers on our rivers and lakes; in Mexico, where he was brevetted for his gallantry, and had become favorably known at Washington for good work in the lighthouse service. Then, finally, in the rebellion all our eyes had been turned to him for the completeness of every work that he had thus far un-

dertaken with his Pennsylvania reserves. He won me
more by his thoroughness and fidelity than by any
show of sympathy or companionship. To me, of
course, he stood in the light of an esteemed, experienced regular officer, old enough to be my father, but
like a father that one can trust without his showing
him any special regard. So we respected and trusted
Meade from the beginning.

CHAPTER XXIV

GENERAL MEADE at once began the sending of his forces so much eastward that we knew that any movement against Lee's rear or the Confederate communications via Harper's Ferry had been given up.

The evening of June 28, 1865, the whole army was at or near Frederick, Md. In his dispatch that evening Meade said: " I propose to move this army to-morrow in the direction of York."

By a glance at the map it will be seen that this plan was the precise opposite of that of Hooker, as indicated by his dispatches two days before. The reason for the change was that Lee was reported not only on our side of the Potomac, but as already occupying Chambersburg, Carlisle, and threatening Harrisburg, and having at least a brigade in the town of York. He did not just then seem to care greatly for his communications, any more than did Hannibal of old after he had once obtained his strong foothold on the Continent of Europe. Lee had now corn, flour, cattle, and horses in abundance, and the farther north he pushed, the more sumptuous would be his supply. Lee's position in Pennsylvania gave ominous threats to Harrisburg and Philadelphia, caused real fright to the loyal people of Baltimore, and to the administration at Washington. The life of the Nation was in its greatest peril— it appeared to hang upon but a thread of hope, and, under God, the thread was *Meade and his army.*

A little later information determined our general to cover more ground, to stretch out in line of corps as he moved forward. An army line in a campaign is now a day's march or more long. After our marches of June 29th, the First and Eleventh Corps were on the left of that extended line at Emmittsburg; the Third and Twelfth at Taneytown, where was General Meade himself; the Second at Frizelburg; the Fifth at Union, and the Sixth at New Windsor.

This grand army line looking northward had most of its cavalry under Pleasonton, well forward—one division under Buford aiming for Gettysburg, and the others fighting and chasing the Confederate cavalry, which daringly swept around our army between us and Washington and Baltimore and Philadelphia. The army of Meade was also well supported by a fine reserve; for Halleck, strange to tell, had given to Meade what he had withholden from Hooker, namely, the force at Harper's Ferry. French moved it, now 11,000 strong, to Frederick, Md. It here constituted a cover to our depots, to Washington communications, and a ready help for any contingency.

The infantry and artillery extended over a large area. Military experts ask: " Was not this an error of Meade's, to so move forward his command, exposing his left to be attacked by at least two-thirds of Lee's army?" Meade's answer is in his own words: " If Lee is moving for Baltimore, I expect to get between his main army and that place. If he is crossing the Susquehanna, I shall rely upon General Couch holding him until I can fall upon his rear and give him battle."

The Battle of Gettysburg Begun

But Lee was already drawing back his scattered forces to the neighborhood of Chambersburg and watching toward Gettysburg, to see what could be behind the bold pushing of John Buford's cavalry division in that neighborhood. He began his concentration before Meade could do so, and upon the flank where he was not expected to concentrate.

On the last day of June a few changes in our position took place. The First Corps, under John F. Reynolds, went to " Marsh Run," about five miles from Gettysburg; the Eleventh, under my command, remained at Emmittsburg for that day; the Third (Sickles's corps) moved from Taneytown to a point near Emmittsburg; the Twelfth (Slocum's) went forward and encamped near Littlestown. The headquarters and remaining corps did not change. Buford's cavalry was kept ahead of Reynolds, in the vicinity of Gettysburg.

On June 30th the Confederate army formed a concave line (concavity toward us), embracing Chambersburg, Carlisle, and York. Ours formed an indented line, extending from Marsh Run to Westminster, the left of that line being thrown far forward. If Lee could bring his men together east of the South Mountain, near Cashtown, it would appear that he might strike us in the flank—before we could assemble—blow after blow, and beat us in detail. Of course, it was a bold undertaking. The safe course of a cautious mind would have been different—probably to have concentrated beyond the South Mountain as Lee had done at Antietam; but Longstreet was at hand, and urged Lee to adopt more risky measures with the hope of obtaining grander results.

So, then, while we were feeling around in the dark-

399

ness of conflicting rumors and contradictory information, Lee, June 29th, designated a point east of South Mountain, behind Cashtown and Gettysburg, for the grand gathering of his forces. When the order came Ewell was near Harrisburg; he had already drawn back Early's division from York. Early's and Rodes's, with the corps chief, coming together, succeeded in reaching Heidelsburg, about ten miles north of Gettysburg, the evening of the 30th, but Johnson's division, obeying the same orders, had gone from Carlisle back toward Chambersburg. He, however, took a left-hand road by the way of Greenwood, and encamped the same night near Scotland, a hamlet west of the mountain. The other two corps—Longstreet's and Hill's— were not far in advance of Ewell's; for, though they had shorter distances they had fewer routes from which to choose. Hill's corps led, and was at or near Cashtown the evening of the 30th.

Longstreet, with two divisions, remained that night near Greenwood, at the west entrance to Cashtown Gap. One division only—that of Pickett—caring for Lee's transportation, remained behind, at Chambersburg. The Confederate commander then had, the night of June 30th, the bulk of his army—probably between 50,000 and 60,000 men—within fifteen miles of Gettysburg. His leading division (Heth's of Hill's corps) had already encountered our cavalry. After Heth had arrived in Cashtown, eight miles from Gettysburg, he sent, on the 30th, Pettigrew's brigade with wagons to that town for shoes and other supplies. Pettigrew was just entering the suburbs at 11 A.M., when he discovered Buford's division rapidly approaching. Pettigrew, who expected only detached militia, being surprised by meeting our cavalry, immediately withdrew and marched back four miles toward his own division, halted at Marsh Run on the Cashtown road, and reported to his chief that Meade's army in force was near at hand.

At that time Stuart's Confederate cavalry was not with the main army to bring him information, but was hastening to Lee's left flank.

In this irregular manner, on the last day of June, the two great armies, each in the aggregate near 100,-000 strong, came so close to contact that Lee's right and our left had exchanged shots at Gettysburg.

In the subsequent operations of our army and in the changes of commanders incident to the coming bloody conflicts, the left (three army corps) was still called *the Right Wing;* but the corps were really located on the extreme left of Meade's general line. Buford's division of cavalry coöperated with this wing, brought its chief all the information it gathered, and handsomely cleared its front. The Comte de Paris remarks of the cavalry leader and of the commander of the wing:

"Meade intrusted the task of clearing and directing his left to two men equally noted for quickness of perception, promptness of decision, and gallantry on the battlefield—Buford and Reynolds." This is just praise.

There were several kinds of officers to serve under, as every man who was in the army for any considerable time as a subordinate will admit. A few were simply tyrants; some were exacting as commanders, but always fair and ready to recognize work; some were courteous enough in deportment, but held subordinates to an extreme responsibility, striving to do so in such way as to clear themselves of all adverse

401

criticism. Others belittled the aid rendered them, and absorbed the credit to themselves and threw all faults at another's door; others, still, who had a steady hand in governing, were generous to a fault, quick to recognize merit, trusted you and sought to gain your confidence, and, as one would anticipate, were the foremost in battle. These generally secured the best results in administration and in active campaigning. To the last class belonged General Reynolds. From soldiers, cadets, and officers, junior and senior, he always secured reverence for his serious character, respect for his ability, care for his uniform discipline, admiration for his fearlessness, and love for his unfailing generosity. He was much like General George H. Thomas, not, however, so reticent and, I should judge, not quite so tenacious of purpose. It was always a pleasure to be under the command of either. I had been for some time during this campaign reporting to Reynolds.

At Emmittsburg, June 30th, I had only changed the position of my corps from the east to the northwest of the village. There was an establishment (probably we should call it a college) under the care of several Jesuit fathers. On my arrival the 29th, in the neighborhood, these met me very pleasantly, and begged me to make my headquarters with them. That day had been cold and rainy, the roads heavy, and the march very tiresome. I yielded to the tempting offer of hospitality, and instead of pitching my tent or stretching my "fly" as usual, I went to enjoy the neat and comfortable bed which was offered me. Here, too, I was to pass the night of the 30th. It was about dark when a message came from Reynolds. He desired me to ride up to his headquarters, situated about six miles off on the Emmittsburg and Gettysburg road, where the Marsh Run crosses it.

Taking Lieutenant F. W. Gilbreth, my aid-de-camp, and an orderly, I set out immediately, and in less than an hour found my way to the little house which Reynolds occupied. It was near the run, on the right-hand side of the road. Dismounting, I was at once shown into a back room near the south end of the house. Reynolds rose to meet me; he was here occupying a room which had in it but little furniture—a table and a few chairs. The table appeared to be laden with papers, apparently maps and official dispatches. After the usual cordial greeting, he first handed me the confidential appeal which General Meade had just made to his army commanders. In this Meade expressed the confident belief that if the officers fitly addressed the men of their commands, they would respond loyally to their appeal. He urged every patriotic sentiment which he felt assured would arouse to enthusiasm and action his whole army, now on the threshold of the battlefield—a field which he felt might decide the fate of the Republic. After reading this communication, we next went over the news dispatches of the day. They were abundant and conflicting. They came from headquarters at Taneytown, from Buford at Gettysburg, from scouts, from alarmed citizens, from all directions. They, however, forced the conclusion upon us, that Lee's infantry and artillery in great force were in our neighborhood.

Longstreet's corps, which had been with General Lee himself at Chambersburg, had come toward us; Hill's, which was lately at Fayetteville, had already passed the mountain and his nearest camp was not more than four miles from Gettysburg.

We spent the entire evening together, looking over the different maps, discussing the probabilities of a great battle, and talking of the part our wing would be likely to play in the conflict.

Reynolds seemed depressed, almost as if he had a presentiment of his death so near at hand. Probably he was anxious on account of the scattered condition of our army, particularly in view of the sudden concentration of the enemy.

At about eleven I took my leave of the general, and rode rapidly back to headquarters. I retired to my comfortable bed in the college and was soon fast asleep. It could not have been an hour before a loud knocking at the door aroused me.

" What is it, orderly? " I asked.

" Orders from army headquarters."

I took the bundle of papers in my hand. The address was to Reynolds as the wing commander. To forestall the possibility of their loss between Emmittsburg and Marsh Run, I opened the dispatches, as was customary, read them, and sent them forward with a note.

The orders were as follows: " Orders—Headquarters at Taneytown — Third Corps to Emmittsburg; Second Corps to Taneytown; Fifth Corps to Hanover; Twelfth Corps to Two Taverns; First Corps to Gettysburg; Eleventh Corps to Gettysburg (in supporting distance); Sixth Corps to Manchester; cavalry to front and flanks, well out in all directions, giving timely notice of positions and movements of the enemy."

With these orders came a clear indication of Meade's opinion of the location of Hill and Longstreet, as between Chambersburg and Gettysburg, while Ewell was believed to be still occupying Carlisle and York.

404

The Battle of Gettysburg Begun

He closed his circular letter with these significant words: "The general believes he has relieved Harrisburg and Philadelphia, and now desires to look to his own army and assume position for offensive or defensive, or for rest to the troops."

The town of Gettysburg covers about one square mile, and is situated in an undulating valley, through which runs Rock Creek. This small stream, fed by three or four smaller ones, courses from the north and flows southeast of the town. The Cemetery Ridge, so often described, begins at Culp's Hill, broadens out on the top westerly to take in the cemetery itself, and then turns to trend due south to Zeigler's Grove; then bends a little south, to ascend gradually a rugged, rocky knoll—Little Round Top. Farther on is a rougher, higher, and larger prominence called Big Round Top. Four important wagon roads traverse the region; the road due east from Bonaughton, just showing Benner's Hill on its north side; the Baltimore pike from the southeast, crossing White Run and Rock Creek, and after passing the cemetery enters the village; the Taneytown road skirting the east slope of the main ridge, going near the Round Tops and entering Gettysburg along one of its main streets; and the Emmittsburg road, which passes by the west side of the Round Tops and Sherfy's peach orchard, and makes a westerly sweep well out from the ridge, comes back to cut the Taneytown road, and ends at the Baltimore pike just below the cemetery and near the town.

The Seminary Ridge lies toward the west, and is nearly parallel with the Cemetery Ridge, and about one mile from it. It is, however, a third longer, and passes considerably beyond the village. The Willoughby Run, with a southern flow bearing off with the ranges of heights, courses between the Seminary Crest and the next higher western ridge.

As the day dawned that memorable July 1, 1863, with somewhat less than 5,000 cavalry, Buford was fully ready. General John Buford was a healthful, hardy cavalry officer, born in Kentucky, a graduate from the Military Academy of the class of 1848. He especially distinguished himself during the war for boldness in pushing up close to his foe; for great dash in his assaults, and, at the same time, for shrewdness and prudence in the presence of a force larger than his own. The night before, he had deployed his brigade beyond Gettysburg so as to cover the approaches from the west, pushing his pickets and scouting far out on the different roads. He knew that he must contend against infantry, so he dismounted his men and prepared them to fight on foot. Devin's brigade held the right and Gamble's the left. Devin was between Chambersburg Railroad and Mummasburg road. Gamble extended his lines so as to cover the space leftward as far as the Middletown road.

The Confederates were early in motion. This time Pettigrew was reënforced by the remainder of Heth's division. Their head of column reached Buford's pickets a little after sunrise, and their skirmishers came within sight of the seminary and Buford's artillery before nine o'clock.

Without hesitation Buford's command opened fire upon them, enfilading the roads with his horse artillery, and confidently breasting against them with small arms from his extended line. Doubtless, Confederate Heth thought there must be something besides a cavalry division in his front, for at once he put his command in order of battle. The cavalry, showing the tenacity of infantry, prolonged the struggle until even the leading corps commander of Lee, A. P. Hill, arrived with Pender's division.

It is said that watchers from the Lutheran Seminary, who could from that high point look westward far out toward Cashtown along the Chambersburg pike and behold the thickening columns of Lee, could also at that moment toward the south see our own bright flags approaching amid the rising mists. The sun in its heat was clearing the valleys, and Reynolds with his First Corps was on the field and soon met Buford near the seminary.

It appears that Reynolds, who commanded our wing, gave that morning the immediate charge of the First Corps to his senior division commander, General Abner Doubleday, who set out for the front with the main body. Reynolds, going rapidly to the position of Gamble, encouraged Buford's weary cavalrymen to hold on a little longer, then he sent his officers as guides to conduct Wadsworth directly from the Emmittsburg road across the fields to the Seminary Hill. He also at this time sent an officer to meet me on the road from Emmittsburg.

Doubleday had now come up, so that there were together the wing, the corps, and two division commanders, yet thus far only two brigades of infantry and the weary division of cavalry to withstand the large corps of A. P. Hill. But Wadsworth's division was well commanded. He himself, of large frame, always generous and a natural soldier, had under him two reliable brigades, Cutler's and Meredith's; the latter, for its tenacity, was dominated the " Iron Brigade." In these were some notable regimental commanders who gave strong character to their regiments.

We noticed how Heth of the Confederates had deployed his columns. Davis's, his right brigade, extended north of the Chambersburg pike and railway, seemed to be aiming for Devin's right, while Archer's, on his (Davis's) left, deployed southward and advanced toward the Seminary Ridge. The firing was brisk and our skirmishers retiring. Archer had reached the edge of a handsome grove of trees that stretched along south of the pike and near Willoughby Run.

Reynolds quickly made his dispositions. Meredith was sent against Archer. He deployed and endeavored to take the grove in front. Wadsworth, with Cutler's brave troops, and Buford still there to help him, deployed, pressed forward, and opened his lively fire upon the enemy's right. Just as General Reynolds beheld the movement of his " Iron Brigade " going into action, he himself, not far in the rear, on the south side of the pike, on a spot now pointed out to every traveler, fell, pierced through the head with a rifle ball.

On July 1st, weary as I was after having been awakened by the ominous orders of the night, it was necessary to be at work again at dawn. I resolved to send Barlow's division by the direct road to Gettysburg; the distance is eleven miles. Steinwehr's and Schurz's were to follow a road, clearer and better, a little farther to the eastward, passing Horner's Mill and entering the route from Taneytown. Being obliged to wait for Reynolds's order of execution, the columns did not start till 8.30 A.M.

Barlow that day, always vigorous and pushing, owing to the heat of the weather, a road full of ruts and stones, and still obstructed by the supply wagons of the preceding corps, made an average of but two and one-half miles per hour.

With my staff and a small escort of horsemen I set out, as the march began, toward Gettysburg, taking the fields and woods, in order to avoid the trains and columns which occupied the roads. Many officers remember the rapidity of that ride. By 10.30 A.M., according to my own time, I was in sight of the village of Gettysburg, when the staff officer which Reynolds had dispatched on his arrival met me. He gave me information of the commencement of the battle.

A battle was evidently in progress, judging by the sounds of the cannon and small arms and the rising smoke, a mile and a half to my left. I could then see the divisions of Doubleday, moving along northwesterly across the open fields toward the seminary. My previous orders were to keep within supporting distance. When neither corps was in action this was interpreted to be an interval of four or five miles, but the aid who met me said: "Come quite up to Gettysburg." I remember distinctly, as if it were but yesterday, asking him where the general desired to place me and the aid replied: "Stop anywhere about here, according to your judgment, at present." The spot where this remark was made was on the Emmittsburg road, near Sherfy's peach orchard. The aid left and the firing continued. I sent Captain Daniel Hall to find Reynolds and bring me word that I might go to him.

Then with my staff, as was my habit in coming to a new field, I began to examine the positions with the view of obtaining the best location in that vicinity for our troops. I rode from place to place, first visiting the high portion of a cross ridge to my left, near the

Emmittsburg road. Not finding a point from which I could get an extended view and noticing higher ground eastward, I turned and rode to the highest point of the Cemetery Ridge. Here was a broad view which embraced the town, the seminary, the college, and all the undulating valley of open country spread out between the ridges. There was a beautiful break in the ridge to the north of me, where Culp's Hill abuts against the cemetery, and touches the creek below. It struck me that here one could make a strong right flank.

Colonel Meysenberg was my adjutant general. We sat on our horses, side by side, looking northward, when I said: "This seems to be a good position, colonel," and his own prompt and characteristic reply was: "It is the only position, general." We both meant *position for Meade's army.*

After observing the whole sweep of the country, I then made up my mind what I would do with my troops, or recommend for Reynolds's wing, or for the army, should my advice be sought, that is, use that Cemetery Ridge as the best defensive position within sight.

Recognizing that one's mind is usually biased in favor of his own theory, I have taken great pains to ascertain the impressions of others who were associated with me as to whether I received any instructions or intimation from any quarter whatever touching the selection of Cemetery Ridge and Hill. The testimony, both direct and indirect, points all one way: that I did not; that I chose the position and used it throughout the first day of the battle, as we shall see. The aid-de-camp of General Reynolds (Captain Rosengarten), who thinks he heard General Reynolds tell my aid-de-camp that I must occupy Cemetery Ridge, is certainly in error. Captain Daniel Hall was the only aid of mine sent to the general; the only one who saw him at all, and he never brought me any such order or intimation. In this connection I may quote Captain Hall's own words in a letter to me: " You directed me to ride forward as rapidly as possible, find General Reynolds, report to him the progress of the Eleventh Corps, and ask for his orders. I followed with all speed and overtook him nearly at the extreme advance of our troops, where the skirmishers and some regiments were already hotly engaged. I spoke to General Reynolds, reported to him the approach of the Eleventh Corps, as directed, and told him you had sent me to obtain his orders. In reply he told me to inform you that he had encountered the enemy apparently in force, and to direct you to bring your corps forward as rapidly as possible to the assistance of the first. General Reynolds gave no order whatever in regard to occupying Cemetery Hill, nor did he make any allusion to it.

" I immediately left him to return to you. Retracing my steps, I met you hurrying into the town, and not far from the cemetery. I communicated to you the order of General Reynolds to bring up your column as rapidly as possible to the assistance of the First Corps, and the order was dispatched immediately back to the columns of Schurz and Barlow. Riding into the town at your side I remember that, as we passed along the road at its base, you pointed to the crest of Cemetery Ridge on our right and said: ' There's the place to fight this battle,' or words to similar effect."

Speaking of the same thing in another letter to a friend in February, 1877, Hall says: " The impression has always been firmly fixed in my mind that the first

411

suggestion that I ever heard about occupying Cemetery Hill was from General Howard."

Once more, in a subsequent letter to me, Captain Hall used these words: " I know to a certainty that nobody anticipated you in seeing the importance of Cemetery Hill, and immediately acting upon that conclusion."

Major E. P. Pearson, of the Twenty-first Infantry, who was then Captain Pearson, commissary of musters, avers the same thing in a letter that lies before me. And certainly there is no official communication or testimony from any quarter whatever that has ever reached me which even claims that any orders for me to occupy Cemetery Hill or Ridge were delivered to me.

After my first visit to the cemetery with my staff, I rode into the village, and we were trying some method of getting into the belfry of the court house, when my attention was called by Mr. D. A. Skelly to Fahnestock's observatory across the street.

Mounting to the top, I was delighted with the open view. With maps and field glasses we examined the battlefield. Wadsworth's infantry, Buford's cavalry, and one or two batteries were nearest, and their fighting was manifest. Confederate prisoners were just then being sent to the rear in large groups from the Seminary Ridge down the street past my post of observation.

We were noting the numerous roads emerging from Gettysburg and from our charts comparing the location and names, when a young soldier riding up the street below, stopped, and looking up, saluted me and said: " General Reynolds is wounded, sir," and I replied to him: " I am very sorry; I hope he will be able to keep the field."

It was not many minutes afterwards that an officer (I now believe it was Captain Hall) stood in the same street and, looking up, said sadly: " General Reynolds is dead, and you are the senior officer on the field." This, of course, put me in the commander's place.

I realized the situation. We had here, deducting our losses, in Lee's front, not to exceed 12,000 men; my corps was yet many miles back and our other troops were very much scattered, and the majority of them far away—too far for this day's work. My heart was heavy and the situation was grave indeed! but I did not hesitate, and said: " God helping us, we will stay here till the army comes," and quickly dictating orders, assumed command of the field; Schurz to take the Eleventh Corps; Doubleday to hold the First, and the cavalry of Buford to remain with him. Reynolds's last call for help had gone through me back on the Emmittsburg and Taneytown roads, to Barlow, Schurz, and Steinwehr. The new orders were carried to them again by Captain Hall to Schurz and to the reserve artillery under Major Osborn; by Captain Pearson to Barlow; then on to Sickles, ordering him up from Emmittsburg. Thence the news was borne to General Meade at Taneytown. A message was also sent to General Slocum, who was my senior. He was, judging from Meade's orders by this time at or near the two taverns.

Under my orders Osborn's batteries were placed on the Cemetery Ridge and some of them covered by small epaulements. General Steinwehr's division I put in reserve on the same heights and near the Baltimore pike. Dilger's Ohio battery preceded the corps, and soon after Wheeler's, the two passing through the town at a trot, to take their places on the right of the First Corps. Schurz ordered General Schimmelfennig (who had Schurz's division now) to advance briskly through Gettysburg and deploy on the right of the First Corps in two lines. Shortly after that the first division, under Barlow, arrived by the Emmittsburg road proper, and advanced through the town on the right of the third division. I rode with Barlow through the city, and out to what is now Barlow Hill.

The firing at the front was severe and an occasional shell burst over our heads or among the houses. When I think of this day, I shall always recall one incident which still cheers my heart: it was that a young lady, after all other persons had quite disappeared for safety, remained behind on her porch and waved her handkerchief to the soldiers as they passed. Our living comrades who were there will not forget this episode, nor the greeting which her heroism awakened as they were going to battle. How heartily they cheered her!

Leaving Barlow to complete his march and deployment near the upper waters of Rock Creek, and sending my senior aid, Major C. H. Howard, to visit Buford, I rode off to the left, passing in the rear of Robinson, had a few words with Wadsworth, and stopped a short time with Doubleday farther to the west. Doubleday's left flank was near the Willoughby Run, and his artillery actively firing at the time.

The first brilliant incidents of the engagements in this quarter were over, but the movements made by General Reynolds did not cease at his death. Meredith under Doubleday's eye made a charge straight forward which resulted in the capture of a Confederate brigade commander (General Archer) and several hundred of his men; but Cutler, farther to the right, was not so fortunate. A charge from Confederate Davis's brigade broke his line; the One Hundred and Forty-seventh New York, near the railway cut, was badly handled and lost much ground; the Fourteenth Brooklyn, Ninety-fifth New York, and Hall's battery were cut off, and in danger of capture; the horses of one gun were all disabled, so that the best thing to do was to retire and leave that gun to the enemy. Just here the corps commander (Doubleday) took the offensive farther to the left; using Fairchild's Second Wisconsin and a piece of artillery, he pressed them forward; then bearing to the right, they fired rapidly into the exposed flank of the Confederate commander Davis, who was too hotly in pursuit of Cutler's men to notice these flankers. Of course, Davis turned upon his new enemy, but Cutler's men, recovering from their temporary discomfiture, pushed forward into action. Two Confederate regiments were thus caught between two fires and in the railroad cut and soon surrendered with their brigade commander.

Immediately after this movement General Robinson, of the First Corps, posted his division more strongly northward of Wadsworth, drawing back his right so as by the aid of Buford to make there a strong flank. It was a little after eleven o'clock and this primary work of the First Corps was over. There was artillery firing and skirmishing, but just then no active effort by either army. The temporary repulse of Cutler and the defeat of Archer and Davis had produced a feeling of caution on both sides, so that there was a period of delay before any organized assault was again attempted.

I returned to my headquarters feeling exceedingly anxious about the left flank. I believed, as soon as Lee should deploy the entire corps of Hill and support his line by Longstreet's men, who could not be far behind, that Doubleday's weak left would be overlapped and pressed back; so, in order to relieve the threatened pressure against the First Corps and at the same time occupy the enemy's attention, I ordered Schurz to push out a strong force from his front and seize a wooded height situated some distance north of Robinson's position; but the order had hardly left me when Major Howard brought me word that Early's division of Ewell's corps was at hand; in fact, the entire corps was coming in from the north and east. Reports from Schurz and Buford confirmed the alarming intelligence.

Barlow against a shower of bullets made a strong effort to advance his lines, but as soon as I heard of the approach of Ewell and saw that nothing could prevent the turning of my right flank if Barlow advanced, the order was countermanded, except to press out a skirmish line. The skirmishers on their arrival found the heights already occupied by Rodes's division of Ewell's corps.

Our lines were much extended, and there was quite an interval between the Eleventh and First Corps, occupied only by the two batteries and skirmishers which I have named, yet Robinson, aided by Schimmelfennig (Forty-fifth New York Regiment), captured in that space another Confederate brigade (Iverson's).

I sent again to General Slocum, hoping that he would be able to come to my relief. After a short time, probably within one hour after I had returned from Doubleday to the cemetery, a lively skirmish arose all along the front. At 3.30 P.M. the enemy renewed his attack upon the First Corps, hotly pressing the first and second divisions. There was a similar movement of Ewell's deployed lines against Schurz. The fighting became severe and reënforcements were called for. I sent from the reserve all that I dared. Steinwehr had then at my instance put one brigade—Coster's—in the edge of the town, behind barricades and in houses, prepared to cover the anticipated retreat. At 3.45 the calls to me for help from Doubleday and Wadsworth were stronger than ever. Schurz was instructed to send one regiment to Wadsworth, as his front was the place at that moment of the hardest pressure. It was only a few minutes after this when the firing, growing worse and worse, showed me that the front lines could not hold out much longer.

I will not attempt to describe the action further. It saddens me to think of the losses on that front. The order that I sent to Doubleday then was this: "If you cannot hold out longer, you must fall back to the cemetery and take position on the left of the Baltimore pike."

But it was not long before I was satisfied that the men were giving way at different points of the line, and that the enemy, who overreached both flanks, were steadily and slowly advancing. I then sent positive orders to Schurz and Doubleday to fall back to the cemetery as slowly as possible and take post—the Eleventh on the right and the First on the left of Baltimore pike. I instructed Buford to pass to the extreme left and extend the new line, making with his cavalry all the show possible.

Speaking of the retreat of the two corps Doubleday remarks: "I think the retreat would have been a very

417

successful one, if it had not been unfortunately the case that a portion of the Eleventh Corps, which had held out very well on the extreme right, had been surrounded and fallen back at the same time that my right flank fell back."

The two corps were entangled in the streets. There was much straggling there for a time, and doubtless many men leaving their ranks found their way eastward along the Taneytown and Baltimore routes. The brigade in the front of the town, put there to help the retreat, lost heavily.

When the men were reaching their new position on the heights, and at the time of the greatest confusion between 4 and 5 P.M., General Hancock joined me near the Baltimore pike; he said that General Meade had sent him to represent him on the field. I answered as the bullets rent the air: " All right, Hancock, you take the left of the Baltimore pike and I will take the right, and we will put these troops in line." After a few friendly words between us, Hancock did as I suggested. He also took Wadsworth's division to Culp's Hill and we worked together in prompt preparations until sundown, when, after Slocum's arrival at that time, Hancock returned to meet General Meade. Slocum's troops had been previously placed in the line.

Gratified by the successes of the day, General Lee made but one more attempt against us that night. This, to turn our right in column, our well-posted batteries thwarted. As the darkness fell General Sickles, having at once heeded my call, had arrived from Emmittsburg, and the remainder of the army, with General Meade at its head, was already *en route*. The First and Eleventh Corps and General Buford's cavalry did their duty nobly that first day at Gettysburg

—fought themselves into a good defensive position for the army, especially good when the whole Army of the Potomac had come up to occupy the Cemetery Ridge.

General Lee, mistaking our numbers from the vigor of our defense, and beholding the great fortification-like appearance of our new stand, contented himself with what he had gained, and postponed further attack till the next day.

When the broken regiments were emerging from Gettysburg upon the open ground just north of the cemetery, my aid, Lieutenant Rogers, was standing by my side, both of us dismounted; a colonel passed by murmuring something in German—his English was not at his command just then; fragments of his regiment were following him.

Seeing the color sergeant and guard as they came between me and the stone wall, near the edge of the city, I called out: "Sergeant, plant your flag down there in that stone wall!" Not recognizing me the sergeant said impulsively: "All right, if you will go with me, I will!" Thereupon I took the flag and accompanied by Rogers, the sergeant and his men, set it up above the wall. That flag served to rally the regiment, always brave and energetic, and other troops.

Ames, who succeeded Barlow, formed his entire division to the right of that regiment. After the battle Slocum, Sickles, and I took our headquarters on the ground near the gatekeeper's cottage. Mrs. Peter Thorn, whose husband was a soldier, with her daughter was caring for the cottage. I had been all day from breakfast at sunrise without food and was nearly famished. Mrs. Thorn, before we had time to ask, brought us some bread and cups of coffee. Those refreshments have never been forgotten.

CHAPTER XXV

WHEN the troops that had gathered on Cemetery Hill went to sleep the night of Wednesday, July 1, 1863 they anticipated that Lee would renew the attack upon them very early the next morning from the direction of our right, for two reasons: one that reports showed that Ewell's men had been working off into that quarter, where they had the shelter of trees. And the other reason was, that we thought that greater immediate results to the Confederates could be expected by promptly crushing our right flank, seizing Benner's, Culp's, and Cemetery hills, and so dislodging us from our strong position embracing those hills and the Round Tops.

Now we know several reasons why General Lee did not do this. He had meditated that plan; in fact, he had given the order to attempt it, provided that Culp's Hill could be carried without too much cost. But, undoubtedly, he was influenced by a reconnoissance of Ewell, who reported an assault impracticable, and by his finding a Union dispatch concerning Slocum's arrival, which showed not only Culp's Hill, but the rough-wooded ground eastward to be already completely occupied. So that though every preparation, even of issuing orders to his officers, had been made to make our extreme right the main point of attack,

420

yet Lee, before daylight of July 2d, had completely changed his mind and plan.

General Lee says: "The preparations for the actual attack were not completed till the afternoon of July 2d."

Ewell occupied the left of his line, Hill the center, and Longstreet the right. The morning of July 2d, when Lee's attack was expected by us, Law's brigade of Longstreet's corps was behind at Guilford for picket duty; and Pickett's division was not yet up from Chambersburg. Longstreet, thinking his present force too weak for attack, determined upon waiting for Law's brigade.

Among the preparations of the forenoon were the locating of the batteries. Pendleton, Lee's chief of artillery, had worked hard during the night. Ewell's batteries were posted, Latimer's holding the easternmost height available. A. P. Hill's guns were mainly on Seminary Hill, within comfortable range. All this was already done by daylight. But General Lee now planned to attack our left, so that General Pendleton, about sunrise, was over there surveying. So close was he to our lines that he captured two of our armed cavalrymen.

Somehow, Pendleton and several other officers—engineers and artillery—spent all the morning in surveying and reconnoitering. Probably the nearness of our troops made the work slow and embarrassing.

Longstreet and Pendleton got together opposite our flank about twelve o'clock. There was now much sharpshooting, and at last, as the Confederate artillery of Longstreet was moving into its selected positions, a "furious cannonade" was opened from our side. This necessitated a quick removal of the marching column—the artillery column—farther off to a better cover.

But, finally, about 4 P.M., Longstreet, having made a long march from his camp, began the battle of the second day in earnest. And, indeed, all this delay was good for us. For one, I am glad that Lee chose our left as his point of attack; glad that Longstreet had considerable marching to do before he could bring his excellent troops into position; glad that Pendleton had much trouble in surveying and spent much time at it, and glad also that General Hunt, our artillery chief, had sharp eyes and quick apprehension, and succeeded for hours in disturbing that artillery so essential to the enemy's success. We could better understand the situation from our side, for we had high points of observation and could take in the field. There was no shrubbery then to obstruct our view.

At 7 P.M. the evening of July 1st I received the first intimation that Hancock, junior to me in rank, had been placed in command. When I read the written order of General Meade, I immediately wrote him asking him if he disapproved of any of my actions during the first day's battle. It is a little surprising how much historic statements differ, and often about the least important affairs. Take the statements of generals made at different places; for example, in the reports in the committee rooms of Congress, and in subsequent writings, often executed far from their records. Those of the same officer, as to time and place, often vary strangely. Others catch up these discrepancies and impute untruth and false intent, till much bad blood is stirred up. Even the time of Meade's arrival at the cemetery gate is a point of controversy; one officer putting it at 1 A.M. of July 2d, another at a later hour. I have been confident that it was about 3 A.M., because the time seemed so short to daylight. He was riding at the head of his escort. I met him just inside the gate. The first words he spoke to me were very kind. I believed that I had done my work well the preceding day; I desired his approval and so I frankly stated my earnest wish. Meade at once assured me that he imputed no blame; and I was as well satisfied as I would have been with positive praise from some other commanders. General Sickles joined us as we were talking. I told Meade at once what I thought of the cemetery position. We could have held it even if Lee had pressed his attack the evening before, for Slocum's division had come up and been placed. Sickles had heeded my call and was on hand with a part of his corps. He and Geary and Buford's cavalry together then took care of the left. Out batteries had been placed, and then the simple fact that so much help had already arrived gave heart to our officers and men, who had become discouraged in losing the Seminary Ridge. Therefore, I said to Meade with emphasis: " I am confident we can hold this position."

Slocum expressed himself as equally confident: " It is good for defense."

Sickles, who had been able to get a glimpse of the Round Tops as he marched past them, and of the ridge, flanked by Culp's Hill and supported by Wolf's Hill, which Slocum's batteries firmly held after his arrival, was prepared with his opinion:

" It is a good place to fight from, general! "

Meade's reply to us pleased me: " I am glad to hear you say so, gentlemen, for it is too late to leave it."

There was a bright moon, so the dawn of day crept

upon us unawares. Before sunrise I rode with General Meade along our lines toward the left. These lines, much extended, with long intervals, did not appear very favorable; a sleeping army, at best, suggests weakness; the general saw the needs. He sat upon his horse as the sun was rising, and with his field glass took a survey of the Cemetery Ridge and its environments. We were upon the highest ground within the cemetery inclosure.

The Confederate artillery was occasionally firing. The skirmishing at intervals was a restless, nervous fusillade near the town and off to the right in the woods. I stood at that same point of observation during the most exciting epoch of the great battle. I was there when the cornerstone of the soldier's monument was laid. I stood at the same center some years later amid a group of friends and explained some of the varied scenes of the conflict, and never without emotion; but the impression of that beautiful morning is ineffaceable. The glorious landscape, with its remarkable variety of aspect, in the fresh morning light, like a panorama was spread before our eyes. I need not rehearse its pictorial summary, for I hardly think Meade was considering the panorama at all — the mountains, the groves and the valleys, with their variety of productions, or the streams of water—except in their evident relationship to his military plans.

What he soon did, after he had ridden away slowly and thoughtfully, is the true key to his thought. For, by his direction, Slocum's entire corps went quickly to the right to hold the rough-wooded slopes from Culp's Hill to McAllister's Mill. Ames, Steinwehr, Schurz, Robinson, and Doubleday, with their respective divisions, remained substantially the same as I had located them on their arrival at the cemetery the day before. These continued their line from Culp's Hill southward to near Zeigler's Grove. Hancock now brought the Second Corps to occupy a short front on the highest ground by Zeigler's Grove. Sickles gathered the Third Corps and tried to fill the whole space from Hancock to the Little Round Top. His formation, finally, was to push far out to the peach orchard and draw back his left to the Devil's Den, and then put Humphreys's division forward beyond the Emmittsburg road, well to the right.

From Humphreys in front of Hancock's left the ground was occupied by Birney's division. These divisions formed an angle at the peach orchard. For a time the Fifth Corps arriving, was placed in reserve; and all the army reserve of artillery Hunt carefully placed in the angle between the Baltimore pike and the Taneytown road. Buford's cavalry had gone to the rear for rest and to protect the trains, and, by some unaccountable misunderstanding, no cavalry whatever was in the vicinity of our left during July 2d. Sickles's position was questioned; it was outside of the natural line from Zeigler's Grove to the Round Tops. But, as there was no cavalry there and no masses of other troops to protect his left, it was a fortunate circumstance that Sickles had pushed out as he did, simply that it gained time for General Meade and secured Little Round Top against capture.

I, myself, from the cemetery could not see the Confederates' attack, for their objective was the rough and precipitous Little Round Top. It took Longstreet over two hours to dislodge and drive back Sickles and the supports Meade sent him, and caused a most dreadful general contest amid this mass of rock and stony hillock.

As soon as the firing began in earnest, Meade rode near his left flank, and ordered up the Fifth Corps, which entered the battle, led by the vigilant Warren, Meade's chief engineer, and held Little Round Top to the end. The grand old Sixth Corps, having made its thirty-two miles, continuing its march through the night, had filed into position in our rear. It was then the strongest corps, well commanded and ready for use. Hancock's corps, too, was well concentrated and near at hand. As the fight waxed hotter, Meade sent for Slocum's two divisions, leaving only Greene's brigade, beyond Culp's Hill, to face the eastern half of Ewell's corps.

Sickles, like Hood, was at last badly wounded and carried from the field. Then Birney took his place.

The battle was almost over when, just before sunset, a Confederate regiment crossed our line through an open space. Colonel Willard was killed there and his men were falling fast. Hancock himself led the First Minnesota to the exposed point, and they drove back the intruders. Williams's division from Slocum had now come to reënforce the Minnesota men.

During this second day my own command played but a small part in the engagement, except the artillery of the Eleventh Corps, which was incessantly at work from the commencement of Lee's assault.

During the afternoon and evening of July 2d General Ewell, who had succeeded Stonewall Jackson, enveloped our right with his corps, Rodes in and near the town, Edward Johnson opposite our right, and Early between the two. Ewell certainly had instructions to attack at the same time that Longstreet opened his fire opposite Little Round Top.

First, neither he nor his generals could distinguish Longstreet's firing; second, a portion of his command was sent off, far to his left and rear, to meet a force of " Yankees " reliably reported to be turning his left flank. Naturally he delayed a while to get back these troops, because, at the best—judging by natural obstacles and artificial hindrances behind which were the bravest of our infantry and a mighty concentration of artillery—he had assigned to him a task not easy to perform. Under these circumstances few generals ever succeed in getting many brigades to act simultaneously, especially where the ground is exceedingly broken and wooded, where few of the troops can see each other.

On the Confederate side, just about the time when the last of Slocum's column was disappearing and the diligent Greene was endeavoring to so extend his one brigade as to occupy the roughly fortified line just vacated, Johnson, the Confederate, was moving forward his division, astonished to meet with almost no opposition. Johnson went into the woods, stumbled over rocks and stones, forded Rock Creek, drove in and captured a few skirmishers and small detachments, and quietly took possession of Ruger's works; but suddenly from the direction of Culp's Hill he encountered a most annoying fire.

Greene had drawn back his line, turning a little on his left as a pivot, until he could bring an oblique fire. Johnson, perceiving this danger menacing his right, turned and attacked Greene's front and right near the Culp's Hill with those two brigades nearest and immediately available. Again and again the assault was renewed with a sort of angry fury and always as coolly repulsed. Greene's men were sheltered and lost but few. The Confederates piled up their dead and wounded to little purpose. One brigade commander fell among the assailants, and the other was obliged at last to discontinue the useless onslaught, but not until between nine and ten at night.

Wadsworth had so extended his lines as to strengthen Greene's, giving him perhaps one regiment of his own for reserve. As soon as the attack commenced, Greene sent to Wadsworth for assistance, to which he readily responded. Afterwards, Greene came and thanked me for the good service done in his night fight by the Eighty-second Illinois, Forty-fifth New York, and Sixty-first Ohio, sent by me to his assistance from the Eleventh Corps. Lieutenant Colonel Otto, of Schurz's staff, who led this detachment, was also highly commended.

I remember well when Otto promptly volunteered to guide these troops into position. Somehow it always affected me strongly to behold a hearty and fearless young man, after receiving an order, set forth without reluctance to execute it under such circumstances that there were few chances of ever seeing him again. So I felt as Otto went forth that night into the gathering gloom.

I count among the remarkable providences at Gettysburg the want of concert of action among the Confederate commanders. When Edward Johnson gave the command "Forward!" it was understood that Jubal Early would move at the same time; yet it was at least an hour later before Early began his attack. He had waited for the return from the flank march of his two brigades. Yet as soon as one had

428

arrived he set his troops in motion. Early's first and second brigades, having been long in position, lying quietly under the cover of the Cemetery Hill on its north side, suddenly, after a new spurt of artillery, and just at dusk, sprang forward to assault my corps. He was governing himself by the adjoining brigade of A. P. Hill's corps on the right. Certainly this was fortunate for us, for the two large brigades that did attack —the one of Louisiana and the other of North Carolina troops—were quite enough. It was after seven o'clock when the first cry, shrill and ominous, was heard in front of Ames's division. The Louisiana men, well named " Louisiana Tigers," came on with a rush, broke through the front of Von Gilsa's brigade and other points of my curved front, and almost before I could tell where the assault was made, our men and the Confederates came tumbling back together. Quickly they were among the intrenched batteries of Major Osborn, whose fire was intended strongly to support that bastioned front of the cemetery. Schurz and I were standing near, side by side. At my request he faced Colonel Krzyzanowski's brigade about, now not over 800 men, and double-quicked them to the relief of Wiederich's battery. When they arrived the battery men had not left their guns. Ames's men were assisting them with their rifles, they were wielding hand spikes, abandoned muskets, sponge staffs, or anything they could seize, to keep the enemy from dragging off their guns. The batteries were quickly cleared and promptly used, but the broken lines were not yet restored. Hancock, quick to understand—not more than a quarter of a mile away—" hearing a heavy engagement " on my front, and judging the firing to be coming nearer and nearer to his position, caused Gibbon to detach the brigade of Colonel S. S. Carroll to my support. Colonel Carroll was at that time a young man of great quickness and dash. His brigade was already deployed in the darkness at right angles to the general front, and swept along northward to the right of Krzyzanowski, past the cemetery fence and batteries, and on, on, with marvelous rapidity, sweeping everything before it, till by his energetic help the entire broken front was completely reëstablished. General A. S. Webb, a generous and coöperative commander, also sent two of his regiments to my aid. The lines were thus reëstablished; then, by the help of General Newton, who commanded the Fifth Corps, I was enabled to shorten my front and have sufficient reserves to prevent the possibility of such a break again.

Early made a few desperate attempts to regain what he had just lost. One of his brigade commanders, Colonel Avery, was killed, and his men were falling rapidly, so that he at last gave up the struggle. Every effort against Culp's Hill, on either flank of it, had come too late to be of any avail in Lee's main attack against the Round Tops, and had been vigorously and promptly met with plenty of troops. But yet, as Geary, next to Greene, and Ruger, nearer McAllister's Mill, began to skirmish back in the night with the hope of resting within their strong barricade, they found to their surprise that these strong lines were held by at least two brigades of the enemy under Edward Johnson. Taking up excellent positions for defense so as to bring an abundant cross fire into those woods and ravines east of Culp's Hill and west of McAllister's Mill, the troops threw themselves on the ground for a brief rest. Meanwhile General Slocum was diligently preparing, determined to regain the stony and log barricades, which an incident of the terrible battle of July 2d had caused him to lose. So ended that day's and that night's conflict.

Thus far it was a drawn battle. We had barely held our own recovered ground temporarily lost at the center, fought desperately and prevented extreme disaster on the left; but we had gone to sleep—Confederates and Union men, many in different parts of the same intrenchments.

The ground was covered with the groanings and moanings of the wounded. While the soldiers were sleeping, the medical men with their ambulances, their lanterns, and their stretchers, aided here and there by a chaplain or a member of the Christian Commission, were going from point to point to do what little they could for the multitude of sufferers. Imagine, then, how we corps commanders felt in view of all this as we came together at Meade's headquarters (on the Taneytown road) for a brief council of war. Two questions were asked: First, "Shall we remain here?" Second, "Shall we remain on the defensive or shall we take the offensive?" We voted to remain and fight, but not to begin an attack. Lee, on his side, indicates his thought in the report of the campaign in his quiet way of writing, as he says: "These partial successes determined me to continue the assault next day."

It is not always the case that the characteristics of a young man at school or college remain the same in after life, but in the case of my classmate, Thomas H. Ruger, the marked characteristics of his school days followed him, to be even more observable in his active manhood. Deliberative, cautious, and yet fearless; persistent, and, if unfairly pressed, obstinate to the last degree; it was a good thing that a division fell to him at Gettysburg.

It was a wise order given by Williams, the corps commander, to send Ruger back to hold the extreme right of Slocum's line, it being the right of our main line, after his troops could be of no further use in rear of Hancock's Second Corps.

It must have been after nine o'clock in the night, when, moving along the Baltimore turnpike, Ruger cautiously covered the left of his column by flankers or by skirmishers, " to ascertain if the enemy held any part of the breastworks, and if not, to occupy them at once." The breastworks held an enemy, so several of Ruger's skirmishers were captured. But Ruger, finding a little farther on, beyond a swale which makes into the Rock Creek, that a portion of his barricaded line which he had left in the morning had not been discovered by Johnson's men, reoccupied it at once and strongly posted his division so as to bring an oblique fire upon the sleeping enemy's stronghold. Geary by midnight had worked himself into a corresponding line near Culp's Hill, prolonging that of Greene's, where the early night battle had been fought. Geary faced so as to take the same sleeping enemy with an oblique fire from the other side of the swale. Ruger's and Geary's lines, when prolonged southward, met somewhere beyond the Baltimore pike. Batteries were located on Power's Hill near that point, in the actual interval between the lines, so as to sweep all the approaches; and, besides, two regiments (the Twentieth Connecticut and the One Hundred and Seventh New York) were deployed in the same interval, so that there should be some little direct opposition should the Confederate general, Edward Johnson, endeavor to seize the famous turnpike, which at daylight he was bound to discover through the slight opening in the wood, the turnpike being only about 700 yards distant.

It appears that the Union commander (in spite of the council of war) and the Confederate had each ordered an attack at daylight. Geary first opened fire with his artillery, continuing it for ten minutes. Then, Geary's troops, or a part of them, began to advance, when the Confederates, also taking the offensive, made a rapid charge along Geary's entire front, shouting as they came; but the Union troops cheered back defiantly, fired rapidly, and yielded no ground.

At last, with Slocum's abundant artillery at Power's Hill and following up Geary's victorious shouting, Ruger's entire division swept forward and, in conjunction with Geary's men, reoccupied those barricades which had by that time cost five hours of hard fighting and carnage which pen cannot describe.

After returning from Meade's headquarters the evening before, as everything was quiet, I made my bed within a fenced lot of the cemetery and took this opportunity, after extraordinary and prolonged effort and want of rest, to get a good sleep, not minding a grave for a pillow. I heard nothing till I was startled by combined artillery and musketry which I have just described, and which appeared near at hand. The roaring of the cannon seemed like thunder, and the musketry may be compared to hail striking a flat roof, growing louder as the storm increases, or lessening as it subsides. I sent immediately to General Meade to inquire what the combat meant. The answer was: "The Twelfth Corps is regaining its lines." Five years afterwards I walked over that rough battlefield. The breastworks of logs and stones, though dilapi-

dated, were still traceable. Trees and old stumps
were full of holes made by rifle bullets and enlarged
by the knives of relic seekers. Quite sizable trees
were fully cut off, some broken and falling or shattered as with lightning bolts. Even the large rocks,
partially covered with moss, by the thousands of dis-
colored spots showed how they had been exposed to the
leaden storm. It would not be strange if Slocum and
his officers felt that the main Gettysburg battle had
been there.

On July 3d the time from the cessation of Slocum's
battle to the beginning of Longstreet's last attack was
about three hours. During this time, when Lee was
making his best preparations for a last effort, our cavalry was doing us good service on the flanks. Stuart,
after his raid, had returned, to be sent by Lee to so
place himself beyond our right as to do us the greatest
possible damage in case of our defeat. But the vigilant General Gregg, with his veteran brigades, was in
that quarter. A severe battle, involving cavalry and
artillery, occurred well out of town and in the vicinity
of the Bonaughton road. Judging by all accounts, it
seems to have been a fierce duel, where both parties
suffered greatly, losing nearly 1,000 men on each side;
but Gregg had the satisfaction of defeating the purpose of his adversary, who was, of course, soon obliged
to withdraw to guard the flanks of his own defeated
army.

On our left, where General Farnsworth fell, Kilpatrick's division contended—often at great disadvantage—with the different portions of Longstreet's infantry. There were only two brigades—Merritt's and
Farnsworth's. They seem to have been intent upon
capturing sundry supply wagons that hove in sight,

when they were obliged to meet and hold in check the best infantry troops of the South. They were badly injured, with heavy losses.

The final effort of General Lee against our left had two parts or periods: first, the work of his artillery; second, the assault of his infantry. He chose for his point of attack not Little Round Top, but "the umbrella trees," a landmark near Zeigler's Grove, which was easier of approach, and he believed would give even better fruits to his hopes if once firmly seized and manned with abundant artillery. It was not easy for our glasses to determine the new position of Lee's guns.

Near the ground occupied by Sickles at the beginning of the battle of July 2d, extending along the Emmittsburg road was a semicircular line of about forty pieces, farther south a few more, and on higher ground, as if in tiers, the remainder of that portion of Lee's artillery assigned to Longstreet, who was to attack the command. There were concentrated in this neighborhood at least 140 cannon. The ranges to the point of attack would vary from 1,000 to 2,000 yards.

Pickett's division of three brigades was to make the main attack. It was formed with Kemper on the right, Garnett on the left, and Armistead in rear. Pickett's main force had in support Willcox's brigade on its right and Pettigrew's six brigades on its left.

On our side, Hunt had arranged the artillery into four divisions:

1. On Cemetery Heights, under Osborn, having a large sweep of the front and right of my positions, 50 cannon.

2. Hazzard had 30 finely located close to the crest near Zeigler's Grove.

3. McGilvery about 40, near Little Round Top, favorable for a direct or oblique fire; and

4. The reserve, which Hunt kept ready under shelter, for quick replacement of any which might become disabled.

The infantry had changed place but little.

The brigades now most exposed to direct assault were those of Smyth and Willard (Hays's division), and Webb, Hall, and Harrow (Gibbon's division).

At last two signal guns were fired. Then, after just interval enough to mark well the signal, the cannonading began in good earnest. At first the hostile fire was unusually accurate, neither firing too high nor too low, and the projectiles were showered upon the space between Zeigler's Grove and Little Round Top about the center of our line.

But as soon as Osborn set his guns in play from the cemetery, and McGilvery had opened up his forty pieces from Little Round Top, the Confederate artillerists undertook to give blow for blow, striking blindly toward the most troublesome points. We concentrated our aim more than they. Over 200 heavy guns now fired as fast as men could load and fire; they filled the whole region of mountain, hill, and valley with one continuous roar, instantly varied by sudden bolts at each lightning flash from the cannon's mouth, and by the peculiar, shrill screech of the breaking shells. Then the crash of destruction, the breaking of carriages, the killing and wounding of men—in one of my regiments twenty-seven fell at a single shot. General Meade's headquarters were for a time in the hottest place; the house was riddled with shot, the chimney knocked in pieces, the dooryard plowed with them, officers and men wounded, and the many patient horses killed, and, what seemed worse, others dreadfully wounded. My horses and those of my staff were nearer the cemetery behind a projecting cliff. The German boy, Charley Weiss, then Colonel Balloch's orderly, was holding a number of them; a fragment of an iron missile struck him, clipping off his left arm. Mrs. Sampson, caring for him, said: "Poor boy, I'm sorry for you!" Weiss sprang up in bed and, lifting his remaining arm, said with vigor: "I'm not a poor boy. General Howard has lost his right arm and I my left. That's all there is about it!"

So every part of that field was visited. Men were killed while straightening their teams; while carrying orders; on horseback; on foot, while talking, eating, or lying down. The lowest ground in our rear was quickly cleared of noncombatants, camp followers, and overcurious civilians. No orders were needed after the first bombshell exploded there. The air was so full of terror and death-dealing fragments that every man at first must have doubted if he should ever see the light of another day. Yet the majority in both armies were now well accustomed to artillery, and, shielding themselves by every possible cover at hand, quietly waited for this firing to cease. We stopped first. We did not want to waste ammunition, and knew what would follow that extraordinary cannonade. Many of the Confederate leaders thought that their fearful artillery had disabled ours and silenced the batteries.

During this artillery duel I had been watching the events, sitting in front of my batteries on the slope of Cemetery Hill. Feeling that my greatest danger came from the strippings of the shells as they flew over my head, I had cracker boxes piled behind us—affording protection from our own cannon. In the lull I suddenly observed beautiful lines of regiments as on parade emerging from the woods in rear of the enemy's cannon. I seemed to see a mile of frontage. The flags, still bright in the thinning haze of the sunlight, waved prettily, and looked like ours. This was Pickett's division and came forward at a rapid pace. Our artillery began with round shot and shells to make openings in their ranks, but they were quickly closed. Nearer, nearer the Confederates came; the front was narrower now and the flanks traceable. It was more like a closed column, and bore to its left and aimed for Zeigler's Grove front. Hays, Gibbon, Doubleday, and their brigade commanders and all their commands, in two lines, were behind the slight barricades and the walls, waiting the word. Hancock was on hand, and General Stannard placed the Vermonters brigade among the trees at an angle so as to fire obliquely. Pickett's right flank was now plain to McGilvery; his 40 guns poured in their deadly shot, and suddenly the whole front of Hancock's line was ablaze with small arms. The Confederates were mowed down like the wheat in harvest; yet not all, for they did not stop.

They advanced in the face of a " galling fire " of both infantry and artillery " to about 20 paces from our wall, when, for a few moments, they recoiled under a terrific fire "; then were " rushing forward with unyielding determination and an apparent spirit of laudable rivalry to plant the Southern banner on the walls of the enemy."

The fighting over the wall became hand to hand, but Pickett's force was too weak. It looked for and " hoped for support, but hoped in vain." The end must come to such an unequal contest. As a sample, one brigade went into action with 1,427 officers and men, and came off with only 300. General Garnett, always cool and self-possessed, was shot from his horse, just in front of the fatal wall. Willcox and Perry, with their supporting brigades, blinded doubtless by the storm of shot and shell, had veered toward the right and Pickett had borne toward the left; thus the right support was lost to the main charge. The support of Pettigrew and others on Pickett's left was more real, but in such a sudden change and quick repulse this force came up only to suffer losses with no substantial result.

The heaviest blow struck Webb's brigade. Armistead reached the wall with about 100 men, but fell inside mortally wounded. Beyond that wall Garnett and Pettigrew had already fallen. The most of that part of Webb's brigade posted here abandoned their position, but fortunately were not put to rout altogether. Webb, with a rifle in his hand broken by a shot and a bleeding head, rallied them to reënforce the rest of his brigade. Plenty of help soon came. I saw our own brigades quickly, in some apparent confusion, with flags flying, charge upon the weakened foe. The Confederates were everywhere beaten back; many became prisoners; many others. threw away their arms and lay upon the ground to avoid the firing, while the whole front was strewn with the dead and dying.

The last operation on the evening of July 3d was a sweep over the field in front of Little Round Top by McCandless's brigade and some few other troops. This was ordered by Meade himself. By this movement the whole of the ground lost the previous day was retaken together with all our wounded, who, until then, mingled with Confederates, were lying on the field uncared for.

Autobiography of Gen. O. O. Howard

It is sometimes said to me that writing and speaking upon the events of the war may have a deleterious influence upon youth. I can conceive of two reasons for such a warning—one, that a soldier by his enthusiasm may, even unconsciously, infuse into his writing and speech the war spirit, and thus incite strong desires in younger minds for similar excitements and deeds; and, secondly, a soldier deeply affected as he must have been in our great struggle for national existence, may not take sufficient pains in his accounts of historic incidents to allay any spirit of animosity or dissension which may still exist.

But with regard to the first, I think there is need of a faithful portraiture of what we may call the after-battle, a panorama which shows with fidelity the fields covered with dead men and horses; with the wounded, numerous and helpless, stretched on the ground in masses, each waiting his turn; the rough hospitals with hay and straw for bedding, saturated with blood and wet with the rain; houses torn into fragments; every species of property ruthlessly demolished or destroyed—these, which we cannot well exaggerate, and such as these, cry out against the horrors, the hateful ravages, and the countless expense of war. They show plainly to our children that war, with its embodied woes and furies, must be avoided, except as the last appeal for existence, or for the rights which are more valuable than life itself.

When I dwell on the scenes of July 4th and 5th at Gettysburg, the pictures exhibiting Meade's men and Lee's, though now shadowy from time, are still full of terrible groupings and revolting lineaments.

There is a lively energy, an emulous activity, an exhilarating buoyancy of spirit in all the preparations

for an expected battle, and these feelings are intensi-
fied into an increased ardor during the conflict; but it
is another thing to see our comrades there upon the
ground with their darkened faces and swollen forms;
another thing to watch the countenances of friends and
companions but lately in the bloom of health, now dis-
figured, torn, and writhing in death; and not less affecting to a sensitive heart to behold the multitude of
strangers prone and weak, pierced with wounds, or
showing broken limbs and every sign of suppressed
suffering, waiting for hours and hours for a relief
which is long coming—the relief of the surgeon's knife
or of death.

Several years ago I wrote: "I saw just before leaving the cemetery, on July 5th, a large plat of ground
covered with wounded Confederates, some of whom
had been struck in the first and some in the second
day's battle, not yet attended to. The army surgeons
and the physicians, who now flocked to their aid by
every incoming railroad train from the North, were
doing their best, yet it took time and unremitting labor
to go through the mass. The dirt and blood and pallor
of this bruised mass of humanity affected me in a manner I can never forget, pleading pathetically for peace
and good will toward men."

As to the second reason, any feeling of personal re-
sentment toward the late Confederates I would not
counsel or cherish. Our countrymen—large numbers
of them—combined and fought us hard for *a cause*.
They failed and we succeeded; so that, in an honest
desire for reconcilement, I would be the more careful, even in the use of terms, to convey no hatred
or reproach for the past. Such are my real convictions, and certainly the intention in all my efforts

441

is not to anger and separate, but to pacify and unite.

That morning (the 5th) I made a reconnoissance with a company of cavalry, the Eleventh Corps headquarters escort. It was immediately commanded by Captain Sharra. Major C. H. Howard, then my senior aid, was to accompany me. As we were moving out westerly, toward the Cashtown road, Captain Griffith, of Philadelphia, another staff officer, who being for that time in charge of making provision for the headquarters mess, had ridden out to see what he could find. Noticing our party in motion he rode quickly up to me and said: "General, you are going toward the enemy; please allow me to accompany you?"

I answered: "Very well, if you desire to do so."

The Confederates had already left the village and the Seminary Ridge. We passed on at a rapid pace till we came to a ridge fringed with trees. We saw the gray coats among the trees. The escort under Captain Sharra formed in order and charged quickly to the crest, and I followed on with my orderlies to find that the men had overtaken a number of stragglers from the Confederates and had taken them prisoners. The same thing was repeated at the next ridge, only this time, from the grove bordering the road, Sharra found a well-set ambuscade. The men in waiting fired upon the too eager horsemen. Major Howard and Captain Griffith had charged with the cavalry.

In my next letter home, written from Emmittsburg the next day (the 6th), I spoke of this scene and of Griffith: "I made a reconnoissance yesterday with some cavalry. We saw some men ahead that looked like stragglers. A dash was made by the cavalry, led

The Battle of Gettysburg

by Charles (Major Howard), Captain Griffith, and other officers. Poor Griffith was very badly wounded by a sudden fire from the woods and thickets; also two or three of his men. We all love Griffith very much. He is a pure-minded, noble man; has a wife in Philadelphia. The ball went quite through him. He is at Mrs. Taylor's in Gettysburg, and is quite comfortable. I talked with him, got strong expressions of his faith in God through Christ; read and prayed with him before leaving. I told him his wound (which afterwards proved fatal) was a punishment to me and not to him. Charles (Major Howard) is well, but we are all pretty well tired out. I long for rest."

Before I left Gettysburg, with Professor Stoever, of the Lutheran Seminary, I paid a last visit to Captain Griffith. I read a few verses from the fourteenth chapter of John. When I said, " That where I am there ye may be also," Griffith with his moist eyes looking in my face, said gently: " I am not afraid to die, General, and only regret to leave you and the dear ones at home."

A member of the Christian Commission who was with Griffith until his good wife came, wrote: " I attended Captain Griffith's funeral on Wednesday (July 8th). I could speak with confidence of his Christian character and hope. He died triumphantly! "

My brother Rowland, of the Christian Commission, looked up our cousin, Major S. P. Lee, of the Third Maine. Lee's arm was shattered and had to be amputated at the shoulder. Lee had first served acceptably in the naval force, but concluded to change into the army, entering my old regiment as lieutenant after I left it by advancement. His gallantry and ability soon won him promotion. When found on the field the

443

major was unconscious and very low. It was not believed that he could recover. Yet by great care and good nursing, first by the friend I have named, and then by his wife, he gradually regained his health and strength.

So each family had its own sorrows and woundings after Gettysburg. Hancock, Gibbon, Webb, Butterfield (Meade's chief of staff), and so many others were wounded that commands changed hands. Meade did not immediately commence the pursuit, and when he did it was not made straight after the foe, but worked off to our left. My command in this moving was, part of the time, the Eleventh and the Fifth Corps combined. For some reason not at the time plain to me we were halted at Emmittsburg. Yet the halt was not long, for July 7th the two corps (the Fifth and the Eleventh) marched thirty miles to the Middletown Valley. The 8th, Schurz's division, was dispatched to Boonsboro. This preferred to support Buford's cavalry, which had some time before met the retreating Confederates and been engaged for hours. My other divisions guarded the mountain pass there till the arrival of other corps. I wrote the next day from Boonsboro (July 9, 1863) : " We are near the enemy. Lee has not yet crossed the Potomac and we must have one more trial. God grant us success in the next battle. He has preserved us so many times, I begin to feel that He might do so to the end."

It was six miles from Funkstown, where I then was the evening of the 12th, when Meade brought together his corps commanders and counseled with them with respect to the position, strength, and intention of Lee, who was intrenched facing us with his back to the river at Williamsport, and with respect to the wisdom of our making an attack upon him there. Meade read us Lee's proclamation, apparently fresh and hearty, wherein ostensibly he courted an opportunity for another trial of strength under more favorable circumstances than those which caused him his reverse at Gettysburg. All regarded that proclamation as something to keep up Confederate courage, and allowed to come to us for " strategic " effect.

We had present, I think, nine corps commanders; six were of the opinion that we had better not assault Lee there. The other three, Wadsworth, Pleasonton, and I, pleaded for an immediate attack. Wadsworth had the First Corps temporarily and Pleasonton the cavalry corps.

A reconnoissance ordered by me on the 13th was made by one of Schimmelfennig's regiments, and Kilpatrick's cavalry, which Pleasonton had sent to Lee's left flank; as soon as the cavalry skirmishers had approached the enemy's line, he opened a brisk fire from infantry or dismounted cavalry. One or two pieces of his artillery also fired at random from a battery near the Williamsport road. After this reconnoissance, and on the information I could collect, I was impressed with a belief that the enemy would retreat without giving us battle, and it was with a hope of being able to make a lodgment on the enemy's left that I asked permission to make a reconnoissance at 3 A.M. of the next day (the 14th). Subsequently the commanding general's order for several simultaneous reconnoissances at 7 A.M. reached me. I also received word, in answer to my request, that orders had already been sent out, which would probably effect the purpose I proposed. But it happened that 7 A.M. was too late.

In a letter of July 14th, dated at Funkstown, Md.,

where we had abutted against Lee's intrenched position till he effected a crossing by the deep ford and by a hastily constructed rickety bridge of boats, I wrote just after the works were emptied of his troops: " The enemy has got away from us again and gone back to the Potomac, having left a strongly fortified position. We do not know yet whether the Confederates have all crossed. . . . Senator Wilson and Vice-President Hamlin visited us while here."

I remember meeting them in the belfry of a large church on July 13th, in Funkstown, from which we could see what appeared to be Lee's extreme left flank. The letter further says: " Captain Harry M. Stinson—good, true, and faithful and brave as ever—has just reported that he had been in the enemy's evacuated works." We hastened on that morning, after we found Lee's lines empty, to Williamsport.

En route I reproached an elderly, gray-haired Pennsylvania volunteer, belonging to a regiment of a very high number, for leaving his regiment and straggling. He said that he didn't think that officers who could let Lee escape that way should say much. In heart I then rather sympathized with his growl. He further remarked that we who rode on horses had a good deal to say. I asked him if he wanted to ride. He said that he would not object to that. I dismounted from my horse, which, by the aid of an orderly, the complaining soldier mounted, not removing his full equipments. It was not long before he found out where he was, and becoming very weary with trying to keep his seat, he begged to be allowed to walk and join his regiment. This was granted.

At the river the inhabitants told us that part of Lee's command had crossed the Potomac at Falling

The Battle of Gettysburg

Waters on a new bridge of boats; a part on flatboats at Williamsport, and more at a deep ford a little above that place; that many horses and men were drowned while fording the river.

The loss of Meade's army at Gettysburg is set down at 23,186, made up as follows: 2,834 killed, 13,709 wounded, and 6,643 missing. According to the hospital record we had 7,262 wounded prisoners and 13,-621 aggregate. I have been under the impression that Meade, who always had strong objections to overstate, has left an underestimate of the actual number of prisoners taken. General Lee's killed were over 5,500. The number that escaped as stragglers, as slightly ill, or having light wounds—many of whom went back to Virginia or farther south—is reckoned as about 10,000. Taking these figures, the aggregate loss of General Lee caused by the battle of Gettysburg is 29,121 from all causes.

If we put the two sums together, 23,186 and 29,121, we have 52,307 *hors de combat*. Aggregating the wounded, we have 20,971 men to be cared for—a large number even for our active and efficient hospital department. More than 20,000 men, a strong army corps in itself!

(For notice of General Stannard see Appendix.)

CHAPTER XXVI

I CONTINUED with the Army of the Potomac till General Meade had not only recrossed the Potomac and marched back southward, following up, by the inside lines, the retreat of the Confederates, but till Meade had crossed the Rappahannock also, established his headquarters at Culpeper Court House, Virginia, and put his forces into good positions for watching every point of the compass. The Eleventh Corps, which I then commanded, spread itself out north of the Rappahannock, in fan-shaped order, facing the rear, with its center near Catlett's, a station on the Orange & Alexandria Railroad. My tents were pitched on Mr. Catlett's farm; and we were suffered to remain so long in one place that we became quite domesticated. By the letters which I have preserved I recall the fact that the officers of my staff and myself had much sympathy and friendship with Mr. Catlett's family. They remained at home in a neighborhood quite overrun by both armies and one already very destitute of comforts and quite barren of vegetation. Writing from this camp to my child, I said: " Little Lottie Catlett, who looks something like yourself, gave me a good, hearty welcome when I returned, and showed me her nice, new doll. . . . One time she understood somebody to say that I had been killed, and she cried very heartily." The monotony of camp life had many reliefs this hot sea-

448

son. At one time a German chaplain preached, and the Thirty-third Massachusetts band came to the service and played the hymns. The band remained at Catlett's over Monday, and we all had a delightful musical treat. At another time, Saturday, September 4, 1863, returning from Manassas Junction, where I had been to review troops, I found Meade, Humphreys, and Pleasonton at my headquarters.

Meade took dinner with me under our fly; he admired the ability of our cook in making strange devices upon an admirable cake. Our German cook's ability exceeded anything found in cities.

At another time, in the same month, my staff rode with me to the village of Greenwich, where I had one regiment. The principal citizen was Mr. Green. He appeared heartily glad to see us. His premises afforded an exception to the prevailing desolation. They were, indeed, in fine condition. He extended to us cordial and abundant hospitality. With fervor and simplicity he asked God's blessing. His neighbors spoke of his charities. His character much impressed me. He was an Englishman, and " British property " was inscribed in plain letters on his gate posts. There were large stacks of good hay untouched, and good-sized beehives full of honey! War had spared nobody else in that region.

At that time, too, as to many others around me, there came news of illness at home.

While we were in the midst of such surroundings and circumstances, which were making up the woof and web of our daily life, with little apparent prospect of change, on September 24th, without previous intimation, the following orders suddenly made their appearance at my headquarters:

"The commanding general directs that you have your command (Eleventh Corps) in readiness to proceed to Washington to-morrow morning by railroad.

"You will at once notify Mr. J. H. Devereux, superintendent of the railroad, Alexandria, at what points you desire to have the trains take up your troops, and the number at each place.

"Your command must have five days' cooked rations. You will not wait to be relieved by other troops, but proceed to Washington the moment the trains are ready to take your command. Please acknowledge.

"By command of Major General Meade.

"S. WILLIAMS, *Asst. Adj't Gen.*"

General Slocum, commanding the Twelfth Corps, had received substantially the same orders. These two corps were placed upon trains of cars and put under the command of General Joseph Hooker, for it had been resolved to recall General Hooker from his retirement to which General Halleck's influence had consigned him the preceding June 28th. These two corps were intended as reënforcements to the Army of the Cumberland at that time still under General Rosecrans.

The battle of Chickamauga had been fought, ending September 21, 1863. The place of this hardly contested field was in Tennessee, east of Lookout Mountain, and several miles south of Chattanooga. It had resulted, notwithstanding our heavy losses and partial defeats, in a substantial success; for Rosecrans had gained that strong place of arms, Chattanooga, and thus firmly seized the left bank of the Tennessee. By the date of our orders, September 24th, he had rendered his position stronger by his forts and intrenchments. There was little present danger of losing this

450

important advantage by assault or by battle; but Bragg had seized the mountains which hemmed in Chattanooga, the range above (that is, Missionary Ridge) and the ranges below (Lookout and Raccoon), and by his cannon and his outposts so controlled the Tennessee River above and below, that there should be no communication with Chattanooga by the usual routes on the same side with the town.

Rosecrans's wagons with supplies came up the convex road on the opposite bank. When they used the river road there, the route was bad enough, being over forty miles in length from the Nashville & Bridgeport Railroad to the pontoon bridge which led into Chattanooga. Soon even this rugged way was shut up by the boldness of the enemy's sharpshooters posted on the south bank of the river and firing across the narrower stretches.

After a longer and safer road had been selected, the supply trains were "raided upon" by guerrilla bands and by smaller bodies of the enemy's cavalry, which at the time ranged wildly through that portion of Tennessee. Soon the question of supplies became a serious one, so it was necessary either to strengthen Rosecrans's hands, so that he could clear himself from a partial siege, or withdraw his army and so lose advantage of a position which had been secured at a costly sacrifice.

It was, therefore, determined to detach us from Meade and make a transfer to Rosecrans. The two corps (the Eleventh and Twelfth) quickly started up from their scattered camps in regiments, loaded up their tents and luggage, and marched to the nearest railway station. We, fortunately for our subsequent comfort, were to leave our army wagons behind as soon as they had been unloaded at the cars. Our artillery and horses went with us. Instead of having a single long train, Mr. Devereux furnished us with several short ones. As soon as the first one was loaded to its full with our material, animals, and men, it moved off, to be followed by the second, filled in like manner. As several stations were used at the same time, it did not take long, with our multitude of helpers, to embark everything which was allowed.

At first our destination was a secret to everybody. By Halleck's instructions I went to Washington and reported to Hooker. I found him at Willard's Hotel. He at once informed me that my corps and Slocum's were to move by rail to the west and join Rosecrans as soon as it could be done. I remember, years afterwards, just after the completion of the Northern Pacific, I waited a day and a night for a train at the junction of the Utah Northern with that railroad. Mr. Henry Villard, the president of the road, and his guests from Europe and from the Eastern States were returning from the occasion of the driving of the "golden spike." It was making a trial trip. Train after train whizzed past my station, keeping regular intervals apart. These had the road all to themselves. They reminded me forcibly of our manner of moving troops during the war. However, we never went as Villard did, at forty or fifty miles an hour. We did well to average fifteen.

After an interview with my commanders I paid a visit to the President. It was during that visit that Mr. Lincoln pulled down his map from the wall and, putting his finger on Cumberland Gap, asked: "General, can't you go through here and seize Knoxville?" Speaking of the mountaineers of that region he de-

clared: " They are loyal there, they are loyal ! " Then
he gave me his mounted map, better for campaigning,
and took my unmounted one, saying: " Yours will do
for me." In answer to the President's question I replied: " We must work in with Grant's plans, as he has
three armies, the Tennessee, the Cumberland, and the
Ohio." And that is what Mr. Lincoln actually did.

With my headquarters I took the rearmost train.
Many men mounted, from choice, on the tops of the
freight cars. It gave them better air to do so, but it
was dangerous at the bridges and in passing through
the tunnels. A few men were swept off and hurt.
When times of excitement, like the present, came on,
some of our men developed an extraordinary desire
for whisky, and citizens were never wanting who
would be prepared, at any station, to press a bottle into
their pockets. This increased the danger to life.
After several fatal falls were reported, I succeeded in
effecting, by telegraph, an arrangement with the town
authorities where we were to stop, even for a few minutes, so that the liquor shops were closed during the
passage of the trains. When we caught an eager
vender, selling bottles secretly in spite of all precautions, we found it a good policy to give him a free ride
for some distance, and then permit him to walk back.

All the way along through Indiana and Ohio we
received an enthusiastic welcome. Multitudes—men,
women, and children—filled the streets of the towns as
we passed and gave us refreshments and hearty words
and other demonstrations of their appreciation. At
Xenia, for example, little girls, gayly attired, came in
flocks and handed up bouquets of flowers to the soldiers; the children and the ladies, too, were the bearers
of little housekeeper bags, needlebooks, and bright

flags, each bringing some small thing for use. Nothing ever inspirited our men more. True, these lovely faces and these demonstrations were reminders of home; but with our soldiers generally such reminders did not depress and cause desertion, but awakened them to fresh energy and exertion to struggle on, and to preserve to their children an unbroken heritage.

Among our people, anywhere from Maine to California, during the great war, when the Nation's life was the issue, we encountered every variety of opinion. There were those who were able to turn everything into money, and who were, at the same time, always unfriendly to President Lincoln and his administration. There were others, not worse, but more blatant in their opposition. We heard from these in every crowd; they called us cutthroats, Lincoln hirelings, nigger savers, or by some other characteristic epithets. Our loyal soldiers denominated them " copperheads," and when there was opportunity for a more forceful rejoinder it was quick to come.

During this trip, however, the loyal feeling, sympathy, and kind words prevailed. At Dayton, Ohio, all discordant voices were drowned quickly by the vast multitudes who came together and shouted their approval. At last, these warm greetings, mingled with tears from those who were mourning for losses already suffered; these presentations of flowers and useful articles; these upturned faces and extended hands were all passed by. We came again to the Ohio, opposite Louisville, Ky.

For some reason, perhaps to save the soldiers from several hours of hard work, our quartermasters and railroad officials decided to move the horses, artillery, the camp and garrison equipage, and all other luggage entirely independent of the help of the soldiers or their officers. Everything was then taken over the river in small transports and put upon freight cars which were in waiting. The provision was a mistake. It took much longer to do the work, and too often this moving was as destructive as fire. Such confusion as resulted I will not undertake to describe. Tents, bedding, clothing, mess kits belonging to one regiment or battery were thrown together or badly mixed with those of another. There was little separation even between the corps, division, and brigade property; so that one can imagine the difficulty of unraveling this wretched entanglement when we reached our journey's end.

It taught every officer who was on those trains to see to it in the future that each organization kept the management of its own material to itself. Let the helpers help, but not control, particularly in such hurried transfers.

On October 1, 1863, I wrote a letter from the Galt House. My infantry was then ahead, and part of my artillery. I had sent back my aid-de-camp (Major Howard) as far as Richmond, Ind., which I pronounced a "gem of a place." He was to bring up some stragglers. I spoke of the move in this way: "I feel that I am sent out here for some wise and good purpose. I believe my corps will be better appreciated. Already the good conduct of the soldiers excites wonder. We shall go straight on to Chattanooga. God grant us success and a speedy close to the war!" It was the prayer on many lips.

After passing over the Ohio we were upon the soil of Kentucky—upon that soil which I had at the outbreak been forbidden by a Kentuckian to touch or cross. But here the battles *pro* and *con* had been

455

fought. Both armies, Northern and Southern, had swept the State. Her citizens, divided, had given their allegiance to the South or to the Government; many hoping vainly to preserve neutrality. Much of this land of superb fertility had become waste and barren, like the battle grounds of Virginia. We thought of Buell and Bragg, of George H. Thomas and Van Dorn, and of other opposing leaders, as we coursed along through this border State. Crowds of welcoming citizens were not at the stations. War had become a desolating curse and terror. For each family the question of existence was uppermost. How shall we live? How can we provide for our own? And, thanks to the armies of the Tennessee and the Cumberland, we could easily go beyond Kentucky and her proud Bowling Green. For Stone River had been fought, and Rosecrans had chased Bragg beyond the Tennessee. So we went peacefully, train after train, through Nashville, Murfreesboro, Wartrace, Tullahoma, Decherd, the tunnel, and Stevenson (Ala.), 120 miles to the southeast, till we intersected the Memphis & Charleston Railroad. We there turned to the east, and steamed away ten or twelve miles farther, till we stopped at a burned bridge—the bridge that once spanned the Tennessee—which Confederate necessities had caused to be destroyed. This point, with its hamlet, was Bridgeport, Ala. The railroad, which crosses at the bridge, keeps up the Tennessee Valley on the other side, without following the curvature of the river, and makes its way through gaps in the mountain ridges and across deep canyons, and, touching the Lookout range at its base and close to the water of the Tennessee, passes into the Chattanooga basin. From Bridgeport to Chattanooga the distance by this railroad route is but twenty-eight miles. On the evening of October 3d, at 9 P.M., my train arrived at Stevenson, a poor town with some half dozen miserable houses. Here we found an accumulation of supplies for Rosecrans's army. He was then obliged to transport everything by wagons from that point by roads north of the Tennessee River to Chattanooga. The next morning, October 4th, we passed on to Bridgeport, where the greater portion of the Eleventh Corps had already arrived and bivouacked as well as it could without wagons and with its mixed-up baggage. The artillery was there, but the horses had not yet arrived. It was a singularly rough country — nothing but abrupt hills and mountains, nothing except the broad river and the crooked railway! Though early in October, the air was very chilly; and the old camps left by the Confederates as they withdrew to the south shore were, as old camps mostly are, very uninviting.

We found left by Rosecrans's army a small guard over a subdepot, a few workmen laboring to build a little steamer (which there was a faint hope might some time be used to take bread to our half-famished comrades at the front), an old broken-down mill, and some quartermaster's shanties. This was about all. At first everybody was homesick. The feeling was not diminished when the next day we heard of a Confederate cavalry raid in our rear. Major Howard, who was now coming forward, was detained by it at Nashville. On October 8th he noted: "The Confederate cavalry has destroyed several bridges below here, and I could not go on to join the corps and the General, who had already reached Bridgeport, on the Tennessee River, his destination for the present. I found Colonel Asmussen, chief of staff, and other officers here. Some of our freight and artillery horses had not yet passed this place. The rear of the corps is all at Nashville now, and we will march by land next Saturday morning, in order that the railroad, as soon as open, may be free for supplies."

Colonel Asmussen—a most energetic worker—had, after many troublesome delays, secured the wagons and artillery horses at Nashville, and was coming on. We had with us ten days' rations for the men, but my poor friends at headquarters were obliged, as Major Howard wrote, " to go a-begging for their food," because the headquarters-mess furniture had all been kept back at Nashville in consequence of the brilliant conduct of the inhospitable raiders. General Slocum, too, was still at Nashville, and his command stopped *en route* and repaired the breakages along the railway.

By these recitals one may form some idea of the anxieties of the commanders in those times. Was it wonderful that General Sherman estimated that 200,-000 men would not be too many to hold this long line in safety and still enable us to go forward and conquer the hostile army which was beyond?

I saw General Hooker after he had received his instructions from Grant to cross over the Tennessee at Bridgeport and march to form a junction with General Hazen, who was the officer selected by General Thomas to come out from Chattanooga, seize the foot of Lookout Valley, lay a pontoon bridge over the Tennessee, and defend it until our arrival. I never saw Hooker apparently so apprehensive of disaster. He said: " Why, Howard, Longstreet is up on that Lookout range with at least 10,000 fighting men. We will be obliged to make a flank march along the side and base of the mountain. I shall have scarcely so many men, and must take care of my trains. It is a very hazardous operation, and almost certain to procure us a defeat."

I did not share Hooker's apprehensions at that time, for I believed that the coöperating forces, both at Brown's Ferry and the remainder of Thomas's army beyond Lookout Mountain, would be on the watch; that if any considerable force of the enemy came against us, he would thus hopelessly divide his army. But a few days later, after a nearer survey of the country around Chattanooga, I saw that Hooker had good reasons for his surmises; for Lookout was like the Grecian Acropolis at Athens—a place for the most extended observations, quite unassailable if defended by a few men well posted, and fine grounds for well-chosen sorties. Neither Brown's Ferry nor Chattanooga could have struck a blow up there. In all this region the hills and mountains are very high, and the valleys are comparatively narrow. The smaller force in the valley was, therefore, always at a great disadvantage.

The early morning of October 27, 1863, found my command full of exhilaration and in rapid motion. We already knew the country pretty well, for we had held a grand guard at Shell Mound, six miles out on the main Bridgeport & Chattanooga Railroad, and had scouted the country to the front and the right much farther. No matter what the danger may be, the men in marching always brighten up and appear happy after remaining for considerable time in a disagreeable camp. The chills and the fevers had begun to worry our men not a little, particularly the bridge guards which had been on the south side of the Tennessee. Many poor fellows who became sallow and shivering in the low grounds, where they were forced to camp, will remember with gratitude the indefatigable surgeon, Dr. Sparling, sometimes called the Charley O'Mally of the Army of the Cumberland, who lived with them in the low ground and cheered them by his jolly stories as well as by his medicines.

The forward movement was caused by a visit of General U. S. Grant, then commanding the military division. One day I was at Stevenson and, while at the railroad station, the Nashville train brought Grant, Rawlins, and one or two more of his staff. On his car I was introduced to him. He gave me his hand and said pleasantly: "I am glad to see you, General." Then I had to do the talking. In a few minutes a staff officer from Hooker came in and offered Grant a carriage to take him to Hooker's headquarters, a quarter of a mile distant—extending also an invitation to the general to stay and partake of Hooker's hospitality. Grant replied: "If General Hooker wishes to see *me* he will find me on this train!" The answer and the manner of it surprised me; but it was Grant's way of maintaining his ascendency where a subordinate was likely to question it. Hooker soon entered the car and paid his respects in person. Grant that day went on with me to Bridgeport and stayed with me in my tent overnight. It was there he said to me: "If I should seek a command higher than that intrusted to me by my Government I should be flying in the face of Providence." Grant was very lame then, suffering from a fall of his horse. The next day at sunrise Rawlins lifted him into his saddle. Then with a small escort Grant rode off by the most dangerous route via Jasper and along the shore of the Tennessee to Chattanooga.

By this journey he set in motion the entire fall campaign against Bragg.

At last we were escaping from this dangerous soil; from the old camps of the Confederates; from guarding long lines of railway; from the work in mud and water to corduroy the roads and lay the bridges. Just what was before us nobody knew. It was at least a change.

My two divisions took the lead. Ahead of my infantry skirmishers I sent out cavalrymen. I had but few horsemen—only two companies at that time. The policy prevailed of organizing as many regiments as possible from each State which had attempted secession, when we came near them, particularly in the West; so we had in the army our First Alabama Cavalry and our First Tennessee. These regiments afforded an asylum to "loyal refugees." In Tennessee the people at home who were full of sympathy for the rebellion were called "Southern men," while in retaliation the others were usually denominated "renegades," or designated by worse names.

From them I obtained two companies, one from each, and it was these who cleared, as well as a few men could, my front and right flank; the near river sufficiently covered my left. General J. W. Geary was in charge of the division of the Twelfth Corps, which was to follow mine. Slocum had sought and obtained a command on the Mississippi; therefore, before this he had left Hooker's command. The remainder of the Twelfth Corps besides Geary's division, in conjunction with some other troops, were to take care of our long line of communications. We made that first day a comfortable march—for it is not wise the first day out of camp to press the men too hard—and met no opposition. We were early at Whiteside's, having marched about fifteen or sixteen miles. One can hardly imagine a rougher country. There were the steepest mountains, abrupt and rocky heights, and narrow canyonlike defiles. We found mines of coal at the summits of high peaks. They were worked with queer tramways and cars so arranged by ropes and machinery as to let down the coal hundreds of feet. The railway bridge had been supported by wooden frames, built like high scaffolding, story by story. This bridge was nearly destroyed. We found at the old Whiteside's Station one poor family consisting of a woman and several children. I then wrote in my notes, referring to this family and others in that mountain region: "How poor and how ignorant all the people are." The poverty and the squalor was pitiable. The actual cause of the war was not known among them. They were made a prey to any unbelievable tale which made its way to the coal mines. One said to me that he had heard that a battle had been fought among the congressmen in the Capitol at Washington, and that the great war had come from that. There was one abandoned house which presented a respectable appearance; it had two fair-sized rooms. We had the rooms swept and fires lighted in the large, open chimney places and then headquarters moved in to enjoy a reasonably comfortable night. Before taking positions for the ordinary guards and outposts we encountered and chased off some of the enemy's cavalry which approached too closely and gave us annoyance. To add a little to our store of information we had captured two cavalrymen, who were held as prisoners. My inspector general, Colonel Asmussen, probed them with questions. By their reluctant accounts the position and strength of the enemy was made more clear. The next morning, October 28th, the command was on hand in good time. At daylight we pulled out of camp and marched in the same order as the day before. Ascending toward Raccoon Divide we soon came upon the Confederate cavalry pickets, who fled before our advance. In the excitement of a slight skirmish and quick movement of the leading troops the ascent was soon made to the highest ground between Whiteside's and the Lookout Valley. The troops becoming somewhat scattered, a halt was called until my division was closed up. During this halt the enemy's watching forces prepared an ambush for us. They seized and occupied a wooded spur of Lookout Mountain, around the foot of which our roadway wound.

It was, perhaps, one mile south of the Wauhatchie depot. Suddenly, as our skirmish line began to feel its way along over the rough ground among the rocks and trees, there came a few rifle shots, and then in a few minutes a brisker fire. I was obliged to send forward an entire regiment before these persistent shooters could be induced to stop their fighting and fall back. We had in this affair one poor fellow killed and a few wounded. The Confederates then fled down Lookout Valley, and our advanced men, now full of excitement, like hunters in the chase, followed their trail as fast as their feet could carry them. But, as my main column shortly after emerged from the thicket and were marching along in the valley, with the lofty range of Lookout on its right, there was, as if we needed it, a new source of inspiration. From the crest of the high mountain Longstreet and his men were taking a good view of us. Just above the perpendicular rocks which crown the highest part of the range,

463

we could discover the Confederate signal officer waving and dipping his small ensign of Stars and Bars in a most lively manner, and then we saw a flash and a volume of smoke, which was soon followed by a double explosion. This at once revealed to us the position of the hostile cannon.

The cannonading began about the time we passed that intersecting road which led south from Brown's Ferry road to a landing on the Tennessee; the firing continued while we were making about two miles more of our march. My column at that time, with the best closing up which could be effected in that rocky country, must have been at least six miles in extent. This included my usual ammunition and baggage train. The Confederate gunners, therefore, had a lengthy artillery practice. They found it difficult to sufficiently depress their cannon to touch our position. At first the screaming shells went far beyond us. Owing to the echoes and reverberations caused by the mountains, the resounding of the artillery was remarkable. Some missiles fell short, but a few came near enough to make our men long for shelter, and to cause them to hasten their steps in order to gain a safer distance. Under this spectacular and noisy cannonade another man was killed and another wounded.

Being ignorant of the country, we were startled to see a considerable force crowning some round hills which suddenly rose up in our pathway. Field glasses were in demand. We could see bright flags — red, white, and blue. The Confederates had in colors the same as we. We could catch the bright gleam of gun barrels and bayonets. But while preparing to approach with great care, to be ready for war or peace, as the case should resolve itself, we heard a welcome sound; it was just like our own sturdy shout; it was Hazen's men who, excited by the cannonading, had left their brigade camp and had come out to meet us. As we neared them and could catch their accents, we took in the memorable words: "Hurrah! hurrah! you have opened up our bread line!" It was a glad meeting; glad for us, who felt that we had accomplished the difficult march; glad for them, who had for some time been growing thin on supplies; for at times they were living only on parched corn, and not enough of that. It is always hard for a soldier or sailor in active service, who is put on half rations and is forced to resist hunger by shortening his waist belt, to continue this weakening operation too long. The slow starvation of a siege is properly more dreaded by them than the exposure in campaign and in battle.

After a few moments of kindly interchange and greeting of those who came together, Hazen's men and mine resumed their ranks. The former returned to their positions, and my command, resting its right at the foothills of Raccoon Range and in echelon with Hazen, faced toward Lookout Mountain and went into camp for the night. General Hooker, who had come on with Geary's division, joined me and established his headquarters near at hand.

Geary, who had in charge a long train of wagons, was instructed to stop back at Wauhatchie, three miles at least from my camp. As he had but little more than one division of the Twelfth Corps, it was for him a hazardous thing to do. General Hooker deemed this necessary to the holding of Lookout Valley, and he further desired to cut off and catch a small force which Bragg had been keeping on the Tennessee River. Those were the hostiles who had been so enterprising and annoying as to break up our roadway on the opposite shore. The Wauhatchie crossroad was the only practicable pathway for their exit from that place, usually called Kelly's Landing. The Tennessee must be clear from Confederates, for Thomas's little steamer — the *Chattanooga* — was at last finished, loaded with hard bread, and already slowly winding its way up the river to supplement our venturesome march.

Still, important as Wauhatchie undoubtedly was, it was like throwing bait without hook and line before a hungry fish, to have a large train of wagons parked there, defended by so small a force as a division, in plain view of Longstreet and his observing army. For he could dart upon the bait, swallow it, and make off to his sheltered nook without much danger to himself.

Longstreet had quickly apprehended the situation and sent a force, as soon as it was dark enough to conceal its movements, to descend from his stronghold, pass westward along the Chattanooga wagon road, cross Lookout Creek, so as to secure a quick retreat in case of any miscarriage or to hold back the Eleventh Corps and Hazen, should we attempt a flank march along that front to succor Geary. All this was done. The low hills were manned and to some extent barricaded, for there were plenty of rocks and trees covering them. A Confederate division was then dispatched to attack Geary.

Some time after midnight, when our weary men were in their soundest sleep, undisturbed by the friendly moon, which was shining brightly that night, and free from apprehensions—for our march had been completed and we had a good, strong position—of a sudden the extreme stillness was broken by the roar of cannon and the rattle of musketry. Everybody who was fully awake said at once: " Our men at Wauhatchie are attacked." Instantly I sent to my division commanders (Schurz and Steinwehr) to put their troops under arms. The word of command had hardly left me when Hooker's anxious message came: " Hurry or you cannot save Geary. He has been attacked! "

The troops were quickly on foot. Schurz's men were that night especially alert and the first under arms. The road ran along at the base of the low hills which I have described, and which the Confederates were already quietly holding. Schurz was ordered to go on to Geary's relief, but he had hardly set out over the rocks and through the thickets, feeling his way to the west and north of the wagon road in the uncertain light, probably not very clear in his own mind just how to get to that heavy and continuous firing, when a skirmish fire began, coming upon his advance troops from those low hills which skirted Lookout Creek.

Just at that time I joined Hooker, who was sitting with Butterfield, his chief of staff, on the side of a knoll, where a fire had been started; for the night was cold. He was evidently disturbed, but not impatient. He thought my command was not pressing on fast enough, but agreed with me that the first thing to do was to clear those low hills along Lookout Creek. Steinwehr was coming up rapidly along the road. He designated Colonel Orland Smith's brigade for this work for his division. A little farther on, Schurz sent General Tyndall's brigade to carry the hills on his left.

As soon as these primary arrangements were effected, I said to General Hooker: " With your approval, I will take the two companies of cavalry and push through to Wauhatchie."

The general answered: " All right, Howard; I shall be here to attend to this part of the field."

Then immediately, with my small squadron, I set out, moving toward our right till beyond range of the enemy's shots. I picked my way along the foothills of the Raccoon Mountain.

I had been gone but a few minutes when Colonel Orland Smith succeeded in deploying his brigade parallel with the road and facing toward the little hills from which a fitful and annoying fire was kept up by the Confederates; they were concealed along a ridge, and doubtless delivered their fire at random, as they fancied, by the noise, that our men were simply trying to march past them in the valley below.

Smith's men then marched with fixed bayonets across the valley road, up the woody slope, through the thickets and over the hindering rocks, still receiving a fire, but not returning it until the crest was reached. The Confederate soldiers were evidently surprised at this bold movement, and as soon as they saw in the moonlight the shimmer of bayonets they gave way at every point.

In a similar way, and at about the same time, Tyndall's brigade cleared the heights near him. What was known as Ellis's house, beyond the low hills, fell between Smith's and Tyndall's brigades. The road being now clear, Colonel Hecker, of the Eighty-second Illinois (the same who was wounded at Chancellorsville, and was now commanding a brigade), made his way as rapidly as possible toward General Geary.

While the brisk work was going on and I was pushing for Wauhatchie as fast as I could, the firing on Geary's front suddenly ceased. As I emerged into an open space I could see numbers of men moving about. I called to the nearest squad: "Who goes there?"

"We are Jenkins's men," was the prompt reply. I knew that we had no such commander there, so I said: "Have you whipped the Yankees?" The same voice replied that they had tried; had got upon the Yankees' flank, but just then their men in front had given back, so that they had lost their way. Meanwhile, we drew near enough and, suddenly revealing ourselves, took them prisoners. We broke through the enemy's cordon and reached Greene, who commanded Geary's left brigade. He was frightfully wounded through the face. I knew him and his excellent work at Gettysburg; his wound now, bad as it looked, did not prove fatal. After a word, I passed on to Geary. He was a vigorous, strong, hearty and cool-headed man, who was astonished to see me suddenly appear at his side in the smoke of battle, and I was surprised to find that as he grasped my hand he trembled with emotion. Without a word he pointed down and I saw that Geary's son lay dead at his feet, killed at his father's side while commanding his battery in this action.

Shortly the complete junction was effected by my troops, and I hastened back to General Hooker to make my report.

Our loss in the Eleventh Corps was put, before the accurate count could be obtained, at 15 to 20 killed, and 125 wounded. Colonel Underwood, of the Thirty-third Massachusetts, was supposed to be mortally wounded. I soon had a conversation with him during his extreme weakness and prostration, and wrote to a friend these words about him: "He has a clear and decided Christian faith; he is a healthy and temperate man and may get well." He was promoted for this action at Wau-

469

hatchie, and did recover, though with a shortened limb, and has lived many years to be useful to his city (Boston), and to be a comfort and a help to his family.

General Thomas said in orders: "I most heartily congratulate you, General Hooker, and the troops under your command, at the brilliant success you gained over your adversary (Longstreet) on the night of the 28th ult. The bayonet charge of Howard's troops, made up the side of a steep and difficult hill, over 200 feet high, completely routing the enemy from his barricades on its top, and the repulse by Geary's division of greatly superior numbers, who attempted to surprise him, will rank among the most distinguished feats of arms of the war."

The mules tied to park wagons became very restive under the noise of the night firing. Many of them as soon as the cannon began to roar broke away and, strangely enough, rushed straight for the enemy. Doubtless in the dim light this was taken by the Confederates for a cavalry charge. This is the battle in which occurred the " charge of the mule brigade! "

CHAPTER XXVII

CHATTANOOGA AND THE BATTLE OF MISSIONARY RIDGE

THE movements which resulted in the battle of Wauhatchie were but the preliminary steps to the execution of Grant's plan of operations.

This embraced a battle with the Confederate General Bragg, who continued to sit threateningly before Chattanooga, and the freeing of East Tennessee of all the Confederate occupancy.

To effect his purpose Grant ordered Sherman to come to us from the vicinity of the Mississippi with as many troops as possible. Two days before our Lookout Valley battle, which took place the morning of October 29, 1863, Sherman received Grant's dispatch while on the line of the Memphis & Charleston Railroad, to wit: "Drop everything at Bear Creek and move toward Stevenson with your entire force until you receive further orders."

Instantly Sherman began his march with four army divisions having infantry and artillery—some 20,000 strong. We had then, during the first week of November, to operate, or soon should have, the old Army of the Cumberland at Chattanooga, under General George H. Thomas; Hooker's two small army corps in Lookout Valley with a part back to protect our lines of communication toward Nashville; Sherman's approaching column and a few small bodies of cavalry.

471

With one line of railway, and that often broken; with the animals weakening and dying, and with the men badly supplied with even the necessities of life, everything for a time at Chattanooga was out of joint.

Still, Grant, in spite of these impediments, pushed on to the front and hurried Sherman to our neighborhood. Of course, many croakers found fault with this and prophesied disaster; yet the most of us were inspired by Grant's quiet confidence and plans. Little by little great regularity and thorough system covered us all. Supplies came on train after train and boat after boat to Kelly's Ferry; the military railroad men, who should have abundant praise, began to rebuild our railroad from Bridgeport to the front; new mules were found to haul everything from Kelly's Ferry or Landing to Brown's Ferry and thence across the two pontoon bridges into Chattanooga; medical stores came up; the mails began to appear with regularity, and even luxuries found their way to the camps, brought from loving hands at home by the indefatigable agents of the Christian and Sanitary Commissions.

While waiting for Sherman, we had our downs as well as our ups. For example, the Confederates kept hurling shells into the valley at our trains and camps. They could see us better in the morning, when the sun was at their backs. They turned around and shelled Chattanooga in the afternoon.

One Sunday, the afternoon of November 15, 1863, at 4 P.M., Colonel Balloch, Captain Pearson, Captain Stinson, Surgeon Hubbard, and Major Howard accompanied me to our corps hospital in Lookout Valley. The orderly took along a basket of grapes. The distance was about a mile from my own tent. We found

472

the religious service in progress on our arrival. The poor sick ones who could leave their beds had gathered near the largest hospital and kept their hats off reverently while the chaplain was praying. The sick inside the different tents could hear everything, as canvas obstructs the sound but slightly. We sang a hymn and then the chaplain preached a sermon about giving our bodies and spirits a living sacrifice. He made many earnest appeals, and I think left a good impression on the men and officers who were present. While he was speaking the Confederates made themselves heard by an occasional shell from Lookout Mountain. The Thirty-third Massachusetts band came near and, as soon as the service was over, struck up some familiar hymns and airs that were sweet and cheering. As I went through the hospital afterwards, I asked the men —ill and wounded—if they liked the music. " Oh, yes; I wish they would play often," was the burden of the responses.

Sherman marched rapidly. By November 13th his advance had reached Bridgeport. He had already obtained the further orders to keep in motion until he found himself in the vicinity of Chattanooga. As soon as he reached that point, Grant requested him to have his troops close up and come on as fast as the bad roads would permit, but hasten in person for an interview and consultation at Chattanooga.

Grant was already there. Sherman arrived the evening of the 14th. Several officers and I among them were present with Grant when Sherman came into the room.

Grant's greeting was cordial and characteristic. He rose, stood still, and extended his hand, and, while his face lighted up with its cheeriest smile, paid Sherman some compliment on his promptitude; then being about to resort to his habitual cigar, offered one to his new guest. Sherman took the cigar, lighted it, and never ceased to talk in that offhand, hearty, manly way which everybody who knew him will remember. He had not even stopped to take a seat. Grant pointed to an old high-back rocking-chair, and said:

" Take the chair of honor, Sherman."

" Oh, no," the latter rejoined; " that belongs to you, General! "

Grant humorously remarked: " I don't forget, Sherman, to give proper respect to age."

Sherman instantly took the proffered chair and laughingly said: " Well, then, if you put it on that ground, I must accept."

There were no formal introductions. It was assumed that all who were present were acquainted. Sherman quickly took the lead of the whole party and brought on a discussion of the military situation or other topics to which the consultation tended.

My real acquaintance with Sherman began that evening. It was a privilege to see these two men, Grant and Sherman, together. Their unusual friendship—unusual in men who would naturally be rivals—was like that of David and Jonathan. It was always evident, and did not grow from likeness, but from unlikeness. They appeared rather the complements of each other—where the one was especially strong, the other was less so, and *vice versa*. It was a marriage of characters, in sympathy, by the adjustment of differences.

Grant in command was, as everybody then said, habitually reticent. Sherman was never so. Grant meditated on the situation, withholding his opinion until his plan was well matured. Sherman quickly, brilliantly gave you half a dozen. Grant, once speaking of Sherman in cadet phrase, said: "He bones all the time while he is awake; as much on horseback as in camp or at his quarters." It was true. Sherman had remarkable topographical ability. A country that he once saw he could not forget. The cities, the villages, the streams, the mountains, hills, and divides—these were as easily seen by him as human faces, and the features were always on hand for use. It made him ever playing at draughts with his adversary. Let the enemy move and Sherman's move was instant and well chosen.

Grant appeared more inclined to systematize and simplify; bring up sufficient force to outnumber; do unexpected things; take promptly the offensive; follow up a victory. It was a simple, straightforward calculus, which avoided too much complication. It made Grant the man for campaign and battle. Sherman was always at his best in campaign—in general maneuvers —better than in actual battle. His great knowledge of history, his topographical scope, his intense suggestive faculties seemed often to be impaired by the actual conflict. And the reason is plain; such a mind and body as his, full of impulse, full of fire, are more likely to be perturbed by excitement than is the more ironbound constitution of a Grant or a Thomas.

Sherman, patriotic all through, was very self-reliant. He believed in neglecting fractions and was not afraid of responsibility. Grant, probably much influenced by his earliest teachings, relied rather on Providence than simply on himself; he gathered up the fragments for use, and was also strong to dare, because somehow, without saying so, he struck the blows of a persistent faith.

As I watched the countenances of those two men that evening I gathered hope for our cause. Grant's faculty of gaining the ascendency over his generals without pretension or assumption then appeared. He chose, then he trusted his leaders. They grew great because he did not desert them even in disaster.

After this interview with his commander Sherman returned to Bridgeport to bring up his troops by the same route over which my command had marched two weeks before. On November 23d he finished his march with a part of his army and had three divisions on the north side of the river nearly opposite Missionary Ridge, not far from the Tennessee. Jeff. C. Davis's division was sent to him for a reënforcement, while my two were brought over into Chattanooga and put into camp near Fort Wood to be ready to coöperate with Sherman after he should lay a bridge.

There were, owing to rains and floods, constant breakages in our bridges, particularly in the one at Brown's Ferry. On account of it, Osterhaus's division of Sherman's corps was completely cut off. Grant changed his first plan, then made up a new command for Hooker—probably was compelled to do so—for it did look like wasting strength to put much force against the impregnable Lookout Mountain. This force consisted of Osterhaus's, Geary's, and Cruft's divisions, eight brigades, with the batteries which belonged with them, and a reserve from my corps of two batteries—Wiedrich's New York and Heckman's Ohio. This force thus organized was gathered together in Lookout Valley, and during November 23d Sherman was getting his bridge boats well out of sight near the

North Chickamauga, opposite Missionary Ridge. Hooker was reconnoitering, perhaps for the fifteenth time, the west face of the huge Lookout Mountain.

The rest of this battle front was the Army of the Cumberland and its indomitable commander, General George H. Thomas, on the Chattanooga side.

This part of Grant's triple force was destined to commence the battle. Some days before, several deserters from Bragg's army had been brought to my headquarters. They reported that after the battle of Wauhatchie Longstreet had been sent away from our front with his corps. This information was afterwards confirmed from other sources. Our dispatch came from Bragg directly, brought in by a flag of truce. It was taken to Grant. It advised the immediate sending away from Chattanooga of all noncombatants, as he (Bragg) proposed the next day to commence a regular bombardment of the town. The officers who had been there for two months under Bragg's bombardments thought that it was a little late for the Confederate general to be filled with compassion and give his warning. Grant smiled as he read the message, and said: "It means that Bragg is intending to run away."

Longstreet's departure to assail Burnside's force, then at Knoxville, and the fear that Bragg might go, had induced Grant to order an attack some days before he was ready; but as Thomas, for want of horses, could not then move his artillery, Grant delayed his order. But now (November 23d), as Hooker on our extreme right and Sherman on our extreme left were in position, Grant concluded to occupy the attention of the enemy while he himself was making ready for his main attack, and so ordered Thomas to make a reconnoissance in force. The Fourth Corps, then commanded by General Gordon Granger, was selected for this duty. It had three divisions under Stanley, T. J. Wood, and P. H. Sheridan. The Fourteenth Corps, under Palmer, was to watch and support the right of the Fourth, while mine (the Eleventh Corps) was kept in reserve near at hand ready to support, should the exigencies of reconnoissance require it, the left, right, or center. There was a considerable hillock or knoll about halfway from Fort Wood to the foot of Missionary Ridge, a third the height of the ridge, called " Orchard Knob." Confederate Bragg held this eminence as an outpost, and had a line of intrenchments well filled behind it, running along the base of the ridge.

Granger was in his element. He deployed Wood's division in plain view, Sheridan's a little farther to the right; and Baird's (of the Fourteenth) was in echelon with that. After the deployment a cloud of skirmishers quickly covered the whole front. I stood near my corps at Fort Wood, where were Thomas and Grant.

We never looked upon a livelier scene—a finer parade. The enemy were attracted by this bold maneuvering, and stood up in groups on their works to look at the Yankee parade. Immediately after the rapid formation the forward movement began. Away the skirmishers went over the rough broken ground, appearing and disappearing among rocks and trees, or emerging from small ravines and hollows; and the main lines followed on at equal pace. The Confederates this time were really taken by surprise. They, however, did not run away; they hurried into position, and commenced their fire. Some of our men fell, but there was no check, no delay; firing, without halting, was opened by our skirmish line. Sheridan and Baird came up abreast of Wood, and all rushed together over the detached rifle pits and over the intrenchments of Orchard Knob. Many of the enemy were killed or wounded or taken prisoners. The remainder ran precipitately to help their comrades at the foot of Missionary Ridge. The march was stopped at Orchard Knob. It had developed artillery and infantry. It had put Bragg on his guard, and secured his fixed attention. It was but a reconnoissance and the troops were under orders to move back. Rawlins, his adjutant general, appeared to us to be pleading earnestly with Grant. He was overheard to say: " It will not do for them to come back." The general for a time smoked his cigar peacefully and said nothing. At last quietly he said: " Intrench them and send up support."

His orders were promptly obeyed. Palmer came up to secure the right, and I reported to Granger at the Knob, while he was expending a little of his extra enthusiasm by showing a battery commander how to point and serve his guns. Soon all the divisions were in place. Very quickly I passed into the woods to our left from brigade to brigade of Schurz and Steinwehr, and brought them up through the thickets to the Citico Creek. In truth, we of the Eleventh Corps were soon ahead of our neighbors and proud of it, for by my direction Von Steinwehr sent out a regiment— the Seventy-third Ohio—which swept the front beyond the creek of all Confederate sharpshooters who were inclined to loiter in that region. Granger was pleased, and, the hard work of the morning being over, he gathered us around him—Sheridan, Baird, Wood, Schurz, Steinwehr and others—to tell us how the battle had been fought and to show us the way to fight all battles. It was, indeed, a successful reconnoissance, and, though not much of a contest, served with its small losses and its real gain to inspirit the whole command.

On November 25th Hooker succeeded in performing his appointed part in his famous battle above the clouds, the thick fog helping his men to climb up narrow passages. At sunrise, in the clear, crisp autumn air, they unfurled the national banner from "Pulpit Rock," on the extreme point of Lookout Mountain overlooking Chattanooga, with cheers that were re-echoed by the troops below.

So much for the first group.

On November 24th, the morning that Hooker started, before 3 A.M., away off as far as the signal officer on Pulpit Rock, had he been there, could have seen without his telescope, far to the northeast, the little steamer *Chattanooga*, without noise, was working its way up the big Tennessee River. It soon disappeared from any view, running up some tributary for rest and shelter.

Earlier than this, a little past midnight, some pontoon boats, carrying over 3,000 of General Sherman's men, had issued from the North Chickamauga. Friar's Island served them as a cover against the enemy's pickets. Silently they floated, the current carrying them swiftly down to the point which Sherman had selected for his bridge. Here the little steamer came in play; by the boats and by the steamer Sherman caused to be sent over opposite to the end of the famous Missionary Ridge between eight and nine thousand fighting men. With this force were plenty of spades, picks, and shovels. The Confederate pickets were surprised; some ran, some were captured. But the movement

480

was evidently not prepared for, and, indeed, Bragg already had enough line to hold with a small army if he came no farther toward Sherman than the Tunnel Hill, where the railway crosses the ridge.

General W. F. Smith superintended the swift bridge building; boats moved out from each shore, were anchored, the slender joists quickly put down and bound with cords, then the men ran with a plank apiece and placed it, and so the roadway grew. On the enemy's shore, where the ground gradually rises toward the foothills of the mountain ridge, a large curve, whose center was at the river, was marked out on the grass by a few stakes; the earth in a few minutes was broken by hundreds of strong men—hearty, cheerful workers. In less than one hour the long ditch was dug and there was ample cover for a large brigade. The bridge was not quite completed, and the last few shovelfuls were not yet thrown when, with Colonel Bushbeck's small brigade from Chattanooga way, I came in sight. Of course, at first, Sherman's men were a little startled. They did not expect anything or anybody from that quarter except the enemy. The picks and shovels were dropped and the rifles were seized; but those were not recruits, so they did not fly nor fire, but simply looked with 16,000 eyes. We had been sent to form a junction and coöperate with Sherman. We had started early, too; had crept quietly along the bank of the old river, through the thickets, the meadows, and across the small streams, in a circuit of four or five miles, encountering but little opposition till that armed host of workmen loomed up before us. At once I recognized our expected friends, and we were not long in getting together. Immediately I went to the bridge, dismounted, and ran out upon it just as the last pon-

481

toon was being ferried into its place. Sherman had
not been able to wait on the other shore; he was on the
opposite stretch and well out toward the growing end.
" How are you, General Howard? That's right! You
must have got up early," and a host of other short sen-
tences, which one who knew Sherman can easily supply, greeted my ears. Before the space was filled with
planking he sprang across the open draw and we
clasped hands. We had met before, but this, I think,
was our first *bona fide* recognition. We were to be
hereafter in several campaigns and in many hard battles together. At no time after that meeting did I
receive aught from Sherman but a frank confidence,
and I am sure that I ever gave to him a cordial and
loyal service. I think a mutual confidence and sympathy between souls springs up suddenly, often by the
simple look into clear, fearless eyes, and these sentiments are sealed by an unreserved grasp of the hands.
Sherman, in his usual pointed, offhand style, explained
the situation to me as he saw it. At the time he believed himself nearer Bragg's right than he really was.
The Missionary Ridge, like the Raccoon Range and the
Lookout, appeared to be continuous, at least along the
crest, but it proved to be otherwise. Not only were
there heavy, rocky, wooded spurs jutting out laterally,
but there were deep chasms and cross ravines cutting
the crest, so that each jagged knoll so separated had
to be approached and taken like an isolated bastion.
General Sherman said: " You must leave me Bushbeck's brigade. I shall need it to keep up connection
with Thomas." Poor Bushbeck looked a little demure
as I turned to him. He wanted to fight with his own
corps, but being a true soldier, he said nothing. I left
him there to struggle hard on Sherman's right flank

482

and lose some—yes, many—of his best officers and men. I then felt sure that before many hours had passed I should bring the remainder of my corps to the same flank. I bade Sherman good morning and turned back to join my headquarters and Thomas's forces near Orchard Knob.

Now consider that Sherman had four bodies of men abreast, and not connected except by the long line of skirmishers which covered this whole front. They—skirmishers and all—prepared to go up the ridge or to skirt along its side slopes. Thus these resolute men set out to perform the part allotted to them—a part, as it proved, next to the impossible, because nature, aided by the Confederate General "Pat" Cleburne, who guarded Bragg's right flank, had made some of these crags impregnable.

Hooker and his men had already "fought above the clouds" and unfurled the emblem of a free country to the breeze on the most prominent rock of Lookout Mountain; Sherman and his divisions had toiled and fought with more vigor the second day than the first, amid unheard-of ruggedness and against odds. It was reserved by Providence to Thomas and his army, already four times depleted, November 25, 1863, to storm heights more difficult than those of Gettysburg, and to capture batteries and intrenchments harder to reach than those of Vicksburg. Grant, who was at times certainly distinguished for his powers of observation and was as remarkable for self-poise, for keeping at bay every impatient impulse, stood there at Orchard Knob with the imperturbable Thomas. Neither of them wasted any time in words. Orders, when given, were brief and pointed. Officers took posts for observing, and orderlies, ready to mount, held the reins for the dismounted, and messengers stood or sat near by with bridles firmly grasped. Aids and dispatch bearers from divisions came to Thomas or to his chief of staff and to Grant from the wings. They came, reported, and went, always moving with a rapid pace. There was constant motion there and in the army, and yet there was quiet and rest—the quiet, however, of a lake about to burst its barriers, the rest of a geyser soon to hurl its pent waters high in air. About 10 A.M. with my corps I was ordered by General Grant to go quickly to Sherman. Colonel Meysenberg, my adjutant general, went ahead to Sherman for orders, and returning to me *en route* reported Sherman's instructions to put my command (all except Bushbeck's brigade) on the extreme left flank of his army. The brigade had already been hotly engaged and suffered severe loss. Grant then waited until I could get into position. He afterwards waited a little longer for Hooker, who was on his other flank. What could that officer of unfailing energy be doing? Early in the day his flags were seen descending the Summertown road of old Lookout. But his columns had disappeared in the rolling valley, going toward Rossville. Could he have met with disaster? It was hardly possible. At last all apprehensions were relieved. A message arrived. Hooker, having the bridge ahead of him destroyed by the enemy, had been delayed by the impassable Chickamauga Creek. That odd stream had so many branches, and they were so crooked, that an officer could hardly tell on which side of the stream he was. It was deep and sluggish, with muddy banks. The Confederate General Breckinridge, who that day commanded Bragg's left, had greatly bothered Hooker's men, but the obstacle was finally overcome, a bridge was built and Hooker had passed over and was working up the slope of the south end of Missionary Ridge, and driving Breckinridge's advance before him. Now was the fullness of battle time.

Bragg was up there with a comparatively short line. He had well-filled intrenchments a little nearer, at the foot of the ridge. The veteran Hardee, against Sherman, commanded his right, and Breckinridge, as we have said, his left against the lines of Hooker steadily ascending in that quarter. The Confederate Chief Bragg himself, in the center, like an elephant between two persistent tigers, had his mind much distracted; who could wonder or who, except the Confederate press of that day, could blame him! It was the "supreme moment." Grant took the cigar from his mouth, cleared his throat, and told Thomas to capture the intrenchments at the foot of Missionary Ridge. The patient Thomas had been ready all day. The six loaded cannon were ready. In an instant, one after another, in slow succession, so as to be distinctly heard, they boomed forth the inspiring signal. Every soldier in Thomas's four divisions understood that call. But to emphasize it, our various batteries, perched on many hills and convenient knolls, at once fired shot and shells toward the doomed ridge.

I am not sure that this previous artillery practice in battle at long ranges does much good, where there are no walls to break down. It may occupy the enemy's artillery and keep it from effective work against our advancing men, but it prevents anything like a surprise. It would seem wiser to give the foe no formal warning, but, like Stonewall Jackson, burst upon his flank or his intrenchments, without a previous cannon shot.

Conceive of Thomas's divisions formed in one line, with one or two regiments a little in the rear and in echelon, to reënforce the flanks and cover the whole front by a double skirmish line, and you have an idea of the attacking force. At the signals, the words of command sounded simultaneously along the whole line, and instantly every man took a quick pace, the skirmishers clearing the front, now at a double-quick, now at a run; when they could they fired upon the enemy's skirmishers, but without slacking their pace. The country was generally wild, broken, covered here and there with thickets, with plenty of rocks, hillocks, and small ravines. On, on the Union soldiers went straight forward. Of course, the numerous guns from the crest all along Bragg's formidable front, opened their frightful mouths and belched forth their death-dealing charges. The sound of cannon and bursting shells seemed to quadruple the effects. The air was filled with missiles, but fortunately for our men the fire from the lower rifle pits was not very effective; probably it was necessary for each hostile brigade to let their own skirmishers come in before a free range could be had, and when they did get them in and began to fire, there was not time to reload before our determined Westerners, skirmish line and all, were upon them. At any rate, every Confederate not already disabled seemed to think that the time for a hasty retreat had come. The top or the crest of the ridge was, like the cemetery crest of Gettysburg, to be the line of defense. Our division, brigade, and regimental commanders, I believe many of them on foot and half out of breath from the roughness of the field, were in their places or coming on, and undertook to obey their orders; their voices seemed for once not to be heard, and their men, many of them, never stopped for any re-formation nor listened to catch the word of command, but immediately followed their retreating foes up the steep.

Thomas and Grant saw the conflict through their glasses from Orchard Knob.

To show the ardor of the troops in this charge without orders I am reminded of the story of my friend, E. P. Smith, then a member of the Christian Commission, who followed hard after the moving lines to be ready for whatever relief he could bring. Just after the action had lulled, he met four stout soldiers carrying a sergeant to the rear. Smith stopped the stretcher bearers for a moment and said gently: " Where are you hurt, sergeant? "

He, as if a little dazed by the question, replied: " Almost up, sir."

" I mean in what part are you injured? "

He looked steadily toward my friend and answered with all the firmness his failing strength could muster: " Almost to the top."

Then Smith folded down the sergeant's coat, or blanket, and saw the bleeding, broken shoulder where the shell had struck him. The sergeant also turned his face toward the wound. " Yes," he exclaimed, " yes, that's what did it; but for that I should have reached the top." The sergeant had held the flag at the time he was struck. His utterance continued to grow fainter and fainter, as he repeated his sorrowful thought, " Almost up! Almost up! " till his lifeblood ebbed and his spirit left the shattered clay.

There were many more than these who fell on the hillside; some were cold in death, and others were repressing every sign of sufferings which had stopped them midway to the goal of their aspiration. Breckinridge's men gave stout resistance to Sheridan and to Hooker, and our sturdy foe, Pat Cleburne, was unwilling to let go. Surely, these were brave men and commanded brave men. Bragg had no right to condemn them and has only injured his own fame in so doing. And Jefferson Davis wronged his soldiers when he said: " The first defeat that has resulted from misconduct by the troops." How hard for Mr. Davis ever to conceive that he might be wrong; that the days of slavery in America were numbered, and that, little by little, our men, equally brave with his, were acquiring unity of action, strength of muscle and experience, and that, with a cause so sacred as ours—namely, the preservation and the purification of our Republic—and with numbers superior to his, there would come times like those of Gettysburg, Vicksburg, and Chattanooga, when the victory would perch on our banners.

The enemy gave way—his lines were broken in six places; and Hooker, with steadfastness, was on his flank and aiming for his rear, and Sherman was clinging to his other side. Yes, Bragg, much as he hated to do so, was forced to abandon his stronghold and retire with haste.

Our men turned their own guns upon the retreating Confederates and broke their flight in places into a rout. But though they were followed up for a few miles, yet the roughness of the country, not yet familiar to our officers, and the darkness of the approaching night closed the action soon after the capture of Missionary Ridge.

General Grant, summing up our losses in the several combats of Hooker, Sherman, and Thomas, gave them as 757 killed, 4,529 wounded, and 330 missing.

Bragg's losses, as nearly as I can get the figures, were 3,000 killed and wounded, and about 6,000 prisoners left in our hands. Forty cannon fell to us, and at least 7,000 small arms. Many of the prisoners were wounded, and of them an. unusually large number of commissioned officers.

The flight of the Confederates was soon evident along Sherman's lines, for the lively cannon firing had ceased and the skirmishers received no return fire; they ventured forward at dark and found that the death-dealing rocks and barricades had lost their terror. As they were reporting this strange story swift horsemen had brought the good news to Sherman. One cannot exaggerate the joy that animated our men at these tidings. You could soon hear the ringing, manly shouts as they rose from valley and hillside. So the victory was inspiring; another break had been made in the long line of Confederate armies, and that at the strongest possible natural bastioned fortress— that of Chattanooga. There was no envy nor jealousy that night. Hooker's men had bled on Lookout, Sherman's near the tunnel, and Thomas's on the broad, steep side of Missionary Ridge. After the first burst of enthusiasm was over, the men got their suppers over brighter fires, drank their coffee a little better made, and, after talking all together for a while between the puffs of their tobacco pipes, they soon retired to their beds on the ground, and—except the sentinels, the wounded, the doctors, their assistants, and the officers of rank—were soon fast asleep.

Nobody can blot out the record, written in men's hearts, and sent with shoutings into the everlasting spaces, that we were there where brave men fought and were victorious, and that, God helping us, we did what we could. If I know myself, I rejoice as much at the good name of the great-hearted Thomas as I do at my own, but I should distrust any writer who should attempt to pull down other great names even to make a pedestal for Thomas, for he already has a better one in the confidence, love, and praise of all true men who served under his command.

Halleck's judgment at one time (if we may credit the reports early in the war) was a little warped in his estimate of Grant, so that I think his dispatch from Washington after our great battle is quite significant and does him honor. It is: " Considering the strength of the rebel position and the difficulty of storming his intrenchments, the battle of Chattanooga must be regarded as the most remarkable in history. Not only did the officers exhibit great skill and daring in their operations in the field, but the highest praise is also due to the commanding general for his admirable dispositions for dislodging the enemy from a position apparently impregnable."

For two days Grant's army pursued the retreating forces of Bragg. We stopped at Greyfield, Ga., and turned back. When Sherman with the Fifteenth Corps and I with the Eleventh were near Mission Mills, Sherman received a brief note from Grant. He said he couldn't get Granger with the Fourth Corps off soon enough for Knoxville, and that Sherman must turn north at once, or Burnside would be overwhelmed by Longstreet.

Sherman answered: " Why not send Howard with me?"

Grant, on receiving Sherman's reply, so ordered it. I was as badly off for transportation and supplies as Granger; but it was another opportunity. With our respective corps Sherman and I marched immediately toward Knoxville; we were about five miles apart, Sherman always east of me.

At the Hiwassee River, Hoffman (my engineer) and I, one day just before sunset, stood by the bank in the village of Athens, Tenn. The bridge was gone. " How long, Hoffman, will it take you to build a bridge here? " I asked.

He scratched his head for a moment and then said: " It is over 200 feet; I can have a good bridge practicable for the men and the wagons in ten days."

" Ten days! " I cried. " Why, Hoffman, we will cross that river at sunrise to-morrow! "

" Impossible! " he exclaimed with impatient emphasis. Yet, by using the sheds and outhouses of the village and binding the side joists with ropes, we made a fine floating bridge, and by sunrise on the morrow began our usual day's march by crossing our new improvised structure. I had been born and bred near a floating bridge and so I showed the able Hoffman how to make one. Sherman, five miles above, felled tall trees for stringers and with his pioneers quickly made a log bridge. At Loudon I found a sufficient number of Confederate wagons for a footbridge through the ford, six miles up the Little Tennessee. Many of the spokes of the wheels were cut or broken. I had the One Hundred and Forty-third New York Regiment (Colonel Boughton) nail cleats from felloe to felloe. They were strong enough for this regiment to drag them the six miles. Boughton and his men worked all night to plant these wagons in the deep ford, and so plank them from wagon to wagon as to make a fairly good footbridge for the men of the corps. All except Boughton and his good regiment

491

had had a full night's rest. The colonel, wading most of the night with the water above his waist, took a severe cold and suffered from acute neuralgia for years in consequence of that exposure. By raising the loads by planks above the wagon bodies and carrying the cannon ammunition upon them in the same way we got across the ford without loss.

Sherman and I came together about thirteen miles from Knoxville. A messenger from Burnside here met us and told the good news that Longstreet, hearing of our approach, had raised the siege and gone off to join Lee's army in Virginia.

Burnside, after the dreadful battle in which Colonel Saunders and hundreds of men were killed, was expecting every day that Longstreet would renew his assault and he feared that he would not be able to hold out against him.

Sherman and I halted our commands and then, while they were resting in a good camp, rode together the thirteen miles. Burnside was delighted to see us, and gave us a turkey dinner. The loyal East Tennessee people had kept him well supplied during all that long siege. I then remembered President Lincoln's words at my last interview with him: " They are loyal there, general! " During my march of 100 miles I was every day made aware of the truth of Lincoln's declaration. Sherman and I marched back to Chattanooga, and with the Eleventh Corps I returned to the old camp in Lookout Valley.

By some singular clerical error Sherman in his memoirs puts Gordon Granger for me in that Knoxville march.

Granger after our return did come up to help Burnside, and later, Schofield, in the holding and picketing of East Tennessee for the winter of 1863 and 1864. During that time Granger had his headquarters at Loudon.

There was quite an interval of time from the close of the Knoxville campaign to the beginning of the spring operations of 1864. After Chattanooga, the Confederate General Bragg withdrew his army, under the pressure we gave him, to the little town of Dalton, Ga., where he himself was soon replaced by General Joseph E. Johnston, whom we have so often met in the battles of the East. Johnston reorganized his army, gave it discipline and drill, and prepared for the spring work which was expected of him. Taking his headquarters at Dalton, he faced northward and eastward. The railway line which brought him supplies from Atlanta, i. e., from the South, here divided, the eastern branch running to Cleveland and toward Knoxville, East Tennessee, and the other bearing off to Chattanooga and the north, and passed through Taylor's Ridge at the famous Buzzard's Roost Gap. This gap Johnston held strongly, pushing an outpost as far forward as the Tunnel Hill.

Such was the situation of affairs at Dalton. This place, with its difficult approaches, was commonly called in the papers the " doorway " of Georgia, and certainly there was never a defile more easy to defend or more deadly in its approaches than that outer gate of Dalton, the Buzzard's Roost Gap.

Meanwhile, General Thomas, who was still commanding the Army of the Cumberland, made his headquarters at Chattanooga; but his army was scattered —part of his rear back at Nashville, part for 100 miles to his left front near Knoxville, and the remainder on the direct line between himself and Johnston. He was forced to this dispersion by the necessities of the situation as well as by orders from his seniors. Bridges were to be built, railways repaired, fortifications to be erected, and stores to be accumulated.

At first he (Thomas) was in hopes that he might drive back his foe, occupy Dalton, and thus swing wide open the door of Georgia preparatory to Sherman's spring proposals.

A bold reconnoissance was made "after ceaseless labor and under the greatest embarrassment." Wading through mud and water and frost, the troops came up in front of the Buzzard's Roost. The gap was occupied by a force as strong as Thomas's own; the Confederates had more artillery and better cavalry; the country was without forage for mules and horses, and it was almost impossible to drag forward the heavy wagons, as one day's rain would render the Chickamauga bottom impassable for them, so that this vigorous forward movement had but one beneficial effect, which was to keep Johnston busy where he was—in the vicinity of Dalton; for on Thomas's approach he immediately called for reënforcements.

While the other troops were very active between Chattanooga, Dalton, and Knoxville, the wing of Thomas's army to which I belonged—probably about 20,000 strong, counting up the remaining divisions of the Eleventh Corps under Schurz and Von Steinwehr, and those of Geary and Ward belonging to the Twelfth Corps, with corps and artillery transportation reckoned in (for the latter especially afforded many diligent employees)—remained in our first camp.

This temporary city in Lookout Valley had General Joseph Hooker for its governor. Its outside intrenchments, better than the walls of a town, running over

MAJOR GENERAL HOWARD'S HEADQUARTERS LOOKOUT MOUNTAIN TENNESSEE JANUARY 1 1864.

the rolling hills and through the ravines, with Lookout for his advance guard and Raccoon for his reënforcement and the broad, swift Tennessee for his left flank, gave to the gallant general a cheerful repose. Hooker that winter and spring held daily court at his pleasant headquarters on the hillside, where officers of every rank came to receive cordial welcome; to review past battles and campaigns and to project new ones.

I still have at my house a charming picture, an etching made by a skillful German soldier. It represents my own headquarters near to Hooker's in the winter camp. There is the large tent made more spacious, vertically, at least, by its log walls; more convenient of entrance by its rough door of plank, and more cottagelike by its lofty chimney of rough stone at the farther end. There were other tents in convenient order of grouping, without military precision; the straggling canvas dining saloons adding to the irregularity of form and the outdoor stables suggesting but brief occupation; a log cottage opposite with living figures about it, contrasting the old time with the new.

I record that on March 28, 1864, Sherman again arrived at Chattanooga and went on the next day to Knoxville. There was a newspaper rumor that the Eleventh and Twelfth Corps would be sent back east to the Army of the Potomac. I then wrote: " I do not expect we shall go back, because I do not see how we can be spared from this army. I am rather anticipating Johnston's undertaking some game before long. If he take the initiative he may bother us considerably." March 29th I rode over from Lookout Valley to Chattanooga and paid a visit to General Thomas. In the course of conversation I inquired of him why he did not take a brief " leave " before the active operations should commence and visit his friends in the North.

"Oh," he said, " I cannot leave; something is sure to get out of order if I go away from my command. It was always so, even when I commanded a post. I had to stick by and attend to everything, or else affairs went wrong."

The escaping slaves made their way to every camp. A family came to mine, a part of which I sent North to employment. " Sam " remained with me. In a home letter I said: " ' Sam ' continues the best man in the world. He reads to me every night and morning, and keeps up his interest in the Bible. Julia (his aunt, a mulatto woman) wants him to become a Christian! He is trying."

On March 19th I gave an account of a scouting expedition, one among many: On Wednesday, a half hour before sunrise, my staff and myself set out for Trenton, Ga. We took an escort from General Ward's command—200 mounted infantry. The road lies between Lookout and Raccoon all the way. Lookout Creek, about sixty feet wide, winds its way through the whole distance for twenty miles, the crookedest stream you ever saw. The valley of this creek is nowhere level, but full of ridges and knolls. We came past many fine farms—one quite large, phenomenal at this time and place—on our return between the creek and Lookout where the depredators have not been. The owner's name was Brock. He had a two-story brick house almost hidden (it being on that byroad) fences all up, sheep in their pastures and negroes at home. Two or three ladies appeared as we passed. (They were **not** unfriendly in their look or manner to our party.)

Trenton is a little village of some half a dozen
496

houses, a church, and a village inn. We stopped at the latter. Widow G——, who lives there, had an aged mother in bed and a little son, some ten or twelve years old. We ate our lunch there and were permitted to put it on her table. All the people of this village were "secesh" and impoverished. It was a mystery from what source they got enough to eat.

Returning, we crossed the Lookout Creek, skirted the mountain, passed Mr. Brock's and other farms hidden away behind the ridges and woods. Some three or four miles to the east of Trenton, walking and leading our horses up the Nic-a-jack trace, we ascended Lookout Mountain. This rough, steep mountain path had been obstructed by the Confederates near the top by fallen trees. They were partially cut away and the gateway was made through their breastwork wall, which did not completely close the road at the top. We now rode along the crest of the great mountain, so as to take in the whole valley at a glance. The top of Lookout is rather rough and for the most part covered with forest. One pretty good road runs lengthwise along its back. We left Lookout, the north side of Summertown, and then descended by a new and steep path, very difficult, plucked the *Epigæa* or Mayflower, already blossoming near that path. We reached camp a little after dark, having made about forty miles in one day, besides ascending and descending the steep, rugged mountain. The next day Charles (Lieutenant Colonel C. H. Howard) and I rode to Rossville, and, accompanied by General J. C. Davis and Captain Daily, his aid-de-camp, went over the battlefield of Chickamauga. We found on reckoning up that we had ridden that day about twenty-eight miles, and I was weary indeed when I got into a chair in my own tent. The first day the weather was cold and raw and this took much from our pleasure. We here in the West were waiting to see what General Grant was going to do. We believed he was proposing to try his hand at Richmond. Such glimpses are suggestive of the thoughts, the plans, the operations, and the situation of the Northern and Southern men, thousands of them then facing each other with arms in their hands and ready for other bloody experiences soon to come.

Not very long after this Sherman set us in motion against Johnston, and Grant in the East began his more dreadful campaign against the Army of Lee.

CHAPTER XXVIII

OF the respective commanders of the armies which were to operate in advance of Chattanooga, namely, of the Cumberland, the Tennessee, and the Ohio, Sherman was fortunate in his lieutenants. He writes:

"In Generals Thomas, McPherson, and Schofield I had three generals of education and experience, admirably qualified for the work before us."

Each has made a history of his own and I need not here dwell on their respective merits as men, or as commanders of armies, except that each possessed special qualities of mind and of character which fitted him in the highest degree for the work then in contemplation.

Certain subordinate changes affected me personally. On April 5, 1864, with two or three officers, I

some eight or ten miles, and visited General Thomas. He explained that the order was already prepared for consolidating the Eleventh and Twelfth Corps into one body to form the new Twentieth, of which Hooker was to have command. Slocum was in Vicksburg, Miss., to control operations in that quarter, and I was to go to the Fourth Corps to enable Gordon Granger to take advantage of a leave of absence.

I was to gain under these new orders a fine corps, 20,000 strong, composed mainly of Western men. It had three divisions. Two commanders, Stanley and T. J. Wood, then present for duty, were men of large experience. A little later General John Newton, who will be recalled for his work at Gettysburg, and in other engagements, both in the East and West, an officer well known to every soldier, came to me at Cleveland, East Tennessee, and was assigned to the remaining division which General Wagner had been temporarily commanding.

I set out promptly for the new command, taking with me my personal staff. The Fourth Corps was much scattered, as I found on my arrival at headquarters in Loudon, April 10th. The first division (Stanley's) Thomas had kept near him. All through the winter it was on outpost duty along his direct eastern front, east of Chattanooga—two brigades being at Blue Springs and one at Ottowah; the third division (Wood's) had remained, after the Knoxville campaign, in the department of the Ohio, near to Knoxville.

Loudon was not far from the mouth of the Little Tennessee. Troops were held there to keep up communication between the two departments of Thomas and Schofield.

After the briefest visit to Loudon and assumption of command, I speedily moved the headquarters of this Fourth Corps to Cleveland, East Tennessee, fifty miles below. My first duty immediately undertaken was to concentrate the corps in that vicinity, inspect the different brigades, and ascertain their needs as to transportation, clothing, and other supplies. Part of the command, under General Wood, had been during the winter marching and camping, skirmishing and fighting in the country part of East Tennessee, so that, as one may well imagine, the regiments coming from that quarter were short of everything essential to a campaign. Supplies were wanting and their animals were weak and thin.

May 3, 1864, Schofield having come down from Knoxville to complete what became Sherman's grand army, had, with his Army of the Ohio, already arrived at Cleveland. With us the preceding month had been a busy one. For both officers and men the discouragements of the past were over. Now, new life was infused through the whole body. Something was doing. Large forces were seen rapidly coming together, and it was evident to every soldier that important work was to be undertaken. On Sundays the churches were filled with soldiers. Members of the Christian Commission had been permitted to visit our camp and were still with us. Among them was D. L. Moody, the Evangelist, a noble soul, so well known to the country for his sympathy and friendship for men. His words of hope and encouragement then spoken to multitudes of soldiers were never forgotten.

I wrote from East Tennessee a few words: " I have a very pleasant place for headquarters, just in the outskirts of Cleveland. The house belonged to the company which owned the copper mill." Again: " We are drawing near another trial of arms, perhaps more terrific than ever. But, on the eve of an active campaign and battles, I am not in any degree depressed. . . . When it can be done, there is a quiet happiness in being able to say, think, and feel, ' Not what I will, but what Thou wilt!' . . . We are hoping that this campaign will end the war!"

With our left well covered by Ed. McCook's

cavalry, our Fourth Corps, at last together, emerging from Cleveland, commenced to move in two columns; the left passed through Red Clay and the other farther west by Salem Church. The morning of May 4th found us at Catoosa Springs. These springs were on the left of General Thomas's army lines. His whole front looked eastward toward Tunnel Hill. Tunnel Hill, Ga., was between the Northern and Southern armies, the dividing ridge; it was the outpost of Johnston's advanced troops, which faced toward Chattanooga. The bulk of his force was behind, at the village of Dalton, covered by artificial works northward and eastward, and by the mountain range of Rocky Face Ridge toward the west. The famous defile through this abrupt mountain was called Buzzard's Roost Gap. From Rocky Face to Tunnel Hill, which is a parallel range of heights, the Chattanooga Railroad crosses a narrow valley, passes beneath the hill by a tunnel and stretches on toward Chattanooga.

The Confederate official returns for April 30, 1864, gave Johnston's total force as 52,992, and when Polk's corps had joined a little later at Resaca his total was raised to 71,235.

Sherman, in his Memoirs, aggregates the Army of the Cumberland 60,773; the Army of the Tennessee, in the field, 24,465; the Army of the Ohio, 13,559; making a grand total of 98,797 officers and men, with 54 cannon.

As Johnston's artillerymen were about the same in number as Sherman's, probably Johnston's artillery, in its guns, numbered not less than Sherman's.

The Army of the Cumberland delayed in the vicinity of Catoosa Springs till May 7th, to enable McPherson, with the Army of the Tennessee, to get around

from Northern Alabama into position in Sugar Valley
to the south of us and to bring down Schofield from
East Tennessee to the east of us. He was located near
Red Clay; that is, near Johnston's direct northern
front. It will be seen that the Chattanooga (Western
and Atlantic) Railroad, which passes through Tunnel
Hill, Buzzard's Roost, and then on to Dalton, where it
meets another branch coming from the north, through
Red Clay, constituted our line of supply and communication. Thomas had early advised Sherman that, in
his judgment, McPherson and Schofield should make
a strong demonstration directly against the enemy's
position at Dalton, while he himself with the Army of
the Cumberland should pass through the Snake Creek
Gap and fall upon Johnston's communications.

Thomas felt confident, if his plan were adopted,
that a speedy and decisive victory would result. I believe that he, as events have proved, was right; but
Sherman then thought and declared that the risk to his
own communications was too great to admit of his
throwing his main body so quickly upon the enemy's
rear, and he then feared to attempt this by a detour of
twenty miles.

Later in the campaign Sherman's practical judgment induced him to risk even more than that when
he sent whole armies upon the enemy's lines of communication and supply; but at this time Sherman
chose McPherson's small but stalwart force for that
twenty miles forward and flanking operation.

The morning of May 7th my corps left camp at Catoosa Springs to perform its part in these operations.
It led off, due east, along the Alabama road till it came
into the neighborhood of a Mr. Lee's house.

Here, under my observation, a partial unfolding of

my troops took place; quite a long front appeared—
Stanley's division on the right, Newton's on the left,
and Wood's in reserve. First, a few cracks of hostile
rifles, then an exciting skirmish on both sides set in,
but there was no halting. Steadily our men pressed
forward, driving back first the Southern cavalry pickets and outer lines till, awakening opposition more and
more, about nine o'clock our foe crowned Tunnel Hill
with considerable force and fired briskly upon our advance. The same angry reception was given to the
Fourteenth Corps, coming up simultaneously southward beyond our right. Then I saw that the Confederate artillery had only cavalry supports, so that immediately I ordered a charge along our lines. Our
troops promptly sprang forward and carried the
" crowned hill."

Now, from Tunnel Hill we had Rocky Face in plain
view. It was a continuous craggy ridge at least 500
feet high, very narrow on top, but having in places a
perpendicular face almost as abrupt as the Palisades
of the Hudson; the eastern steeps, favorable to Johnston's ascent and defense, were more gradual.

Through Buzzard's Roost Gap, which cuts in two
the Rocky Face, there were both a railway and a
wagon road, also a small stream of water.

This the Confederates had so dammed up as to present a formidable obstacle. They had further so arranged their batteries and their infantry intrenchments as to completely sweep every hollow and
pathway in that formidable defile.

Thomas, however, as he always did, pushed us forward with steadiness and vigor—Fourteenth Corps in
the center, Fourth and Twentieth on the left and right.
Meanwhile McPherson was steadily winding his way

through Snake Creek Gap toward Resaca, and Schofield constantly pressing his heavy skirmish lines from Red Clay toward Dalton, to unveil from that northern side Johnston's half-concealed intrenchments.

A couple of miles away to my right, southward, on May 9th, the Twentieth Corps, under Hooker, had hard 'fighting indeed. Fifty men were killed and a large number wounded. My personal friend, Lieutenant Colonel McIlvain, Sixty-fourth Ohio, was killed here. Every regimental commander in this hard struggle was wounded. The Fourteenth Corps also, under Palmer, nearer to us, had its own brisk work.

From this command, the Sixty-sixth Illinois kept working forward by the side of the dangerous gap, drawing fire, and driving in the enemy's outer lines. The soldiers finally obtained shelter, without being able to get farther forward, within speaking distance of their foes. One enterprising corporal made a bargain with some Confederates who were throwing heavy bowlders from above, that if they would refrain from their bothersome work, he would read to them the President's famous amnesty proclamation. He did so, and comparative quiet was kept during this strange entertainment.

On May 8th General Newton, with my second division, had managed, after working up some two miles north of the gap, to push a small force up the slope, and then, taking the defenders by a rush drove them along southward on the ridge until he had succeeded in capturing from the Confederates at least one-third of the ridge. Here he established a signal station. He next tried, but in vain, to seize and capture a Confederate signal party, which he deemed too actively talking by the busy use of their flags.

Stanley and Wood, on Newton's right, stretched out their own lines to some extent, and gave Newton all the support they could in that difficult ground near the west palisades of the ridge. During the night his men dragged up the steeps two pieces of artillery, and by their help gained another 100 yards of the hotly disputed crest.

On May 9th another experiment was tried. Under instructions I sent Stanley's division for a reconnoissance into that horrid gap of Buzzard's Roost, until it had drawn from the enemy a strong artillery fire, which redoubled the echoes and roarings of the valleys and caused to be opened the well-known incessant rattle of long lines of musketry.

It was while making preparations for this fearful reconnoissance that a group of officers were standing around me, among them General Stanley and Colonel (then Captain) G. C. Kniffin, of his staff. The enemy's riflemen were, we thought, beyond range; but one of them, noticing our party, fired into the group. His eccentric bullet made three holes through the back of my coat, but without wounding me, and then passed through Kniffin's hat, and finally struck a tree close at hand. The group of observers speedily changed their position.

McPherson, now near Resaca, was not so successful as Sherman had hoped. Though there were but two Confederate brigades at that town, the nature of the ground was, for McPherson, unpropitious in the extreme. The abrupt ravines, the tangled and thick wood, and the complete artificial works, recently renewed, which covered the approaches to Resaca, made McPherson unusually cautious, so that the first day, after an unsuccessful effort to strike the railroad,

Johnston's main artery, he fell back to a defensive line near the mouth of the gap and there intrenched his front.

Just as soon as Sherman had received this news, he altered his plan and sent his main army, except Stoneman's cavalry division and my corps, by the same route. General Stoneman, with his force, had just arrived from Kentucky.

With this comparatively small force I kept up on the old ground a lively and aggressive work during Thomas's and Schofield's southward march with perhaps even more persistency than before; yet probably the withdrawal of Schofield from Red Clay by Sherman, and the replacement of his skirmishers by cavalry, together with the report that McPherson was so near to his communications, made the always wary and watchful Confederate general suspicious that something in the enemy's camp—that is, in my part of it—was going wrong for him.

Therefore, on the 12th he pushed a sizable force out northward toward Stoneman, and made a strong reconnoissance, which, like a handsome parade, I beheld from Newton's Ridge and which in the ravines and thickets and uncertain light was magnified to large proportions in the lively vision of our soldiers beholding it.

At first some of our officers feared that Johnston, letting his communications go, would attempt a battle, so as to crush my Fourth Corps. But soon the tide turned, and the tentative force retired within the Confederate intrenchments.

Under cover of the night ensuing, Joe Johnston, as he did many times thereafter, made one of his handsome retreats; no man could make retreats from the front of an active, watchful enemy with better success than he. At daylight of the 13th I pressed my moving forces with all speed after the foe as boldly as possible, but was delayed all day by the enemy's active rear guard, the roughness of the country affording that guard successive shelters. It took time to dislodge the fearless hinderers, yet I did finally before dark of the same night succeed in forming substantial junction with Sherman, who, in person, having hastened on the day before, was at that time near McPherson on ground to the west of Resaca. Meanwhile, Johnston, with his main body, was obstructing, by his peculiar asperities, the roads to that town and getting ready for the next day's battle.

To show the costliness of such operations, in my corps alone there were already in the little combats about 300 wounded. My march following Johnston had been rapid and full of excitement. My mind had been bent upon the situation, watching against any sudden change; sending scouts to the right and left; getting reports from the cavalry in front, or beating up the woods and thickets that might conceal an ambuscade. After my arrival in the evening came the arrangement of the men upon the new ground; then the essential reports and orders for the next day; then followed the welcome dinner that our enterprising mess purveyor and skillful cook had promptly prepared. Here around the mess chest used for a table my staff sat with me and spent a pleasant hour chatting, and leisurely eating the meal, discussing events of the past day and the hopes of the morrow.

Of the movement at Resaca Joseph E. Johnston says: "The two armies" (Sherman and his own) "were formed in front of Resaca nearly at the same time, so that the federal army could give battle on equal terms, except as to numbers, by attacking promptly, the difference being about 10 to 4."

There is evidently a great mistake in this statement. In all Confederate writings this claim of disparity of numbers is noticeable and difficult to be accounted for. General Polk had arrived and the Confederate army at this place was admitted by Hood to have been about 75,000. Sherman's force was at first, as we have seen, 98,797; then, diminished by a thousand casualties at Rocky Face and vicinity and increased by Stoneman's cavalry, which did not exceed 4,000, we had a new aggregate of about 101,797. It is difficult to understand how Johnston can make it anywhere near 10 to 4, or even 2 to 1, against him! It is well, however, to remember what we have before frequently noticed, that our opponents used the word " effectives," counting the actual number of men carrying rifles and carbines, plus the enlisted artillerymen actually with their guns; whereas our officers counted in all present for duty, officers and men, no matter how multitudinous and varied the details might be. It is plain, however we come to estimates, that the disparity between the actual armies was not very great at the battle of Resaca. We could not possibly put into line of battle, counting actual fighting elements, more than four men to Johnston's three.

On May 14, 1864, Polk, with the new corps, had already come up.

As always in this campaign, this Confederate army was promptly marched into position, and without delay intrenched. On the other hand, our forces approaching Resaca through the gap on the one side and from Dalton on the other, had to work slowly and carefully to feel for the enemy's pickets and for each other in that blind, rough, broken, wild, tangled, unknown region.

It was near twelve o'clock of May 14th before we had formed solid junction with each other, and, after that, the lines had to be changed while we worried forward. Sometimes long gaps between brigades troubled the division commanders, and sometimes an astonishing overlapping of forces displaced regiments as they advanced.

The 14th, then, was mainly spent by Sherman in placing McPherson on our right, near the Oostanaula, Schofield next, and Thomas on the left. My corps reached the railroad and formed Sherman's left, and was faced against the strong position of Hood. As the Connasauga beyond Hood bent off far to the east, it was quite impossible for my left regiments to reach that river, so that, after examining the ground, I was again forced to have the left of my line "in the air." But Stanley's excellent division stationed there, by refusing (drawing back) its left brigade and nicely posting its artillery, formed as good an artificial obstacle against Hood as was possible.

Sherman had instructed McPherson after his arrival from Snake Creek Gap, and just before the remainder of the army joined him, to work toward his right and forward, and make an effort to seize Johnston's railroad line near Resaca. To this end, during May 14th, several lively demonstrations were made by McPherson to carry out Sherman's wishes.

The importance of McPherson's capture of some heights, situated between Camp Creek and the Oostanaula, cannot be doubted, for that high ground manned with our guns spoiled all Confederate transit

510

by the railway and the wagon road bridges, and caused the Confederates to lay a new bridge of boats farther up the river.

General Schofield with his "Army of the Ohio," consisting of but one corps, the Twenty-third, fought near the center of our line.

It was worse and worse for Schofield (Judah's division) as he pressed forward. By the help of my troops, Cox's division was enabled to hold its ground. His soldiers acted as did McPherson's later at Atlanta: aligned themselves on the outside of their enemy's trenches and sheltered their front by making small trenches till help came. I remember well that swinging movement, for I was on a good knoll for observation. It was the first time that my attention had been especially called to that handsome, gallant young officer and able man, Jacob D. Cox. He was following his troops, and appeared full of spirit and energy as he rode past the group of officers who were with me. I was watching the movement so as to find where his lines would finally rest in order to support his left. This part of our work was exciting, for the air was already full of bursting shells and other hissing missiles of death. It was much like the first Bull Run, where my brigade was detained for several hours within hearing of the battlefield. I experienced the same feeling again here at Resaca while beholding from my high ground Cox's and Wood's divisions going so rapidly forward into battle. The noise was deafening; the missiles carried the idea of extreme danger to all within range, and the air appeared for the time as if doubly heated.

The effect was like that of a startling panorama of which one forms a part. There was a sense of danger, deep and strong, relieved by a magnificent spectacle and the excitement of the contest. Such moments afford unusual glimpses of an extraordinary mental world, which leave impressions of interest and memory not easily explained.

CHAPTER XXIX

THE partial discomfiture of Judah's enterprising men early on May 14, 1864, brought to them one of my divisions (Newton's).

Newton steadily breasted the Confederates, driving them back and causing them heavy losses, and his men, counting out a few stragglers, kept their lines perfectly and behaved like old soldiers. Newton showed here his wonted tenacity. He secured all the ground he could gain by a steady advance, and, stopping from time to time, returned fire for fire, until the fierce artillery and rifle fusillade on both sides diminished to a fitful skirmish. Palmer's corps was doing similar work to my right.

Farther toward the left, over the rough ground east of Camp Creek, and amid the underbrush and scattered chestnut trees, I beheld my third division in line. Thomas J. Wood commanded it; covered by a complete skirmish front, every man and officer was in his place. He waited, or he advanced cautiously, so as to support Newton.

I came forward and was with him as his men advanced into place. The movement was like a dress parade. I observed Wood's men with interest. How remarkably different the conduct of his veteran soldiers compared with new troops! They were not, per-

513

haps, braver, but they were less given to excitements, and knew always what was coming and what to do.

I remember, when suddenly the enemy's skirmish fire began, Wood's main lines immediately halted and lay prone upon the ground. They returned the fire, but never too rapidly.

When Wood was completely ready, he caused a quick advance, drove back the enemy's skirmishers, and seized the detached rifle pits, capturing a few prisoners. Every Confederate not killed, wounded, or captured ran at once to his breastworks proper, and for a short time the fire of artillery and infantry from his main line was brisk and destructive enough. At last, Wood, by planting and covering his own batteries with epaulements, and by intrenching and barricading his men, was able to give back blow for blow.

Stanley's division of my corps came up by my instructions on Sherman's extreme left. His men and batteries were well located, as well as could be done with the whole left flank in air. Stanley endeavored, by his reserve brigade, and by his artillery carefully posted behind his lines, through its chief, Captain Simonson, to so reënforce his left as to make up for want of any natural obstacle. Though he protected the railway and the main Dalton wagon road, yet there was a long stretch of rough ground between Stanley's left and the Oostanaula; the bend of the river was so great that an entire corps, thrust in, could hardly have filled the opening.

Stanley had the same lively advance as the others, and was well up and in position before 3 P.M. of this day, May 14th. My secretary, Joseph A. Sladen (then a private of the Thirty-third Massachusetts Infantry, afterwards my aid-de-camp and by my side in campaign and battle for twenty-three years) voluntarily did such distinguished service that day that he was awarded the Congressional Medal of Honor. The coolness and courage of his example and, as he told me, equally energetic work of my brother, Lieutenant Colonel C. H. Howard, inspired panic-stricken troops to turn and repel fierce assaults. Johnson was quick to detect anything so tempting as a "flank in air," and so he directed Hood to send heavy columns against and beyond my left flank.

The front attack was handsomely met and the batteries well used, but Stanley, finding the turning force too great for him, sent word to me, then near Wood, that the enemy was rapidly turning his left.

Knowing the situation exactly, I took with me Colonel Morgan of the Fourteenth Infantry (colored troops), who was temporarily on my staff, and galloped to Thomas, fortunately at the time but a few hundred yards off. I explained to him the alarming condition of things on my left, and begged for immediate reënforcement.

Thomas (Sherman being present) directed Hooker at once to send me a division, and with no delay Hooker detached from his Twentieth Corps the veteran division of A. S. Williams. Colonel Morgan, acting for me, guided them as fast as foot troops could speed straight to Stanley's flank. The division came when most needed.

Deployed at double time at right angles to Stanley's line, instantly with the batteries Williams opened a terrific, resistless fire. The hostile advance was checked, the tide turned, and the Confederates were swept back and driven within their intrenchments.

Our losses were great. In my corps that day 400 men were put *hors de combat*.

Next morning very early I reported for joint work to Hooker, my senior in rank. At his headquarters I learned what points of Johnston's line he intended to assail and I had him carefully describe to me the manner in which he would form his troops, and agreed with him how best to give him my prompt support.

At last, after some more irksome delays, everything was in readiness. Hooker's corps was drawn up in column of brigades—that is, each brigade in line, and one following another with no great intervals between them. My support was placed, at call, on his right and left. I was so to breast the enemy along my whole front that they could not detach brigades or regiments against Hooker; and, further, as Hooker gained ground, I had so arranged as to follow up his movement and aid him to seize and hold whatever he should capture. Besides all this, I had a clear reserve, which was kept ready for him in case of disaster or other extraordinary need. The ground in our front was very rough, appearing to our observation like detached stony knolls more or less covered with trees.

The noise of musketry and cannon and shouting and the attending excitement increased as the forces neared each other. Hooker appeared to gain ground for some time. His men went on by rushes rather than by steady movement. Two or three sets of skirmish trenches were captured before Butterfield's leading brigade had run upon a strong Confederate lunette.

After desperate fighting, the enemy, behind cover, would break Hooker's men back, only to try again. Finally, the latter seeing a covered position close by, a rush was made for it. Butterfield, aided by Geary, secured it. So near to the guns and beneath a crest were the men that they by their fire almost paralyzed their use against our advance lines. These guns, however, at intervals did bloody work, using canister and shells against brigades farther off.

During this advance of Hooker, which, we confess, was not very successful and attended with loss, the Twenty-third Corps, or a good part of it, was brought over to aid Hooker and me at any instant when Hooker should make a break through the enemy's main line.

It is said one regiment, the Seventieth Indiana, sprang from a thicket upon the lunette and, as they came on, the Confederate artillerists blazed away without checking our men. They entered the embrasures; they shot the gunners.

In this effort Ward was badly wounded. Colonel Benjamin Harrison immediately took his place and gallantly continued the work.

The fire from intrenchments behind the lunette became severe, being delivered in volley after volley; too severe to render it proper to remain there; so that Harrison, getting ready to make another vigorous advance, drew back his line a few yards under cover of the lunette hill.

Here a color bearer by the name of Hess, One Hundred and Twenty-ninth Illinois, chagrined to hear the shrill, triumphant cry of the Confederates, at once unfurled his flag, swinging it toward them in defiance. He instantly fell, but other hands grasped the flag, and it came back only to return and wave from the very spot where its former bearer fell.

In the most determined way those four guns were now defended by the blue and gray, costing many lives; but there they stayed hereafter in the middle

517

space, unused by either party, till dark. The Confederates then made a bold charge to retake them, but our men promptly and successfully repelled the charge. Finally, the picks and spades were brought up by our soldiers, and our defenders dug their way to the guns. At last these costly trophies were permanently brought into our possession. The Confederate commander names this as an advanced battery of Hood's, put out beyond his front, on the morning of May 15, 80 or 100 yards.

We now know that Hood, in front of Hooker, had been constantly reënforced by Hardee and Polk, and that just as Hooker started his column Hood had pushed out his attacking lines, so that the first shock beyond the Confederate trenches was severe, each side having taken the offensive.

Finally, Hovey led a movement at double-quick, and encountered a dreadful fire, but succeeded in routing the Confederates' obstinate attacking column and driving it to its own cover; I was watching and my corps bore its part. Artillery and musketry had been kept active all along my front and strong demonstrations with double-skirmish lines were made for my center and right. We succeeded at least in keeping the Confederates from seizing any point on my ground. Brigadier General Willich was severely wounded in this engagement; Harker and Opdycke of Newton's division were also wounded, but able to remain on the field.

Sherman's aggregate loss in the whole battle of Resaca was between 4,000 and 5,000. Nearly 2,000 were so slightly injured that they were on duty again within a month. By referring again to the comments of the Confederate commander in his reports, we see that the cause of his retreat is not ascribed to the persistent fighting which I have described. He says:

"It was because two (new) bridges and a large body of Federal troops were discovered the afternoon of the 14th at Lay's Ferry, some miles below, strongly threatening our communications, indicating another flanking operation, covered by the river as the first had been by the ridge."

By instructions from Sherman, McPherson had early sent a division of the Sixteenth Corps, commanded by the one-armed General Sweeny, to Lay's Ferry. He was to make a lodgment on the other bank of the Oostanaula and protect the engineering officer, Captain Reese, while the latter laid his pontoon bridge.

Sweeny found some force there which he dislodged; but, getting a report, which then seemed to him very probable, that the Confederates were crossing above him and would cut him off from our army, he withdrew and retired at least a mile and a half from the river; but the next day, the 15th of May, he made another attempt to bridge the Oostanaula, which was more successful. This time Sweeny had, after crossing, a serious engagement with a division which the Confederate commander had detached against him. In this Sweeny lost 250 men killed and wounded. Nevertheless, Sweeny, using his intrenching tools, established his bridgehead on the left bank of the Oostanaula, drove off the opposing Confederate force and opened the way for our cavalry to operate upon Johnston's communications.

We were up bright and early on the morning of the 16th. The sunlight gave a strange appearance to the smoke and fog among the tree tops. During our deep sleep between midnight and dawn a change had been wrought. Not a cannon, not a rifle, not a carbine was over beyond our front there to give defiant shots. The tireless Newton was on the *qui vive* and, the first to move, his skirmishers soon bounded over the parapets of Hood to find them empty.

When my report at Resaca, that Newton occupied the abandoned trenches at dawn of May 16th, reached Sherman, he instantly ordered pursuit. One division of our cavalry, under Garrard, was scouting off toward Rome, Ga., so now the infantry division of General Jeff. C. Davis was hurried down the Oostanaula Valley, keeping on the right bank of the river, to support the cavalry, and, if possible, seize Rome and hold it.

Two bridges were already in good order at Lay's Ferry. Sweeny's division, as we have previously seen, was across the river, so that at once McPherson began his movement and pushed on southward, endeavoring to overtake the retreating foe. A few miles out, not far from Calhoun, McPherson's skirmishers encountered the Confederates, and a sharp skirmish speedily followed.

Johnston did not long delay in his front and yet he was there a sufficient length of time to cause McPherson to develop his lines, go into position, and get ready for action. The expected affair did not come off, for Johnston had other points demanding his attention.

The next morning, finding the enemy gone, McPherson continued his movement down the river road to a point—McGuire's Crossroads—which is about due west of Adairsville, and eleven miles distant.

Meanwhile, Thomas, with my corps and the Fourteenth, took up a direct pursuit. The railroad bridge over the Oostanaula had been partly burned, but a rough floating bridge was quickly made from the timbers at hand.

My corps led in this pursuit; we also, just after McPherson's skirmish, began to exchange shots with Johnston's rear guard; we made during the 16th but slow progress.

General Stewart's Confederate division constituted Johnston's rear guard, which we were closely following. The severe skirmish of the evening was a brief one between Stanley's division and Johnston's line at Calhoun.

Early the next day (the 17th) our column, passing the enemy's empty works at Calhoun, continued the march; Newton's division, starting at half-past five, was followed by Stanley's. Newton took the Adairsville wagon road, while Wood, a little farther to the right, came up abreast along the railroad. I was near Newton. Our progress was continually interrupted.

As we neared Adairsville the resistance increased. Wood, sent by me across the railway, kept extending his skirmish line and strengthening it till it abutted against the enemy's main line west of Adairsville. Newton, under my immediate direction, east of Wood, did the same, deploying farther and farther to the left and doubling his advance line.

It was four o'clock in the afternoon when Newton's men, rushing into a grove of trees, brought on from the Confederates a heavy fire. It was a little later than this when Sherman came riding up with his staff and escort and, joining me, led off to the highest ground. There he was observing with his field glass till he drew the fire of a battery.

The skirmishing on both sides had grown into brisk and rapid firing just as I was approaching Sherman,

Newton and his staff with me. Our group, so large, attracted attention. A hostile battery of several guns was quickly turned upon us. The shells began to burst over our heads at our right and left. One of them disabled the horse of Colonel Morgan, my senior aid, another that of Colonel Fullerton, my adjutant general; Newton's aid, Captain Jackson, was wounded; two orderlies' horses were disabled, and still another horse belonging to the headquarters' cavalry was crippled. One piece of a shell in the air slightly wounded Captain Bliss, also of Newton's staff, carrying away the insignia of rank from his shoulder.

It was evident, as there was fighting along the front of two divisions—which had been increased and reenforced — that the Confederates were making a strong stand here at Adairsville; so we prepared for battle and I made haste to bring up my reserves for a decided assault. However equipped and supplied, it always required time to get an attacking column in readiness for action. Quite promptly the columns were in motion; but as soon as the vigorous movement was inaugurated, Thomas, then by my side, said to me that it was too near night for me to take the offensive. He advised me further to simply do what was needed to hold my position, and postpone, if possible, any general engagement till daylight the next morning.

One battery of artillery, however, drew another into action. Our batteries one after another were quickly brought up, and fired with their usual spirit and vigor. The sun went down upon this noisy, unusual, and bloody conflict, where probably both parties, could they have had their way, were really disposed to wait till the morning.

It was nine o'clock at night, and very dark, before

we could entirely disengage. Then the rattling musketry with an occasional boom of cannon continued further into the night, then gradually diminished to a fitful and irregular fire.

The losses in my corps resulting from this combat at Adairsville were at least 200 killed and wounded.

During the night the Fourteenth Corps came within close support, and McPherson moved from McGuire's so much toward Adairsville as to connect with Thomas's right flank. But there was no general action; the next morning at dawn (May 18th), I found that Johnston had made another clean retreat. The reason for it we will find by taking the map and following the movement of Sherman's left column. This column was Schofield's, reënforced by Hooker's corps. Sherman had sent Hooker to follow Schofield over the ferries that ran across the branches of the Oostanaula above me, because our new bridge at Resaca had not sufficient capacity for all, and probably, furthermore, to give greater strength to his flanking force.

The left column, setting out at the same hour with me, was obliged to make a wide detour eastward and to cross two rivers instead of one, to wit, the Connasauga and the Coosawattee. Schofield laid his bridges at Fite's and Field's crossings. The cavalry forded the rivers, these made two columns coming up beyond my left. Johnston heard during the night, by reports from his active cavalry scouts, that Hooker and Schofield were beyond his right and aiming for Cassville, thus threatening the Allatoona Bridge, which was to be his main crossing of the Etowah. He knew, too, that McPherson, as we noticed, had already turned his position on the other flank, and was resting between McGuire's Crossroads and Adairsville, and he also had tidings that a division of cavalry, supported by infantry, was much farther west in the immediate vicinity of Rome, and that this column was likely to carry the weak forts there by assault, and so swoop up his foundries and important mills. Surely things were not favorable for a long delay at Adairsville. Unless the Confederate commander was prepared to take the immediate offensive against Thomas in the morning, his army would be before many hours hemmed in on every side. No wonder he drew off before such a day had dawned.

Judging by Confederate accounts, I am inclined to think that there was no complete report of losses on the part of the enemy. Johnston intimates that, as they fought mainly behind breastworks at Resaca, the loss of the Confederates, compared with ours, was not large. One who was present remarks: " A regiment was captured by Howard, and a few vagabond pickets were picked up in various places." Another declares that, besides the wounded, " prisoners (Confederate) at the hour I write, 9 A.M., May 16th, are being brought in by hundreds." On the 18th we were busy destroying the Georgia State Arsenal at Adairsville; we visited the wounded that the Confederates had the night before left behind, and picked up a few weary stragglers in gray coats.

All this show of success gave us increased courage and hope. It should be noticed that our Colonel Wright, repairing the railways, was putting down new bridges with incredible rapidity. When we were back at Dalton his trains with bread, provender, and ammunition were already in that little town. By May 16th, early in the morning, while skirmishing was still going on with the rear guard of Johnston, across the Oostanaula, the scream of our locomotive's whistle was heard behind us at Resaca. The telegraph, too, was never much delayed. Major Van Dusen repaired the old broken line, and kept us constantly in communication with our depots and with Washington, and at Adairsville we received word from our commissaries at Resaca that there was at that subdepot, at our call, abundance of coffee, hard bread, and bacon.

Here, we notice, from Tunnel Hill to Adairsville, Sherman, in less than ten days, had experienced pretty hard fighting, but he had also overcome extraordinary natural obstacles which, according to writers in the Southern press, had been relied upon as impregnable against any enemy's approach, supported and defended as they were by the brave army of Joe Johnston behind them—obstacles such as Tunnel Hill, Taylor's Ridge, Snake Creek Gap, and the Oostanaula with its tributaries. True, the Confederate army was not yet much reduced in numbers, yet the spirit of the men, though not broken, was unfavorably affected by Johnston's constant retreats.

General Johnston was becoming every day more and more conservative and cautious. He continued to stand on the defensive; while under Sherman our more numerous men were pressing against his front, and moving to the right and left of his army with Napoleonic boldness.

Thus far we had experienced hardly a check, as, like heavy waves, these forces were rolling on toward the sea.

That morning, near Adairsville, in a little nook to the right of the road, while we were marching toward Kingston, we caught sight of a group of young ladies standing on the green; they appeared somewhat nervous and excited on our approach.

In a courteous manner I accosted the one who had most self-possession, and who had stepped out in front of her companions:

"Young lady, can you tell me whose residence this is?"

She answered curtly: "It belongs to Captain Howard."

"Ah, Captain Howard! That is my name. My name is Howard. Perhaps we are connections."

She replied sharply: "We have no relations whatever North, sir!"

I then asked: "Is Captain Howard at home?"

She replied: "No."

"Where is he?"

"Captain Howard is with the Confederate army, where he ought to be."

"Ah, indeed, I am sorry! Where is that army?"

"I don't know anything about the Confederate movements. I told you, sir, that I had no relations North."

"Well, then, the blood of all the Howards does not flow in your veins."

At this time, turning to a staff officer, and within hearing of the group of young ladies, I remarked, as the sound of skirmishing reached our ears: "That house will make an excellent field hospital."

The speaker and her companions were frightened at this unexpected reply and ran to the house and appeared shortly after on the upper porch. Before we had left the premises, a middle-aged lady came hastily toward me, and besought me not to take her house for a hospital. I replied that I had been treated rather cavalierly by the young people, and that my courtesy met only with rebuff.

"Oh, sir," she said, "you must not mind those girls. They talk flippantly!"

Fortunately for the family, there was nothing but a slight skirmish in their neighborhood, and the lovely house and other buildings near at hand, so prettily ensconced beyond the green in the grove of trees, were not used for the dreaded army purpose.

I have since found that this Georgia family remembered my visit, and had spoken highly of me, probably more highly than I deserved.

I have lately pleasantly met them at Atlanta. Prejudice has given way to time and change.

After leaving this place we proceeded to Kingston, where General Sherman had already established his headquarters, and where they were to remain during the few days' rest after Johnston's Confederate forces had crossed the Etowah.

CHAPTER XXX

I N the forward movement from Adairsville, May 18, 1864, our three armies were a little mixed.

One division under the enterprising Jeff. C. Davis, with Garrard's cavalry, became detached from Thomas and went directly to Rome, and on the 18th drove out the small garrison of Confederates there; they captured some ten heavy guns, other war material, supplies of all kinds including a trainload of salt, and a few prisoners of war.

Johnston had fully determined to give Sherman battle at Cassville. To this end he had selected certain well-defined positions, which were most favorable, and covered them with the usual temporary intrenchments.

Places for artillery were carefully chosen by good engineers and artillerists, and epaulements set up for proper cover. Strengthened by a small reënforcement, he located Hardee's corps so as to meet all the Army of the Cumberland and of the Tennessee, which were likely to approach Cassville from the west or from the Kingston route; Polk's command in the center would meet Hooker's corps with sufficient force to hold him in check, and have strong enough reserve to strengthen Hood, who, on Johnston's extreme right, was directed to meet and withstand Schofield's army.

528

Battle of Cassville

With regard to position at this time, Johnston had greatly the advantage of his adversary, because his troops were concentrated. He could move on inner lines. Sherman was coming in upon Cassville, after having his four columns greatly separated the one from the other. The nature of the country was such that it was next to impossible, before actual conjunction, for Thomas to send help to Hooker, and worse still for McPherson or Thomas to reënforce Schofield in a reasonable time.

But Sherman was so anxious for battle on the more favorable ground north of the Etowah, rather than upon the ragged country south of it, that he declared to his commanders as in his dispatch to Schofield: " If we can bring Johnston to battle this side of the Etowah, we must do it, even at the hazard of beginning battle with but part of our forces."

It is very evident that Johnston hoped to be able to dispose of Hooker and Schofield by striking with a superior force and crushing them before help could come. Johnston's intention to make an " offensive defensive " battle appears plain from his own language and the instructions that he gave. He says in effect after consultation with his engineer officer, who was questioned over the map in the presence of Polk and Hood, who were informed of his object, that he found the country on the direct road open and favorable for an attack; that the distance between the two Federal columns would be greatest when those following the railroad reached Kingston. Johnston's chief of artillery warned him that our artillery, planted on a hill a mile off, could enfilade his right. Johnston ordered traverses to be constructed, though he declared that such artillery firing, more than a half-mile away, could do little harm, seeing that there were many protecting ravines.

My corps, as we already know, followed the wagon road nearest the railway, turning to the left of Kingston about 8 A.M., May 18, 1864. We had hardly passed through this much-scattered hamlet, when skirmishing opened southeast of the place. Pressing back the skirmishers, we delayed any positive action till about 11 A.M., waiting for other troops to come into position, when my command again took up the march.

Then, shelling the low ground, mostly covered with broad patches of thick underbrush and straggling trees, we moved slowly forward, forcing back the outer lines of the enemy. These obstinate divisions retired perforce, skirmishing all the time, to within two miles of Cassville; we now, with thick timber all around, appeared to be in front of the Cassville Confederate works.

Hooker's troops had done the same thing as mine, but on the direct Adairsville and Cassville road.

Palmer's corps, off to my right, had at least one division (Baird's) deployed.

About this time a deserter came into our lines and reported that Johnston had received reënforcements of 6,000 men. Just at this juncture we reckoned his forces to be fully 70,000 strong.

With reference to the Fourth Corps, which I commanded, the journal of Lieutenant Colonel Fullerton, my adjutant general, has given an animated account of the series of combats which took place between Kingston and Cassville:

"3.50 P.M., advance commenced. . . . The enemy was driven by us. We again took up the march in column, and again met the enemy one mile beyond his first position at 5.30 p.m.; 5.40 p.m., General Sherman ordered General Howard to put thirty or forty pieces of artillery in position; to form two or three brigades in line of battle; then to shell the woods in our front vigorously, afterwards, to feel the enemy."

This was done. The journal continues:

" 6.30 p.m., firing ordered to cease and skirmishers ordered forward, followed by main lines."

Here we connected with Palmer's corps on the right and Hooker's on the left.

" Now the line advanced, trying to move to Cassville; skirmishing very heavy, and progress slow."

At 7 o'clock, apparently within about one mile of Cassville, I halted my command in place, and all slept in line of battle that night. The day had been warm and clear, but the roads were very dusty.

In these exchanges of artillery shots ten of our men had been killed and thirty-five wounded.

The whole of Johnston's force was before us in Cassville. Johnston meant to strike Hooker before we got up. The enemy had strong rifle pits and works, and Johnston had published an order to his troops, saying that he would make his fight there; this was issued the night we arrived.

That General Johnston did intend and expected to make a stand here will be seen from the tenor of this order, which was as follows:

" Soldiers of the Army of the Tennessee: You have displayed the highest quality of the soldier— firmness in combat, patience under toil. By your courage and skill you have repulsed every assault of the enemy. By marches by day and by marches by night you have defeated every attempt upon your communications. Your communications are secured.

You will now turn and march to meet his advancing columns. Fully confiding in the conduct of the officers, the courage of the soldiers, I lead you to battle. We may confidently trust that the Almighty Father will still reward the patriots' toils and bless the patriots' banners. Cheered by the success of our brothers in Virginia and beyond the Mississippi, our efforts will equal theirs. Strengthened by His support, those efforts will be crowned with the like glories."

McPherson, under Sherman's orders, had also turned to the left toward us, and was close in support of Thomas's right.

It was, however, Schofield's cavalry, under Stoneman, some horse artillery being with it, that appeared off to the right and eastward of Hood's command during May 18th. It was decidedly to our advantage that the valiant and indomitable Hood was thus deceived by a force which dismounted and acted as infantry. Stoneman deserved special recognition from Schofield and Sherman for this good work.

Captain David B. Conyngham, who was present at Cassville as soon as we occupied that village, says three men of the Twenty-third Corps entered a house and were betrayed to a detachment of Confederate cavalry by some of the inmates. They barricaded themselves in the house and resisted several attacks. Just as the Confederates were setting fire to the house " a squad of Stoneman's cavalry heard the firing and hastened to the spot. The Union cavalry attacked the besieging party in the rear, soon putting them to flight, and so released their friends." Of course, one bird does not make a summer, but these three infantrymen may indicate the presence of more of the same sort near the cavalry of Stoneman.

Battle of Cassville

With reference to the enfilading, Johnston spoke of the bare possibility of our enfilading him with artillery. The report of one of my officers, Lieutenant White, Bridge's Illinois Battery, says: " At 6 p.m. General Howard brought this battery, with others, into position, from which we were able to fire with raking effect upon the flank of the Confederate lines occupying Cassville, while their front was facing the attack of Hooker."

This operation took place, as we have before seen, the evening of May 19th, and will account for some of the serious impressions of Polk, if not of Hood, as they were subsequently evinced at their council.

This council doubtless indirectly caused Johnston's dismissal at Atlanta, and resulted in Hood's accession and his series of disasters and his ultimate complete discomfiture by Thomas at Nashville. It rendered possible the great " March to the Sea," and the more troublesome ordeals of the Carolinas, which ended in Bentonville and bore no small weight upon the operations in Virginia—those operations which closed the war. The details of that council show that Hood, believing his right flank hopelessly turned, had shown Johnston that his position at Cassville was absolutely untenable. Here is Johnston's account:

" On reaching my tent, soon after dark, I found in it an invitation to meet the lieutenant generals at General Polk's quarters. General Hood was with him, but not General Hardee. The two officers, General Hood taking the lead, expressed the opinion very positively that neither of their corps would be able to hold its position next day, because, they said, a part of each was enfiladed by Federal artillery. The part of General Polk's corps referred to was that of which I had conversed with Brigadier General Shoup. On that account they urged me to abandon the ground immediately and cross the Etowah.

"A discussion of more than an hour followed, in which they very earnestly and decidedly expressed the opinion, or conviction rather, that when the Federal artillery opened upon them next day, it would render their positions untenable in an hour or two."

Hardee's note is of interest. He wrote:

"At Cassville, May 19th, about ten o'clock in the evening, in answer to a summons from General Johnston, I found him at General Polk's headquarters, in company with Generals Polk and Hood. He informed me that it was determined to retire across the Etowah. In reply to my exclamation of surprise, General Hood, anticipating him, answered: 'General Polk, if attacked, cannot hold his position three-quarters of an hour, and I cannot hold mine two hours.'"

The results of this remarkable council appear in Johnston's concise statement which follows: "Although the position was the best we had occupied, I yielded at last, in the belief that the confidence of the commanders of two or three corps of the army of their inability to resist the enemy would inevitably be communicated to their troops, and produce that inability.

"Lieutenant General Hardee, who arrived after this decision, remonstrated against it strongly, and was confident that his corps could hold its ground, although less favorably posted. The error was adhered to, however, and the position abandoned before daybreak."

In the fearful skirmishes which took place on

Battle of Cassville

May 19th in the rough woodland between Kingston and Cassville, Kingston served as a field hospital.

Small tents were erected for the wounded, and for the many others who fell sick.

It is gratifying to think these comrades had double care from the faithful hospital attendants and from the Christian Commission. The delegate of the Commission would sit by the bedside of a young man and act as amanuensis; so that a last message, too sacred for publication, often found its way to a sorrowing household beyond the scenes of war.

The second day after Johnston's departure from Cassville and Cartersville, Georgia (May 22, 1864), was Sunday. Sherman had his headquarters, for railway convenience and to be accessible to all his commanders, at the village of Kingston. General Corse was at the time his chief of staff. Sherman and he occupied a small cottage on the south side of the main street.

While Sherman sat at the window, apparently in a deep study, occasionally transferring his thoughts to paper, he was interrupted by the sudden and then the continued ringing of the church bell. Thinking that some fun-loving soldiers or some of the already enterprising " bummers " were practicing with the bell, perhaps with a view to his annoyance, he told Corse to send over a patrol and arrest the bell ringers. My friend, Rev. E. P. Smith, representing the Christian Commission, had gone to the church and prepared it for service. Not being able just then to get anyone to help him, he was obliged to climb up to ring the bell, the rope having disappeared. As he dropped down he caught the bottom of his trousers and slit them to his waist. Just then a corporal with a file of men opened the church door and said to him: "Fall in."

My friend said: "What for?"

The corporal answered: "To take you over there to General Sherman's headquarters."

Smith pleaded: "Can't go in this plight; take me where I can fix up."

Corporal answered: "Them's not the orders—fall in."

Corse, standing by the back door, received him and said:

"You were ringing that bell?"

"Yes, it is Sunday and I was ringing it for service."

Corse dismissed the guard and, as he stood in the doorway, he reported the case to Sherman, who stopped his work for an instant, looked up at Corse's face, and glanced over toward Mr. Smith as Corse said:

"It is Sunday and he was ringing the bell for service."

Sherman answered: "Sunday, Sunday! Didn't know it was Sunday; let him go."

That morning we had a church well filled with soldiers. I was present and enjoyed immensely the religious service conducted by my friend.

It was at my camp near Cassville that Sherman came to my aid in an unexpected way. It will be remembered how I had taken a radical stand with regard to strong drink, believing and insisting then, as I do now, that the poison of alcohol used as a drink is not only injurious to the mental and moral life of a soldier, but that, though it may be a spur in an emergency for an attack, it is always attended with so speedy

536

a reaction as to be detrimental to steady and persistent garrison or field work. Of course, I abstained from alcoholic drinks. This conduct naturally subjected me to constant remark by those who thought me extreme; and many were the criticisms promulgated at my expense.

A number of officers were having a chat in groups about my bivouac at Cassville on the morning of May 21st, when, it being about refreshment time, some officer proposed that the whole party go over to his tent, and have a drink all around.

General Thomas John Wood, one of my division commanders, eminent in war, undertook to rally me on my oddities and exclusiveness. He wound up by saying: "What's the use, Howard, of your being so singular? Come along and have a good time with the rest of us. Why not?"

Sherman interposed with some severity, saying: "Wood, let Howard alone! I want one officer who don't drink!"

There is a letter which I wrote from that Cassville camp, which, coming back to me, has in it some new items:

NEAR CASSVILLE, May 22d, 1864.
. . . I haven't written you for several days, and am not sure about this letter getting back, but will try and send it.

Charles (then Lieutenant, Colonel Charles H. Howard), Gilbreth (Lieutenant Gilbreth, aid-de-camp), Stinson (Mr. Blaine's nephew, captain and aid-de-camp), Frank (my secretary, Frank G. Gilman, of Boston), and myself are all well.

Instead of three days we have had some twelve or thirteen days' fighting. It is not always engaging our main lines, but heavy skirmishing. The Confederates have a rear guard of cavalry supported by infantry. They arrange barricades

537

of rails and logs along the line. When driven from one, another force has another barricade ready some half or three-quarters of a mile on. In this way they manage to check and hinder our march.

We have driven them across the Etowah, and are now resting and collecting supplies for further progress. You will possibly see accounts of our operations in the newspapers. We have had to charge or turn well-constructed breastworks, and at times the fighting has been severe. General Willich and Colonel (now General) Harker in our corps were wounded. We had quite a battle at Dalton, at Resaca, then at Adairsville, and lastly here, near Cassville.

A kind Providence has protected me and my staff in the midst of constant dangers. We have been fired upon by sharp-shooters, small arms and artillery. Two or three have had their horses shot, and I had one bullet through my coat, but none of us have received any harm.

We are preparing for a march, and if you don't get a letter you must not think it strange, for communication may be much interrupted. I long to get this work done that I may return to you all, if God is willing. I do feel as though my work was not yet done, but we ought always be ready. . . .

The country this side of Resaca is very beautiful. Large, luxuriant farms, magnificent trees. It is no wonder our enemies are not starving in such a country as this. This is a pleasing change of scenery from the mountains near Chattanooga, and really of great practical benefit to the horses and mules; plenty of grass to eat. The people have nearly all gone away. . . .

God bless and keep you. . . .

How much we owed to our transportation! That well-organized railway performed wonders.

Before our three days' rest at Cassville was over, the railway that our enemy had destroyed had been constructed as far as Sherman's headquarters at

538

Kingston, and not only supplies of all kinds were giving the men refreshment, but letters from home were flooding our camps; for the mail service was keeping abreast of that of the road builders.

Home news and home cheer gave our hearts new courage and energy for additional trial and enterprise.

The forward march cut us off from communication, which, as I mentioned in my letter, was to begin May 24th. It required twenty days' supplies. We were to veer to the southwest and endeavor to turn Johnston's left flank. We must impede ourselves as little as possible with wagons, so as to move with celerity and strike quick blows. In the three days of rest, there was not much real resting. It was a busy command throughout. We hadn't much luggage before the halt, but, as Wood said, " We razéed still more." We distributed the food and rations, reorganized some commands, selected garrisons for Cartersville and Rome, and, in brief, stripped ourselves of all surplusage, and reëquipped every department for crossing the Etowah—that small stream just ahead of Schofield's head of column near the Allatoona Bridge, and within sight of other portions of the army from Allatoona to Rome, thirty miles west. The Confederate commander had not been idle. As always, " Joe " Johnston had instinctively apprehended just what our Sherman was planning as Sherman sat by the window at Kingston, " drumming with his pencil upon the window sill and thinking."

The decision, impatiently made by Johnston after the council with Hood and Polk on the night of May 19th, to retire behind the Etowah River, though conceived in vexation, was followed by prompt action. His army, led from the Cassville line straight to the

Etowah, crossed that river in some haste near the railroad bridge.

After the crossing, and during the afternoon, the bridges, including the railroad structure, were disabled by fire.

On the night of the 20th Johnston had established his headquarters in citizen Moore's house, at which point Hardee also had his. This house was near the point where the railroad intersected the Allatoona wagon road, and about a mile and a half from Allatoona. The Confederate commanders remained there during May 21st and 22d.

Johnston, having passed the Etowah, disposed his army somewhat as follows: Facing northward, and occupying a rocky ridge south of that river, appeared his front line. On his right he placed the famous Wheeler, with his swift-footed cavalry in observation; on his left, General Jackson with his cavalry. The bulk of the Confederate army was to the rear, in and about Allatoona, concentrated, and ready for a sudden move.

On the 21st Johnston's extra supply trains were farther off, south of the Chattahoochee, while other wagon trains were collected nearer at hand, south of Allatoona, in the open country.

In addition to guarding the Etowah in his immediate front and his flanks, as we have hinted, Johnston placed an extended picket line along a tributary of the Etowah—Pumpkin Vine Creek. This positively indicates that as early as May 21st or 22d he at least suspected just the movement westward which Sherman was considering. Johnston was, indeed, as was usual with him, holding his entire army in observation, while Sherman was preparing to move to the westward, so as to at least turn Allatoona. The Etowah, in Johnston's front, it is true, concealed to some extent Sherman's movements, so that it was difficult for the Confederate commander to keep the national forces under the close observation which the situation from his standpoint required; therefore, Johnston was continually probing and feeling for the movements of his adversary. For example, on May 22d he ordered Wheeler to cross back with his cavalry five or six miles to his (Wheeler's) right, and to push on toward Cassville, with a view to gathering reliable information. There were so many contradictory stories! Wheeler managed somehow to get over the river, marched rapidly to Cassville, and here, on May 24th, seized a wagon train carelessly left behind, the last of Sherman's supply.

The important fact was that Wheeler brought back the information he was after. He reported that Sherman's army was in rapid march, and he showed to Johnston the direction it had taken. Wheeler's report that the Union forces were moving westward, as if to cross the Etowah at Kingston, had been anticipated by Confederate Jackson's cavalry; while Wheeler was marching toward Cassville, Jackson, with his cavalry, on the Confederate left, had discovered Sherman's march toward the bridges laid near Stilesboro, and had seen Union forces already crossing the river there. This news came promptly by signals the morning of the 23d. Surely Allatoona was to be turned, and not attacked in front as Johnston had greatly hoped.

On the receipt of these tidings, he grasped the entire situation. Swiftly and energetically he made his dispositions to meet Sherman's new moves. In fact, on the 23d, before Wheeler's return, he had ordered Hardee to march at once by New Hope Church to the road leading from Stilesboro through Dallas to Atlanta. Polk was directed to go to the same road by a route farther to the left, and Hood was to follow Hardee's march the day following.

By the 25th, Sherman's army, still in motion, was pushed southward toward New Hope and Dallas. McPherson's army, increased by Davis's division, coming from Rome, was well to the right, near Van Wert. From here Davis took an eastern country road and joined Thomas, who kept the main road as far as Burnt Hickory, passing through a strange land, a country desolate and uninhabited. It seemed like forests burned over, with here and 'there an opening. There were innumerable knolls of light soil, dotted with half-burned trees, almost without limbs, every shape and size.

The march from the Etowah was a sad and gloomy one, possibly ominous. At Burnt Hickory, Thomas sent Palmer with his and me with my corps off toward the right to catch somewhere the Van Wert and New Hope road, while Hooker went on straight toward the same destination by the main highway, using wood and farm roads as far as he could to help forward his divisions. Ed. McCook's cavalry was a little in advance of Hooker, well spread out.

Schofield, farther to the left, with his cavalry under Stoneman cared for the left flank, and moved southward more slowly.

Garrard, on the right, with his troops of cavalry, had pressed back the Confederate horse toward Dallas, and discovered the left of Johnston's new line; Garrard kept within easy reach of McPherson.

Battle of Cassville

It was a terrible country, as hard to penetrate as the Adirondacks, where Johnston chose his position. Hardee was put at Dallas, Hood at New Hope, and Polk between them, nearer to Hood than Hardee, causing some thin lines.

Yes, there was here great natural strength like that of Culp's Hill at Gettysburg and worse than any of the Antietam banks; and every hour made and increased the log barricades and earth embankments covered and concealed by abatis and slashings. Johnston's commanders were never better prepared for a defensive battle than on our steady approach in strong columns.

Personally, I would have been glad then to have known that rough, blind country and our enemy's position as well as we all do now.

The character of the country traversed, and the rapidity with which our army moved, gave strong indication of its excellent *morale* and of its physical strength. Abundant was its confidence in itself—a confidence born of its prowess in the bloody encounters of the campaign thus far.

The Confederates were also confident as they prepared for another stand, here in a dense forest, and there in broken ground, while they were deployed along the new front.

Johnston's army had had the same advantage of rest that we had, and from the fearless and obstinate stand made so soon after the depressing effects of the retrograde movement and our successes, it would seem as if its spirit was equal to any emergency.

Part of Hood's front was, by the time the Yankees came, even better prepared than the rest. We knew from past experience that now it did not take the

Yankee or Confederate very long to thoroughly cover himself by some sort of barricade or intrenchment. Notwithstanding all this, a few commands had little protection when the battle began, those especially who came out to meet us as far as the famous Pumpkin Vine Creek.

On the morning of the 25th Ed. McCook's cavalry, in front of Burnt Hickory, had ventured beyond that creek and captured a dispatch from Johnston to Jackson. This informed Sherman that some Confederate troops were still in motion toward Dallas. This news led Sherman to hold back his left for a short time, till the army of the Tennessee could come well forward on the right.

All the columns were thus making a partial wheel, so as to arrive substantially parallel with Pumpkin Vine Creek. Hooker kept advancing his three columns along or not far from the direct Dallas road. The two corps, Palmer's and mine, had made a considerable detour that morning, hoping to reach the Van Wert-Dallas road about three or four miles from Dallas. The skirmishing had begun. When Geary's division (Hooker's center) had come forward and was near Owen's Mills, he found the enemy's cavalry engaged in burning the bridge which crossed Pumpkin Vine Creek. Geary, with Hooker's escorting cavalry and infantry, drove the hostile cavalry off, extinguished the fire, and crossed his command. Hooker now began to believe that the enemy held his strongest force near New Hope Church, and so he ordered Geary to take the fork of the road leading that way.

Pressing on, on the top of a rising ground, Hooker first encountered the infantry of Hood. Here our men met a stubborn resistance. Geary had to

strengthen and greatly extend his line, and, as Geary
was apt to think, he believed that he was dealing with
a much larger force than that actually before him.
The combat that suddenly came on was sharp and
lasted half an hour. There were brave charges by
Geary's men, and fierce countercharges by the Confederates, which were repulsed by Candy's Union brigade, that had been deployed. Our men finally made
a steady advance till they stood upon another ridge
opposite that on which Hood had aligned his forces.
Geary had at last driven the advance back. Geary,
as was customary with us all, made hastily such shelter as he could for his troops, using logs for temporary cover, behind which he might with comparative
safety await the Confederates' further development.

As soon as Sherman heard the firing he hastened
to the front. He ordered Hooker to bring his two
remaining divisions, Williams's and Butterfield's,
promptly into position. He declared that an attack
by Hooker should be made at once. By this Sherman
undoubtedly wished to develop the force in his immediate front before darkness set in. The time of the
approach of the new forces is somewhat in question.
Thomas reported their arrival as 3 P.M., but Geary
about 5 P.M. Thomas probably referred to heads of
column and Geary to the complete arrival.

At any rate, the whole corps was assembled by the
latter hour. Hooker used it as at Resaca, by deploying it into heavy columns of brigades, and then moved
almost *en masse* with a narrow front to the attack.
It was a shock; a quick attack made through a wood,
greatly obstructed by a dense undergrowth. This
bothersome timber generally covered the slopes on
either side of the valley.

Hardly had Hooker's advance struck the obstructions when not only the iron hail but a *rainstorm* with terrific thunder broke upon the contending forces. The loud, crashing noise of the thunder did not, however, drown the rattle of musketry and roar of cannon. Through all the dreadful tempest the loud and ominous sounds of battle penetrated to the columns marching from the rear. They resounded even as far back as Burnt Hickory, and told of the phenomenal conflict raging in front. Soon after the thunder a most abundant deluge of rain followed, which continued falling all through that long night. From 5 P.M. until 6 the attempts to force Hood's line were several times made by Hooker's corps alone. By the latter hour one division of my Fourth corps, moving *au cannon*, was brought up to Hooker's support. The entire corps through rain and mud was coming forward as fast as it could to Hooker's left, and getting into position as soon as possible; the leading division (Newton's) arrived first, and the rest of the command, somewhat delayed by the mass of Hooker's wagons stretched along the roads, fetched in at last. All that evening and far into the night we assaulted Hood's works again and again; we tried amid the storm to dislodge his troops, but in vain. In the face of sixteen Confederate pieces of artillery using canister and grape, and the musketry of several thousand infantry at close range and delivered, much of it, from behind breastworks, it became simply impossible even to gain a foothold anywhere upon the enemy's barricades.

I was near the head of my column, and so came up to Hooker before six o'clock. At his request, before I saw General Thomas, I deployed one division, ac-

546

cording to Hooker's desire, near his left, and abreast of his troops. The firing from the enemy's cannon along the line and the constant discharges of the Confederate rifles wounded or killed some of Hooker's men and mine at every discharge. In spite of the danger, however, camp fires soon began to appear here and there as the darkness came on. These still more drew the enemy's artillery fire, and for some time increased the danger. Still, the chill of the night and the wet clothing called for fires. At last there was a lull in the battle, though not an entire cessation from cannon and rifle firing. Then you could see the torches borne by ambulance parties as they went hither and thither, picking up the wounded and bearing them to the rear. As soon as I could get my several commands in hand and arrange for the reliefs of working parties along our exposed front, I went back a short distance to the little church, which was used for a hospital. The scene in the grove there and in the church can never be forgotten. There were temporary operating tables with men stretched upon them; there were diligent medical officers, with their attendants and medical helpers, with coats off and sleeves rolled up, and hands and arms, clothes and faces sprinkled with blood. The lights outside and in were fitful and uncertain; smoky lights, for the most part, from torches of pine knots. It was a weird, horrid picture, and the very heavens seemed to be in sympathy with the apparent confusion. It was hard to distinguish between the crashing of the thunder, the sound of the cannon, and the bursting of shells. The rain never ceased to pour during the night. At one time, as I went out, I met General Schofield, who, in spite of a severe injury to his leg, caused by the stumbling of his horse against a tree, had come to offer Hooker and me his assistance. As I now look back upon the whole affair at New Hope Church, I wonder that we did not approach those well-chosen Confederate lines with more caution. But we did not know. We thought that the Confederates were not yet thoroughly prepared, and we hoped that by a tremendous onslaught we might gain a great advantage, shorten the battle, and so shorten the war.

I am glad that military knowledge now insists on thinner lines. Brigade line following brigade line produced awful results. There a single bullet would often kill or wound six men, on account of the depth of such a column of brigades; and who can tell the destruction of a single cannon shot or shell in bursting, whose fragments, fan shaped, went sweeping through every rank from front to rear!

To us military folk it is interesting to note the advantage of thin lines, when soldiers are well trained and well handled.

As must have been noticed in all these accounts of combats during the series of marches and battles, the skirmishers were more and more used as the campaign progressed. It was always, when taking the offensive, a wise thing to do, to increase the skirmish line enough to give the men confidence, and then push forward till a waiting enemy—one in defensive position—was sufficiently revealed to enable the commander to determine his next order. On the defensive, a skirmish line well out, and admirably located, would bother an approaching foe as much as a battle line, and at the same time lose but few lives. The breech-loading arms and magazine guns now make thin exposed lines an imperative necessity. Our double skirmish order has indeed become a veritable line of battle.

By vigorous skirmishing, putting batteries in place and into action and constant threats of advance, the Confederates were kept all the night, like ourselves, on the watch.

By morning not a few but many logs were piled up in barricades, and as much dirt as possible thrown beyond them. Neither of us had a " stomach " for attack or for battle at that time. Hood and Hooker were willing to wait.

CHAPTER XXXI

THAT was a stubborn fight at New Hope Church on May 25, 1864. Hooker's corps, as we have seen, supported by the greater part of my corps, endeavored to break Johnston's line near its center. Sherman had hoped to seize the railroad south of Allatoona Pass, toward Marietta, and hold it; but he found the works in his front too strong. His enemies had ample time during their resting days and in the night after Hooker's bold charges to make these lines next to impregnable. It therefore became necessary to adopt some other means of gaining the end in view. Johnston's forces extended nearly parallel to ours between four and five miles, from near Dallas on his left to the vicinity of Pickett's Mill on his right.

Sherman, after this last bloody battle, returned again to his tactics of moving by the flank; the next movement contemplated was to gain ground toward our left.

Thomas and Schofield, with the majority of their troops, were engaged in completing their deployments extending from McPherson, near Dallas, toward Johnston's right, and this unfolding brought us steadily nearer to the railroad at Ackworth. The marching of all moving columns had to be in rear of our front line, which was at all times in close contact with the enemy

550

—so close, in fact, that there was a continual skirmish fire kept up.

Johnston seemed to discern the nature of this new plan of ours as soon as it was undertaken. He firmly believed that Sherman was feeling for his right. He therefore withdrew Polk, who was located at his center, and marched him parallel to those of us who took up the movement, always keeping time and pace with our march to the left. Then began and continued for a considerable time a race of breastworks and intrenchments.

The race of trenches was well on by May 27th. In accordance with the plan of our leader, one division of my corps, Wood's, and one of the Fourteenth, R. W. Johnson's, were drawn back from the fighting line, and early on the morning of the 27th started on their leftward march. These two divisions constituted a detachment, and I was sent in command.

All day we plodded along pretty far back, but within sound of the skirmish firing of the front line. The march was over rough and poor roads, when we had any roads at all. The way at times was almost impassable, for the " mud forests " closed us in on either side, and the underbrush shut off all distant objects. On we marched till 4.30 in the afternoon, when we reached the vicinity of Pickett's Mill.

Our march, necessarily somewhat circuitous, had during the day been often delayed for the purpose of reconnoitering. Wood would send his advance to skirmish up quietly toward the supposed Confederate lines, and when near enough, officers with their field glasses would make as close observations as the nature of the thickets or more open fields would permit.

At this time, nearly an hour before the final halt

551

and the direct preparation for a charge, I was standing in the edge of a wood, and with my glass following along the lines of Johnston, to see where the batteries were located and to ascertain if we had reached his limits. My aid, Captain Harry M. Stinson, stepped boldly into the opening. He had a new field glass, and here was an excellent opportunity to try it. I had warned him and the other officers of my staff against the danger of exposure, for we were not more than 700 yards from the hostile intrenchments.

Stinson had hardly raised his glass to his forehead when a bullet struck him. He fell to the ground upon his face, and as I turned toward him I saw that there was a bullet hole through the back of his coat. The missile had penetrated his lungs and made its way entirely through his body. I thought at first that my brave young friend was dead, and intense grief seized my heart, for Harry was much beloved.

After a few minutes, however, by means of some stimulant, he revived and recovered consciousness. He was taken back to camp, and soon sent to Cleveland, Tenn., where good air and good nursing brought him so near to recovery that he joined me again during this campaign at Jonesboro. "I think Harry Stinson was the most unselfish man I ever saw," was the remark of another of my aids, Captain J. A. Sladen.

Wood's division was at last drawn out of the marching column and formed in lines of brigades facing the enemy's works, one behind the other; while R. W. Johnson's division passed beyond Wood's and came up near his left for support. This was far beyond Schofield's left. Wood touched a large clearing, turned to the southeast, and moved forward,

552

keeping in the edge of the clearing, toward what would be the natural extension of Johnston's lines.

Pushing quickly through the undergrowth, Wood rectified his formation. Coming to me about 5.30 P.M., he said:

" Are the orders still to attack? "

Fully believing, from a careful study of the whole position, that we had at last reached the end of Johnston's troops, I answered:

" Attack! "

The order was promptly obeyed. The men sprang forward and made charges and a vigorous assault.

I found Johnston's front covered by strong intrenchments. A drawing back of the trenches like a traverse had deceived us. Johnston had forestalled us, and was on hand fully prepared. In the first desperate charge, Hazen's brigade was in front. R. W. Johnson's division was in echelon with Wood's, somewhat to its left. Scribner's brigade was in that front. The plan had been, though not carried out, that McLean's brigade of Schofield's command, which was the intended support on our right, should show itself clearly on open ground, attract the attention of the enemy to that part of the line, while Wood and Johnson moved upon what was supposed to be the extreme right of the Confederates' position.

In this conflict Wood, the division commander, during this gloomy day met with a loss similar to mine. An officer, Major J. B. Hampson, One Hundred and Sixty-fourth Ohio, aid to General Wood, to whom he was personally greatly attached, was struck in his left shoulder by a musket ball, which broke the spine and ended his life in a few hours. He was a general favorite, and his death produced unfeigned sadness among his comrades.

Wood had always seemed to me masterful of himself and others who came in contact with him; he had a large experience in such battles as Stone River and Chickamauga. I was therefore unprepared to see him on this occasion exhibit stronger feeling than any of us. For a few minutes, sitting beside his dying friend, he was completely overcome. It has appeared to me at times that the horrors of the battlefield had hardened men; but these cases of exceptional affection served to confirm the expression: "The bravest are the tenderest!"

When the advance was made, our men pushed rapidly forward, driving the opposing skirmishers before them. As Hazen pressed on, the left of his brigade still seemed to overlap his enemy's right, and everything appeared to indicate that our tedious march was to conduct us to a great success. But, while Hazen and the remainder of Wood's division were gaining ground, Johnson's division, which was at Hazen's left, was going on toward Pickett's Mill. This was situated on a branch of the Pumpkin Vine Creek. Here the leading brigade received quite a severe fire against its left flank, and was compelled to face in the new direction, and so stopped the whole division from moving up abreast of Hazen. This halting and change left Wood's division completely uncovered, and, worse still, Wood was now brought between a front and flank fire. It did not take long to discover that what we had supposed was the end of the Confederate intrenched line was simply a sharp angle of it. The breastworks where Hazen's devoted men first struck them were only trending to the Confederate rear. Wood's men were badly repulsed; he had in a few minutes over 800 killed.

While this attack was going on, Newton's and Stanley's divisions of my corps near New Hope Church were attempting to divert attention by a strong demonstration, but the Confederates there behind their barricades did not heed such distant demonstrations. The whole engagement, an hour long, was terrible. Our men in this assault showed phenomenal courage, and while we were not successful in our attempt to turn the enemy's left, which, as a matter of fact, we had not yet found, nevertheless considerable new space was gained, and what we held was of great importance. As soon as Wood's division had started, the enemy shelled our position. A shell after striking the ground to my left threw the fragments in different directions. One of these struck my left foot as I was walking forward. It cut through the sole of my boot and through the up-leather and badly bruised me. My foot was evidently lifted in walking—but the boot sole was very thick and somewhat protruded and so saved me from a severer wound. For the instant I believed I had lost my leg, and was glad, indeed, to find myself mistaken. There, wounded, I sat among the maimed till after midnight; meanwhile I was reorganizing broken lines and building forts and lines of obstruction.

During the war a few sad scenes impressed me more than any others. One was the field after the battle of Gettysburg. A second scene was the battlefield of Antietam. But these things, not happy to relate, were matched at Pickett's Mill. That opening in the forest, faint fires here and there revealing men wounded, armless, legless, or eyeless; some with heads bound up with cotton strips, some standing and walking nervously around, some sitting with bended forms, and some prone upon the earth—who can picture it? A few men, in despair, had resorted to drink for relief. The sad sounds from those in pain were mingled with the oaths of the drunken and the more heartless.

I could not leave the place, for Colonel C. H. Howard and Captain Gilbreth, aids, and other officers were coming and going to carry out necessary measures to rectify our lines and to be ready for a counter attack of the Confederates, almost sure to be made at dawn.

So, for once, painfully hurt myself, I remained there from 8 P.M. to participate in that distress till about one o'clock the next morning. That night will always be a sort of nightmare to me. I think no perdition here or hereafter can be worse.

Is it not an argument in favor of every possible arbitration? After our tedious night's work, my fortifying in the enemy's front had rendered an attack at daylight by Johnston useless.

The character of the country gave us more openings in the forests on all approaches to Dallas than at New Hope or Pickett's Mill. Still, the greater part of the Confederate front was strung along threading a rugged forest country, with excellent positions for artillery, and rough ridges which were easily fortified and hard to take.

Hardee, at Dallas, had in his vicinity a " grand military position," which it would do a West Pointer good to survey—well chosen, well manned by the best of troops thoroughly seasoned in war.

McPherson, opposite Hardee, had just now not more

than 20,000 men, for Blair's troops, marching at the time from the Far West, had not yet joined him. But Davis's division of the Fourteenth Corps (about 5,000 men) was sent back by Sherman to strengthen McPherson's command, because McPherson was so widely separated from the rest of us.

From Van Wert, McPherson had hastened on, with Dodge's corps in the lead. Dodge never said much in advance of what he proposed to do, but he was a most vigorous commander and inspired the men who served under him with his own energy. Well protected by skirmishers, he now approached the Pumpkin Vine Creek, and encountered the enemy's skirmishers and advance guards and drove them steadily back.

During May 25th, while Thomas was assailing Hood at New Hope Church, Jeff. C. Davis, prompt, systematic, and active, extended and thoroughly protected Dodge's left at Dallas. Meanwhile, John A. Logan, commanding the Fifteenth Corps, had taken on the inspiration of fighting—like a horse just ready for battle—and was veering off to the right of Dodge.

On Logan's right, clearing the way, and, like the cavalry opposite, securing all approaches and occupying as much attention as possible, was Garrard's cavalry command.

Logan was intensely active on the approach of battle. His habitual conservatism in council was changed into brightness, accompanied with energetic and persistent activity.

Dodge, as he left him, was moving along in a column, and the cavalry, assisted by Logan's artillery, were noisily driving in the enemy's light troops far off to the right beyond the crossroads at Dallas.

Logan's and Dodge's advance, substantially two

heavy skirmish lines acting conjointly, with some artillery protected by cavalry, drove everything before them for about two miles.

While the battle of Pickett's Mill was fiercely going on, both Logan and Bate kept up between them artillery firing and skirmishing. In the afternoon of that day a stronger demonstration was made by the Confederate General Bate. This demonstration was promptly checked by Dodge crossing Pumpkin Vine Creek, and pushing forward until he had cleared his entire front up to Hardee's works. From that time on there was no peace between those opposing lines, for skirmishers and artillery were busy and noisy all the time on both sides.

In his general movement to the left, Sherman had ordered McPherson to relieve Davis and send him back to Thomas, and McPherson was preparing to do so and to close his army in to the left, when he sent the following dispatch to Sherman:

"We have forced the enemy back to his breastworks throughout nearly the whole extent of his lines, and find him occupying a strong position, extending apparently from the North Marietta or New Hope Church road to across the Villa Rica road; our lines are up within close musket range in many places, and the enemy appears to be massing on our right."

It will thus be seen that McPherson was loyally preparing to carry out his instructions, and was, indeed, ready to do so with his usual skill and promptness, when Hardee's dispositions warned him of his danger in uncovering his flank and of making the movement in the face of an active and energetic enemy. Hardee was pressing his lines constantly, probably in anticipation of just such a movement.

Battle of Pickett's Mill

The battle began at 3.30 P.M. The attacking column of the Confederates had been able to form out of sight in the woods for the most part; those in front of Oosterhaus's division (of Logan) gathered under shelter of a deep ravine, and then rushed *en masse* to within fifty yards of his line, where they were mowed down by the hundred.

The Sixteenth Corps (Dodge's) had also a considerable part in this battle. Walker's Confederate division had found its way at first, with the design of a demonstration only, quite up to the well-prepared barricades of Dodge.

This assault, though most desperate and determined, was promptly and gallantly met and repulsed.

The other Confederate division (Cheatham's) opposite Davis simply strengthened its skirmish line and pushed it forward briskly and persistently in front of Davis's gallant men, resulting, of course, in some losses on both sides. These vigorous efforts of Walker and Cheatham had the effect, as Hardee intended, namely, to keep Dodge and Davis in place and prevent them from reënforcing Logan.

Within an hour and a half the attack upon the whole right had proven a costly failure to the enemy, and his lines had been hurriedly withdrawn to the earthworks from whence they had sallied forth. Hardee in this combat left many of his wounded and slain to us to care for.

It will be noticed that my battle of May 27th at Pickett's Mill was a determined assault of one division supported by another against Johnston's right flank, and that the battle of Dallas, whether by General Johnston's orders or not, was a correspondingly heavy assault of Bate's and part of Walker's divisions, supported by the rest of Walker's and the whole of Cheatham's, against Sherman's right flank. There was a decided repulse in each case. The scales were thus evenly balanced.

After the failure of Hardee on the afternoon of May 28th, he withdrew within his own intrenchments, and, besides the skirmish firing which was almost incessant during those days, no other regular attack for some time was made.

On the 30th, shortly before midnight, Hardee made a moderate demonstration against our lines, possibly in the belief that we were evacuating, but finding the men in their places and on the alert, he desisted.

Thus matters remained until June 1st, when Sherman's characteristic movement from right to left began again in good earnest, and McPherson left the Dallas line and marched over beyond us all to relieve and support the troops which were lying between New Hope Church and Pickett's Mill. The last three battles—New Hope, Pickett's Mill, and Dallas—were at best but a wearisome waste of life and strength, blows given and taken in the dark without visible result.

Steadily the movement of the Union army toward the left, for the purpose of reaching the railroad, had been continued, and, at last, on June 1, 1864, the diligent McPherson fully relieved Hooker's corps and my own remaining divisions, and spread his men so as to guard all that part of the line lately occupied by Hooker, Schofield, and myself. In this he was still assisted by Jeff. C. Davis's division. Thomas and Schofield were then free for the leftward operation.

Schofield with his three divisions of the Twenty-third Corps promptly marched away eastward; Hooker followed and supported him as far as the " Burnt Hickory Church," at the point where the Allatoona wagon road crosses that from Burnt Hickory to Marietta.

Schofield now promptly deployed his line and pushed southward toward Marietta, his left *en route* touching the Marietta wagon road. Every foot of his way was contested by skirmishing Confederates, but now, slowly and steadily, without general battle, the enemy was forced back to a partially new intrenched position, south of Allatoona Creek, back as far as the forks of the Dallas-Ackworth road. Here, charging across the creek in a terrific thunderstorm, Schofield's men forced their way close up to the Confederate works. They were as near to them as 250 yards, tenaciously holding the ground gained and actively intrenching. Meanwhile, Stoneman, beyond Schofield, with his cavalry had already seized the village of Allatoona, near the pass, getting there June 1st, where, taking a strong position, the work of repairing the railroad northward and southward began, and progressed with little or no opposition.

At the time Schofield and Hooker were steadily advancing, Thomas was also moving the rest of us to the left from the vicinity of Pickett's Mill, Thomas being on the lead himself with Baird's division. Thomas's army in this effort gained ground eastward about three miles.

Sherman's forces were then in position by June 3d to catch in flank the Confederate line of intrenchments, which still were manned, and extended from Pickett's Mill first due east and then almost north.

When on that date Johnston learned of the extension of Schofield's and Hooker's commands, he saw that his old position, that of New Hope, was no longer tenable. Now, leaving New Hope, he began to move back with remarkable quickness to the new line partially prepared by his engineers. This line, about ten miles long, ran, in general, from southwest to northeast, and was doubtless intended only for a temporary resort.

At last, McPherson, still going toward the east, reached and followed the Ackworth Railroad, and then moved out and went beyond us all near to Bush Mountain.

Thomas, after another leftward effort, was next in place to McPherson, near to and advancing upon Pine Top, while Schofield remained nearer the angle at Gilgal Church. Our line, like that of the Confederates', was about ten miles long, and conformed to all the irregularities of Johnston's intrenchments. The Georgia mud was deep, the water stood in pools, and it was hard to get fires to cook our food and dry spots sufficiently large upon which to spread a tent fly or soldier's blanket.

A young man from Boston who joined me, Mr. Frank Gilman, and who became my private secretary, though well and strong when he arrived, and full of patriotic fervor, with an earnest desire to remain, could not bear the wear and tear of our mud bivouac here near Big Shanty. He lost his appetite and little by little his flesh; then, being attacked by chills and fever, was obliged to seek the hospital, and, finally, to save his life, he returned to his home. But the most of the soldiers were now veterans, and so inured to hardships that the mud and water seemed hardly to affect them at all; they thought the soft places around the camp fires preferable for beds to the rough rocks which they had had a few days before.

Battle of Pickett's Mill

On June 14th, Sherman, after reconnoitering the lines of the enemy as well as he could in rough ground and forest, with a view to finding a weak place through which to force a column, came to my temporary station near Pine Top. He noticed that several of us had been for some time watching in plain sight some Confederate intrenchments and a group of Confederate gentlemen about 600 yards from our position, and some evidently observing us with their good-sized field glasses. Sherman said to me: "How saucy they are!" He told me to make them keep behind cover, and one of my batteries was immediately ordered to fire three volleys on the group. This would have been done by me, except that Thomas had instructed me to use artillery ammunition only when absolutely necessary.

It would appear from the Confederate accounts that Johnston had ridden from Marietta with Hardee and Polk till he reached Pine Mountain (Pine Top). Quite a number of persons had gathered around them as they were surveying us and our lines. Johnston first noticed the men of my batteries preparing to fire, and cautioned his companions and the soldiers near him to scatter. They for the most part did so, and he himself hurried under cover. But Polk, who was quite stout and very dignified, walked slowly, probably because he did not wish the men to see him showing too much anxiety on account of the peril. While leisurely walking, he was struck in the breast by a fragment of an exploded shell, and was instantly killed.

We were apprised of Polk's death by our vigilant and skillful signal officers, who, having gained the key to the Confederate signals, could just read their messages to each other: " Why don't you send me an ambulance for General Polk's body?" was the one from Pine Top. In this way the story that Sherman himself had fired the gun that killed Polk, which was circulated for a time with much persistency, was explained.

Nobody on the Union side knew who constituted the group. The distance was too great to distinguish whether the irregular company, at which the volleys were fired, was composed of officers or soldiers.

What Sherman and I noticed and remarked upon more than any gathering of men, were the little tents which were pitched in plain sight on our side of the hill-crest. It seemed to us unusually defiant. After our cannon firing the hostile tents disappeared.

On June 15th, Thomas, of whose command my corps and Hooker's formed a part, was near Pine Top. Hooker's men had carried some Confederate works after a struggle, accompanied by rifle firing and cannonading. These works, some of them detached, connected Johnston's principal line from Lost Mountain with Pine Top.

Schofield, about the same time, drove a line of skirmishers away from a small bare hill near Allatoona Creek, placed his artillery upon it, and thence worked a cross fire into the enemy's intrenchments, driving Johnston's men, thus newly exposed in flank, back to near Gilgal Church. We were all along so close to our enemy that the constant skirmish fire of the New Hope line was here repeated. In the meantime, Johnston, continuing his inimitable defensive and delaying tactics, had prepared another new line along Mud Creek. This line followed the east bank of this creek, and was extended so much as to cross the direct wagon road between New Hope and

Marietta. It was the same line that ran from Lost Mountain.

Here Hardee, who had now retired to the new works, on the night of the 16th posted his batteries. The position covered the open ground toward us on the other side of the creek for a mile, and through this open ground the road coursed along, running between some steep hills that shaped the valley. There stood near by one bare hill, almost as high as the bluff where the Confederate batteries were posted, apparently unoccupied or weakly held. This was the position of Hardee on the morning of June 17th. It was formed by a dropping back of Hardee's men after being relieved from their place held the previous day. They had fallen back some three miles to cross "Muddy Run." Our observation of what was going on was so close that no time was lost in following up Hardee's backward movement. Thomas and Schofield, now in the right wing of our army, early in the morning of the 17th went straight forward, skirmishing with Jackson's cavalry and driving it before them, until they reached the Marietta Crossroads. Cox (of Schofield's), with his division, was feeling forward for the new right flank of Hardee.

Soon the valley of Mud Creek was reached, and the Confederate batteries on the bluff were exposed to full view. Schofield's men made a rapid rush across the open ground to the shelter of the "bare hill" above referred to; there they lay for a time under its protection. They were well formed in two lines— while Cockerell's battery and another from Hooker's for over an hour were storming the batteries of the enemy and gradually advancing their guns.

Here it was that Cockerell took advantage of the

565

bare hilltop as a natural breastwork. Unlimbering
out of sight, he opened his fire, with only the muzzles
of the guns exposed. His keen perception of this advantage saved his men, while the other battery, exposing itself fully on the crest, lost heavily.

The guns opposite Cockerell were silenced; then
the deployment of our infantry was continued. My
own corps (the Fourth) as well as the Twentieth
(Hooker's) were occupied during this forward swing.
Having left their Pine Top lines early in the morning
of the 17th, they marched at first substantially abreast.
Hooker, having the right, sped over the abandoned
intrenchments of the enemy, and turning gradually toward the southeast, so as to face Hardee's refused
lines, was coming upon the Confederates, who were
already in place, as we have seen, behind Mud Creek,
and strongly posted. I did the same on Hooker's
left flank.

Palmer's corps (the Fourteenth) came up also on
my left as soon as there was room. Thus Thomas
with the Third Corps worked forward with his left
touching the Ackworth Railroad, and soon made all
proper connections with McPherson, who was advancing on the other side of the same railway.

Part of my corps (General C. G. Harker's brigade), at this time under the cover of a heavy artillery
fire instituted by the division commander, charged
a portion of Hardee's salient angle with great vigor,
effected a lodgment in part of it, where the roads gave
him some protection, and then carried and held several rods of these works, capturing the defenders.

This was one of the few cases in which intrenchments, strongly constructed and well manned were
during the war, carried by direct front assaults.

Battle of Pickett's Mill

I first remarked the neatness of Harker's brigade, even during our rough field duty. At inspections and musters his men had on white gloves, and excelled the lauded Eastern troops in the completeness and good order of their equipments. The unusual pains taken by him and his brigade to appear clean and properly attired and well equipped did not, as we observed, detract from its energy and success in action.

In the afternoon Ed. McCook's cavalry followed up this success by getting around the left flank of Hardee, and pursued his cavalry down along the Dallas-Marietta wagon road and across Mud Creek. McCook in his venturesome sallies succeeded in getting within five or six miles of Marietta. He captured two hospitals with five commissioned officers and thirty-five men, also several attendants and nurses.

While securing these partial successes I saw, near my right, the most remarkable feat performed by any troops during the campaign. Baird's division (Palmer's corps), in a comparatively open field, put forth a heavy skirmish line, which continued such a rapid fire of rifles as to keep down a corresponding well-defended Confederate line of men, while the picks and shovels behind Baird's skirmishers fairly flew, till a good set of works was made but 300 or 400 yards distant from the enemy's and parallel to it.

After the action at Mud Creek, above described, with the forcing back of Hardee's flank, the situation was dangerous for Johnston. He, however, had fortified, with his usual foresight, another new defensive position nearer to Marietta, and work was going on in that quarter while the battle of the 17th was raging. Colonel Prestman, Johnston's military chief of engineers, had traced the proposed intrenchments, which were destined for the last stand of the Confederates before the abandonment of Marietta; it was their last strong defense north of the Chattahoochee.

Meanwhile, early on June 18th our batteries were put under cover on the hills in front of Hardee's salient angle. This angle was in front of Palmer's and my corps, so that our guns, which we had located the preceding day, could play with an enfilading fire upon the Confederate works. After some cannonading, seeing the evident intention of a further movement to the rear, I thrust Newton's and Wood's divisions into action early in the day; charging with great vigor, they captured the works in their front, taking about 100 prisoners.

Confederate efforts by countercharges and battery firing were made to delay our advance, but all attempts were frustrated and the enemy each time repulsed. The brigade of the enterprising Harker already held the intrenchments which he had captured, and seeing the great advantage of securing them, I hurried in the whole of Newton's division.

The situation then was such that Johnston could no longer delay his retrograde movement.

Just before Johnston left Muddy Creek, Sherman declared: "His" (Johnston's) "left was his weak point so long as he acted on the 'defensive'; whereas, had he designed to contract the extent of his line for the purpose of getting in a reserve force with which to strike 'offensively' from his right, he would have done a wise act, and I" (Sherman) "was compelled to presume that such was his object."

On the afternoon of the 20th, Kirby's brigade of Stanley's division was holding "Bald Knob," a prominent knoll in our front. The Confederates, using artillery and plenty of riflemen, suddenly, just about sundown, made a spring for that knoll. Kirby's men were taken by surprise and were driven back with loss. The enemy quickly fortified the position and thus had a break in Sherman's line, where the enemy the next morning could follow up this advantage and begin an offensive movement for which we were not prepared. I was much annoyed, and as soon as Thomas and Sherman heard of the break they were also worried. I telegraphed Thomas that I would recover that " Bald Knob " on the morrow without fail. I ordered General Wood on the right of the Knob to have his left brigade (Nodine's) ready under arms before sunrise, and Stanley to have Kirby's brigade there in front and to the left of the Knob also under arms and prepared to make an assault. One of Wood's artillery officers spent the night in putting in place four cannon and covering them by a strong field work, just in the edge of heavy timber near his left and well to the front, whence he could shell the enemy now intrenched on the Knob. Very early, with a couple of staff officers, my faithful orderly, McDonald, and private secretary, J. A. Sladen, Thirty-third Massachusetts (afterwards my aid-de-camp), I rode to the four-gun battery; leaving my comrades I took a stand on the improvised fort where I could see and direct every move. A Confederate battery shelled us fearfully and we replied with vigor. My situation was so perilous that my officers entreated me to leave it and get a safer place. But in this particular action I would not, for I wanted to be with my men in the action when it came on. When Kirby's skirmishers were well out, and Nodine's also, and our battery very active filling the air over the Knob with bursting shells, I saw an officer standing behind Nodine's line not far from me. I mistook him for Colonel Nodine; I called him to me, and as soon as he was near enough to hear my voice amid the roar and rattle of the conflict, I said: " Colonel, can't you now rush your men forward and seize that Bald Knob? "

He answered: " Yes, sir, I can."

I then said: " Go ahead!"

He sounded the advance and all the men of the Fifteenth Ohio Infantry sprang forward, and, at a run, within fifteen minutes had crowned the knoll. It was Colonel Frank Askew, and he had done with 200 men what I had intended Nodine tō do with his entire brigade. Leaving orders for Nodine and Kirby to hurry up their brigades, I mounted and, followed by McDonald and Sladen, galloped to the front and stayed there with the gallant Fifteenth Ohio men till the reënforcements with shovels and picks had joined them. The suddenness of our charge and the quickness of our riflemen cleared the " Bald Knob " and restored the continuity of Sherman's front.

The concentration of Johnston's forces compelled us at this time to be on the lookout for just such offensive movements.

Before, however, bringing our troops forward into immediate contact with the Kenesaw barricades and abatis, it is necessary to give an account of an affair which cost many lives; only a drawn battle was fought, but it was fraught with consequences which seriously affected the remainder of the campaign. The affair is usually denominated " Kolb's " or " Culp's Farm," and took place June 22, 1864.

CHAPTER XXXII

THE weather continued stormy, and it was not until June 22, 1864, that any positive advance could be made. On that date, as he often did, Sherman rode from end to end of our line, in order that he might thoroughly understand the position of his army.

He ordered Thomas to advance his right corps, which was Hooker's; and he instructed Schofield by letter to keep his whole army as a strong right flank in close support of Hooker's deployed line. It will be remembered that Schofield's Twenty-third Corps at this time constituted Sherman's extreme right.

Hooker came next leftward, and then my corps. Hooker, in accordance with his orders, pressed forward his troops in an easterly direction, touching on my right.

There was heavy skirmish firing along the whole front. As Hooker went forward he first drove in the enemy's cavalry. The movement was necessarily slow and bothersome; and at 2.30 P.M. the contest became very hot. The enemy took a new stand near Manning's Mill about 5 P.M. The Confederate advance was made boldly in force.

During the progress of this engagement, which became an assault upon Hooker's right flank, he called upon me for some help, asking me to relieve his left

571

division (Butterfield's), so that it might be sent off for a reënforcement to his right. This request I complied with at once, using every regiment of mine not then in line. These replacing troops were five regiments of Colonel Grose's brigade.

In this manner Hooker was given the whole of Butterfield's division for a reserve, or for resting any troops that had been long engaged; so his left flank was thoroughly secured.

Just as soon as the Union troops all along these lines had recovered from the first shock of the battle and re-formed wherever broken, so as to restore the unity of their defense, all hands became confident. In those places where the small breaks had occurred, several attempts were made by Hood to reanimate his men and push on, but all in vain. This was called the battle of Kolb's Farm. In this battle, at one time the firing, on a part of my corps front, was rapid. I rode to a high plateau where I could see considerable of the ground where the contest was sharpest. I had sent my staff away with important messages, and had with me only my orderly, McDonald, and my secretary, Sladen. We three were on our horses, anxiously watching the results of the Confederate attacks, my horse being a few yards ahead of the others. Suddenly McDonald rode up to my side and said: " General, I am wounded."

" Where, McDonald? "

" In my left foot, sir, right through the instep."

He was very pale and evidently suffering intensely. He looked me in the face, and in a low voice said: " General Howard, I shall die from this wound! "

" Oh, no, McDonald, you will not die! A wound like that through the foot is very painful, but not fatal. You go back to the field hospital, and when this battle is over I will visit you there."

After he began to ride back from me, he turned his horse about, and, with tears bedimming his eyes, he looked in my face again and said: " Oh, general, I am so glad I was wounded and not you!"

When, near sunset, I went to the field hospital, I learned that McDonald had been sent back with other wounded to the general hospital on the top of Lookout Mountain. And he did die from that severe wound and was buried among " the unknown."

Some very peculiar controversies, in which Sherman, Thomas, Schofield, and Hooker were involved, grew out of this battle.

During the battle, Hooker was asked by Sherman from a signal station: " How are you getting along? Near what house are you?"

He replied as follows: "*Kolb's House,* 5.20 P.M. We have repulsed two heavy attacks and feel confident, our only apprehension being from our extreme right. Three entire corps are in front of us."

This latter dispatch was not received by Sherman until after the battle, about 9.20 P.M. He then wrote to Thomas, who was Hooker's army commander. After citing to Thomas two dispatches, he telegraphed as follows:

I was at the Wallace House at 5.30 and the Kolb House was within two miles, and though I heard some cannonading I had no idea of his being attacked; and General Hooker must be mistaken about three entire corps being in his front. Johnston's army has only three corps, and I know there was a very respectable force along McPherson's front, so much so that his generals thought the enemy was massing against them. I know there was some force in front of Palmer and Howard, for

I was there. Still, it is very natural the enemy should meet Hooker at that point in force, and I gave Schofield orders this morning to conduct his column from Nose's Creek, on the Powder Springs road, toward Marietta and support Hooker's right flank, sending his cavalry down the Powder Springs road toward Sweet Water and leaving some infantry from his rear to guard the forks. . . .

It was natural for Hooker to make reply, for Sherman had asked questions of him. And, naturally, at such a time there was some excitement at Hooker's headquarters. As soon as Sherman received this disturbing message directly from Hooker, he first answered thus:

Dispatch received. Schofield was ordered this morning to be on the Powder Springs and Marietta road, in close support of your right. Is not this the case? There cannot be three corps in your front; Johnston has but three corps, and I know from full inspection that a full proportion is now, and has been all day, on his right and center.

Sherman also sent for his adjutant general, Captain Dayton, and made inquiry as to whether or not those most important orders had been sent to Schofield and received by him. Dayton immediately brought him the envelope which had on it the receipt of Sherman's instructions, signed by Schofield himself.

After that assurance, Sherman was more confident than ever that the Army of the Ohio had been all the time in place, and close up to Hooker's right flank.

When Sherman had passed from his left to his right, he had found evidence to satisfy him that Confederate Loring held all the long breastworks of the Confederate right opposite McPherson; Hardee held the center and much of the left opposite Thomas's three corps, which were in line from left to right, viz., Palmer's, Howard's, and Hooker's. Hood had simply passed partially beyond Hardee's left and come up to make his reconnoissance and attack, so that Hooker's men encountered only a part of Hood's and a part of Hardee's commands.

Schofield breasted the remainder of Hood's divisions and the cavalry of Wheeler, which supported Hood's moving left flank. In view of these plain facts Sherman was incensed that Hooker should have made such a fulsome report, and some words of Thomas increased his vexation—words that we find in a letter written by Thomas to Sherman himself, about ten o'clock the same night, for example:

I sent you a dispatch after my return to my headquarters this morning that Hooker reported he had the whole rebel army in his front. I thought at the time he was stampeded, but in view of the probability that the enemy might believe that we intended to make the real attack on our right, and would oppose us with as much of his force as he could spare, I ordered one division of Howard's to be relieved by Palmer and placed in reserve behind Hooker.

Hooker's position is a very strong one, and before I left him he certainly had his troops as well together as Howard has had for the last three days, and Howard has repulsed every attack the enemy has made on him in very handsome style. . . . The enemy cannot possibly send an overwhelming force against Hooker without exposing his weakness to McPherson.

Taking these things into account, Sherman took occasion the next day after the battle (June 23d) to ride down to Kolb's Farm, fully determined in his own sharp way to call Hooker to an account for his exaggerations. Sherman's determination to do so was increased when he found Hooker had used during the combat but two of his own divisions, for Butter-field's, kept back in reserve, had not been engaged at all during the day. Again, he saw, as before reported, one of Schofield's divisions properly placed abreast of Hooker's right, constituting what Sherman denominated a strong right flank.

Just after this personal reconnoissance, with its results in his mind, Sherman met both Schofield and Hooker near there on the field of battle. At once Sherman showed Hooker's dispatch to Schofield. Sherman said: " Schofield was very angry, and pretty sharp words passed between them," i. e., Schofield and Hooker. Schofield insisted that he had not only formed a strong right flank, as ordered, but that in the primary engagement the head of his column, part of Haskell's division, had been in advance of Hooker's corps, and were entitled to that credit. He affirmed, also, that dead men from his army were yet lying up there on the ground to show where his lines had been.

Hooker, thus called to account, made answer, apologetically, that he did not know this when he sent the dispatch. But Sherman, considering that the original statement of Hooker had reflected to his hurt upon an army commander without cause, and that Hooker's exaggeration had led Thomas to weaken other portions of his line—something that might have led to disaster—and that the dispatch came near causing him to do the same as Thomas, administered in his own blunt manner a caustic reprimand.

Sherman, as I think, was unaware of his own severity. He justified himself in this phrase: " I reproved him more gently than the occasion warranted." The result of this reproof was that from that date to

July 27th following, Hooker felt aggrieved. On that day he was relieved, at his own request, by General A. S. Williams.

This battle of Kolb's Farm was wholly on the Kenesaw line extended southward. Sherman, on account of guerrilla and cavalry attacks far in his rear, upon his own line of railroad, was greatly distressed concerning his communications. They were not secure enough, he declared, to permit him to break away from his base of supplies.

The Kenesaw Mountain—sometimes called the Kenesaws, probably on account of an apparent cross break in the range giving apparently two mountains —is the highest elevation in Georgia, west of the Chattahoochee. It is the natural watershed, and was in 1864, upon its sides, mostly covered with trees. From its crest Johnston and his officers could see our movements, which were believed to be hidden; they have recorded accounts of them in wonderful detail. The handsome village of Marietta, known to Sherman in his youth, lying eastward between the mountain and the river, could be plainly seen. Johnston could not have found a stronger defensive position for his great army.

Prior to the battle of Kolb's Farm the entire Confederate army had taken substantially its new line; the Confederate right, which abutted against Brush Mountain on the north, took in the Kenesaw; the line passing down the southern slope of that mountain, continued on to the neighborhood of Olley's Creek. It was virtually a north and south bending alignment, convex toward us. Its right was protected by rough Brush Mountain and Noonday Creek. Its center had Nose's Creek in front of it, but the strength of its almost impregnable part was in the natural fortress of the south slope of Kenesaw.

The intrenchments or breastworks everywhere, whatever you call those Confederate protecting contrivances, were excellent. They had along the fronting slopes abundant " slashings," that is, trees felled toward us with limbs embracing each other, trimmed or untrimmed, according to whichever condition would be worse for our approach. Batteries were so placed as to give against us both direct and cross fires.

To my eye, Kenesaw there, at the middle bend of Johnston's long line, was more difficult than any portion of Gettysburg's Cemetery Ridge, or Little Round Top, and quite as impossible to take. From extreme to extreme, that is, from the Confederate infantry right to the actual left in a straight line, must have been six miles.

The reports show that Johnston had just before the battle of Kenesaw received reënforcements from the Georgia militia under G. W. Smith. His numbers at this terrible battle are not now easily discovered, but standing so much as Johnston did on the defensive behind the prepared works, his losses were hardly ever as great as ours; so that, I think, at Kenesaw he had as many men as at Resaca. My judgment is confirmed by the surprisingly long defensive line which he occupied. Hood, at first, had the right, covering all the wagon approaches and trails from Ackworth and the north, and the wagon and railroads that ran between Brush Mountain and the Kenesaw.

Loring, the Confederate commander who now replaced Polk, for his custody and defense had all the Kenesaw front, including the southern sloping crest and the ground passing beyond the Marietta and Canton wagon road.

Hardee's corps began there, crossed the next highway (the Marietta and Lost Mountain road), and gradually drew back till his left was somewhere between Kolb's Farm and Zion's Church, that part of his force looking into the valley of Olley's Creek.

On our side, Blair, with his Seventeenth Corps, had now come to us from the west. He brought enough men to compensate for Sherman's previous losses; so that, like Johnston, Sherman had about the same numbers as at Resaca. The Army of the Tennessee, with Blair on the left, faced Hood. A short distance beyond, eastward, was Garrard's cavalry, trying to keep back the Confederate cavalry of Wheeler.

Thomas, with his three Union corps, touched the middle bend opposite Loring and part of Hardee. Hooker's corps made Thomas's right; then came, on the extreme right, the Twenty-third Corps and Stoneman's cavalry, under Schofield. The Union right, already by June 20th reached as far south as Olley's Creek. The whole infantry stretch of Sherman's front was at that time fully eight miles.

There are four distinct combats which ought to come into this battle of Kenesaw:

1. The combat with Wheeler's cavalry near Brush Mountain.

2. The cavalry combat against Jackson.

3. The battle of Kolb's Farm on June 22d.

4. Our determined attacks and repulses at different points all along the Kenesaw line during June 27th.

General Sherman's field orders notified us that he and his staff would be " near Kenesaw Mountain " on

June 27th. I recall, in general, the character of the country near to Kenesaw, mostly wild, hilly, and rugged, and thickly covered with virgin trees, oak and chestnut, with here and there a clearing made for a small farm, or a bald opening that seemed to have come of itself, though I but dimly remember Sherman's temporary headquarters, which were fixed on Signal Hill for a few days only.

Mr. J. C. Van Duzer (a superintendent of telegraph lines) telegraphed to the Assistant Secretary of War at 9.30 P.M. on June 24th: " Sherman moved to a point in field three miles west of Marietta, and Thomas to a new headquarters camp half a mile farther to our right, about the same distance from Marietta."

Van Duzer thus, by the wires keeping up his connection with Washington, united our commands. He used for us what was called the " field line " of telegraph wire, and connected his railroad line with Sherman, and Sherman with Thomas half a mile distant, and with Schofield, at least two miles in the same direction; also northward from Sherman two miles with McPherson.

Here, then, like the arrangements of Von Moltke in the Franco-Prussian War, we have our commander in a central position on high ground, about one mile in our rear, connecting his spreading rays in fan-shaped order with his army commanders; and they by signal stations and swift messengers with their corps commanders, the latter with division leaders, and so on to include brigades and regiments.

Johnston did well to go up to the Kenesaw crest. Here he had in the battle similar but better advantages over Sherman than Meade had over Lee from the famous Cemetery Hill.

Battle of Kolb's Farm and Kenesaw

Sherman's plan was, as ordered, for Thomas to make a heavy assault at the center with his army while McPherson made a feint on the left and Schofield a threatened attack on the right. Orders:

I. The corps of Major General Howard will assault the enemy's intrenchments at some point near the left of Stanley's and Davis's divisions, which will be selected by General Howard after a careful reconnoissance. He will support his attack by such disposition of his artillery as, in his judgment, is best calculated to insure success.

II. Major General Palmer will, with his column on the right of General Howard's, coöperate with the latter by carrying the enemy's works immediately in his front. The batteries of General Baird's and Davis's divisions will remain as at present posted until the contemplated movement is made. General King's division will occupy its present position, but hold itself in readiness to follow up any advantage gained by the other troops.

III. Major General Hooker will support General Palmer on the latter's right with as much of his force as he can draw from his lines, selecting positions for his artillery best calculated to enfilade the enemy's works to his left and on General Palmer's front. In supporting General Palmer's movement, General Hooker will watch carefully his own right flank, and be prepared to meet any demonstration of the enemy upon it.

IV. The troops must get into position as early as possible and commence the movement at 8 A.M. to-morrow, precisely. All the troops will be ready to follow up with promptness any success which may be gained.

I will risk wearying the reader by quoting here my own brief orders for the same battle:

In pursuance of instructions from headquarters, Army of the Cumberland, an attack will be made upon the enemy to-morrow at 8 A.M. by this corps (the Fourth) in conjunction with the Fourteenth Corps. The points of attack are selected near the present position of Colonel Grose's brigade.

II. General Newton will lead the assault, being prepared to cover his own left.

III. Major General Stanley will retain one of his brigades in position extending from General Palmer's left to the ravine, and will be prepared, with his other two brigades well in hand, to follow closely General Newton's movements.

IV. General Wood will occupy his present front and extend to the ravine on his right with one brigade, while he will hold his other two brigades in readiness to follow up the movement of the attacking column.

V. The points for massing the troops of General Stanley's and Wood's divisions will be pointed out in the morning.

General Newton will commence his movement for the attack at sunrise, keeping his troops as well concealed from the enemy's view as possible.

Thomas and his two corps commanders most concerned, Palmer and I, were for hours closeted together. I went with my division commander, Newton, and we examined the ground which our juniors had selected that seemed least objectionable. Newton used the column of regimental divisions, doubled on the center. That formation seemed best for the situation; first, to keep the men concealed as well as possible beforehand and during the first third of the distance, the ground being favorable for this; second, to make as narrow a front as he could, so as to make a sudden rush with numbers over their works. But for the slashings, abatis, and other entanglements, all proving to be greater obstacles than they appeared to our glasses, the little column would have lost but a few men before arriving at the barricades. Had they done so, and broken through the Confederate works, as our men did in the night fight in Lookout Valley, and as Harker's men did at Muddy Creek, deployed

582

lines were ready to follow up the forlorn hope and gain a success.

At a preconcerted signal the columns pushed rapidly forward, driving in the enemy's skirmishers, and were not checked until they reached the entanglements in front of the enemy's works. At this place the artillery and infantry fire became so galling that the advance was stopped. Harker made a second advance, when he received the wound which caused his death. Some of his men succeeded in reaching the enemy's works, but failed to secure a lodgment. As soon as it became evident that the enemy's intrenchments could not be carried by assault, the command was directed to resume its former position. Our losses were very heavy, particularly in valuable officers.

"General Harker's brigade," says Newton, "advanced through the dense undergrowth, through the slashing and abatis made by the enemy, in the face of their fire, to the foot of the works, but" (the men) "were unable to get in, and fell back a short distance. General Wagner's brigade passed through similar obstacles, and" (his men) "were compelled to stop their advance a short distance from the enemy's works. . . . Apart from the strength of the enemy's lines, and the numerous obstacles which they had accumulated in front of their works, our want of success is in a great degree to be attributed to the thickets and undergrowth, which effectually broke up the formation of our columns and deprived that formation of the momentum which was expected of it. Besides the enemy's musketry, our troops were exposed to a heavy fire of case shot. . . . The loss of the division in the assault was 654 killed and wounded."

583

Colonel Opdycke, with the One Hundred and Twenty-fifth Ohio, led Harker's charge. Harker went into the action mounted, and so was a conspicuous mark. At the bugle call the column was started. The mass paid no attention to the enemy's scattered out-watchers, but rushed at once for the hostile skirmish line, protected by deep detached rifle pits. The skirmish fire made but little impression. But here came the "tug of battle"—musketry before them, hot in their faces, direct and cross firing! On they went up the slope, but not many yards, when a Confederate battery, well located for the purpose, poured grape and shells into their flank, cutting in halves their column and confusing the regiments in rear. Still many men kept on, pulled the abatis apart, sprang over or kept under the felled trees, and tried to mount the high parapet. Some were killed, some were seized and pulled over to become prisoners. This terrible trial lasted a little more than an hour, when Harker's brigade gave up the assault and fell back for better shelter, bringing their dead chief, General Harker, with them.

Wagner's assault was equally brave—six regiments in column, Colonel Blake, with the Fortieth Indiana in the lead.

The Confederates, at one time eagerly pursuing, sprang over their works and undertook to charge Wagner's repulsed brigade, but gained nothing.

Palmer, commanding the Fourteenth Corps, selected Jeff. C. Davis's division. Davis chose what seemed to be the most vulnerable point in the enemy's breastworks. He designated McCook's and Mitchell's brigades, placing McCook on his right and Mitchell on his left, in the rear of my right division (Stanley's).

Morgan's brigade he held in reserve. His front line was about 600 yards from the point of attack. There the ground was uneven and rocky, covered with the usual trees and undergrowth.

" The signal," writes Davis, " was given a little before nine o'clock, and the troops, following the example of their admired leaders, bounded over our own works in the face of the enemy's fire, and rushed gallantly for the enemy, meeting and disregarding with great coolness the heavy fire, both of artillery and infantry, to which they were exposed, until the enemy's works were reached. Here, owing to exhaustion produced by too rapid execution of the movement, the exceedingly rough ground, and the excessive heat, the troops failed to leap over and carry the works to which their noble, daring, and impetuous valor had carried them."

A renewal of the assault in the present exhausted condition of the troops was exceedingly hazardous. Under the circumstances, after a thorough examination of the ground and the enemy's works, I reported to Major General Thomas, and recommended that the position be held and the troops intrenched where they were. This he ordered to be done. . . . Colonel Daniel McCook, long the admired and gallant commander of his brigade, fell with a severe wound, of which he subsequently died at his home in Ohio. Colonel Harmon of the One Hundred and Twenty-fifth Illinois succeeded him in command, but fell immediately after. He was a brave and skillful officer. The death of these two noble leaders was at the time a great misfortune to the troops, and will ever be to the army and country a great loss. General Davis's losses were 770.

Sherman still hoped against hope that Schofield, followed by Hooker, might make a lodgment upon

Johnston's weakened flank. Schofield's dispatch at 10 A.M. was encouraging: " Colonel Reilly has carried a position on the Sandtown road and driven the enemy back. Cox will push forward as much as possible. Hascall is using his artillery freely and pressing strongly, but finds the enemy too strong to give hope of getting his works."

But at last Cox's dispatch, received at 4.30 P.M., showed that nothing more could be done. Cox and Stoneman, routing a Confederate detachment and driving it back, seizing and holding an important Confederate outwork, had done good service for future operations, but that, important as it was, just then afforded poor consolation to our defeated commander.

On the Confederate side, when General Johnston left the Kenesaw heights and retired to his headquarters he was greatly rejoiced with the triumphs of that day. In his modest account of his victory were these words in praise of our gallant attack against him: " The Federal troops were in greater force and deeper order, and pressed forward with the resolution always displayed by the American soldier when properly led."

The entire Confederate loss was 522 against 2,500 for Sherman. It is a wonder our loss was not greater.

Among our greatest losses was that of General Harker, who was in characteristics much like McPherson. Would that he could have lived to have realized some of his bright hopes, and the country to have reaped still more benefit from his grand and heroic qualities! I wrote at the time of him:

HEADQUARTERS FOURTH CORPS, July 15, 1864.
MY DEAR COLONEL: . . . I knew General Harker as a cadet while I was on duty as instructor at West Point. He was then

remarkable for independence of character and uprightness of conduct. I was particularly happy to renew my acquaintance with him after I came West. I was surprised and pleased to find that so young a man had won the complete confidence of the commanding general of the department. On taking command of this corps Harker was still a colonel, and as I was a comparative stranger in the corps, I was anxious to get him to serve as my chief of staff. He assured me he would do everything in his power to aid me in my duties, but if I would excuse him he greatly preferred command in the field. His choice I soon learned to appreciate. Strict and exact in the performance of his own duty, he obtained the most willing and hearty coöperation from all his officers without apparent effort. The only complaint I ever heard was that if Harker got started against the enemy he could not be kept back. Yet I never found him other than cool and self-possessed. Whenever anything difficult was to be done—anything that required pluck and energy—we called on Harker.

At Rocky Face, where his division wrested one-half of that wonderful wall of strength; at Resaca, where he tenaciously held a line of works close under fire; at Dallas, where he held on for several days with thin lines in connection with his brother officers and hammered their works at a distance of less than 100 yards; at Muddy Creek, where he reënforced the skirmishers and directed their movements with so much skill and vigor as to take and hold a strong line of the enemy's earthworks; in fact, at every place where the corps had been engaged, this noble young man earnestly and heartily performed his part.

On June 27th (upon his horse) he led in that terrible assault on the enemy's breastworks. We did not carry them, but part of his command reached the works. A sergeant bearing the colors was bayoneted as he was climbing over. Our beloved and trusted young general was close by, pressing forward his column, when the fatal wound was received. I never saw him after the fight began. I do not yet realize that he is gone— one so full of rich promise, so noble, so true a friend, so patriotic a soldier. God grant that we may live like him, and, if called to die, have as good an earnest of enduring peace in heaven as had our lamented General C. G. Harker.

I am, colonel, respectfully, your obedient servant,

O. O. HOWARD, *Major General.*

To COLONEL G. P. BUELL, commanding fifth-eighth Indiana.

General Daniel McCook, who fell about the same moment as Harker, was once Sherman's law partner, and brother of Major General A. McD. McCook, of the army. Sherman felt his loss as he would that of a brother.

CHAPTER XXXIII

UNTIL they reached Kenesaw, Johnston's and Sherman's men alike had been working along, by swingings and twistings, it is true, but yet mainly and gradually gaining ground toward the southeast. Between the point where the railroad from Marietta crosses the Chattahoochee and Howell's Ferry five miles below, is that singular stream, the Nickajack.

It runs north, then east, then stopping a mile from the great river, it turns south and gradually approaches the Chattahoochee.

The Nickajack thus, by the help of a traverse brook flowing directly east and passing into the Chattahoochee far above us, almost completes a square about three miles on a side. Ruff's Mills were on the Nickajack near the northwest corner of this remarkable square.

As the banks of the river and all the creeks near here are very high, that Nickajack square afforded the Confederate commander unusual advantage for an extensive bridgehead against us. Letting his left rest above the mouth of the Nickajack, Johnston had his forts and trenches made bending around behind that creek. He extended these works to the right, northward beyond the Nickajack square, across the railroad and as far as Power's Ferry, near Vining's

589

Railway Station. His outer lines, considerably away from the river, were also intrenched in the Nickajack square, having that winding creek and Ruff's Mills for protection.

News brought us from scouts declared that from 1,000 to 1,200 slaves had been there employed.

On June 29th Sherman had everything clearly mapped out. He was heaping up stores to enable him to cut loose from his railroad. He now aimed to get upon that railroad somewhere below Marietta by turning around Schofield as a door around a free hinge.

In a telegram sent to Halleck, at Washington, the last day of June, Sherman showed what he was doing:

To-morrow night I propose to move McPherson from the left to the extreme right. . . . This will bring my right within three miles of the Chattahoochee and about five of the railroad [at the place where the railroad crossed the river]. By this movement I think I can force Johnston to move his army down from Kenesaw to defend his railroad crossing and the Chattahoochee. . . . Johnston may come out of his intrenchments and attack Thomas, which is what I want, for Thomas is well intrenched parallel with the enemy south of Kenesaw.

The proposed march was only to proceed " down the Sandtown straight for Atlanta."

On July 1st, from Sherman's " Signal Hill," he had issued a set of general orders, which, germinating ever since, at last came out:

" King's division of Palmer's corps was designated to go off northward to puzzle the Confederate Kenesaw watchers, and with Garrard's cavalry to take the place of all McPherson's army. The next morning by 4 A.M. McPherson drew out one division (that of Morgan L. Smith) and marched it ' trains and troops,' back

590

of us all, and on down river to Schofield, whom he was to aid and support till the remainder of his corps should arrive.

"Something delayed King all that day, but the night of July 2d King was on hand, and McPherson was about to pull out the remainder of his troops from their lines, when Harrow, one of his division commanders, reported that when he tried to withdraw, the enemy advanced in column and were forming in line of battle near his picket line.

" Sherman, watching this news by the wires, ordered Harrow to stay where he was, and in fact, all of McPherson's men still there, to delay; and announced that all of us would do what we could during the night to get at the facts. But he said: ' We must not attempt any night movement with large forces, because confusion would result, but must be prepared at break of day to act according to the very best information we can gather during the night.' "

That Friday night was a feverish one on our lines, and, I doubt not, a troubled one on the Confederate side; for until after twelve midnight, I had kept on pressing skirmishers as near their wary foes as could be done, and here and there throwing a shell, but nothing definite could be found out, so many skirmishers did the Confederates keep in our front—nothing sure till about 2.45 A.M. of July 3d. The enemy then had gone, and Stanley's skirmishers were in their works! At three o'clock similar reports came from Wood and Newton.

Immediately my corps was assembled. At 5 A.M. it was light enough to move, without danger of running upon other troops. Stanley's division, full of excitement, the front covered by a good skirmish line, pushed

591

on toward Marietta. Soon after this, my column, having made three miles, was at the Academy just south of the city, and found the enterprising Hooker already there. Hooker was crossing the column at an angle and obstructing it.

This shows somewhat the confusion that arose as divisions and corps, apparently on their own motion, were each moving for Marietta, striving to get there first.

McPherson was not long delayed, for he drew out from Johnston's front that very night of July 2d, leaving Garrard's dismounted cavalry in his place; he moved on down behind Thomas, "stretching to the Nickajack." But Logan's Fifteenth Corps delayed and passed through Marietta after the retreat.

Doubtless, Johnston, who had suspected just such a movement when Cox first appeared across Olley's Creek, was sure of it when, after the failures of the 27th, Sherman kept his cavalry and infantry creeping on and on down the Sandtown road, till Stoneman, on the lead, had actually touched the Chattahoochee River; and we had already in the morning of July 2d Morgan L. Smith's division as far down as the Nickajack square in conjunction with Schofield.

Sherman's quickening orders, given under the inspiration of what he had discovered on the sides of Kenesaw, and what he hoped for, came to me through Thomas. Sherman and some members of his staff rode as rapidly as they could past the marching troops which filled the roads into Marietta. There he found my skirmishers, some of Palmer's, and certain fore-runners of Hooker's corps, coming in at once from four directions. All, for the time, seemed absorbed in taking in the sights about the little city, of which they had heard so much during the preceding fortnight, and of which they had here and there distant glimpses; now they were actually there! It was, in fact, coming out of the woods and desert places into the brightness of civilization. The very few people who remained were frightened. Their eyes were troubled and often their lips trembled and their cheeks grew pale as they spoke to these hearty Yankees, who, counting their capture another victory, were somewhat saucy and buoyant.

It was at this time that Sherman, with mind intent on the retreat of Johnston, who really was a night ahead, rode into the center of the city and dismounted.

I had halted my head of column till Thomas could stop Hooker's cross march and let me take the road down river.

It was precious time to lose; but it took half an hour for Thomas's staff to bring matters into some order, and another half hour was lost by me in their marching King's division back to Palmer athwart my path. At last we were ready to advance. I had the left, Hooker and McPherson the right, as we went.

At a short distance below Marietta I came upon the Confederate rear guard to the left of the railway. Leaving the right to Palmer, I began the usual method of pressing forward, now making direct attacks against the enemy's temporary barricades; now flanking their positions on their right or left, and making a run for some choice grove or knoll that, when taken, would hasten our progress.

It was 3 P.M. when we passed the Dow Station. Not far below—from Marietta some six miles, near the Smyrna camp ground—we came upon the Confederate works; first, their little detached pits, sometimes a hole dug deep enough for protection and only large enough for a single man, and sometimes large enough for five or six.

Here the skirmishing became more and more obstinate. I called a halt and carefully reconnoitered. Confederate main works, stronger than usual, in a very advantageous position, were discovered.

At 3.30 of that day I caused Stanley to deploy lines well supported just behind his own skirmishers, and put the other two divisions of my corps in column ready to face to the left in case of need. We had since daylight captured many prisoners, probably a thousand, and a few negroes had come in. Johnston's army, the most of these newcomers asserted, was at that very time behind those formidable works.

Garrard, with his cavalry, had advanced as fast as he could down the Chattahoochee and turned off from my left flank eastward on a river ferry road; then pushed on, skirmishing till he came to a ridge defended strongly by Confederate infantry. He picketed what he took to be the Pace's Ferry roads, connecting his outer line with mine, all within plain sight of the Confederate outposts.

On my right, King's division, also connecting with mine, was close up to the Confederate skirmishers, and intrenched.

The previous movements of Schofield had forestalled and prevented any contact with the enemy by Hooker, or even by Blair and Dodge, till they had passed beyond him. They picked up a few stragglers.

Dodge (of McPherson's army), this Saturday, July 3d, did a good work; he marched down to a place near Ruff's Mills and went into camp near the Nickajack square, while sending forward one division to intrench close by Nickajack stream, and having that division send over two regiments to fortify the cross-roads beyond the mills and hold the high ground. He arrived too late to attempt anything beyond securing his camp for the night and an opening for a clear advance on the morrow. There were thick woods all around him, but after dark, large fires starting up in his front revealed the position of the Confederate forces behind their newly occupied intrenchments.

Sherman was impatient over the general confusion and, after a short, worrisome stay in Marietta, pushed on with his escort three miles down the railroad. He established there his headquarters.

General Sherman instilled into us some of his energy in the following words to Thomas:

"The more I reflect, the more I know, Johnston's halt is to save time to cross his material and men. No general, such as he, would invite battle with the Chattahoochee behind him. I have ordered McPherson and Schofield to cross the Nickajack at any cost, and work night and day to get the enemy started in confusion toward his bridges. I know you appreciate the situation. We will never have such a chance again, and I want you to impress on Hooker, Howard, and Palmer the importance of the most intense energy of attack to-night and in the morning, and to press with vehemence, at any cost of life or material."

Sherman was sending McPherson with Stoneman's cavalry ahead down by the Nickajack to the Chattahoochee far below Johnston's forces.

Garrard had now gone back two miles above the Roswell factories to occupy the attention of the enemy's cavalry there, and clear the way for future operations in that direction. My own corps (the Fourth) had already worked its way up to the intrenchments on the Smyrna camp-meeting grounds.

Early Sunday morning Sherman himself made me a Fourth of July call. His mind was impatient because he had done so little. He did not believe that any regular works were in our front, and desired to have the troops which were north of Ruff's Mills so occupy the attention of the Confederates as to prevent their accumulation of force in front of McPherson and Stoneman. He and I were walking about from point to point in a thin grove of tall trees near a farmhouse, where were Stanley's headquarters.

" Howard," Sherman remarked,- " what are you waiting for? Why don't you go ahead?"

I answered: " The enemy is strongly intrenched yonder in the edge of a thick wood; we have come upon his skirmish line."

" Nonsense, Howard, he is laughing at you. You ought to move straight ahead. Johnston's main force must be across the river."

" You shall see, general," I rejoined.

I sent for Stanley, who held my leading division, and gave him instructions:

" General, double your skirmish line and press forward! "

The men sprang out, passing between the Confederate rifle pits. They took nearly all the occupants as prisoners of war. Our soldiers had hardly passed these outer defenses when they met, straight in their faces, an unceasing fire from a set of works that had been hitherto but dimly seen, running along in the edge of the thick wood.

In a few moments several batteries opened slowly from unexpected points, sending their shot and shell

crosswise against our lines. Many of these shells appeared to be aimed at the very place where Sherman,
Stanley, and myself, with officers gathered around us,
had formed a showy group. In fact, the officers were
obliged to cover themselves by trees as well as they
could. Our men on Stanley's front did as skirmishers
are always instructed to do; those who had not fallen
gave themselves protection by using detached Confederate rifle pits, or, where that was not practicable,
they dropped on their faces, then by rushes they took
advantage of every ridge or depression of the ground.
The main part of the skirmish charge had been across
an extensive wheat field, with an ascending slope.
Meanwhile, Sherman himself passed from tree to tree
toward the rear.

It was not ten minutes after the enemy's lines
had opened fire before Sherman saw plainly that for
some reason Johnston had stopped on our side of the
river; and he remarked as he rode away, " Howard,
you were right."

Following out the instructions already given, all
my divisions, after coming up and extending the line,
had seized continuous rifle pits; and we soon made
works of our own along the enemy's front. The other
corps of Thomas's army did the same thing. These
operations often gave rise to so much fighting that
at times it was as brisk and noisy as a regular engagement. In this strange manner on Sunday morning
did our countrymen on opposite sides of intrenched
lines, by the use of loaded rifles and shotted cannon,
celebrate the Fourth of July.

At daybreak this bright morning Dodge followed
up his leading brigade. His whole force went over
the creek, and part of it was deployed into line; he

597

covered his front by a skirmish exhibit much stronger than usual, then all moved briskly forward. Dodge stirred up quite as brisk a contest in Nickajack square as we did near Smyrna camp ground. He ran into Stevenson's division, but could not go beyond the first line of detached rifle pits. " The order was gradually executed, the outworks taken, and some fifty prisoners captured." Stoneman now held our side of the river to Sandtown.

The position of the Confederate army was in two lines running across the Atlanta Railroad at right angles near where the railroad bent off toward the river. Loring's corps was on the right and Hardee's on the left of that road. Hood's stretched off toward the extreme left, where was G. W. Smith with his Georgia troops supporting General Jackson's cavalry. Wheeler's cavalry division watched the extreme right.

Hood was made uneasy by McPherson's works. " The enemy," he wrote, " is turning my left and my forces are insufficient to defeat this design or hold him in check." Johnston instantly on this report dis- patched (Cheatham's) division. That, however, was not enough.

In the evening of that same Fourth of July G. W. Smith declared that the Yankee cavalry was pressing him with such force that he would have to abandon the ground he had been holding and retire before morning to General Shoup's line of redoubts.

As soon as Johnston received this ominous dis- patch, which, as he said, threatened an important route to Atlanta and one that was nearer to that city than his main body, he instantly declared " the neces- sity of abandoning the position and of taking a new line"; and so before the morning he drew back from the outer lines to the inner lines of the bridgehead, sending his cavalry and some artillery to the south bank of the Chattahoochee. From all quarters as early as 4.30 A.M. the morning of the 5th, we found the strong outer works in our immediate front empty.

A Confederate officer, who had been a pupil of mine when I was an instructor in mathematics at West Point, left a note upon a forked stick in the abandoned trenches addressed to me, saying: "Howard, why didn't you come on and take my works? I was all prepared for you. I am ashamed of you." One of the officers who picked it up brought the note to me. It was plain enough after our experience at Kenesaw why I did not charge over my pupil's lines.

But now from all parts of the front we rushed forward with the hope of overtaking some portion of the retreating army, but we were again too late. I did take, however, about 100 prisoners of war. At 10 A.M. we reached Vining's Station on the railroad, and soon after pushed off to the left into the wagon road that leads to Pace's Ferry. Now from that station we came upon Wheeler's cavalry dismounted and skirmishing from behind barricades.

Our infantry skirmishers soon cleared the way and drove this cavalry back. So closely were they followed that they did not have time to destroy their pontoon bridge across the river, but we could not save the bridge, because a few Confederates, at the risk of their lives, stayed back and cut it loose from the north side so that the current quickly caused it to swing to the other shore.

Thus we had possession of every part of the Chattahoochee below the Nickajack, and also from Pace's Ferry northward to Roswell's factories.

Colonel Frank T. Sherman for some reason was riding leisurely across the opening, when suddenly he came upon the Confederate skirmish line and was captured. He could hardly realize where he was when he saw the rifles aimed at him, and heard a clear-cut command to surrender. As his name was Sherman the rumor ran through the Confederate army that the terrible " Tecumseh " had been captured.

Colonel Sherman, an active, intelligent, and healthy man, full of energy, had aided me greatly during this trying campaign. No officer could have been more missed or regretted at our headquarters than he. Our picket line was completed, but this did not relieve us from the chagrin caused by the loss which slight care might have prevented.

In the minds of the readers of a military campaign wonderment often arises why there are so many delays. Our people at home and the authorities at Washington, at the time of which we write, were always impatient at such delays, and could not account for the waste of so many precious days behind the Chattahoochee. " Hadn't Joe Johnston cooped himself up there at the railroad crossing? Why not now be bold and strike below him for Atlanta, already in plain sight, and for Johnston's lines of supplies? "

We who belonged to Thomas pushed up a few miles against those inner lines; the Confederate cavalry had crossed the river and taken on the other high bank fine positions for their cannon—cannon to be well supported by mounted and dismounted men. Every crossing within reach was diligently watched by our foes, and every possible effort put forth to prevent our attempted passage of the river; Colonel Jackson and his active cavalry were working below the Confederate army, and Wheeler above the Marietta and Atlanta railway crossing of the Chattahoochee, to and beyond the Roswell factories; besides, Forrest, the Confederate cavalry leader, was worrying the posts far behind us, guarding our single line of supply. Sherman attended to that matter in a most effectual manner by appointing a district command with its headquarters at Chattanooga, and putting (Steedman) with detailed instructions, at the head of it. He had given him additional troops and adequate authority to combine his men and give blow for blow.

Believing that this annoyance could be even better removed by imitating Forrest's raids, Sherman sent out General Rousseau from the Tennessee border far down into Alabama, to swing around, destroy railroads as far south as Talladega and Opelika; and then, if possible, to return to him near Atlanta. Rousseau started from Decatur, Ala., July 9th. This remarkable raid was successful. His cavalry made a lodgment upon the Southern Railroad west of Opelika and destroyed some twenty miles of it. He defeated every Confederate troop sent against him with a loss of but twelve killed and thirty wounded; and he brought back a large number of captured mules and horses. Rousseau astonished the inhabitants everywhere by his unexpected visit, and did not join us, after his consummate raid, until July 23d.

To make our connections complete, two railway breaks, a long one above Marietta and one shorter below, near Vining's Station, had to be repaired. During July 6th the first gap was announced as restored, and the second was in progress.

Thomas had found it impracticable to cross the river in face of the fortified points on his front or left.

The water, which had risen from the recent rains, was now too high for fording. Sherman saw, however, that the water was slowly falling and that in a short time all the fords would be practicable; so that, by and by, something more than cavalry with its artillery would be required by the Confederate general over there to keep us back.

On Tuesday, July 6th, in a dispatch, Sherman indicated briefly what he was then meditating:

" All the regular crossing places are covered by forts; but we shall cross in due time, and instead of attacking Atlanta direct, or any of its forts, I propose to make a circuit, destroying all its railroads." After the rain and mud beyond Kenesaw, we were now having fair weather—at times a little too hot for comfort or safety; but the region afforded us high ground and the army had no prevailing sickness. Sherman did not delay all his operations. Something important was going on all the time.

Sherman by July 8th had determined to make his first crossing near the Roswell factories; he ordered Garrard's cavalry division to go there. As soon as Garrard could charge into the place he drove out the detachment of Wheeler's cavalry and destroyed the factories. The Confederate guard had rushed over the Chattahoochee bridge, and succeeded in destroying it. McPherson was to go up there, ford the river, and clear the way for a bridgehead and repair the bridge. Who could build a trestle bridge like his general, G. M. Dodge, who was not only a superb commander of men in battle, but was already an eminent practical engineer?

Garrard crossed at 6 A.M. with little loss, and Newton, of my corps, followed him during the morning; the ford by this time had become practicable. The men were not long in putting up a strong work for a bridgehead, and so the upper crossing was secured.

Meanwhile, something else even more important had been done. As soon as Schofield had been crowded out by Johnston contracting his lines from the " outer " to the " inner " protection of his railroad over the Chattahoochee, Sherman brought Schofield's corps back near to Thomas's left and rear, and lo_cated him at Smyrna camp ground, near where I fought on the Fourth of July. Sherman set him to reconnoitering for a convenient river crossing some_where near Thomas.

He discovered a practicable ford just above the mouth of Soap Creek. There was but a small picket of the enemy's cavalry opposite, and a single section of artillery. The whole work of preparation and ap_proach was done so well that the enemy suspected no movement there until Schofield's men about 3 P.M. July 8th were making their way over by ford and by de_tached pontoon boats.

I had sent the pontoons with Colonel Buell and his regiment, and had, in order to aid him, already made a display of force below Schofield, in front of Pace's Ferry. My demonstration began about sundown the night before with a completeness of preparation that attracted the attention of the Confederate watchmen opposite. While there was yet light enough we opened all our artillery that was near and practiced until we got the range; then we ceased till a fixed time in the night, when all sleepers were startled by an alarming cannonade that continued for half an hour. Mean-while, our officers had detachments in secure places near the river's bank and were moving about and giving commands. This was a ruse!

General T. J. Wood's entire division was kept under arms during the whole demonstration, and at hand during the night, ready for any work that might come. A mere ruse? No, not exactly, for we would have gladly made a crossing there had not the enemy been too strong at that point; but we wanted to draw more and more of the preventing foe to our neighborhood.

At 6 A.M. of July 8th I had taken a regiment with me and gone some five miles northward to find the right of Schofield's command and to protect his bridge across a broad creek, called Rottenwood, that separated him from us.

Newton, on the morning of the 9th waited for Dodge to replace him at the Roswell village and let him return to me.

Johnston, not far from Atlanta, with his three corps, now passed behind Peach Tree Creek, whose direction in its flow is northwest; so that his army faced substantially to the northeast, covering mainly all approaches to Atlanta, which lay between the Marietta and the Augusta roadways. Johnston showed consummate generalship when he took Peach Tree Creek instead of the Chattahoochee as a line of defense.

Johnston, full of hope and courage, located his splendidly disciplined and veteran troops as follows: Stewart, succeeding Polk, on the left touching the Chattahoochee; Hood on the right from Clear Creek around to some point near the Augusta Railroad; and Hardee holding the center. Hood's right was strengthened by General G. W. Smith with his Georgia troops. Wheeler with his cavalry watched the front and right, and Jackson the left.

Just as Johnston had put everything in capital shape to repulse us if possible, he received, on July 17th, a startling telegram from Richmond.

It announced his failure to arrest Sherman's progress; complained that he expressed no confidence of success in repelling Sherman, and ordered him to turn over his army to Hood. It is plain that Hood himself was taken unawares, and naturally felt unprepared for so large a contract as that now imposed. Johnston says:

"At Hood's earnest request I continued to give orders until sunset." And further: "In transferring the command to General Hood, I explained my plans to him."

We will not delay upon these plans, for Hood tried to carry them out. The difference was not in the plans, but in the execution. Johnston was cautious, wary, flexible, full of expedients; Hood was incautious, blunt, strong-willed, and fearless of Sherman's strategy. He was not the general to execute any plan but his own; and then he ought not to have had a Sherman or a Thomas for an opponent.

By the 14th Sherman wanted Stoneman back from the crossing below us of the Chattahoochee, at least as far as Sandtown, so as to let all of Blair's division go up and join McPherson at the Roswell factories.

Schofield's bridge was over Phillip's Ferry. Power's Ferry was also bridged by a pontoon, and later by another, a rough pier log structure, which Stanley made to the island, and Newton finally finished to the east shore. Over Phillip's and Power's ferries my divisions crossed, and, staying there, put trenches on

Schofield's right; Newton, after his return from Roswell, soon went over to strengthen the line; Wood later moved down east of the river, sweeping away the Confederate cavalry detachment and pickets, till Pace's Ferry (near Vining's Station and Palmer's front) was uncovered; then Palmer's pontoon bridge was laid there in safety. We had an occasional reconnoissance by the redoubtable Wheeler, which stirred up all hands. About this time Sherman relieved all suspense in the langour of hot weather by ordering us forward and then said:

"A week's work after crossing the Chattahoochee should determine the first object aimed at; viz., the possession of the Atlanta and Augusta road east of Decatur, Ga., or of Atlanta itself."

Having the same Fourth Corps under Thomas I was already near the middle of our concave line: Palmer the rightmost, Hooker next, and I next, then Schofield, then McPherson. Stoneman was back by the night of July 16th, so that we were all in active march the morning of the 17th.

By July 19th, army, corps, and division commanders had pretty well fulfilled Sherman's preliminary orders, having made what he denominated his "general right wheel." Thomas, after much skirmishing and driving back first cavalry and then infantry, had secured three crossings of the Peach Tree Creek. One lodgment over the creek was in front of Palmer, on the right of the army, below Howell's Mills; two in front of me, one near the mouth of Clear Creek, the other over a north fork of the Peach Tree Creek where the road via Decatur to Atlanta passes. Stanley saved a part of the bridge from Confederate flames and immediately rebuilt it.

Battle of Smyrna Camp Ground

Sherman was now with Schofield. The night of the 9th the latter with his Army of the Ohio was at the Peyton farms, and had already made good a crossing of the south fork of the Peach Tree Creek. McPherson, having to make twice the march of Thomas's center, had gone on too rapidly for Hood's calculations. He had already in long gaps broken the railroad to Augusta, and was so swiftly approaching Atlanta from the east that Hood had to stretch his lines farther around the great city to the east and south, thus thinning his lines before Thomas.

As my orders appeared a little confusing, I rode back at daylight of the 20th to General Thomas near Buckhead, where he had slept the night before. Here he instructed me to take my two divisions, Stanley's and Wood's, to the left two miles off from Newton, leaving Newton where he was, on the direct Atlanta wagon road.

This, creating a broad, uncovered space along my front, was done owing to the nature of the country—rough and woody with much thick underbrush—but particularly to fulfill Sherman's express orders to keep connection with Schofield.

"We must not mind the gap between your two divisions. We must act independently," said Thomas, with almost a smile. Fortunately for me, Thomas was to be near Newton's troops during the tough conflict at Peach Tree Creek, which was to burst upon us that day. His clear head and indomitable heart never were so cool and unconquerable as in desperate straits.

CHAPTER XXXIV

THE morning of July 20, 1864, McPherson was swinging toward Atlanta on the left of all Sherman's troops. Schofield pressing on in the center, and my two divisions, Wood's and Stanley's, touching Schofield's right by extended picket lines, were still following the Atlanta road via Decatur.

All these troops situated or in motion nearly two miles to the left of the gap that existed between Wood and Newton, constituted this day a maneuvering army by itself. Sherman, with Schofield, near the center, here took direct cognizance, as far as he could, of all that was going on. Sherman, knowing Hood's characteristics, felt that he would attack him and believed that he would make his first offensive effort against McPherson or Schofield, because the movements of these commanders were aimed threateningly against all his communications. Already the Augusta road was cut by them in several places and miles of it destroyed.

Wheeler, with Confederate cavalry, opposite McPherson, being driven by artillery, was slowly falling back toward Atlanta. Hood, much troubled by McPherson's steady approach, directed Wheeler in his own blunt way to fight harder, and assured him that G. W. Smith with his troops was behind him, and would vigorously support his resistance.

608

Battle of Peach Tree Creek

McPherson's left division, farthest south, drove Wheeler's cavalry constantly backward, though slowly, toward Atlanta. This division of McPherson's army was commanded by General Gresham (in after years Secretary of State with Harrison). Gresham's advance was fearless and well timed.

Some points were vastly more important than others. A round hill, free of trees, which Gresham approached, leading on his men, was attempted. We may say that his position was indeed the keypoint to the splendid defense made two days later by the Army of the Tennessee. It was here that Gresham while ascending the slope, was severely wounded by a sharpshooter. He was not only an able and gallant officer in action, but excellent in council. His loss from the front at this time was much felt.

Of course, an important position like this hill, in plain sight of the Atlanta forts, Hood's division commander on his right essayed again and again to regain, but Leggett's division and Gresham's stoutly held their ground and repelled every hostile assault.

Sherman and Schofield were on the Cross Keys road. It is the one that passes the "Howard House" *en route* to Atlanta. After driving back the cavalry, Schofield found the enemy's outworks crossing this road obliquely and making an acute angle with it. Of course, his skirmishers came upon the usual short pits that the enemy put out in front of every permanent line. Cox's division was stopped and constrained to deploy considerable force. As the resistance became stronger, the other division, Hascall's, was hurried up upon Cox's left, extending the line southward.

In person I accompanied the column of Stanley and Wood. About 8.30 A.M. we were at the south fork of Peach Tree Creek, where the enemy met and resisted us with infantry skirmishers. This point was about a mile to the right of Schofield's main column, but the roads for Schofield and Stanley advancing were now converging toward Atlanta. We had found the bridge over the south fork burned. While our skirmishers were wading the creek and driving those of the enemy back, our bridge men were vigorously employed rebuilding.

By ten o'clock the bridge was done and Stanley moved his skirmishers beyond it. A little more than half a mile from the bridge the firing became more lively and exciting; the enemy resisted from behind piles of rails and other barricades. Soon the main Confederate works were uncovered. A battery of artillery slowly opened its annoying discharges against Stanley's advance. At this time, being with Stanley, I received a message directly from Sherman: "Move forward and develop the enemy; see whether he is in force." From some prisoners taken I ascertained that I was again engaging Stevenson's division. We put in our batteries, covering them by slight epaulements and supporting them by infantry regiments. Then we proceeded in the usual way to carry out Sherman's brief order, moving forward a strong line till we received such resistance as made us more careful. Sherman himself came over to my position about two o'clock in the afternoon. He intimated that he believed that the enemy was withdrawing or would withdraw from my front to meet McPherson, for, up to that time, from his last accounts, McPherson had encountered nothing but artillery and cavalry.

About 3.30 P.M. we succeeded by change of position in driving the Confederates from a strongly constructed line of skirmish rifle pits. In this advance we captured some fifty prisoners. A little later, Stevenson, leaving his works, made a charge upon us along Stanley's front; but his impulsive effort was bravely met and quickly repelled. Before night set in we had succeeded in my part of the line in gradually working up Stanley's division till we occupied the position lately held by the enemy's skirmishers, so connecting us with Schofield's army upon our left. Wood's division had gone the same as Stanley a little farther to Stanley's right. This business of approaching prepared parapets, from the rough nature of this wooded country, was perplexing and dangerous.

In the general turning toward Atlanta, Dodge, who came next beyond Schofield, had been crowded out of the line, so that Logan with his deployed front running nearly north and south, came in facing toward Atlanta, not far from the Howard House; and Blair was stretching to the left and south as far as he could to "Bald Hill" which, ever since the battle of Gresham and Leggett, has been called "Leggett's Hill"; it was situated just in front of his left flank. Meanwhile, some of our cavalry, with a brigade of infantry, was busy in the work of destruction along the Augusta railroad as far back as Stone Mountain.

This July 20th had been to Sherman, with his extended command, a long and trying day, with operations very much like all our advances from the beginning of the campaign up to that time.

Thomas, who took his headquarters near Newton's right flank, just back of Peach Tree Creek, commanded the remainder of the army to the right of the open interval. The whole valley of Peach Tree Creek, with its tributaries, furnished an overplus of woodland, often with low ground, some swamps, and much thick underbrush. There was high land between the creeks which are tributary to the Peach Tree, entering as they do from the south side. There was, indeed, no position from which a general, like Wellington at Waterloo, could see the whole battle front.

The activity of our troops in the vicinity of Leggett's Hill caused Hood first to delay the beginning of the battle, and afterwards, at the most critical period of Hardee's attack, to take from his reserve Cleburne's division and send it off to his extreme right, so as to oppose McPherson's vigorous operations.

Of course, if Hood, commanding the entire Confederate army, had not done that, McPherson would have come up on the evening of the 20th or the morning of the 21st much nearer to Atlanta, without receiving effective opposition. The assault upon Thomas was to be made from the right of Hardee to the left of Stewart in a sort of echelon movement; that is, for Bate's division to move *first*, Walker's a *little later*, Maney's *later still* some 200 yards or more behind and leftward, and so on, including Loring's and Walthall's divisions, to the left of Hood's attacking force. French's division in reserve watched the left flank.

There was one other hindrance to Hood's advance; it was that, though he had the inner lines, enabling the speediest reënforcement, he must gain more ground with his whole force toward the right or else expose some point, altogether too weak, for Sherman to strike.

This gaining of ground to the right, equal to the front of one division, occupied considerable time. Possibly he did this wisely in order to push his moving troops into the interval which I have described on our side, between my position and that of General Newton.

Hood gave imperative orders to his right corps commander, Cheatham, to hold everything firmly for more than a mile of frontage. His soldiers were to stand behind his parapets all the way from the Georgia railroad to that Clear Creek (on some maps erroneously called Pea Vine) which entered Peach Tree Creek near Newton's position. This Cheatham was doing all day opposite my left divisions, also opposite Schofield's and part of McPherson's.

John Newton could never be surprised. He was advancing, as instructed, toward Atlanta; but feeling himself in the presence of an enterprising foe, and believing that he would deliver battle before many hours, Newton had his bridge over Peach Tree Creek well and strongly built. His officers were next assuring him that Ward's division of Hooker's corps was near and about to follow over his bridge and form on an important knoll off to his right. At one o'clock Newton crossed the bridge and moved forward to the crest of a hill nearly half a mile beyond. The enemy's skirmishers fell back as they were met and engaged. Newton found a good position, and as if he knew there must be a battle just there, he stretched out *Blake's brigade* to the left of the road, covering also a crossroad that here went eastward toward Collier's Mill, and *Kimball's brigade* toward the right. He located a battery of four guns near the junction of these two brigades and left the other brigade (Bradley's) just as it had marched from the bridge in column of fours, filling the road for at least a quarter of a mile back. Newton's men on the front threw down before them small piles of rails, and shoveled as much dirt over them as they could in an hour's work with the few spades and shovels they had with them. I call this whole formation " Newton's Cross."

Newton was just sending out a fresh line of skirmishers from his position when, about 3.30 P.M., he discovered Bate's Confederate division coming on to his left front. The shrill Confederate cheer beginning over there to his left, and extending all along before his brigades, could not be mistaken. His skirmishers delivered their shots and hurried back behind the other troops. It was a moment of excitement. Every man made what readiness he could. There first appeared to Newton the front of a Confederate brigade. His own ranks looked slender; the enemy's solid and strong!

The few minutes before battle to the waiting soldiers are always the hardest. Bradley's brigade of Newton's division had long since been faced eastward, and the battery turned that way to the left for action.

The oncoming force appeared like a mass that would strike obliquely against Bradley's front. Bate's leading Confederate brigade must have rushed down the Clear Creek Valley with all its entanglements. As they came into the open and began to ascend the hill Newton ordered: " Commence firing; fire steady and low! " At first not much impression; then the Confederates also fired, and advanced firing; but as they stopped to load, the long line of Union rifles and the fearful pieces of artillery raked them obliquely. They could not face so much; many fell wounded or slain. There was wavering in their ranks; then hesitancy; then a more general falling back to get under cover. Who could blame those brave soldiers? Not enough to take the battery could have lived to reach its commanding place.

Battle of Peach Tree Creek

Bradley had hardly begun to check their fierce assault, when the next installment ran against Blake's brigade. Blake in a few moments was hard at work, and the battery was rolled around to help him, when amid the smoke and confusion the same strong echelon movement of Confederates was carried on to Kimball and beyond. All these soldiers on our side were partially covered by rails and on a crest, so that their losses were not heavy. Walker's division of Confederates, coming straight up on both sides of the road, was without protection. They were cut down like grass before the scythe, as Newton's men had been at Kenesaw less than a month before. Walker's men on the direct front—those who had not fallen—soon retired to rally their strength, but all beyond Kimball's right passed on and made him bend back more and more to meet them, till Bradley and the convenient cannon faced about to help him. It was almost too much for Newton to be outflanked on both sides and to have two whole divisions, each larger than his own, launched against him.

General Ward, the successor in the division of General Butterfield, had three brigades: one under Coburn of Indiana; a second under Colonel James Wood, from Northern New York; a third under Benjamin Harrison, afterwards President. Ward for support had been all the time in Newton's mind, but where was he at that critical moment? Just as he began to worry about his right flank, Kimball caught glimpses of finely led brigades appearing at the crest of that height, 800 yards off. It was a refreshing sight. There were Ward's skirmishers. They did not retire at the prolonged yell of their opponents, nor at the brisk fire of the first rifle shots aimed against them. They kept

615

their advanced positions till Ward could make his deployments behind them. Following the impulse of a soldier's instinct, Ward did not suffer his men to wait without cover, pale and sick at heart as men are apt to be at such a juncture, but put them at once into rapid motion, ascended the hill, absorbed his skirmishers as they went, and met the Confederate charge with a vigorous counter charge. Bradley's new front, facing west, and flank were thus quickly relieved.

The struggle in Ward's front proper was a little prolonged by fitful and irregular firing from everywhere, it seemed; and as his men had nothing for cover his losses were considerable. Three hundred well prisoners and 150 wounded, many battle flags and a cleared field were his within an hour.

The succession of Confederate blows continued leftward—the several brigades of Maney and Loring, striking Williams's division, next after Ward, and carrying it on so as to involve at least one brigade of Palmer's corps.

Taking the division commanders and considering them in succession, we first come to Geary. Our Geary had been compared to Napoleon's Marshal Ney, from his large proportions, his cheerful deportment, and his unfailing energy. His eyes were always wide open, so that he examined every approach to his position, and watched with clear vision for some high point if he could get one. He reconnoitered without regard to personal danger. His men had skirmished up a hill abreast to Ward and Newton, across the Shoal Creek. Geary was in the outset with his skirmishers preparing to bring up to the crest his battle lines. While thus diligently and fearlessly engaged he heard the distant Confederate cry. His left just then had an open front, while his right ran down into low ground and was obstructed by entangling undergrowth. This wood, troublesome to the foot soldiers and impassable to cavalry, caused quite a gap between him and Williams's division. He had left enough force near the creek to occupy and defend the bridgehead. Like Newton's men, in the place where they found themselves, Geary's were just commencing to intrench and barricade, when the sound of battle reached them suddenly. In his own front, without shouting, almost without noise, in apparent masses the Confederates, with their quick, springy step, charged Geary's skirmishers.

The movement was so adroitly executed that most of those in Geary's outer line were captured. Here the sharp firing commenced. Geary galloped to the vicinity of his own battery, where all his left wing, now thoroughly warned, began a rapid and continuous fire. This firing was so strong and well directed that it checked and broke up the Confederate charge. Successive efforts to breast this Union storm on the part of the Confederate officers in immediate command were unsuccessful. Geary's right wing, however, had a much harder struggle. Under cover of the treacherous woods a Confederate column furtively penetrated between him and Williams, and his right flank for a time was completely enveloped. His right brigade commander, Colonel P. H. Jones, soon supported by all the rest, changed front as soon as he could, but too late to check the onset, so that nearly the whole right wing was forced back to the bridgehead near the Peach Tree Creek.

The battle was perhaps not severer in Geary's

front than elsewhere, but the immediate results were not so decisive for him. The limbs of trees and the underbrush were as badly broken and cut up as those had been on Geary's front the last day at Gettysburg. Geary persisted here, as he did everywhere, in reenforcing and making renewed attacks till near night, when the Confederates before him retired. Their commander, General Walthall, had doubtless discovered before his withdrawal that the general attack had altogether failed. The successive advances of Stewart's Confederate corps passed on beyond the ravine westward, and struck Williams a heavy blow. His left was held by Robinson's brigade. The blow came while Robinson was in motion by the left flank endeavoring to get into the ravine and connect with Geary. General Hooker, watching the well-matched combat, had ordered this important junction. Troops could not be worse situated to resist an attack. Sheridan's division at Chickamauga was broken to pieces under such conditions. Yet, Hooker was proud to say, Robinson's men coolly faced toward the enemy and stood fast, giving volley for volley. They lost heavily but they not only maintained their ground but helped Geary's right in recovering what he had lost. Williams, commanding the division, was at all times a faithful officer at his post. He had heard the distant sound of battle, which proved a favorable signal to him and his veterans. At once he caused his batteries to gallop to the nearest hill, and soon to bring an oblique fire to bear upon not only those before his direct front, but upon all who were attacking Geary and Robinson.

As the stormy echelon wave passed along it dashed upon Knipe's and Ruger's brigades with undimin-

ished force and fury. Having had a little more warning than the others, they were fully prepared when
the storm burst; and so they steadily met the shock
of battle, and succeeded in repelling their assailants
without loss of ground.

The last strong effort made by the Confederates
in this engagement took place on Hardee's right. It
was evidently Bate's division, supported by Walker,
which was making the final effort to turn the flank of
the Army of the Cumberland. It was an effort to take
Newton in reverse through the gap between my divisions. Thomas, who could move quickly enough when
duty demanded it, hastened Ward's artillery to the
proper spot near Newton's bridge where it could be
most effective to sweep the Clear Creek bottom and
the entangled woods that bordered it.

Not only artillery but all the cannon that belonged
to Newton's division was ranged in order, and began
and followed up with terrible discharges, using solid
shot, shells, and canister, their brisk fire beginning
just as the Confederate brigades emerged from the
shelter of the woods and were aiming to cross the
Peach Tree Creek itself. This artillery fire, combined
with all the oblique fire that Newton could bring to
bear, broke up the assaulting columns and rendered all
attempts to turn Thomas's position futile.

While this was going on there was again a renewed
supporting effort put forth by all the Confederate
divisions, from Walker's right to French, to sustain
their attack, but Thomas's men from Newton to Palmer's center were still watching, and easily stopped and
drove back the advancing lines.

The loss on both sides was heavy: on our side not
far from 2,000 men *hors de combat*. The Confederate

loss cannot be accurately ascertained. It was between 4,000 and 5,000 killed, wounded, and made prisoners.

Thus ended in defeat Hood's execution of Johnston's plan for a general battle at Peach Tree Creek.

A brigade commander, Colonel Cobham, One Hundred and Eleventh Pennsylvania; Colonel William K. Logie, One Hundred and Forty-fourth New York, and Lieutenant Colonel G. B. Randall were among those who fell. We had a great impulse of joy because we had won the battle. The Confederates had at this time, besides the affliction of death, a great sense of chagrin because they had lost.

- Net Zero
  dangerous Trap

- Lewis Powell *Memorandum*
  1971

Made in United States
North Haven, CT
14 March 2023